SCRIBES AND SCHOLARS
AT SALISBURY CATHEDRAL

c. 1075–c. 1125

TERESA WEBBER

CLARENDON PRESS · OXFORD

1992

Oxford University Press, Walton Street, Oxford OX2 6DP

Oxford New York Toronto
Delhi Bombay Calcutta Madras Karachi
Petaling Jaya Singapore Hong Kong Tokyo
Nairobi Dar es Salaam Cape Town
Melbourne Auckland
and associated companies in
Berlin Ibadan

Oxford is a trade mark of Oxford University Press

Published in the United States
by Oxford University Press, New York

British Library Cataloguing in Publication Data
Data available

Library of Congress Cataloging in Publication Data
Webber, Teresa.
Scribes and scholars at Salisbury Cathedral, 1075–1125/Teresa Webber.
(Oxford historical monographs)
Revision of author's thesis.
Includes bibliographical references and index.
1. Cathedral libraries—England—Salisbury—History. 2. Canons,
Cathedral, collegiate, etc.—England—Salisbury—Books and reading.
3. Learning and scholarship—England—Salisbury—History—Medieval,
500–1500.   4. Manuscripts, Latin (Medieval and modern)—England—
Salisbury.   5. Paleography, English—England—Salisbury.
6. Scriptoria—England—Salisbury—History.   7. Scribes—England—
Salisbury.   8. Transmission of texts.   9. Salisbury Cathedral.
I. Title. II. Series.
Z725.S3W4   1992
091'.09423'19—dc20   92–5533
ISBN 0–19–820308–X

Typeset by Cotswold Typesetting Ltd., Gloucester
Printed and bound in
Great Britain by Biddles Ltd.,
Guildford and King's Lynn

To my parents

PREFACE

THIS book represents a revised version of my D.Phil. thesis. I should like to express my gratitude to the individuals and institutions who have assisted me during my years of graduate research, and subsequently in the preparation of this volume. First, my study of the Salisbury manuscripts would have been impossible without either the permission of the Dean and Chapter of Salisbury Cathedral, who allowed me to make such a prolonged study of their books, or the assistance of Suzanne Eward, the cathedral librarian, whose help and interest made my frequent visits to the library a pleasure, even when the temperature dipped below 50°. I am also grateful to the librarians and staff of the following libraries for allowing me to consult their manuscripts, or for providing me with microfilms and photographs: Aberdeen University Library; the British Library; the Bodleian Library; the Musée des Archives Nationales, Paris; and the libraries of Corpus Christi College, Cambridge; Durham Cathedral; Exeter Cathedral; Keble College, Oxford; Trinity College, Cambridge; and Trinity College, Dublin.

My research was also made possible by financial assistance from the British Academy; the Richard Newitt Fund; the President and Fellows of Wolfson College, Oxford; the President and Fellows of Magdalen College, Oxford; and the Faculty of Arts Research Sub-Committee, University of Southampton.

I am particularly indebted to those who instructed me in the techniques of palaeographical and historical research: to Professor Andrew Watson, Professor Karl Leyser†, Pierre Chaplais, and most of all, Malcolm Parkes, who supervised my thesis, providing a seemingly inexhaustible supply of ideas, information, enthusiasm and constructive criticism. In addition, I am most grateful to my two D.Phil. examiners for their unfailing generosity with advice in the process of preparing my thesis for publication: to Henry Mayr-Harting who has acted as subeditor of this book, and to Diana Greenway, who made the results of her research on the chapter at Old Sarum available to me in advance of publication. Thanks are also due to the many other scholars who have assisted me, in reading and commenting upon all or parts of my thesis or drafts of the book, or providing me with references, among them Professor Christopher Brooke, Professor J. E. Cross, George Bernard, Ernest Blake, Vincent Gillespie, Brian Golding, Michael Gullick, John McGavin, Bella Millett, Alan Piper, Daphne Stroud, and Rodney Thomson.

Academic research can be a lonely business. That this has not been my experience has been due, in large part, to the friendship and stimulus offered by two groups of people: first, the members of The Seminar in the History of the Book to 1500, and in particular its prime movers, Linda Brownrigg and Peggy Smith; and secondly, my fellow medievalists and colleagues at Southampton.

My final acknowledgement is to my husband, Geoffrey, without whose support neither my thesis nor this book could have been undertaken or completed.

T.W.

University of Southampton
1991

CONTENTS

LIST OF PLATES   x

CONVENTIONS AND ABBREVIATIONS   xi

Introduction   1

1 Book Production at Salisbury in the Late Eleventh
   and Early Twelfth Centuries   8

2 The Content and Composition of the Book Collection   31

3 Salisbury and the Transmission of Latin Literature   44

4 Intellectual Interests   82

5 The Religious Life   113

Conclusion   140

APPENDIX 1. Group I Manuscripts: Texts and Scribes   143

APPENDIX 2. Group II Manuscripts: Texts and Scribes   158

APPENDIX 3. The Scala Virtutum   171

BIBLIOGRAPHY   184

NOTES TO THE PLATES   197

INDEXES   203

LIST OF PLATES

between pages 196 and 197

1–5. Salisbury scribes in the late eleventh century: the Group I scribes

 1. (*a*) Salisbury Cathedral, MS 165, fo. 23. Scribes i and xii
    (*b*) Salisbury Cathedral, MS 165, fo. 135. Scribe ii
 2. Salisbury Cathedral, MS 154, p. 153. Scribe iii
 3. Salisbury Cathedral, MS 78, fo. 128. Scribe v
 4. Salisbury Cathedral, MS 168, fo. 14. Scribes ix and xi
 5. Salisbury Cathedral, MS 10, fo. 22. Scribes iii, vi and viii

6–10. Salisbury scribes in the early twelfth century: the Group II*a* scribes

 6. (*a*) Salisbury Cathedral, MS 64, fo. 9. Scribe 3
    (*b*) Salisbury Cathedral, MS 64, fo. 81. Scribe 6
 7. Salisbury Cathedral, MS 61, fo. 34. Scribes 3 and 7
 8. Salisbury Cathedral, MS 162, fo. 15ᵛ. Scribe 8
 9. (*a*) Salisbury Cathedral, MS 124, fo. 3. Scribe 9
    (*b*) Salisbury Cathedral, MS 110, fo. 22ᵛ. Scribe 12
 10. Salisbury Cathedral, MS 162, fo. 19. Scribe 11

11–14. Salisbury scribes in the early twelfth century: the Group II*b* scribes

 11. Salisbury Cathedral, MS 223, fo. 54. Scribes 14 and 17
 12. Salisbury Cathedral, MS 59, fo. 175. Scribe 14
 13. Salisbury Cathedral, MS 59, fo. 85. Scribe 15
 14. Salisbury Cathedral, MS 115, fo. 20. Scribe 16

15–16. The study of the Bible on the eve of scholasticism

 15. Oxford, Keble College, MS 22, fo. 6. A late eleventh-century glossed copy of the Pauline Epistles
 16. Salisbury Cathedral, MS 160, fo. 98. An early twelfth-century Psalter commentary.

Plates 1–14 and 16 are reproduced by permission of the Dean and Chapter, Salisbury Cathedral; plate 15 is reproduced by permission of the Warden and Fellows of Keble College, Oxford.

CONVENTIONS AND ABBREVIATIONS

THE following conventions have been adopted for transcriptions. Punctuation and capitalization have been modernized, but the orthography of the original has been preserved. Faulty word separation has been corrected, and abbreviations expanded silently. Gaps in the original, or passages no longer visible because of damage are represented by square brackets; the missing text has been supplied wherever possible. Editorial comments or emendations are enclosed within round brackets.

I have observed the following principles when referring to manuscripts. A folio number alone (e.g. 'fo. 101') indicates the recto page; a folio number followed by 'v' (e.g. 'fo. 101ᵛ') indicates the verso; a folio number followed by r–v (e.g. 'fo. 101ʳ⁻ᵛ') indicates the whole leaf. When reference is made to manuscripts in two columns, the left-hand column is referred to as 'a', and the right-hand column as 'b'. Thus 'fo. 101ᵛᵃ' refers to the left-hand column of the verso of folio 101. The terminology I have employed when referring to the constituent parts of a letter is best explained with reference to examples: **m** consists of three minims, **d** consists of a lobe and a shaft, **a** consists of a lobe and a headstroke. Strokes which extend above the height of minims (as in the letter **l**) are called ascenders; strokes which descend below the ruled line (as in the letter **g**) are called descenders.

The following abbreviations have been used (full details of the works cited are in the Bibliography):

ASE	*Anglo-Saxon England*
BHL	*Bibliotheca hagiographica latina*
BIHR	*Bulletin of the Institute of Historical Research*
Bischoff, 'Wendepunkte'	B. Bischoff, 'Wendepunkte in der Geschichte der lateinischen Exegese im Frühmittelalter'
CCCM	Corpus christianorum: continuatio mediaevalis
CCSL	Corpus christianorum: series latina
CLA	*Codices latini antiquiores*
Clavis	*Clavis patrum latinorum*, ed. E. Dekkers
CSEL	Corpus scriptorum ecclesiasticorum latinorum
EEMF	Early English Manuscripts in Facsimile
EETS	Early English Texts Society, Original Series
EHR	*English Historical Review*
GCS	Die griechischen christlichen Schriftsteller der ersten drei Jahrhunderte

Greenway, *Fasti*, iv	D. Greenway, ed., J. Le Neve, *Fasti Ecclesiae Anglicanae, 1066–1300*, iv: *Salisbury Cathedral*
Greenway, 'The False *Institutio*'	D. Greenway, 'The False *Institutio* of St Osmund'
Ker, 'Beginnings'	N. R. Ker, 'The Beginnings of Salisbury Cathedral Library'
Ker, *English Manuscripts*	N. R. Ker, *English Manuscripts in the Century after the Norman Conquest*
Ker, 'Salisbury Cathedral Manuscripts'	N. R. Ker, 'Salisbury Cathedral Manuscripts and Patrick Young's Catalogue'
Ker, 'Three Old English Texts'	N. R. Ker, 'Three Old English Texts in a Salisbury Pontifical, Cotton Tiberius C I'
MGH	Monumenta Germaniae historica
PL	*Patrologia cursus completus, series latina*, accurante J.-P. Migne, 221 vols. (Paris, 1844–64)
Rev. bén.	*Revue Bénédictine*
Römer	F. Römer, *Die handschriftliche Überlieferung der Werke des heiligen Augustinus*, ii/i
RS	Rolls Series: i.e. Rerum Britannicarum medii aevi scriptores
RTAM	*Recherches de théologie ancienne et médiévale*
Stegmüller	F. Stegmüller, *Repertorium biblicum medii aevi*
William of Malmesbury, *GP*	William of Malmesbury, *De gestis pontificum anglorum*

Biblical passages in English are taken from the Douay–Rheims translation of the Latin Vulgate.

INTRODUCTION

THE late eleventh- and early twelfth-century manuscripts of Salisbury Cathedral form the largest group of manuscripts to have survived from any English centre in the fifty or so years after the Norman Conquest. They are our best evidence of the interests and concerns of the men associated with the cathedral at Salisbury in the first few decades after its establishment. The manuscripts are a witness to the energetic scribal and scholarly activities of a community of intelligent and able men, and they place Salisbury in the forefront of intellectual developments in England after the Conquest.

Studies of the early history of Salisbury Cathedral have hitherto been based, for the most part, upon the documentary sources; their principal objective being to gain an understanding of the organization and composition of the cathedral chapter, and to examine it within the context of the history of secular cathedral chapters in England in the Middle Ages.[1] This monograph, by contrast, sets out to form an impression of the interests and activities of the canons from the evidence provided by their books.[2] It does not attempt either to reassess the documentary evidence or to present a thorough account of the structure of the cathedral chapter in the first decades after its establishment, the individuals who composed it, and their duties. Nevertheless, a brief review of the current state of our knowledge concerning the establishment of the chapter and its character in the early years is necessary here, in order to provide a background against which to study the canons and their manuscripts.

A cathedral was established at Salisbury in the last quarter of the eleventh century—one of several changes made to the organization of the English Church in the wake of the Norman Conquest. In 1075 a Council

---

[1] The principal studies are K. Edwards, 'The Cathedral of Salisbury', in *The Victoria History of the Counties of England, A History of Wiltshire*, ed. R. B. Pugh and E. Crittall (London, 1956), iii. 156–64, and K. Edwards, *The English Secular Cathedrals in the Middle Ages*, 2nd edn (Manchester, 1967), and, most recently, D. Greenway (ed.), J. Le Neve, *Fasti Ecclesiae Anglicanae, 1066–1300, iv, Salisbury* (London, 1991). See also D. Greenway, 'The False *Institutio* of St Osmund', *Tradition and Change: Essays in Honour of Marjorie Chibnall*, ed. D. Greenway, C. Holdsworth and J. Sayers (Cambridge, 1985), 77–101, and C. N. L. Brooke, *The Medieval Idea of Marriage* (Oxford, 1989), 78–89.

[2] A preliminary examination of the post-Conquest Salisbury manuscripts was undertaken by N. R. Ker, 'The Beginnings of Salisbury Cathedral Library', *Medieval Learning and Literature: Essays presented to Richard William Hunt*, ed. J. J. G. Alexander and M. T. Gibson (Oxford, 1976), 23–49; this study provided an invaluable starting point for my examination of the manuscripts.

held at London granted permission to Hereman, bishop of the united sees of Sherborne and Ramsbury, to move his episcopal see from Sherborne.[3] He chose as his new see the ancient fortified hill settlement now known as Old Sarum (some three miles to the north of the present Salisbury Cathedral), near by one of his episcopal manors, and already the location of a royal castle. Hereman initiated the building of a cathedral just outside the inner fortifications of the castle, but he died in 1078, before it could be finished.[4] He was succeeded by Osmund, during whose pontificate (1078–99) canons were established at Salisbury and the cathedral itself was completed and dedicated.[5]

Documentary sources for the early history of Salisbury Cathedral are scarce, and the information they offer is, from our point of view, disappointingly lacking in detail and precision.[6] They provide incomplete or ambiguous evidence for many aspects of the establishment and organization of the early chapter. First, they are completely silent for the period between the granting of permission to move the see in 1075, and the years 1089–91 which saw the formal establishment of canons at Salisbury. An entry in the Chronicle of Holyrood Abbey for 1089 is the first dated or datable mention of canons at Salisbury: it states that in that year Osmund established thirty-six canons in the church of Salisbury.[7]

---

[3] It invoked the decrees of Popes Damasus and Leo and of two General Councils of the early Church, those of Laodicea and Sardica, which declared that episcopal sees situated in small villages should be moved to larger centres: *Councils and Synods with other Documents relating to the English Church, 1, AD 871–1204,* ed. D. Whitelock, M. Brett, and C. N. L. Brooke (Oxford, 1981), ii. 613. On the motives which may have lain behind the transfer of sees at this time, see C. N. L. Brooke, 'Archbishop Lanfranc, the English Bishops, and the Council of London of 1075', *Studia Gratiana,* 12 (1967), 52–3. An entry for 1070 in John of Worcester's Chronicle (written in John's own hand over an erasure), almost certainly in error, goes against all other evidence in attributing the move to this year: 'Herimannus etiam episcopus, qui jam praesulatus sedem a Scireburna transtulerat Salesberiam, cum quibusdam aliis, eius interfuit consecrationi' (Florence of Worcester, *Chronicon ex chronicis,* ed. B. Thorpe (London, 1849), ii. 7). I am grateful to Patrick McGurk for this information.

[4] William of Malmesbury, *De gestis pontificum Anglorum,* ed. N. E. S. A. Hamilton, RS (London, 1870), 183. For the most recent study of the archaeological evidence for the size and structure of the cathedral as it was originally built, see R. Gem, 'The First Romanesque Cathedral at Old Salisbury', in *Medieval Architecture and its Intellectual Context: Studies in Honour of Peter Kidson,* ed. E. Fernie and P. Crossley (London, 1990), 9–18.

[5] William of Malmesbury, *GP* 83–4; *A Scottish Chronicle known as the Chronicle of Holyrood,* ed. M. O. Anderson, Scottish Historical Society, 3: 30 (Edinburgh, 1938), 110–11; Annals of Multifernan and Annals of Waverley (cited ibid. 22–3); Florence of Worcester, *Chronicon ex chronicis,* ii. 30. Osmund's foundation charter of 1091 is printed in D. Greenway, 'The False *Institutio*', 97–100.

[6] All the more disappointing when one compares them with the plentiful and detailed records extant from the later Middle Ages. But the contrast may well reflect differences between the administrative habits and attitudes of the two periods rather than the accidents of survival, cf. K. Edwards, *English Secular Cathedrals,* p. x.

[7] 'Mlxxxix. Osmundus episcopus constituit canonicos xxxvi in ecclesia Salisberiensi' (*The Chronicle of Holyrood,* 110). It is one of a series of entries which appear to derive

But we lack firm evidence which might indicate whether this group of canons was formed from scratch or whether a group of *clerici* or *presbyteri* already existed (perhaps as part of Osmund's itinerant *familia*, or based at Salisbury or another of his episcopal manors), who might have formed the basis of the first chapter at Salisbury Cathedral.[8] Still less do we know what kind of communal life, if any, such men might have lived, or from whence they derived the necessary means for their sustenance. Domesday Book (1086) lists the lands of the bishop of Salisbury but makes no mention of canons or any other clerics in connection with Salisbury.[9]

Furthermore, the sources do not permit firm conclusions to be drawn concerning the organization of the canons once they had been formally established at Salisbury, nor the kind of religious life they led. By contrast, the structure of the chapter at Salisbury in the later Middle Ages is well documented.[10] It was a type of chapter which, in common with the chapters at the eight other English secular cathedrals, was characterized by an elaborate hierarchical structure, headed by four dignitaries: the dean, cantor, chancellor, and treasurer, and which maintained few of those practices of the full common life which had been considered appropriate for cathedral clergy in the early Middle Ages, namely the holding of all property in common, with a shared refectory and dormitory. Instead, the canons dwelt in separate houses, and derived a substantial part of their income from individual territorial prebends. But we possess insufficient evidence to determine with any certainty to what extent, if at all, the first chapter at Salisbury resembled such an

from annals made in the locality of Salisbury, and which also occurs in the Annals of Multifernan (which shares other common material with the Holyrood Chronicle): ibid. 22–3. The Annals of Lacock likewise assign the introduction of canons at Salisbury to the year 1089: '[Osmundus episcopus po]suit canonicos in ecclesia Sar' (London, BL, MS Cotton Vitellius A VIII, fo. 126ᵛ); a similarly worded entry for 1089 occurs in annals probably written at St Nicholas, Exeter (London, BL, MS Cotton Vitellius D IX, fo. 8ᵛ). On these entries, see Greenway's introduction to *Fasti*, iv. Osmund's foundation charter of 1091 which refers to the canons as having already been established ('Ego Osmundus Seriberiensis ecclesie episcopus . . . notifico . . . ecclesiam Seriberiensem me construxisse et in ea canonicos constituisse': Greenway, 'The False *Institutio*', 98) need not conflict with 1089 as the date when canons were established at Salisbury.

[8] Nothing is known of the character or composition of Osmund's *familia* before the establishment of canons at Salisbury. It is not clear whether William of Malmesbury's claim that Osmund attracted learned *clerici* from far and wide, and persuaded them to remain, refers only to the period after the formal establishment of canons at Salisbury, or to the period before as well (*GP* 184). Osmund's predecessor, Hereman, attracted to his household at least one scholar, the hagiographer Goscelin: see *The Life of King Edward who rests at Westminster*, ed. F. Barlow (London, 1962), 93–4.

[9] Of those holding estates at the two earlier episcopal sees, Sherborne and Ramsbury, Domesday Book records only the monks of Sherborne Abbey, and priests at Ramsbury, who held four of the 90 hides of the episcopal manor there.

[10] For what follows, see Edwards, *English Secular Cathedrals*.

arrangement. Diana Greenway's recent demonstration that the so-called *Institutio Osmundi*, purporting to date from 1091, was in fact compiled in the mid-twelfth century, has considerably modified the previously held opinion that the first chapter at Salisbury possessed most, if not all, of the characteristic features of the English secular cathedral chapter of the later Middle Ages.[11] The *Institutio* appeared to represent the introduction to England of a very different kind of chapter from any which had existed there previously, and was also believed to have acted as a blueprint for other secular cathedral chapters established in England as well. In the light of Dr Greenway's findings, our picture of Osmund's foundation, and the nature of its significance for the history of the English secular cathedrals, are much less clear.[12]

The text of Osmund's foundation charter of 1091 has survived, and its authenticity is not in doubt. But it provides no details concerning how the canons were to be organized, nor the kind of the religious life Osmund expected them to follow.[13] It merely states that he made his endowment to them 'viventibus canonice', and 'ut exigit regularis censura canonice'. But precisely what he meant by 'living canonically' or 'regular discipline' is not specified here or elsewhere. How far, in practice, the Salisbury canons' conduct of the religious life differed from that of regular canons who led the full common life, under the discipline of a named rule, cannot be established from the extant authentic documents.[14]

This study of the Salisbury Cathedral manuscripts represents an attempt to stand aside from many of the difficult questions posed by the meagre documentary remains, and to approach the early history of the canons from a different angle. It draws upon the evidence offered by all aspects of the manuscript books (their physical characteristics as well as their contents) in order to gain an insight into the canons' intellectual and spiritual interests, attitudes, and concerns, and to place them within the context of intellectual life in England and on the Continent at this time.

[11] Greenway, 'The False *Institutio*', 77–101. She points out (77 n. 2) that Dr Edwards had already expressed certain reservations concerning the authenticity of parts of the text of the *Institutio* as it appears in the extant witnesses, the earliest of which dates from the first quarter of the 13th cent. ('The Cathedral of Salisbury', 156–8, and *English Secular Cathedrals*, 12–19, 181–3).

[12] Professor C. N. L. Brooke, while accepting these findings, maintains that the establishment of secular canons at Salisbury and elsewhere in England around 1090 marked the deliberate reversal of the trend to bring cathedral chapters under the discipline of a rule either for canons or for monks, which was current in England from the 1050s to 1080s, and that it represented the collaborative effort of several English bishops to introduce secular chapters to England. He asserts that such a policy only became possible after the death of Lanfranc, who had been active in promoting the establishment of monastic chapters: see Brooke, *Marriage*, 78–89.

[13] For the text, and its authenticity, see Greenway, 'The False *Institutio*'.

[14] For the evidence of the manuscript books, see below, Ch. 5.

The book begins with a detailed palaeographical study: an essential preliminary to using the manuscripts as historical evidence.[15] Every aspect of a manuscript book, from the parchment of which it is composed to the text it carries, constitutes a form of evidence. But how we interpret that evidence depends upon establishing as far as possible when and where the book was made, by whom and for whom. For example, manuscripts owned by a community at any one time cannot be used unreservedly as evidence of intellectual life there at that time. Some collections were built up over several centuries, and therefore represent a cumulation of the differing interests of successive generations. Collections of books were also assembled by individuals, such as bishops and abbots, who only subsequently donated or bequeathed their books to their communities; such collections would represent the interests not of the community to whom they were given, but the man by whom they were assembled.

Thus the historical interpretation and conclusions offered in this book rest upon the results of the palaeographical study offered in Chapter 1. This study concludes that the general characteristics of the manuscripts, the number of scribes at work, and the patterns of participation between them, together indicate that the books were produced as a collaborative effort, at (or near) Salisbury, and that they were produced by some at least of those for whom the books were intended, in other words, the Salisbury canons.[16] The books were produced over a comparatively short space of time (scribal activity was at times very intense), but datable specimens of the work of some of the scribes combined with the patterns of collaboration between them, demonstrate that manuscript production began during the episcopacy of Osmund, and continued well into that of Roger. It is therefore unlikely that the books were produced either for, or as the initiative of, a single man, but that they are a remarkable expression of the foremost concerns of the canons in the first few decades after their establishment.

A palaeographical study of the manuscripts does more than establish that they were produced by and for the canons themselves. The physical

[15] Cf. the remarks made by Michael Gullick, 'The Scribe of the Carilef Bible: A New Look at Some Late-Eleventh-Century Durham Cathedral Manuscripts', in *Medieval Book Production: Assessing the Evidence, Proceedings of the Second Conference of The Seminar in the History of the Book to 1500, Oxford, July 1988*, ed. L. L. Brownrigg (Los Altos Hills, 1990), 76.

[16] Throughout the book I refer to manuscript production 'at Salisbury'. This is a phrase of convenience, and should not be taken to imply a 'scriptorium' located at Old Sarum in any concrete sense: manuscript production did not require a room set aside for the purpose. The nature of collaboration between the scribes indicates that they were working closely together in the same locality, but that need not preclude the possibility of some perambulation, with copying taking place neither solely at Salisbury nor at any one of the bishop's other estates.

characteristics of the manuscripts reveal much about the canons' attitude towards the texts they contain, and the needs which they were intended to serve. The phases of scribal activity exhibited by the patterns of participation between scribes indicate the order in which texts were copied. From this we can establish the canons' priorities in acquiring texts.

The remainder of the book is concerned with the content of the manuscripts. It examines the content of the collection as a whole, and the principles which lay behind its formation. When they are compared with what is known of collections formed elsewhere in England before and after the Conquest, the Salisbury books stand out as one of the earliest and most thorough collections of the works of the Latin Fathers to have been compiled by any English centre in the centuries after the Viking invasions.

The importance of the Salisbury collection within the context of intellectual life in post-Conquest England becomes still more clear when one examines Salisbury's role in the transmission of Latin literature in England after the Conquest. Many of the texts copied at Salisbury were not widely available (if at all) in England at this time, and several exemplars were imported from the Continent. Canterbury has already been identified as an important centre for the transmission of such texts in England. But many of the texts copied at Salisbury do not depend on Canterbury exemplars, and a number of them belong to different textual traditions altogether. Some texts copied at Salisbury are either very rare, or bear witness to textual traditions represented by few other manuscripts (in some cases, only one). They point to independent contacts between Salisbury and centres of learning on the Continent, and highlight the somewhat unusual and eclectic interests of the canons.

A more detailed examination of the content of the collection, and of certain texts in particular, makes possible a closer analysis of the canons' interests and concerns. Foremost among those interests was scholarship, since the content of the collection goes far beyond what would have been required for purely spiritual purposes. Texts were acquired at Salisbury primarily to support a programme of biblical and theological study, based heavily upon the works of the Fathers. This kind of study was becoming increasingly popular in the Continental schools, especially in northern France, at centres such as Bec and Laon. Chapter 4 assesses the evidence for scholarly activity at Salisbury, and examines in detail two manuscripts, a copy of the Pauline Epistles with glosses, and a Psalter commentary, which demonstrate that the Salisbury canons were well abreast of contemporary developments in biblical exegesis on the Continent.

The canons' scholarly activities were a manifestation of their approach to the spiritual life. The texts of spiritual guidance and edification which they acquired, illustrate their spirituality and allow us to compare it with that of communities which, unlike Salisbury, were subject to the discipline of a named rule. The texts chosen by the canons, and annotations made to them, shed light upon the conduct of the religious life at Salisbury, and point to an underlying similarity with the spirituality of the regular orders in this period. Two texts, the *Scala virtutum* and the *Meditationes Godwini*, are of special importance since they provide rare evidence of the spiritual attitudes and concerns of secular canons in the late eleventh and twelfth centuries. Almost all of the texts of spiritual edification copied at Salisbury had been composed or compiled by monks, but these two texts promote a pattern for the conduct of the religious life clearly intended for those who were not monks but who, none the less, aspired to lead a life of apostolic perfection. Neither text has been printed before, and I have therefore included a transcription of the shorter of the two (the *Scala virtutum*) as Appendix 3. There was not space to include a transcription of the *Meditationes Godwini* in this book: an edition of this text is an important *desideratum*.

I chose the early canons of Salisbury Cathedral and their books as an example of the evidence manuscript books can provide for historical study. The number of manuscripts which have survived, and the unusual nature of the collection allow us to form a clear picture of the canons' interests and activities. In particular, they bring to light the range and level of the canons' scholarly interests and abilities. Moreover, in the course of my research, I unexpectedly found that three or possibly four of the scribes who were active in producing books for the first canons at Salisbury, had also played an important part in the writing of the Exon Domesday (the draft return for the south-western circuit in the Domesday Survey of 1086).[17] These were indeed versatile men, involved thus in royal administration, whilst at the same time (or perhaps just about to begin) producing one of the earliest and most comprehensive collections of exegetical and theological manuscripts to have survived from any English centre in the Anglo-Norman period.

[17] T. Webber, 'Salisbury and the Exon Domesday: Some Observations Concerning the Origin of Exeter Cathedral MS 3500', *English Manuscript Studies 1100–1700*, 1 (1989), 1–18. N. R. Ker had already identified the hand of one Salisbury scribe in the Wiltshire geld accounts, also datable to 1086, now bound with the Exon Domesday ('Beginnings', 34–8).

I

BOOK PRODUCTION AT SALISBURY IN THE LATE ELEVENTH AND EARLY TWELFTH CENTURIES

A LARGE number of manuscripts dating from the half century following the establishment in 1075 of a see at what is now called Old Sarum, remain in the cathedral library at Salisbury. It is the largest group of manuscripts of this date to have survived from any one centre in England. None of the manuscripts contains a scribal colophon, a contemporary *ex libris* inscription, or any other explicit evidence of origin or early history.[1] However, an examination of the general appearance of the manuscripts, their script, and the patterns of scribal co-operation provides convincing evidence that the manuscripts were produced in one place, and that the place of production, as N. R. Ker has suggested, was Salisbury.[2]

PHYSICAL CHARACTERISTICS

The manuscripts display a general similarity in their construction and physical appearance, which suggests a common origin. Most of them are small, easily portable books. Even those which contain major patristic texts, such as Jerome's biblical commentaries, have a written-space of under 250×150mm; others are much smaller (see, for example, Pl. 4). Some are composed of several originally separate booklets each consisting of as little as a single quire of eight to ten leaves.[3] The

---

[1] No medieval book lists have survived from Salisbury. Apart from the few books mentioned by Leland, the earliest book list is that compiled by Patrick Young in 1622 or 1623 (now Salisbury Cathedral, MS 225): see N. R. Ker, 'Salisbury Cathedral Manuscripts and Patrick Young's Catalogue', *Wiltshire Archaeological and Natural History Magazine*, 53 (1949–50), 153–83; T. Webber, 'Patrick Young, Salisbury Cathedral Manuscripts and the Royal Collection', *English Manuscript Studies 1100–1700*, 2 (1990), 283–90.

[2] Ker, 'Beginnings', 23–49.

[3] Booklets may be identified within a composite manuscript by a combination of such features as blank leaves at the ends of quires, different sequences of quire numeration, and different systems of ruling. Salisbury Cathedral, MS 165, for example, consists of six originally independent booklets with blank leaves occurring at the end of four of them. For a discussion of the characteristics of booklets, see P. R. Robinson, 'The "Booklet": A Self-Contained Unit in Composite Manuscripts', *Codicologica*, 3 (1980), 46–69, and 'Self-Contained Units in Composite Manuscripts of the Anglo-Saxon Period', *ASE*, 7 (1978), 231–8.

parchment used for all of the manuscripts is very poor: it is discoloured and marred by imperfections in many places. Its quality varies considerably even within a single manuscript: leaves are of different sizes, and some lack straight edges. The manuscripts also exhibit a general similarity of layout and decoration. Many of the manuscripts were copied in long lines rather than the two columns which was the more usual layout for the longer patristic texts in this period. The ruling itself is sometimes untidy and uneven. None of the manuscripts is richly decorated; the decoration does not act as embellishment, but indicates in a simple but effective way the beginnings of new texts, or the major divisions within them. Few of the manuscripts have retained their original bindings, but from a study of those that have, Graham Pollard was able to conclude: 'There is a stark community of style in ... (the) bindings, which are mostly small and noticeably narrow folios with square unbevelled boards covered in thinnish whittawed leather; and each board is nearly as thick as the book itself.'[4] Taken together, such physical characteristics give the manuscripts a certain 'home-made' quality. As N. R. Ker commented, 'one would not expect to find such untidy writing, such poor parchment ... and such faulty ruling in books commissioned or given.'[5]

A similar impression is given by the handwriting of the books. They were not copied in a recognizable 'house style'—that is, a distinctive style of script exhibiting a common treatment of letter forms, which is followed consistently by the scribes within a single scriptorium. The handwriting of most of the scribes found in these manuscripts is nevertheless a distinctive form of minuscule derived from Carolingian minuscule, which differs from that copied in the major monastic scriptoria in England after the Norman Conquest. It is smaller, less formal, and exhibits several variant letter forms.[6]

Small, informal hands are not confined to manuscripts from Salisbury. Therefore they cannot be used on their own as a criterion for assigning a manuscript to Salisbury. In this period such handwriting was rarely used as a text hand in manuscripts produced in England, but it was used in many eleventh- and twelfth-century Continental manuscripts. These Continental manuscripts are similar to the Salisbury manuscripts in other

---

[4] H. G. Pollard, 'The Construction of English Twelfth-Century Bindings', *The Library*, 5: 17 (1962), 21.

[5] Ker, 'Beginnings', 23.

[6] Note the different treatment of letter forms employed by the two hands in Pl. 1*a*, which indicates the absence of a house style. Compare the hands in this plate with the hand of a scribe from Christ Church, Canterbury who wrote Cambridge, University Library, MS Kk.I.23, fo. 46 (reproduced in N. R. Ker, *English Manuscripts in the Century after the Norman Conquest* (Oxford, 1960), Pl. 7). This scribe wrote a formal book hand which exhibits the characteristics of the Christ Church, Canterbury style: see Ker, ibid. 26–9.

respects—in their size, booklet format, parchment, irregular ruling, and a lack of elaborate decoration. Many can be shown either to have connections with people who studied or taught at the Continental schools, or contain texts studied at the schools. For this reason the hands which they contain have been called small 'academic' hands.[7]

The general impression derived from the appearance of the manuscripts preserved at Salisbury is that they were produced by scribes associated with the place for which they were intended. That a group of over fifty manuscripts of this period remains at Salisbury makes it likely that the place of origin was Salisbury. Other evidence supports this likelihood. William of Malmesbury states that many books were acquired at Salisbury during the episcopacy of Osmund (1078–99), and indicates that at least some of them were produced at Salisbury since he tells us that Osmund himself did not disdain to copy and bind books.[8]

Moreover, N. R. Ker observed that two scribes who appear in the Salisbury manuscripts also made additions to a Pontifical (now London, BL, MS Cotton Tiberius C I) which demonstrate that the book was being adapted for use at Salisbury:[9] on fos. 112^v–113^v they collaborated in copying the order for the benediction of an abbot in which the bishop asked the abbot whether he would, in all things, maintain canonical obedience to the holy mother church of Salisbury.[10]

The hands of a large number of scribes may be identified in these manuscripts. The numbers of scribes at work, and the patterns of co-operation which emerge from a study of the hands provide firm evidence that almost all of the late eleventh- and early twelfth-century manuscripts which have survived at Salisbury were produced there. The degree to which the scribes co-operated suggests that they were working in the same place, and the nature of the co-operation confirms this. Several of these scribes are to be found within a single manuscript, each responsible for several stints, sometimes only a few lines long; several changes of hand may appear on a single opening (see, for example, Pl. 5).

However, the patterns of collaboration also indicate that not all the scribes were active at the same time. Several hands appear together in a number of the manuscripts and form a coherent group of co-operating

---

[7] For a discussion of small 'academic' hands, and the characteristics of the manuscripts in which they appear, see M. B. Parkes, 'The Date of the Oxford Manuscript of *La Chanson de Roland* (Oxford, Bodl. Libr., MS. Digby 23)', *Medioevo Romanzo*, 10 (1985), 165–70.

[8] 'Librorum copia conquisita, cum episcopus ipse nec scribere nec scriptos ligare fastidiret.'(*GP* 184.)

[9] See N. R. Ker, 'Three Old English Texts in a Salisbury Pontifical, Cotton Tiberius C I', *The Anglo-Saxons: Studies in some Aspects of their History and Culture presented to Bruce Dickins*, ed. P. Clemoes (London, 1959), 269–70.

[10] 'Vis sanctę matri ęcclesię Seriberiensi canonicam per omnia subiectionem exhibere?' (London, BL, MS Cotton Tiberius C I, fo. 112^v.)

scribes (Group I). A second group of scribes (Group II) copied the other Salisbury manuscripts. This second group of scribes not only copied complete manuscripts but also made additions and corrections to manuscripts copied by Group I scribes, which suggests that they were at work in the same place, but at a later date. The identification of individual hands in these two groups enables us to identify manuscripts which were produced at Salisbury but are now located elsewhere.

The work of many of these scribes is readily identifiable. They were clearly well practised, and had developed highly personal or idio-syncratic styles of handwriting. Some wrote very accomplished hands and may be quickly identified by the particular way in which they formed certain letters, or added serifs, or from the duct of their handwriting.[11] Other scribes, although not as careful in their attention to calligraphic detail, also wrote very distinctive hands. They may be identified by the duct of their handwriting supported by reference to certain details, although these details may not always appear together in the same stint.

Not all the scribes stand out as individuals. Because the small 'academic' hand is characterized by the variety of letter forms within the hand of a single scribe, the less practised scribes, lacking the discipline of a house style, and not having developed a style of their own, either admitted variation to an extent which precludes identification, or did not develop a duct which is immediately recognizable. For the most part such scribes did not copy large portions within any one surviving manuscript. They may therefore have been regarded by their fellows as being less able. The Salisbury manuscripts thus contain a number of stints executed by hands I have not yet been able to identify. It is possible that some of these stints may be the work of scribes already identified but operating in unfavourable circumstances, because considerations of space forced them to write larger or smaller than they were accustomed to; others may represent lapses of concentration on the part of a scribe already identified. In some cases it is not clear whether, or at what point, a different scribe has taken over.

GROUP I SCRIBES

Group I comprises seventeen scribes who each copied all or parts of two or more manuscripts. They were assisted by several more scribes whose hands each appear in only one manuscript. Together these scribes

---

[11] 'Duct' is the distinctive manner in which a scribe traced the strokes on the page, consisting of a combination of such factors as the angle at which the pen was held in relation to the way in which it was cut, and the degree of pressure applied to it. Compare, for example, the different ducts of the hands in Pls. 1*a* and 1*b*.

produced over fifty extant manuscripts or originally independent booklets within extant manuscripts.[12] The patterns of co-operation which emerge from a study of their work indicate that they were copying manuscripts during the same period. Six of the eight principal scribes of the group co-operated with all of the other principal scribes, two more did not co-operate with each other, but did co-operate with the other six.

I have listed the scribes in order according to the number of manuscripts or booklets in which they appear, since such a listing indicates the relative importance of the scribes more clearly than a list according to the amount of text they copied. Scribe i, for example, copied few leaves of text, but his activity in glossing, correcting and setting the line-spacing for a number of manuscripts indicates that he acted as a director. In the lists of manuscripts which follow, 'part' indicates that the scribe wrote one uninterrupted stint, 'shared' indicates that he wrote more than one; if neither 'part' nor 'shared' is indicated, the scribe copied the entire manuscript or booklet.

Scribe i (Ker's scribe C)[13] copied:[14] Aberdeen, University Library, MS 216 (last 11 lines), London, BL, MSS Cotton Tiberius C I (additions, shared),[15] Royal 5 E xix, fos. 1–20 (shared), Royal 5 E xix, fos. 21–36 (shared), Oxford, Bodl. Libr., MS Bodley 756 (first 4 lines), Oxford, Keble College, MS 22 (part), Salisbury Cathedral, MSS 10 (shared), 25 (3 lines), 63 (shared), 78 (17 lines), 106 (21 lines), 119 (shared), 128 (shared), 128 flyleaves (5 lines), 138 (shared), 140 (first 14 lines), 140 flyleaves (first 7 lines), 154 (12 lines), 165, fos. 11–20 (text heading only), 165, fos. 23–87 (first 6 lines), 168 (shared), 179 (shared), 221 (15 lines).

Scribe i added glosses to Oxford, Bodl. Libr., MS Bodley 444, fos. 1–27; Oxford, Keble College, MS 22; Salisbury Cathedral MSS 78 and 154.

Scribe i made corrections in Aberdeen, University Library, MS 216, London, BL, MSS Cotton Tiberius C I, Cotton Vitellius A XII, fos. 72–77, Royal 5 E xix, fos. 37–52; Oxford, Bodl. Libr., MSS Bodley 392, Bodley 444, Bodley 756, Bodley 765, fos. 10–77, Bodley 768, Bodley 835, Rawlinson C. 723; Oxford, Keble College, MS 22, Salisbury Cathedral, MSS 6, 10, 25, 37, 63, 67, 78, 88, 106, 119, 128, 129, 135, fos. 1–24, MS 135, fos. 25–59, MSS 140, 154, 159, 165, fos. 23–87, MSS 221, 222.

Scribe ii (Ker's scribe B3)[16] copied:[17] Dublin, Trinity College, MS 174 (shared),

---

[12] For a list of the manuscripts in which Group I scribes appear, and for details of their scribal stints, see App. 1.

[13] Ker, 'Beginnings', 41–7.

[14] For specimens of scribe i's handwriting, see Pls. 1a and 15, and also J. J. G. Alexander and M. T. Gibson, *Medieval Learning and Literature: Essays presented to Richard William Hunt* (Oxford, 1976), pls. VIa and VIb (lines 1–4).

[15] For these additions, see Ker, 'Beginnings', 41–2.

[16] Ibid. 40–1.

[17] For specimens of scribe ii's handwriting, see Pl. 1b; see also T. Webber, 'Salisbury and the Exon Domesday: Some Observations concerning the Origin of Exeter Cathedral MS 3500', *English Manuscript Studies 1100–1700*, 1 (1989), pls. 5–6, and É. Chatelain, *Paléographie des classiques latins* (Paris, 1884–92), i, pl. IVa.

London, BL MSS Royal 5 E xvi (headings only), Royal 5 F xviii (part), Royal 15 C xi, fos. 113–94 (shared); Oxford, Bodl. Libr., MS Bodley 835 (shared); Salisbury Cathedral, MSS 6, 9 (21 lines), 33 (shared), 63 (shared), 67 (shared), 78 (shared), 88 (shared), 120 (11 lines), 128 flyleaves (3 lines), 135, fos. 1–24 (part), 135, fos. 25–59, MSS 154 (additions), 165, fos. 122–78, MS 168 (shared).

Scribe ii also copied over 240 entries relating to Dorset and Somerset in the Exon Domesday (Exeter Cathedral, MS 3500).[18]

Scribe iii (Ker's scribe A)[19] copied:[20] London, BL, MSS Cotton Tiberius C I (additions, shared),[21] Royal 5 E xix, fos. 1–20 (34 lines); Oxford, Bodl. Libr., MSS Bodley 765, fos. 1–9 (shared), Bodley 765, fos. 10–77 (shared); Salisbury Cathedral, MS 10 (shared), 24 (1 leaf), 33 (shared), 63 (shared), 106 (part), 114, 128 (shared), 138 (shared), 140 (shared), 154 (shared), 179 (5 lines), 221 (shared), 222 (shared).

Scribe iii also copied parts of the Wiltshire Geld Accounts B and C which are bound with the Exon Domesday in Exeter Cathedral, MS 3500.[22]

Scribe iv (Ker's scribe D3)[23] copied:[24] London, BL, MSS Cotton Tiberius C I (additions, shared), Royal 5 E xix, fos. 1–20 (shared); Oxford, Bodl. Libr., MSS Bodley 392 (shared), Bodley 444, fos. 1–27; Oxford, Keble College, MS 22 (shared; he also added the prologues to the Epistles as a whole, and to Romans); Salisbury Cathedral, MSS 12, 33 (part), 63 (shared), 78 (shared), 119 (shared), 120 (part), 154 (additions), 165, fos. 1–10 (part), 168 (1 leaf), 169 (shared).

Scribe v[25] copied:[26] Dublin, Trinity College, MS 174 (shared), London, BL, MS Cotton Tiberius C I (additions, shared); Oxford, Bodl. Libr., MS Bodley 756 (shared); Salisbury Cathedral, MSS 24 (shared), 33 (shared), 78 (part), 128 (13 lines), 129, 179 (shared), 222 (shared).

Scribe vi copied:[27] London, BL, MS Royal 8 B xiv, fos. 154–156ᵛ (fragment); Salisbury Cathedral, MSS 10 (shared), 33 (shared), 63 (shared), 106 (shared), 138

---

[18] Scribe ii is scribe D2 in my analysis of the scribes of Exeter Cathedral, MS 3500: Webber, 'Salisbury and the Exon Domesday', 6, 13–14.

[19] Ker, 'Beginnings', 34–8.

[20] For specimens of scribe iii's handwriting, see Pls. 2 and 5, lines 5–14 'tantum'; see also Alexander and Gibson, *Medieval Learning*, pls. IV*a*–*c*, and Webber, 'Salisbury and the Exon Domesday', Pls. 1–2.

[21] For these additions, see Ker, 'Beginnings', 36.

[22] Ibid. 35. He is scribe E in my analysis of the scribes of Exeter Cathedral, MS 3500: Webber, 'Salisbury and the Exon Domesday', 4, 14.

[23] Ker, 'Beginnings', 48. Ker called this scribe, scribe X in his study of the additions made to London, BL, MS Cotton Tiberius C I: 'Three Old English Texts', 268.

[24] For a specimen of scribe iv's hand, see C. F. R. De Hamel, *Glossed Books of the Bible and the Origins of the Paris Booktrade* (Woodbridge, Suffolk, 1984), Pl. 3: Scribe iv copied the biblical text and the last six and a half lines of the gloss in the lower margin. The other glosses are in the hand of scribe i.

[25] Ker called this scribe, scribe VIII in his study of the additions made to London, BL, MS Cotton Tiberius C I: 'Three Old English Texts', 268.

[26] For a specimen of scribe v's handwriting, see Pl. 3; see also *Bodleian Library Record*, 3, no. 31 (1951), pl. I*a*.

[27] For a specimen of scribe vi's hand, see Pl. 5, lines 1–4.

(17 lines), 140 (7 lines), 168 (shared), 169 (part), 179 (shared), 221 (shared), 222 (shared).

Scribe vii (Ker's scribe B2)[28] copied:[29] London, BL, MSS Royal 5 E xix, fos. 1–20 (shared), Royal 5 E xix, fos. 21–36 (shared); Oxford, Bodl. Libr., MSS Bodley 756 (shared), Rawlinson C. 723; Salisbury Cathedral, MSS 24 (shared), 63 (10 lines), 120 (part), 138 (6 lines).

Scribe viii (Ker's scribe B1)[30] copied:[31] London, BL, MS Cotton Vitellius A XII, fos. 4–71; Oxford, Bodl. Libr., MS Bodley 765, fos. 1–9 (4 lines); Oxford, Keble College, MS 22 (shared; additions), Salisbury Cathedral, MSS 10 (shared), 25 (part), 33 (23 lines), 128 (part).

Scribe viii's hand also occurs in a manuscript which was neither produced at, nor for, Salisbury: Utrecht, Universiteits-bibliotheek, MS 86.[32]

Scribe ix copied:[33] Oxford, Bodl. Libr., MS Bodley 756 (11 lines); Oxford, Keble College, MS 22 (shared); Salisbury Cathedral, MSS 63 (shared), 165, fos. 1–10 (part), 168 (shared), 221 (5 lines).

Scribe ix also copied parts of the Wiltshire Geld Accounts A, B, and C, and over 150 entries relating to Dorset and Somerset in the Exon Domesday (now bound together as Exeter Cathedral, MS 3500).[34]

---

[28] Ker, 'Beginnings', 39–40.

[29] Scribe vii wrote a distinctive English Caroline minuscule, characterized by short, firm minim strokes, tall ascenders, and vertical strokes finished with wedge-shaped serifs. The *punctus versus* is sometimes formed with the comma placed a little to the left of the point.

[30] Ker, 'Beginnings', 38–9.

[31] For a specimen of scribe viii's hand, see Pls. 5 (lines 14 'modo'–25) and 15 (biblical text; other scribes copied the glosses).

[32] Utrecht, Universiteitsbibliotheek, MS 86 comprises four volumes of an originally six-volume copy of Gregory, *Moralia in Iob*. Scribe viii's hand occurs in vol. 3. For reproductions of his hand in this manuscript, see K. van der Horst, *Illuminated and Decorated Medieval Manuscripts in the University Library, Utrecht: An Illustrated Catalogue* (The Hague, 1989), Pls. 12–14. His hand is easily recognized from the clumsy two-tier **s** (Van der Horst, pl. 14, line 14 'suis'; compare with a specimen of his hand in a Salisbury manuscript (Pl. 5 below, line 16 'precepisse'). Compare also the form of *punctus elevatus* which he employs, in which the 'tick' faces to the right: Van der Horst, pl. 14, line 10, after 'solent'; Pl. 5 below, line 25, after 'filia'.) All four volumes were owned by St Paul's Abbey, Utrecht, but their origin is unknown. They are written in a number of Continental hands such as are found in the Salisbury books, but, in their general appearance, and, in particular, in the quality of decoration, they differ greatly from manuscripts produced at Salisbury. None of the extant late 11th- and 12th-cent. English copies of the *Moralia* were made in six volumes: one, two, or three volumes being the normal format. However, Brussels, Bibliothèque royale, MSS 1246–9, comprise the first four volumes of a 12th-cent. six-volume set from another centre in the Low Countries: St Laurent, Liège (s.xii). It thus seems likely that Utrecht 86 was made on the Continent, and probably in the Low Countries.

[33] For specimens of scribe ix's hand, see Pl. 4, lines 1–7 and 14 'nosse'–26, and also Webber, 'Salisbury and the Exon Domesday', pls. 3–4.

[34] Scribe ix is scribe D1 in my analysis of the scribes of Exeter Cathedral, MS 3500: Webber, 'Salisbury and the Exon Domesday', 4, 12–13.

Scribe x copied:[35] Aberdeen, University Library, MS 216 (part); Oxford, Bodl. Libr., MS Bodley 756 (part); Salisbury Cathedral, MSS 37 (part), 179 (shared).

Scribe xi copied:[36] London, BL, MS Royal 5 E xix, fos. 37–52; Salisbury Cathedral, MSS 25 (part), 140 flyleaves (part), 168 (7 lines).

Scribe xii copied:[37] Salisbury Cathedral, MS 138 (part), MS 165, fos. 1–10 (part), MS 165, fos. 11–22, MS 165, fos. 23–87 (part).

Scribe xiii copied:[38] Salisbury Cathedral, MSS 25 (shared), 109+114+128 flyleaves (shared), 138 (shared).

Scribe xiv copied:[39] Oxford, Bodl. Libr., MS Bodley 765, fos. 10–77 (shared); Salisbury Cathedral, MS 33 (1 page). Scribe xiv also added glosses to Oxford, Keble College, MS 22.

Scribe xv copied:[40] Oxford, Bodl. Libr., MSS Bodley 768 and Bodley 835 (part).

Scribe xvi copied:[41] Salisbury Cathedral, MSS 221 (31 lines) and 222 (shared).

Scribe xvii copied:[42] Salisbury Cathedral, MSS 67 (32 lines) and 162 flyleaves.

A scribe whose hand does not appear in collaboration with a Salisbury scribe already identified, copied Salisbury Cathedral, MS 132 and London, BL, MS Royal 5 F xiii, a manuscript which was almost certainly at Salisbury in the early twelfth century, since it contains corrections in the hand of Group II scribe 10 (see below). The hand of the scribe of these two manuscripts is a good example of English Caroline minuscule, probably datable to the second half of the eleventh century. It is possible that this scribe was not active at Salisbury, and that the books were acquired from elsewhere.

[35] Scribe x employed the variety of English Caroline minuscule which is characterized by a relatively light stroke production. For specimens of his handwriting, see Alexander and Gibson, *Medieval Learning*, pl. VIb, lines 5–7, and M. R. James, *A Catalogue of the Medieval Manuscripts in the University Library Aberdeen* (Cambridge, 1932), pl. 22 (facing p. 81).

[36] For a specimen of scribe xi's hand, see Pl. 4, lines 8–14 'quam'.

[37] For a specimen of scribe xii's hand, see Pl. 1a, lines 6 'V. Propitiatorii'–14.

[38] Scribe xiii wrote an English Caroline minuscule which exhibits a slight forward lean and a tendency to be laterally compressed.

[39] For a specimen of the hand of scribe xiv, see Pl. 15, all but the first line of the gloss in the lower margin.

[40] Scribe xv wrote a very small Continental 'academic' hand. Its most distinctive characteristic is the ampersand in which the final stroke rises almost vertically, extending well above the rest of the ligature.

[41] Scribe xvi wrote a large, formal English Caroline minuscule formed with heavy pen strokes. The formation of the letter **g** is distinctive: the lobe which forms the lower part of the letter is not appended directly to the base of the upper part (as, for example, in the hand of scribe iii, see Pl. 2), or joined to it by means of a short vertical stroke (as in the hand of scribe x) but curves upwards to join the left-hand side of the upper lobe.

[42] Scribe xvii wrote a relatively informal English Caroline minuscule in which both round-backed **d** and **a** formed without a headstroke occur. The lower part of the letter **g** is formed with a particularly large lobe.

The patterns of co-operation between scribes indicate that the Group I manuscripts were copied within a relatively short period—N. R. Ker suggested a period of less than twenty years.[43] It is probable that most, if not all, of the Group I manuscripts were produced during the episcopacy of Bishop Osmund (1078–99), since we know from the testimony of William of Malmesbury that many books were acquired during that time, and that Osmund himself took part in copying and binding books.[44] Furthermore, the additions made by scribes i and iii on fo. 112ᵛ of the Pontifical (London, BL, MS Cotton Tiberius C I), indicate that they were at work after the see had been transferred from Sherborne to Salisbury.[45]

It is more difficult to establish whether manuscript production began soon after permission had been granted to move the see from Sherborne (1075), or only after the formal establishment of a community of canons at Salisbury, sometime between 1089 and 1091. At least three of the Group I scribes (scribes ii, iii, and ix) were working together as scribes before 1089, since they collaborated to produce parts of the Wiltshire Geld Accounts and the Exon Domesday (Exeter Cathedral, MS 3500) which are datable to 1086.[46] It is possible that part, if not all, of the Exon Domesday was produced by scribes associated with Salisbury, since it bears many similarities with the Group I Salisbury manuscripts, in its physical construction, quality of parchment, and handwriting.[47] The palaeographical evidence can be supported with historical evidence. A passage added to the Exon Domesday, and incorporated into Domesday Book itself, mentions Salisbury in connection with the Survey. And it was to Salisbury that William the Conqueror summoned his council and all landholding men to swear an oath of fealty to him there on 1 August 1086, an occasion which, according to J. C. Holt, should be viewed as being closely associated with the Domesday Survey.[48] In addition, Osmund had been royal chancellor before becoming bishop of Salisbury,

[43] Ker, 'Beginnings', 23.

[44] *GP* 184. N. R. Ker made the tentative suggestion that Osmund might be the scribe-corrector (scribe i): 'Beginnings', 33. This scribe made numerous annotations chiefly concerned with clerical discipline in Salisbury Cathedral, MS 78, a copy of Lanfranc's abridgement of Pseudo-Isidore, Decretals, and Canons of Councils. Such activity might, however, reflect the interests and concerns of an archdeacon: for a possible identification, see below, Ch. 5.

[45] See above, n. 10.

[46] For the date of the Geld Accounts, see V. H. Galbraith, 'The Date of the Geld Rolls in Exon Domesday', *EHR* 65 (1950), 1–17, and also J. F. A. Mason, 'The Date of the Geld Rolls', *EHR* 69 (1954), 283–9. A scribe who copied seven leaves of a Group I manuscript (Salisbury Cathedral, MS 119, fos. 74–80) may also have contributed to the Exon Domesday. He wrote a hand which is very similar to that of scribe C of the Exon Domesday, who copied over 90 entries relating to Cornwall: see Webber, 'Salisbury and the Exon Domesday', 7–8, 12, pls. 7–8.

[47] For this and what follows, see Webber, 'Salisbury and the Exon Domesday', 1–18.

[48] J. C. Holt, '1086', in *Domesday Studies: Novocentenary Conference, Royal Historical Society and Institute of British Geographers, Winchester 1986*, ed. J. C. Holt (Woodbridge, Suffolk, 1987), 41–64.

and his administrative skills may well have been called upon for such a project. If the Exon Domesday was produced at, or near, Salisbury, as this evidence would seem to suggest, then it is possible that the Salisbury scribes who collaborated to produce it were already collaborating to produce manuscripts for Osmund and his *familia.*

A high level of activity by scribes at Salisbury during this period is indicated by the level of production—at least fifty books and booklets were produced in the space of twenty years, or less, if book production did not begin until after the establishment of the cathedral chapter. The scale of activity is also indicated by the numbers of scribes and assistants at work. The patterns of co-operation within many of the manuscripts suggest that the copying was done in great haste, possibly because exemplars had to be sent back to their owners or to another 'scriptorium'. In several manuscripts a principal scribe was assisted by one or more scribes who relieved him for several short stints. This practice usually occurs towards the end of a lengthy manuscript, presumably as pressure mounted to finish the copying. Scribe ii, for example, having copied almost all of a copy of Augustine, Homilies on St John's Gospel (Salisbury Cathedral, MS 67) was helped out by assistants who copied seven short passages. Some manuscripts show signs of extreme haste, since they were copied by a large number of scribes. In a copy of Cassian, *Collationes* (Salisbury Cathedral, MS 10), copied by no less than eight scribes, several changes of hand appear even on a single opening, often occurring within *sententiae* (see, for example, Pl. 5). The fact that several manuscripts did not pass through the finishing stages where initials and headings would have been filled in, may be a further indication of the haste in which the manuscripts were produced.

Nearly all the manuscripts of Group I appear to have been copied continuously across quire boundaries: changes of hand occur within quires rather than at the beginnings or endings of quires. This indicates that, for the most part, collaboration did not take the form of simultaneous copying: the exemplar being divided into individual quires to be distributed among two or more scribes who would then work simultaneously to produce the copy. However, blank leaves or lines do occur at the ends of quires in the middle of a few manuscripts which contain especially lengthy texts: for example, Salisbury Cathedral, MS 33 (Gregory, *Moralia in Iob*), and Salisbury Cathedral, MS 25 (Jerome on Isaiah). This might indicate simultaneous copying, but an alternative explanation is that each of these manuscripts was originally intended to form two volumes.

Handwriting

Most of the Group I scribes wrote small 'academic' hands. Their handwriting is smaller than the formal book hands associated with books from the major monastic scriptoria in England, such as Christ Church, Canterbury, Durham, and Rochester. In formal book hands the bodies of letters are comparatively large, and ascenders are less than twice the height of minims.[49] By contrast, in many Salisbury hands the bodies of letters are small and laterally compressed, while ascenders are usually at least, if not more than, twice their height. This difference in proportion necessitated a different treatment of the script. In formal hands the bottoms of minims often received as careful calligraphic treatment (in the form of serifs) as the tops of ascenders, but in the Salisbury hands the minims are too short and compressed to allow such treatment; serifs are on the whole confined to the tops of ascenders. The handwriting of the Group I scribes includes the variant forms characteristic of small 'academic' hands, but which are not commonly found in monastic book hands: **d** with a curved shaft (e.g. Pl. 2, line 2 'ad') as well as the more formal form with a straight shaft (e.g. Pl. 2, line 1 'benedictio'); **a** without a headstroke (e.g. Pl. 1*b*, line 2 'formatarum'); **f** and long **s** with the shafts descending below the line (e.g. Pl. 3, line 4 'officio suo'), and the tironian sign for *et* (**7**) as well as the ampersand. Their handwriting also contains more abbreviations and ligatures than is usual in formal book hands: the ampersand and the tironian sign for *et* are used as ligatures in all positions within a word; ligatures of **N** and **T**, and of **N** and **S** are also found, especially at line endings. All of these variations are space- or time-saving devices. These two criteria seem to be behind what might otherwise be interpreted as evidence of a poor scribe—cursive elements, a forward or backward slope, and the same letter form or ligature produced in a number of different ways, especially complicated forms such as **g** and **&**.

Some of these scribes were very experienced. Scribes iii and viii, for example, wrote handsome, upright, and regular hands. Scribe ii, when he wrote small, could write a fine hand, but when he wrote larger the letter forms became irregular and untidy. Likewise the writing of scribe v varies greatly in quality according to its size.[50] The hands of scribes i and vi, although untidy in appearance, nevertheless have a well-developed duct and are readily identifiable. Some scribes, however, were clearly in-experienced. The scribe, for example, who copied fos. 286ᵛ/4–17 and 286ʳ⁻ᵛ of Salisbury Cathedral, MS 222, formed his letters with large, clumsy pen strokes which often failed to connect.

---

[49] See, for example, Ker, *English Manuscripts*, pls. 3 (from Exeter Cathedral), 8b (from Durham Cathedral Priory), and 12*a* and *b* (from Rochester).

[50] Compare the specimen of his hand in Pl. 3 with that in *Bodleian Library Record*, 3, no. 31 (1951), pl. I*a*.

Not all of the Group I scribes wrote small 'academic' hands. Some wrote varieties of English Caroline minuscule.[51] A few, for example, scribes x and xiii, wrote the variety characterized by relatively light stroke production, others, such as the scribe who copied fos. 89–120ᵛ of Salisbury Cathedral, MS 222, wrote the more 'monumental' variety with heavier pen strokes. Scribe iii, perhaps the most accomplished of the Group I scribes, wrote a hand which displays some 'English' characteristics, such as his formation of the letter **g**, but his hand also incorporates some of the characteristics of the small 'academic' hand, for example, the two forms of **d** with straight or curved shaft (see Pl. 2).

Scribal practices

The number of variations in scribal practice that appear in these manuscripts suggests that the scribes arrived at Salisbury with their own scribal practices fully developed. However, there are signs which indicate a certain amount of direction of the copying. N. R. Ker pointed out scribe i's role as a director.[52] This scribe not only corrected a number of the books but also determined the layout of several, by commencing the copying of the first text (see, for example, Pl. 1*a*, lines 1–6 'arce').

There also appears to have been some degree of consistency in such practices as layout, ruling, decoration, and quire signatures. All the manuscripts of Group I were ruled in long lines, with the exception of Salisbury Cathedral, MSS 33 and 67, which are in two columns. The usual practice was for sheets of a whole quire to be pricked and ruled at the same time, so that after folding each opening would have an equal number of equally-spaced lines. However, some quires contain bifolia with different numbers of lines, which indicate that each bifolium was ruled separately before inclusion with the other sheets for folding.[53] A large number of the manuscripts were ruled according to the same pattern with two vertical bounding lines on each side of the written-space extending to the edge of the leaf, and with the first two and last two horizontal lines extending beyond the written-space into the margins. In a few manuscripts, however, the first and third, and third last and last horizontal lines extend into the margins. This is also the practice most

---

[51] For the distinctive features of English Caroline minuscule at the time of the Conquest, see Ker, *English Manuscripts*, 22–3; and for a detailed description of the different varieties of English Caroline minuscule, see T. A. M. Bishop, *English Caroline Minuscule* (Oxford, 1971), pp. xxi–xxiv.

[52] Ker, 'Beginnings', 41.

[53] For example, quire 3 in London, BL, MS Royal 5 E xvi (fos. 15–22): bifolium 1 (fos. 15 + 22) has 34 lines; bifolium 2 (fos. 16 + 21) has 30 lines, and bifolia 3 and 4 (fos. 17–20) have 29 lines.

commonly found in the manuscripts of Group II, a fact which might suggest that the Group I manuscripts which exhibit this pattern were among the later manuscripts of that group to be copied. The following Group I manuscripts have this pattern of ruling: London, BL, MS Royal 5 E xvi, and Salisbury Cathedral, MSS 33, 67, 138 and 169. Scribe ii co-operated with Group II scribes in two manuscripts: London, British Library, MSS Royal 5 F xviii and Royal 15 C xi, fos. 113–19, both of which are ruled in this way.

In order to ensure that the individual quires were bound into the codex in the correct order, scribes added quire signatures on the first or last leaf of each quire. In many instances these signatures were trimmed off during binding. From those that remain it seems that the most common practice followed by the Group I scribes was to number each quire in sequence with a Roman numeral placed in the lower margin of the last verso of the quire, either in the middle or at the outer edge. However, quires are numbered on the first recto as well as, or instead of, the last verso, in London, BL, MS Royal 15 C xi, fos. 113–94, and Salisbury Cathedral, MSS 10, 25, 37, 88, and 106. In some manuscripts there is an experimental use of catchwords—unusual in England at this time.[54] They appear spasmodically in Oxford, Bodl. Libr., MSS Bodley 392 and Bodley 756; and Salisbury Cathedral, MSS 9, 12, 33, 169, 221, and 222.

Corrections

The correction of the completed texts seems to have been the responsibility of just one of the Group I scribes: scribe i. Well over half of the Group I manuscripts contain his corrections. For the most part these corrections were made as a result of checking the copy against the exemplar, and noting scribal errors, such as homoeoteleuton (the omission of a passage as a result of the copyist's eye skipping from one word to the same or a similar word a line or more below). But some of his activity approached that of an editor. For example, he collated the text of Augustine, *De adulterinis coniugiis* in Salisbury Cathedral, MS 128 with that in a second exemplar, and emended it accordingly (see below, Ch. 3). During the twelfth century, formal provision was made for such activity:[55] a charter of Bishop Jocelin (1142–84), datable to *c.*1180 records the grant of a virgate of land which 'ab antiquo' was wont to be used for the correction of the books of the Cathedral, to Philip of St

---

[54] J. Vezin, 'Observations sur l'emploi des réclames dans les manuscrits latins', *Bibliothèque de l'École des Chartes*, 125 (1967), 5–33.

[55] Ker, 'Beginnings', 31.

Edward, on condition that he undertake the duty of correcting the books.[56] In the early thirteenth century these duties, together with the virgate of land, were assigned to the Chancellor.[57]

Decoration

The Group I manuscripts contain little elaborate decoration: there are no historiated initials, and only a very limited use of colour. The decoration, such as it is, is uniform in character. The initials are usually only two to four lines high. They are either plain black or red, or decorated with tiny trefoils, curls, lines, and berries. These decorated initials are found largely in the books copied and miniated by scribe ii. Good examples of his work may be seen in Salisbury Cathedral, MS 88 and London, BL, MS Royal 15 C xi, fos. 113–94.[58] In London, BL, MS Royal 5 E xvi he appears solely as a miniator. Colours other than red, or initials constructed with more than one colour, appear only in the following manuscripts: Oxford, Bodl. Libr., MS Bodley 768, fo. 1 (green, red and blue), and fos. 47ᵛ and 64ᵛ (green), and Salisbury Cathedral, MSS 78, *passim* (green and red), 159 *passim* (green), 168, fo. 2 (blue), and 221, fo. 1 (red and blue).[59] Headings are in Rustic capitals or minuscule, in red or black. In some manuscripts the heading for the first text is in a mixture of capitals and uncials, written in black with red infilling. All but one of the scribes left blank spaces for the heading and initials to be filled in later. The guide letter for the initial was written in the margin, while the words for the heading were written vertically along the edge of the outer margin. Scribe ii was the only scribe who did not leave gaps, but miniated as he wrote. This is evident from the several cases where he wrote a word or part of a word across an initial which he had already painted.[60] Scribe i often seems to have filled in initials and headings when he came to correct the texts, using the ink with which he wrote the corrections. But there are several instances where the gaps left for the initials and headings were never filled in.

---

[56] *Statutes and Customs of the Cathedral Church of the Blessed Virgin Mary of Salisbury,* ed. C. Wordsworth and D. Macleane (London, 1915), 38–9.

[57] Ibid. 54–5.

[58] See, for example, É. Chatelain, *Paléographie,* pl. IVa.

[59] On fo. 37 of Salisbury Cathedral, MS 128, there is an initial with distinctive decoration which is also found in a number of the Group II manuscripts, and it is possible that this initial, like the plain blue or green initials which appear just once or twice in a few of the Group I manuscripts, was added at a later date.

[60] As, for example, on fo. 155 of London, BL, MS Royal 15 C xi, where the text encroaches on top of the red initial **M**.

GROUP II SCRIBES

Group II comprises nineteen scribes who each appear in two or more manuscripts. Together they produced no less than forty books and booklets, and made additions to eight earlier manuscripts.[61] Group II may be subdivided into two smaller groups on the basis of the way in which the scribes collaborated (Groups II*a* and II*b*). The scribes of Group II*a* did not co-operate with one another to the same extent as the principal scribes of Group I. This pattern suggests that they may not all have been at work at the same time, but may suggest the order in which they worked. Two Group II*a* scribes (scribes 1 and 2) co-operated with scribe ii from Group I, and hence belong to the phase at the beginning of Group II's activity. I have listed the remaining scribes according to the way in which they collaborated with scribes 1 and 2, and with each other. Group II*b* consists of six scribes who worked together, but do not appear to have co-operated with any of the Group II*a* scribes. One other scribe was also working at Salisbury during this period—the scribe who added the Salisbury *titulus* to the Mortuary Roll of Abbot Vitalis of Savigny (Paris, Musée des Archives Nationales, MS 138). I have not, however, been able to identify his hand in any of the other surviving manuscripts from Salisbury.

Group II*a*

Scribe 1 copied:[62] London, BL, MS Royal 15 C xi, fos. 113–94 (part); Salisbury Cathedral, MSS 11 (part) and 131 (part).

Scribe 2 copied:[63] London, BL, MS Royal 5 F xviii (part), Salisbury Cathedral, MSS 12 (fos. 56–60ᵛ, an addition to a Group I manuscript), 118 (shared), 169 (fos. 77–91, an addition to a Group I manuscript).

Scribe 3 (Ker's scribe D1)[64] copied:[65] London, BL, MS Royal 6 B xv (part); Salisbury Cathedral, MS 61, fos. 1–10, MS 61, fos. 11–20 (rubrics), MS 61, fos.

---

[61] For a list of the manuscripts in which the hands of Group II scribes appear, and for details of their scribal stints, see App. 2.

[62] Scribe 1 wrote a regular, well-proportioned, upright hand. He employed both the straight-backed **d** and the less-formal, round-backed **d**. The letter **g** is the most distinctive feature of his hand: the right-hand side of the upper lobe of the letter is formed with a vertical stroke; the lower lobe is appended to the base of the upper part of the letter without an additional connecting stroke.

[63] Scribe 2 wrote a clumsy and irregular hand; serifs are untidy, and vertical strokes have a tendency to taper towards the base of the stroke. Round-backed **d** is preferred to **d** formed with a straight shaft.

[64] Ker, 'Beginnings', 47–8.

[65] For specimens of scribe 3's hand, see Pls. 6*a* and 7, lines 1–32 'sermone'.

21–30, MS 61, fos. 31–52 (shared), MSS 64 (part), 116, 131 (shared), 139 (shared), 197+London, BL, MS Royal App. 1 (shared), Salisbury Cathedral, MS 198.

Scribe 4 copied:[66] Cambridge, Trinity College, MS R.16.34 (shared); London, BL, MS Cotton Tiberius C I, fo. 202^v (addition);[67] Salisbury Cathedral, MS 11 (part).

Scribe 5 copied:[68] Salisbury Cathedral, MSS 118 (6 lines), 125 (shared), 130.

Scribe 6 (Ker's scribe D2)[69] copied:[70] Salisbury Cathedral, MSS 4, 64 (part), 109, 112, and 136.

Scribe 7 copied:[71] London, BL, MS Royal 6 B xv (part); Salisbury Cathedral, MSS 58 (23 lines), 61, fos. 31–52 (shared), MS 65 (shared), MS 162, fos. 19–27 (part), 165, fo. 178^v (an addition to a Group I manuscript).

Scribe 8 copied:[72] London, BL, MS Royal 15 C xi, fos. 1–58 (36 lines), Salisbury Cathedral, MSS 5, 57 (shared), 58 (13 lines), 65 (23 lines), 110 (11 lines), 110 flyleaf (fragment), 162, fos. 3–18.

Scribe 9 copied:[73] London, BL, MS Royal 15 C xi, fos. 1–58 (part); Salisbury Cathedral, MS 124 (shared).

Scribe 9 also supplied replacement leaves for Salisbury Cathedral, MSS 139 (fos. 88–89^v, fo. 106$^{r–v}$), and made corrections in London, BL, MS Royal 15 C xi, fos. 1–58; Salisbury Cathedral, MSS 58, 139, and 165, fos. 23–87.

Scribe 10 copied:[74] Dublin, Trinity College, MS 174 (part); Salisbury Cathedral, MSS 9, fos. 60^v-81 (part, an addition to a Group I manuscript), 101 (fo. 32, an addition to a tenth-century manuscript), 124 (part), 165, fos. 88–107.

Scribe 10 also supplied replacement leaves for: Salisbury Cathedral, MSS 139 (fos. 94–103^v), 165, fos. 23–87 (fos. 72–6), 197 (fos. 55–6), and made corrections in London, BL, MSS Royal 5 F xiii, Royal 6 B xv; Salisbury Cathedral, MSS 4, 5, 11, 25, 57, 65, 110, 112, 130, 165, fos. 23–87, MS 197+London, BL, MS Royal App. 1.

Scribe 11 copied:[75] London, BL, MS Cotton Vitellius A XII, fos. 79–86^v; Salisbury Cathedral, MS 162, fos. 19–27 (shared).

Scribe 12 copied:[76] London, BL, MS Royal 15 C xi, fos. 1–58 (shared); Salisbury

---

[66] Scribe 4 wrote an irregular 'academic' hand which exhibits a tendency to lean backwards; he added serifs (in a somewhat rough fashion) to the base of descenders, placing them at an acute angle.

[67] This is Ker's scribe XIII in his analysis of the scribes of this manuscript: 'Three Old English Texts', 269.

[68] Scribe 5 also wrote an 'academic' hand with generally upright letter forms but which exhibits considerable variation in the formation of individual letters.

[69] Ker, 'Beginnings', 48.

[70] For a specimen of scribe 6's hand, see Pl. 6*b*.

[71] For a specimen of scribe 7's hand, see Pl. 7, lines 32 'dominum'–35.

[72] For a specimen of scribe 8's hand, see Pl. 8.

[73] For a specimen of scribe 9's hand, see Pl. 9*a*.

[74] Scribe 10 wrote an informal small 'academic' hand, with a rapid duct, which exhibits a marked preference for forms which could be traced swiftly. For example, he formed the letter **g** with just three strokes—two lobes (each consisting of a single stroke), one below and to the right of the other, connected by a single curved stroke.

[75] For a specimen of scribe 11's hand, see Pl. 10.

[76] For a specimen of scribe 12's hand, see Pl. 9*b*.

Cathedral, MSS 57 (shared), 58 (part), 110 (shared), and 162, fos. 19–27 (29 lines).

Scribe 13 copied:[77] Salisbury Cathedral, MSS 7, 9, fos. 60ᵛ–81 (part, an addition to a Group I manuscript).

Group II*b*

Scribe 14 copied:[78] Dublin, Trinity College, MS 174 (part); Salisbury Cathedral, MSS 59 (shared), 221 (fos. 223/17–224ᵛ: an addition to a Group I manuscript), 223 (shared).

Scribe 15 copied:[79] Dublin, Trinity College, MS 174 (part); Salisbury Cathedral, MSS 59 (shared), 223 (shared).

Scribe 16 copied:[80] Salisbury Cathedral, MS 115+London, BL, MS Royal 15 B xix, fos. 200–5 (shared), MS 223 (shared).

Scribe 17 copied:[81] Oxford, Bodl. Libr., MS Bodley 698; Salisbury Cathedral, MSS 35 (shared), 223 (shared).

Scribe 18 copied:[82] Salisbury Cathedral, MSS 35 (part), 59 (11 lines), 137 (shared), 223 (shared).

Scribe 19 copied:[83] Salisbury Cathedral, MSS 35 (shared), 137 (shared).

The majority of the manuscripts in Group II were probably written in the early twelfth century. They were produced by scribes who were active after all but one of the Group I scribes whose industry seems to have coincided with the episcopacy of Osmund (1078–99).[84] Group II scribes 2, 7, 10, 13 and 14 made additions to manuscripts which contain the hands of Group I scribes,[85] and, in one instance, Group II scribes made a copy of a manuscript produced by Group I scribes.[86] The very small

---

[77] Scribe 13 wrote a large, irregular and clumsy hand. He preferred to use the *punctus versus* to mark the end of a *sententia* rather than a simple point which, by the early twelfth century, had become the more usual mark of punctuation for this purpose.

[78] For a specimen of scribe 14's hand, see Pls. 11 (lines 9–16) and 12.

[79] For a specimen of scribe 15's hand, see Pl. 13.

[80] For a specimen of scribe 16's hand, see Pl. 14.

[81] For a specimen of scribe 17's hand, see Pl. 11, lines 1–8.

[82] Scribe 18 wrote a somewhat ponderous hand which exhibits variant forms of the same letter. The letters **a** and **g** are particularly prone to variation: **a** is sometimes formed with a pronounced headstroke, and sometimes without one at all; the lower part of the letter **g** is formed with a particularly large lobe which is sometimes open (in the form of a reversed **c**), and sometimes closed.

[83] Scribe 19 employed a rapid, generally rounded hand. He formed **a** without a headstroke, and the lower lobe of **g** is invariably closed.

[84] Group II scribes 1 and 2 collaborated with Group I scribe ii to produce London, BL, MSS Royal 5 C xi, fos. 113–94 respectively.

[85] Additions were made to London, BL, MS Cotton Tiberius C I, and Salisbury Cathedral, MSS 9, 12, 165, 169, and 221.

[86] Salisbury Cathedral, MS 65 is a direct copy of Salisbury Cathedral, MS 138.

number of overlaps between the two groups of scribes suggests that the activity associated with Group II may have been due to a fresh impetus, and was not merely a continuation of the work of Group I. The patterns of co-operation between the Group II scribes suggest that not all of them worked at the same time, and that the group may have been active over a longer period of time than Group I.

The only scribe active at Salisbury in the early twelfth century whose work is datable is the scribe who added the Salisbury *titulus* to the Mortuary Roll of Abbot Vitalis of Savigny in 1122/3.[87] His hand exhibits a number of similarities with those of the Group II*b* scribes, which suggests that they too were active in the 1120s. Although it is impossible to put a date to the end of the Group II activity, it seems likely that it ceased not long after the beginning of the second quarter of the twelfth century.

The copying of the manuscripts of Group II seems to have been a less hurried affair than that of the manuscripts of Group I. Many Group II scribes copied manuscripts largely or entirely on their own, and there are no instances of large numbers of scribes co-operating to produce a single manuscript. The principal scribes usually received help from assistants only when copying especially long texts, for example, Augustine, *Enarrationes in psalmos i–l* (Salisbury Cathedral, MS 57).

The exemplars for most of the Group II manuscripts, like those for Group I, seem to have been copied straight through, and not divided for copying. Exceptions to this are Salisbury Cathedral, MS 64 (divided between scribes 3 and 6: scribe 3 copying the first ten quires (as they are currently bound), and scribe 6, the remaining nine),[88] and also Salisbury Cathedral, MSS 131, 139 and 197. In these last three manuscripts scribes 9, 10, and two unidentified scribes copied individual quires in manuscripts otherwise copied by scribe 3. However, these three manuscripts are almost certainly not examples of simultaneous copying. Although scribe 3 always finished precisely at the ends of the last versos of the quires he copied, large gaps occur at the ends of the quires copied by the other scribes. This may have been because they were less expert at fitting their portions of text into the space given them. But there is another more likely explanation: that they were working subsequently from a second exemplar, and were replacing defective parts of the text originally copied by scribe 3. In Salisbury Cathedral, MS 131, for example, the third quire (fos. 17–20) now consists of only four leaves written by scribe 3, but four

---

[87] For the date of the Mortuary Roll, see *Rouleau mortuaire du b. Vital, Abbé de Savigni*, ed. L. Delisle (Paris, 1909), 15. The Salisbury titulus is no. 186, reproduced in Delisle (ed.), pl. xliv.

[88] The original quire numbers indicate that the quires are at present bound in the wrong order: the quires originally numbered 10–19 now precede the quires numbered 1–9.

more leaves have been cut away, leaving only the stubs. The next quire seems to have been a replacement for these leaves since the text continues without a break but the quire was written by a different scribe. Scribe 10 made a similar replacement in a booklet otherwise copied by a Group I scribe (Salisbury Cathedral, MS 165, fos. 72–6). In Salisbury 139, a copy of Eusebius, *Historia ecclesiastica*, it is clear that scribe 9 was collating the manuscript with a second exemplar which bore witness to a different tradition of the text, since he not only corrected several readings but also drew attention to a portion of text which is lacking from manuscripts which represent the tradition of the text to which the second exemplar almost certainly bore witness (see below, Ch. 3).

Handwriting

No Group II scribe wrote the kind of English Caroline minuscule written, for example, by scribes x and xiii of Group I. The handwriting of some Group II scribes also reflects developments which had subsequently taken place within the small 'academic' hands since they had been used by many Group I scribes.[89] Several Group II scribes, for example, scribes 9 and 10, exhibit no such developments, but others attempted to write larger versions of these hands, using heavier strokes. The enlargement of the script caused difficulties for many scribes, apparent in the clumsy and irregular way the strokes were put together resulting in even more variations in the formation of complicated forms. Some scribes, in the course of copying a lengthy text, lapsed into the smaller script with which they were more comfortable. This is evident in Salisbury Cathedral, MS 58, a copy of Augustine, *Enarrationes in psalmos li–c*. The main scribe (scribe 12) began the volume writing in a fairly large formal hand, but as he copied he gradually decreased the size of his hand, and made the letter forms with strokes which required less care.

The employment of larger letter forms and heavier strokes is particularly characteristic of the hands of all but one of the Group II*b* scribes (see Pls. 11–14), and the hand of the scribe of the Salisbury *titulus* in the Mortuary Roll of Abbot Vitalis.[90] The variant letter forms characteristic of 'academic' hands are still present, for example, **a** without a headstroke (Pl. 11, line 15 'salutifera'; Salisbury *titulus*, line 1, 'Salesberiensis'), and **d** with a curved shaft (Pl. 11, line 12 'deo'; Salisbury *titulus*, line 2, 'defunctorum'). However, the letter forms are larger, and the proportion of the ascenders to the minims has altered—the ascenders are now less

[89] For an account of these developments, see Parkes, 'The Date of the Oxford Manuscript of *La Chanson de Roland*', 168–70.

[90] *Rouleau mortuaire*, no. 186, reproduced in Delisle (ed.), pl. xliv.

than twice the minim height. Calligraphic details such as serifed or 'split' ascenders, and feet on minim strokes have been added, but these can appear clumsy and exaggerated. M. B. Parkes argues, using the example of the scribe of the Digby manuscript of *La Chanson de Roland* (Oxford, Bodl. Libr., MS Digby 23—to which he assigns a date only a little later than that of the Mortuary Roll of Vitalis) that these scribes produced clumsy-looking work because they were 'grappling with a new and comparatively unfamiliar quality of style—an element of calligraphy—in the handwriting'.[91] He demonstrates that the addition of calligraphic details borrowed from the formal book hands of the period, and the increased size of letter forms, is particularly characteristic of the 'academic' hands written in the latter part of the first quarter, and the beginning of the second quarter of the twelfth century.

Scribal practices

None of the Group II scribes appears to have acted as a director. Scribes 9 and 10 corrected several manuscripts (in some instances, collating the text with that in a second exemplar) but they did not set the page layout in the way that Group I scribe i had done. There are, however, signs of attempts at consistency in scribal practices, and some changes from the practices followed by the Group I scribes.

All of the Group II manuscripts are ruled in dry-point. Many of them are ruled with the first and third, and third last and last horizontal lines extending into the margins (see, for example, Pl. 9*b*). Some are ruled in two columns (Oxford, Bodl. Libr., MS Bodley 698, and Salisbury Cathedral, MSS 35, 57, 58, 59, 137, and parts of 223). No consistent practice was observed with regard to the number of vertical lines ruled for each column. The scribes had great difficulty in making these lines perpendicular to the horizontal lines (see, for example, Pl. 11, left-hand margin). Many of the Group II manuscripts, especially those in two columns, are rather larger than those of Group I; this larger size may have been the source of the scribes' difficulty.

The scribes were less consistent in their method of numbering quires than the scribes of Group I. Although they did not take up the experimental catchwords introduced by some Group I scribes, the use and position of Roman numerals followed no set pattern. Roman numerals in red or black appear in various positions in the lower margin of the last verso, first recto, or both. The signatures in Oxford, Bodl. Libr., MS Bodley 698 consist of minuscule letters written on the first recto, but they may have been added at a later date.

[91] Parkes, '*Chanson de Roland*', 171.

Decoration

As in the manuscripts of Group I, gaps left in Group II manuscripts by the scribes for initials and headings often remain unfilled (see, for example, Pl. 11), or have been filled in very roughly in the ink used for writing texts. The initials which were executed are on the whole larger, a little more elaborate, and sometimes exhibit a greater use of colour than those in Group I. A distinctive type of line-drawn initial in pale brown ink is found in Salisbury Cathedral, MSS 61, 64 (see Pl. 6*a*), 65, 109, 116, 131, and 198. These are manuscripts almost entirely produced by scribes 3 and 6, which suggests that this type of initial may be the work of either one or both of these scribes. A number of decorative motifs are employed in the initials in Oxford, Bodl. Libr., MS Bodley 698, and 'insular' style initials appear in Salisbury Cathedral, MS 59 (see Pl. 12).[92]

CONCLUSION

The nature of the scribal activity and the physical appearance of the books produced in the two phases of manuscript production at Salisbury give us several insights into conditions there, and the activities and interests of the canons. The smaller, more informal script, and the absence of elaborate presentation of texts in the Salisbury manuscripts, indicate that the intent of the Salisbury scribes differed from that of scribes in monastic scriptoria. The latter—whether monks or specialist scribes—produced, for the most part, fine-looking decorated books in formal hands, for the use of the community and for export.[93] By contrast, the Salisbury manuscripts are more akin to the small, plain manuscripts copied by scholars for their personal use, and this feature almost certainly indicates that the Salisbury scribes were producing books for use in their own immediate community. The obvious implication is that at least some of the Salisbury scribes were themselves canons. This assertion is supported by other evidence. It is unlikely that all of the Salisbury scribes were hired specially for the purpose of producing books in response to urgent demand; the sheer number of scribes who comprise Groups I and II would make this improbable. Moreover, the general appearance of the manuscripts is not what one would expect of

---

[92] Initials in imitation of an earlier insular style also appear in a Group I manuscript, Oxford, Keble College, MS 22: see De Hamel, *Glossed Books*, pl. 3.

[93] William of Malmesbury and the scribes who collaborated with him are an exception to this general rule. Several of these scribes wrote informal hands, and William wrote both a formal and a smaller, informal hand: see R. M. Thomson, *William of Malmesbury* (Woodbridge, Suffolk, 1987), 76–97, in which he likens the scribal activity at Malmesbury to that at Salisbury a little earlier.

work executed by specialist scribes for a patron. Rather it indicates that the Salisbury scribes' primary intent was to obtain accurate copies of the texts they themselves required—hence the careful attention paid to details such as word-separation, punctuation and correction. The appearance and 'finish' of the manuscripts was of only secondary importance.

Unlike the monastic communities at Abingdon and St Albans, the Salisbury canons did not employ specialist scribes.[94] Nor did they import more than a few manuscripts produced at other centres, in spite of the difficulties they faced in obtaining adequate supplies of parchment.[95] Instead they copied for themselves the texts they required with whatever materials they could obtain. This suggests that funds were not available either for purchasing manuscripts or for employing scribes, but were being channelled towards other purposes. This is not surprising since the manuscripts were being produced at a time when the cathedral was under construction, and the diocese, newly formed from the two dioceses of Sherborne and Ramsbury, was being organized. The pattern of hasty copying evident from the number of co-operating scribes and the short length of some stints, indicates that the scribes had duties elsewhere and fitted in some copying whenever they could.

That manuscripts were copied in such adverse circumstances indicates the high priority given to obtaining copies of desired texts. Some texts were copied twice, others were copied even from damaged exemplars, and whenever words were illegible in the exemplar, gaps were left to be filled in if, or when, another copy of the text could be obtained (see, for example, Pl. 8). The copies were carefully corrected, and were sometimes collated with a second exemplar.

The patterns of co-operation, and the numbers of scribes at work also indicate the scale of the demand for texts at Salisbury. The first phase, represented by the work of Group I, was one of intense activity in order to provide the canons with essential texts; scribes copied portions of manuscripts when and as they could, sometimes managing only a few lines at a time. The phase of activity represented by the work of Group II was not as intense, which would suggest that the immediate need for texts had been somewhat satisfied. In the mid-twelfth century few, if any, manuscripts were copied at Salisbury, presumably because the canons had by then acquired all the texts they needed. Major accessions of books were resumed only in the late twelfth century, with the acquisition

---

[94] For an account of the employment of specialist scribes at Abingdon, see *De abbatibus Abbendoniae*, ed. J. Stevenson, in *Chronicon monasterii de Abingdon*, RS (London, 1858), ii. 289; and at St Albans, see R. M. Thomson, *Manuscripts from St Albans Abbey 1066–1235* (Woodbridge, Suffolk, 1982), i. 13.

[95] For the manuscripts acquired by the Salisbury canons from other centres, see below, Ch. 3.

of glossed books of the Bible, and other texts emanating from the Paris schools in the second half of the twelfth century.

The patterns of scribal co-operation have indicated that the scribes were all working in the same place. Other evidence has pointed to that place as being Salisbury. However, the Salisbury scribes differed from those of the scriptoria of monastic houses such as Christ Church, Canterbury, Rochester, and Worcester since they did not develop a 'house style' of script. This was because they were not subject to the conditions necessary for scribes to produce a 'house style': to be trained in the same place, and to work together over a considerable period without constant exposure to external influences. Such conditions are more likely to have existed in a monastic scriptorium staffed with monks bound by the rule of stability. The script and practices employed by the Salisbury scribes demonstrate that they had been trained in different places, and had been exposed to a number of different influences. The experimental use of catchwords, for example, indicates foreign influence, since the appearance of catchwords in English manuscripts at this time is very unusual: the practice only began to spread from Spain into Italy and southern France towards the end of the eleventh century.[96] Moreover, there is evidence that at least one Salisbury scribe was active on the Continent, namely Group I scribe viii, who collaborated with other Continental scribes to produce Utrecht, Universiteitsbibliotheek, MS 86.

We know that several of the Salisbury canons and *clerici* associated with the cathedral had contacts with the Continent. Some of them had studied abroad at the Continental schools: in 1113 the canons of Laon paid a visit to Salisbury as part of their fund-raising among *alumni* in England.[97] Among the Salisbury canons named by the Laon account are Nigel and Alexander, nephews of Roger, bishop of Salisbury (1107–39).[98] William of Malmesbury, writing of the episcopacy of Osmund (1078–99), also tells us that learned *clerici* from far and wide came to visit Salisbury, and were encouraged to stay. And he goes on to add that the Salisbury canons were more famous for their learning and chant than those from anywhere else:

Clerici undecunque litteris insignes venientes, non solum libenter retenti, sed etiam liberaliter coacti ut remanerent. Denique emicabat ibi magis quam alias canonicorum claritas, cantibus et litteratura juxta nobilium.[99]

The picture presented by the appearance of the Salisbury books and the texts they contain supports his claim.

[96] Vezin, 'L'Emploi des réclames', 5–33.
[97] *Hermanni monachi de miraculis s. Mariae Laudunensis*, ii. xiii: *PL* 156. 982–3.
[98] Nigel and Alexander themselves subsequently became bishops: Nigel became bishop of Ely (1133–69), and Alexander, bishop of Lincoln (1123–48).
[99] *GP* 184.

2

THE CONTENT AND COMPOSITION OF
THE BOOK COLLECTION

THE acquisition of texts was one of the foremost concerns of the men associated with the new cathedral at Salisbury. The physical characteristics of the books and the degree of scribal collaboration are vivid evidence of the urgency of the demand. An examination of the texts copied and the order in which they were produced allows us to form a picture of the needs which these texts were intended to supply.[1] The first phase of book production was one of intense activity, and this suggests that the texts copied at that time were considered to be essential. Activity in the second phase was not so intense, which suggests that the demand for essential texts had been somewhat satisfied, and that the texts which were copied may reflect special interests developed by the canons in the early twelfth century. A comparison of the content of the Salisbury book collection with that of collections formed elsewhere enables us to set these interests within the context of learning in England in the eleventh and early twelfth centuries, and thus should bring to light the special characteristics of the interests and activities of the Salisbury canons.

Approximately half of all the surviving Salisbury manuscripts contain patristic texts: the works of the great Church Fathers—Cyprian, Hilary, Ambrose, Jerome, Augustine, and Gregory. Such works had a twofold importance. First, they acted as a definitive body of writings which bore witness to the orthodox doctrine of the Universal Church—the *veritas catholica*.[2] Secondly, they were considered to be essential to the interpretation of the Bible. Cassiodorus described them as rungs in the ladder reaching to the understanding of divine scripture:

On this account, most beloved brothers, let us climb unhesitatingly to the Divine Scripture by means of the laudable expositions of the Fathers, as if by a certain ladder in Jacob's vision, in order that, borne aloft by their words, we may deserve to reach an effectual contemplation of the Lord.[3]

[1] For handlists of the manuscripts copied by the scribes of Groups I and II, and the texts they contain, see App. 1 and 2.

[2] Vincent of Lerins, for example, in his *Commonitorium* (AD 434), defined the Fathers as those writers 'qui suis quisque temporibus et locis in unitate communionis et fidei permanentes magistri probabiles exstitissent': quoted in B. Altaner, *Patrology*, tr. H. C. Graef (Freiburg/Edinburgh/London, 1960), 3.

[3] *Cassiodori senatoris Institutiones*, ed. R. A. B. Mynors (Oxford, 1937), 4; tr. L. W. Jones as *An Introduction to Divine and Human Readings* (New York, 1946), 68.

But despite the acknowledged importance of the works of the Fathers, they were not represented with equal thoroughness in every medieval book collection. Some collections appear to have contained few patristic texts, others indicate an emphasis on the works of particular Fathers. Moreover, patristic texts were not always represented in their complete form but sometimes in compilations of extracts.

The patristic content of the Salisbury book collection, however, is particularly impressive. As well as significant numbers of texts by all the principal Latin Fathers noted above, the collection includes Latin translations of some texts by Eastern Fathers, such as Ephraim and Eusebius. Augustine, the most prolific of all the Latin Fathers, is the author best represented in the collection. Furthermore, the canons acquired these texts, for the most part, not in compilations of extracts but in *originalia* (that is, the works of an author in full in their immediate proper context of the writer's *œuvre*). This thoroughness, and the preference for works by Augustine, characterizes the copying of texts in the first phase of book production as much as that of the second phase. Thus, it is clear that the canons made the acquisition of patristic texts a priority from the start.

The number and character of the patristic texts contained in the Salisbury book collection differ considerably from what we know of the content of the book collections formed in England during the two centuries before the Norman Conquest.[4] As far as we can tell from extant manuscripts and booklists, the patristic content of such collections was somewhat limited. Manuscripts containing patristic texts, which can be shown to have been copied in, or imported to, England before the Conquest form only a small proportion of the items in the handlist of manuscripts copied or present in England before 1100, compiled by H. Gneuss.[5] Certain texts which had been available to authors such as Bede and Aldhelm appear to have been no longer available in England by the late ninth and tenth centuries, since copies were imported from the Continent; even some of Bede's own works seem to have been re-

[4] On the content of Anglo-Saxon book collections, see T. J. Brown, 'An Historical Introduction to the Use of Classical Latin Authors in the British Isles from the Fifth to the Eleventh Century', *Settimane di studio del Centro italiano di studi sull'alto medioevo XXII, 1974* (Spoleto, 1975), 237–93; D. Dumville, 'English Libraries before 1066: Use and Abuse of the Manuscript Evidence', in *Insular Latin Studies: Papers on Latin Texts and Manuscripts of the British Isles: 550–1066*, ed. M. W. Herren (Toronto, 1981), 153–78, and H. Gneuss, 'Anglo-Saxon Libraries from the Conversion to the Benedictine Reform', *Settimane di studio . . . di studi sull' alto medioevo XXXII, 1984* (Spoleto, 1986), 643–88. For comparisons of the character of collections formed in England before the Conquest with those formed afterwards, see Ker, *English Manuscripts*, 7–8, and more recently, R. M. Thomson, 'The Norman Conquest and English Libraries', in *The Role of the Book in Medieval Culture*, ed. P. Ganz (Turnhout, 1986), ii. 27–40.

[5] H. Gneuss, 'A Preliminary List of Manuscripts Written or Owned in England up to 1100', *ASE*, 9 (1981), 1–60. This list is currently being updated and revised.

introduced to England in this way.[6] This impression is reinforced by those booklists which can be established to represent collections of books formed in England in the two centuries before the Conquest.[7] Even where a particular text can be shown to have been present in England before the Conquest, it should not be assumed that the text was widely available.

It is possible that the evidence of surviving manuscripts and booklists may be an unreliable guide to the content of Anglo-Saxon book collections, since they may be unrepresentative of the content of the total number of books copied or imported. Studies of the Latin sources employed by English authors writing in both Latin and Anglo-Saxon may provide additional information.[8] But there are difficulties associated with using the findings of source studies as evidence for the availability of texts.[9] For example, it is not always possible to determine whether the English author gained his knowledge of the source first hand, or indirectly, from a quotation used by another author or from a compilation of extracts. None the less, thus far, source studies have not substantially altered the picture presented by extant manuscripts and

[6] For a list of these manuscripts, see F. A. Rella, 'Continental Manuscripts acquired for English Centers in the Tenth and Early Eleventh Centuries: A Preliminary Checklist', *Anglia*, 98 (1980), 107–16, and for his discussion of these manuscripts, see 'Some Aspects of the Indirect Transmission of Christian Latin Sources for Anglo-Saxon Prose from the Reign of Alfred to the Norman Conquest', B.Litt. thesis (Oxford University, 1977).

[7] The booklists are surveyed and edited in M. Lapidge, 'Surviving Booklists from Anglo-Saxon England', in *Learning and Literature in Anglo-Saxon England: Studies presented to Peter Clemoes on the Occasion of his Sixty-fifth Birthday*, ed. M. Lapidge and H. Gneuss (Cambridge, 1985), 33–89. A somewhat different picture is presented by two of the lists edited by Lapidge—no. VIII (*c*.1070) books donated by Saewold to the Church of Saint-Vaast, Arras, and no. XIII a late 11th- or early 12th-cent. list probably from Peterborough. Both lists include patristic texts otherwise unrepresented in surviving manuscripts or booklists from Anglo-Saxon England. However, although certain items in both of these lists can be identified as manuscripts which can be demonstrated to have been present in England before the Conquest, the lists in their entirety should not have been accepted unreservedly as evidence for the content of Anglo-Saxon book collections. Saewold's list may well include manuscripts acquired on the Continent, after he had left England, whilst the Peterborough list was compiled *c*.1100, and probably includes manuscripts copied after the Conquest.

[8] J. D. A. Ogilvy, *Books known to the English, 597–1066* (Cambridge, Mass., 1967) is in need of revision. See also J. D. A. Ogilvy, 'Books known to the English, 597–1066: *Addenda et corrigenda*', *Mediaevalia*, 7 (1984), 281–325. A collaborative project, Sources of Anglo-Saxon Literary Culture, has been initiated to supersede it: see *Old English Newsletter*, 23/1 (1989), 30–1. In addition, a data-base, *Fontes Anglo-Saxonici*, has also been established in order to compile a register of written sources used by authors in Anglo-Saxon England: see *Old English Newsletter*, 19/2 (1986), 17–19.

[9] On such problems, see Gneuss, 'Anglo-Saxon Libraries', 648–9, and the subsequent discussion, 692–5. For an illustration of the difficulties, compare the interpretations and conclusions of T. H. Bestul and P. Sims-Williams concerning the knowledge of the Latin versions of the works of Ephraim in Anglo-Saxon England: T. H. Bestul, 'Ephraim the Syrian and Old English Poetry', *Anglia*, 99 (1981), 1–24; P. Sims-Williams, 'Thoughts on Ephrem the Syrian in Anglo-Saxon England', in *Learning and Literature in Anglo-Saxon England*, 205–26.

booklists. Furthermore, they indicate the importance of *florilegia*, penitentials and homiliaries as a means by which English authors gained a knowledge of the Fathers.[10] As yet, no evidence has come to light which might indicate that, in the two centuries before the Conquest, any English centre made a deliberate attempt to form a thorough collection of the works of the Fathers such as that formed at Salisbury in the late eleventh century. Instead, F. A. Rella has concluded from his study of the transmission of Christian Latin authors in England in the tenth and eleventh centuries, that only a limited number of patristic texts were copied or acquired in England in the tenth century and first half of the eleventh, and that these were texts which promoted the spiritual and scholarly aims of the monastic reform movement: 'the interest of the English monks in nonliturgical material was not intellectual but ethical, leading to the multiplication of texts suitable for a reforming element in a monastic community.'[11]

The Salisbury canons appear to have formed their collection according to different principles from those which influenced the acquisition of patristic texts in pre-Conquest England. The quantity of patristic texts acquired at Salisbury, and the choice of authors, indicate that such texts were required for more than the predominantly devotional and spiritual needs which the limited number of patristic texts in Anglo-Saxon collections were intended to serve. Instead they reflect the recommendations made by Cassiodorus in book I of the *Institutiones*, a text in which he set out a programme for the study of the Bible, and the patristic reading which should accompany it. He gave special prominence to the works of Hilary, Cyprian, Ambrose, Jerome, and Augustine.[12] His recommendations greatly influenced the composition of reading on the Continent, especially in the Carolingian period. In 822, for example, it was to these writers that the Council of Valence affirmed submission.[13]

---

[10]   Rella, 'Indirect Transmission'.

[11]   Ibid. 95. The only Latin Father whose works survive in any numbers from Anglo-Saxon England is Gregory the Great. His writings were held in the highest esteem by monastic reformers both in England and on the Continent because they were seen to promote an essentially monastic spirituality. At the newly refounded monastery of Saint-Évroul in Normandy, Abbot Thierry (1050–7) gave priority to the copying of biblical texts and the works of Gregory; the works of the other Latin Fathers were copied only subsequently: Orderic Vitalis, *Historia ecclesiastica*, bk. III, ed. M. Chibnall (Oxford, 1968), ii. 48–51. In addition, Gregory occupied a special place in the affections of the Anglo-Saxons, since it was he who had initiated the conversion of the English. Bede, for example, in his letter to Bishop Acca (which forms the preface to his exposition of Luke's Gospel), singled out the writings of Ambrose, Augustine, and Jerome, but above all, Gregory (*In Lucae evangelium expositio*: CCSL 120, 7.)

[12]   Cassiodorus, *Institutiones*, I. xviii–xxii, ed. R. A. B. Mynors (Oxford, 1937), 58–61.

[13]   'Indubitanter autem doctoribus pie et recte tractantibus verbum veritatis ipsisque sacrae scripturae lucidissimis expositoribus, id est Cypriano, Hilario, Ambrosio, Hieronymo, Augustino … submittimus' (quoted by J. de Ghellinck, *Le Mouvement théologique du xiie siècle*, 2nd edn (Bruges, 1948), 514).

Book I of Cassiodorus's *Institutiones* was unknown in England before the mid-eleventh century; Salisbury possessed one of the earliest English copies (Salisbury Cathedral, MS 88). It was copied at Salisbury from a ninth-century Continental manuscript, now Hereford Cathedral, MS O.iii.2.[14] This exemplar had reached England by the mid-eleventh century, and its existence is the earliest evidence that book I of the *Institutiones* was known in England. Not only was it the examplar from which all of the earliest English copies of book I of the *Institutiones* were derived but it was also the source for the circulation in England during the course of the twelfth century of a corpus of texts ancillary to the study of the Bible.[15] Hereford O.iii.2 contains, in addition to the Cassiodorus, Jerome, *De viris inlustribus* and the continuations by Gennadius and Isidore; the *Decretum Gelasianum*; Augustine, *Retractationes*; Isidore, *Prooemia, De ecclesiasticis officiis* (I. xi–xii), *De ortu et obitu patrum*, and the *Allegoriae*, and a short anonymous text on the historical interpretation of Scripture.[16] Together these texts provide the basis for an organized programme for the study of the Bible, which supports and amplifies the guide-lines set out by Cassiodorus. The first part of the manuscript contains texts which provide guides to patristic reading. Jerome's biographical list of writers, the *De viris inlustribus*, and the continuations made to it by Gennadius and Isidore, act as finding lists. The *Decretum Gelasianum*, the earliest list of Christian writers accepted or rejected as orthodox, supplements Jerome's list of writers by determining their orthodoxy. (For example, it distinguishes between Origen's orthodox and heretical writings, a distinction not made by Jerome.) Augustine's list of his own writings (the *Retractationes*), acts as an alternative finding list for his writings to that provided by Possidius's *Indiculus*.[17] The second half of the manuscript contains rudimentary texts concerned directly with the interpretation of Scripture. In this manuscript, and those copied from it, the four Isidore texts are presented as a single group under the collective title *Prooemia* (i.e. 'Introduction'). The extract from the *De ecclesiasticis officiis* sets out the canon of the books of the Bible and lists their writers; the *Prooemia* itself, the *De ortu et obitu patrum* and the *Allegoriae* provide useful summaries of background information concerning the different books of the Bible, and the allegorical significance of the people who appear in them. The final,

---

[14] Cassiodorus, *Institutiones*, pp. xv–xvi.

[15] Ibid. pp. xv–xvi, xxxix–xlix.

[16] This text is printed in full in Cassiodorus, *Institutiones*, p. xv, n. *.

[17] Augustine, *Retractationes* and Cassiodorus, *Institutiones*, I, together with Bede's list of his own works at the end of the *Historia ecclesiastica* were used as finding lists in the 9th cent. by the monks of Murbach. Their library catalogue contains lists, derived from these works, of the texts they still required: see W. Milde, 'Der Bibliothekskatalog des Klosters Murbach aus dem 9. Jahrhundert', *Beihefte zum Euphorion*, 4 (1968).

anonymous item explains a method to discover the historical (i.e. literal) sense of the Bible, and this complements the allegorical methods employed by Isidore.[18]

Salisbury Cathedral, MS 88 is probably the earliest of the surviving copies made from Hereford O.iii.2, and is the only copy to contain the entire contents of the exemplar. However, Hereford O.iii.2 was not the only exemplar of some of these texts available to the Salisbury canons. Oxford, Bodl. Libr., MS Bodley 444, fos. 1–27 (like Salisbury 88, a Group I manuscript), also contains copies of Isidore, *Allegoriae, De ortu et obitu patrum*, and the *Prooemia*. But this manuscript was copied from a different exemplar, since its readings belong to a different textual tradition from those in Hereford O.iii.2. The implication is, therefore, that Hereford O.iii.2 was not copied in its entirety merely to acquire texts which the canons would otherwise have lacked, but because the canons viewed this manuscript as having a unity of content and purpose, since the texts it contains were significant as a group which provided a valuable bibliographical introduction to the study of the Bible.

Not only is Salisbury 88 the earliest extant copy of Hereford O.iii.2 but the Salisbury collection as a whole represents the earliest English attempt to adopt the recommendations of Cassiodorus, *Institutiones*, book 1 and the other bio-bibliographical guides associated with it in Salisbury 88. Indeed, the thoroughness with which these recommendations were followed at Salisbury is very striking: no less than thirty-one of the texts specifically mentioned by Cassiodorus,[19] and thirty-four of those listed by Augustine in the *Retractiones* were copied there.[20]

---

[18] The text ascribes this historical method of interpretation to Terrentius. The only known Christian writer or teacher of that name is the Irish grammarian Terrentius, whose writings have not survived but who is mentioned in the works of a 7th-cent. Irish grammarian, Vergilius Maro: see L. Holtz, *Donat et la tradition de l'enseignement grammatical* (Paris, 1981), 317–18.

[19] *Institutiones*, 1. i: Augustine, *De genesi ad litteram, Contra Faustum Manichaeum, Contra adversarium legis et prophetarum, Confessiones*; Origen on Exodus and Leviticus (Salisbury Cathedral, MSS 114, 116, 128, 6, 159); *Inst.* 1. iii: Jerome, Commentaries on Isaiah, Jeremiah and Ezekiel; Ambrose, *De prophetis* (Salisbury Cathedral, MSS 24, 25, Oxford, Bodl. Libr., MSS Rawlinson C. 723 and Bodley 835); *Inst.* 1. iv: Augustine, *Enarrationes in psalmos*; Cassiodorus, *Expositio psalterii* (Salisbury Cathedral, MSS 57, 58, 59); *Inst.* 1. v: Ambrose, *De Isaac et anima* (Oxford, Bodl. Libr., MS Bodley 698); *Inst.* 1. vii: Jerome, Commentary on Matthew; Augustine, Homilies on St John's Gospel (Salisbury Cathedral, MSS 137, 67); *Inst.* 1. x: Augustine, *De doctrina christiana* (Salisbury Cathedral, MS 106); *Inst.* 1. xvi: Hilary, *De Trinitate*; Ambrose, *De fide*; Augustine, *De vera religione, De doctrina christiana, De agone christiano, Speculum, Quaestiones v de novo testamento ad Honoratum, De diversis quaestionibus lxxxiii, Retractationes,* (Salisbury Cathedral, MSS 4, 140, 106, 106, 63, 35, 63, 168, 88); *Inst.* 1. xvii: Eusebius, tr. Rufinus, *Historia ecclesiastica*; Jerome, *De viris inlustribus*; Gennadius, *De viris inlustribus* (Salisbury Cathedral, MSS 139, 88); *Inst.* 1. xix: Cyprian, *De oratione dominica* (Salisbury Cathedral, MS 9); *Inst.* 1. xxii: Augustine, *Confessiones, De fide et symbolo, De haeresibus* (Salisbury Cathedral, MSS 6, 198, 165).

[20] *De beata vita* (Oxford, Bodl. Libr., MS Bodley 698), *De quantitate animae, De libero*

Similar collections had been formed on the Continent in the ninth century, and had been formed upon similar principles.[21] In the eleventh century there was a renewed impetus in the copying or acquisition of patristic texts by communities on the Continent who lacked the kinds of collections held by houses such as Corbie and Fleury.[22] The Benedictine abbey of Mont-Saint-Michel appears to have been one of the first of the newly founded or refounded Norman communities to initiate an intensive programme of copying patristic texts in the mid-eleventh century;[23] by the end of the century, several Norman communities had followed its example.[24] In post-Conquest England the cathedral communities were the first to acquire significant numbers of patristic texts.[25] Of these, the community at Salisbury appears to have been the first to undertake an intensive programme of copying.

An examination of the content of the products of each of the two phases of scribal activity at Salisbury (i.e. the manuscripts of Groups I and II)

arbitrio, De magistro, De vera religione, De utilitate credendi (Salisbury Cathedral, MSS 106, 106, 118, 106, 63), *De duabus animabus* (Oxford, Bodl. Libr., MS Bodley 698), *De fide et symbolo, De genesi ad litteram imperfectus, De diversis quaestionibus lxxxiii* (Salisbury Cathedral, MSS 198, 197, 168), *De mendacio* (Oxford, Bodl. Libr., MS Bodley 765), *De agone christiano, De doctrina christiana, Confessiones, Contra Faustum Manichaeum, De natura boni, De baptismo, Ad inquisitiones Ianuarii, De opere monachorum, De genesi ad litteram, De peccatorum meritis, De unico baptismo, De gratia novi testamenti, De spiritu et littera* (Salisbury Cathedral, MSS 35 (also 63 and 198), 106, 6, 116, 61 (also 63), 64, 165 (also 198), 197, 114, 64, 64, 63, 64), *De videndo Deo, Contra sermonem Arianorum, De nuptiis et concupiscentia, De anima et eius origine, De adulterinis coniugiis, Contra adversarium legis et prophetarum* (Salisbury Cathedral, MSS 35, 128, 65 (also 138), 128, 128, 128), *Contra mendacium* (Oxford, Bodl. Libr., MS Bodley 765), *Contra Iulianum, De cura pro mortuis gerenda, De octo quaestionibus Dulcitii* (Salisbury Cathedral, MSS 65 (also 138), 198 (also Oxford, Bodl. Libr., MS Bodley 765), 106 (also 109 and 169).

[21] On the influence of the corpus of texts represented by Hereford O.iii.2 on the content of Carolingian book collections, see K. W. Humphreys, 'The Early Medieval Library', in *Paläographie 1981: Colloquium des Comité International de Paléographie München, 15.-18. September 1981*, ed. G. Silagi (Munich, 1982), 65–7, and also R. McKitterick, *The Carolingians and the Written Word* (Cambridge, 1989), ch. 5, esp. 200–9.

[22] R. Kottje, 'Klosterbibliotheken und monastische Kultur in der zweiten Hälfte des 11. Jahrhunderts', *Zeitschrift für Kirchengeschichte*, 4: 18 (1969), 145–62. Books produced in the second half of the 11th cent. not only imitate the content of Carolingian book collections but also the appearance of the books themselves, for example: an absence of elaborate decoration, and a corresponding emphasis on the text itself, with the employment of the decorated initial as one element in a hierarchy of scripts used to articulate the structure of the text: see J. J. G. Alexander, *Norman Illumination at Mont St Michel 966–1100* (Oxford, 1970), 45–58.

[23] For the patristic texts copied at Mont St Michel, and the dates which may be assigned to the scribal activity there, see Alexander, *Norman Illumination*, 23–43.

[24] G. Nortier, *Les Bibliothèques médiévales des abbayes bénédictines de Normandie* (Paris, 1971) examines the formation of the book collections of eight Benedictine houses in Normandy: Fécamp, Bec, Mont Saint-Michel, Saint Évroul, Lyre, Jumièges, Saint-Wandrille, and Saint-Ouen.

[25] Ker, *English Manuscripts*, 7–9, 22–32; Thomson, 'The Norman Conquest and English Libraries'.

brings to light the priorities of the canons in their acquisition of patristic and other texts. The texts contained in the Group I manuscripts indicate that the canons' first objective was to acquire copies of major patristic commentaries: alongside the commentaries of Jerome on Ezekiel, Jeremiah, and Isaiah (Oxford, Bodl. Libr., MS Rawlinson C. 723, Salisbury Cathedral, MSS 24 and 25) are Gregory, *Moralia in Iob* (Salisbury Cathedral, MS 33), Augustine, Homilies on St John's Gospel and the *De Genesi ad litteram* (Salisbury Cathedral, MSS 67 and 114), and Origen on Exodus and Leviticus (Salisbury Cathedral, MS 159). In addition to these, more recent commentaries were copied: Bede on the Apocalypse and Luke (Aberdeen, University Library, MS 216 and Salisbury Cathedral, MS 37), Alcuin on the Song of Songs (London, British Library, MS Royal 5 E xix, fos. 37–52), and Berengaudus on the Apocalypse (surviving as flyleaves to Salisbury Cathedral, MS 162). Some of the texts contained in Group II manuscripts show that in the early twelfth century the canons' choice of texts became more eclectic, and they acquired some texts which were unusual for England at this time: for example, Augustine's shorter work on Genesis, the *De Genesi ad litteram imperfectus* (Salisbury Cathedral, MS 197+London, BL, MS Royal App. 1), the earliest surviving English copy of this text, and the only surviving twelfth-century English copy.[26] Even more striking are the copies of Hilary on Matthew, and the Irish Pseudo-Hilary on the seven Catholic Epistles (Salisbury Cathedral, MS 124), Pelagius on the Pauline Epistles (Salisbury Cathedral, MS 5), and an Irish compilation in dialogue format on all the books of the Bible (Salisbury Cathedral, MS 115);[27] I know of no other surviving English copies of these four texts.[28]

[26] For a list of manuscripts in British libraries containing copies of Augustine, *De genesi ad litteram imperfectus*, see F. Römer, *Die handschriftliche Überlieferung der Werke des heiligen Augustinus*, 2/i, *Grossbritannien und Irland, Werkverzeichnis*, Österreichische Akademie der Wissenschaften, phil.-hist. Klasse, Sitzungsberichte, 281 (Vienna, 1972), 95.

[27] This compilation appears to be a hitherto unrecognized copy of the exegetical compilation now known as *The Irish Reference Bible*. For this compilation, see B. Bischoff, 'Wendepunkte in der Geschichte der lateinischen Exegese im Frühmittelalter', *Sacris erudiri*, 6 (1954), 189–281, esp. 223–30; reprinted in his collected papers, *Mittelalterliche Studien* (Stuttgart, 1966), i. 205–73, esp. 231–6; an English translation of a revised and enlarged version of this article is printed in *Biblical Studies: The Medieval Irish Contribution*, ed. M. McNamara (Dublin, 1976), 74–160. The text in Salisbury Cathedral, MS 115 is similar to that in Paris, Bibliothèque Nationale, MS lat. 614, extracts from which are printed in Stegmüller, nos. 10301–19 (Bischoff's Group IB: 'Wendepunkte', 224 (*Mitt. Stud.*, 231; *Bibl. Stud.*, 97)); see also, below, App. 2.

[28] For extant copies of Hilary on Matthew, the Irish Pseudo-Hilary on the seven Catholic Epistles, and Pelagius on the Pauline Epistles, see *Hilaire de Poitiers sur Matthieu*, ed. J. Doignon (Paris, 1978), i. 46–54; *Tractatus Hilarii in septem epistolas canonicas*, ed. R. E. McNally, *Scriptores Hiberniae minores*, CCSL 108 B (Turnhout, 1973), i. pp. x–xi; *Pelagius's Expositions of Thirteen Epistles of St Paul*, ed. A. Souter, Texts and Studies, 9 (1922), i. 201–344. Neither Doignon nor McNally knew of Salisbury Cathedral, MS 124.

The quantity of commentaries, and the nature of some of them, show that the canons' copying programme went far beyond what would have been required for the *lectio divina*—the slow, prayerful, meditative reading of the Bible for the spiritual nourishment of the reader. Their eagerness to acquire commentaries on as many books of the Bible as possible, and more than one commentary on several of them (Genesis, the Psalms, the Song of Songs, St Matthew's Gospel, the Pauline Epistles, and the Apocalypse), suggests that they were interested in the text of Scripture for the knowledge it could impart; that their reading was of a scholarly more than a spiritual nature, its purpose being not merely personal, spiritual edification, but to provide answers to the theological, doctrinal, and moral questions which would be encountered in an active pastoral ministry. Some of the books of the Bible which appear to have aroused most interest at Salisbury—Genesis, the Psalms, St Matthew's Gospel, and the Pauline Epistles, were the books valued especially for their theological content.[29]

Other patristic texts copied at Salisbury support the impression that the canons were interested in theological questions, and that their reading was undertaken for intellectual as well as spiritual purposes. Although these texts include major doctrinal treatises by Augustine, Ambrose, and Hilary,[30] the majority are short texts by Augustine; some, such as the *De mendacio, Contra mendacium* (Oxford, Bodl. Libr., MS Bodley 765), and *De coniugiis adulterinis* (Salisbury Cathedral, MS 128), show that the canons were interested in treatises and tracts on specific moral questions, others, such as the *De libero arbitrio* and *De natura boni* (Salisbury Cathedral, MS 106), indicate an interest in doctrinal and philosophical questions. The special emphasis given to Augustine at Salisbury is a further indication of these interests, since of all the Fathers Augustine addresses himself in his writings most often to individual pastoral and theological problems. The extent to which he was held as an authority in these matters is indicated by the number of texts on such topics written by others, which were attributed falsely to him. Many of these texts were also copied at Salisbury, probably because the canons were under the impression that they were by Augustine.

Some Salisbury manuscripts indicate the canons' efforts to collect texts on specific topics. The canons collected a number of texts concerned with the doctrine of the Eucharist. In the late eleventh century extracts from Paschasius, *De corpore et sanguine domini*, and from a Paschasian *catena* of patristic proof texts were added to a glossed copy of the

---

[29] For a more detailed discussion of the scholarly interests and activities of the Salisbury canons, see below, Ch. 4.

[30] For example, Augustine, *Contra Faustum Manichaeum* (Salisbury Cathedral, MS 116), Ambrose, *De fide* (Salisbury Cathedral, MS 140), and Hilary, *De Trinitate* (Salisbury Cathedral, MS 4).

Pauline Epistles (Oxford, Keble College, MS 22) to supplement glosses on the doctrine of the Eucharist already present in the volume. In the early twelfth century, the canons made copies of the full text of Paschasius, *De corpore et sanguine domini* (Salisbury Cathedral, MS 130) and of an enlarged list of patristic proof texts known as the *Exaggeratio*, together with another treatise on this subject by Heriger of Lobbes (Salisbury Cathedral, MS 61). There is also evidence that the Salisbury canons made a deliberate effort to bring together texts on similar subjects within the covers of a single book. Group II scribe 2, for example, added two texts concerned with the spiritual life—Eutropius, *Sermo de districtione monachorum*, and the *Rule of the Four Fathers*—to a Group I manuscript (Salisbury Cathedral, MS 12) which already contained a copy of Smaragdus, *Diadema monachorum*.

The canons were not only interested in biblical studies and theological questions. The same thoroughness, and in the early twelfth century, eclecticism, which characterizes their copying of texts concerned with the study of the Bible, also characterizes their copying of other texts. For example, in the late eleventh century they made a copy of the largest collection of Latin saints' lives surviving from England in this period (Salisbury Cathedral, MSS 221 and 222),[31] yet these were supplemented by further groups of Latin saints' lives (now Dublin, Trinity College, MS 174 and Salisbury Cathedral, MS 223).[32] The Salisbury scribes also produced the earliest extant English copies of a number of texts on the spiritual life: the so-called 'Rule of St Augustine' (Salisbury Cathedral, MS 169), Augustine, *De opere monachorum* (Salisbury Cathedral, MS 197), the *Rule of the Four Fathers*, Eutropius, *Sermo de districtione monachorum* (Salisbury Cathedral, MS 12), and a text which seems to have been the antecedent of the *Liber graduum* which later accompanied the Sarum *Martyrologium* (Salisbury Cathedral, MS 162).[33]

[31] Formerly Oxford, Bodl. Libr. MSS Fell 4 and 1. These two manuscripts, together with Oxford, Bodl. Libr., MS Fell 3 (now Salisbury Cathedral, MS 223) were returned to Salisbury in August 1985. A contemporary or slightly earlier copy of this same collection of saints' lives, produced at Worcester Cathedral Priory, survives as London, BL, MS Cotton Nero E I+Cambridge, Corpus Christi College, MS 9.

[32] By contrast with other English communities, the Salisbury canons do not appear to have been interested in Anglo-Saxon saints' lives (with the exception of Latin lives of the most prominent Anglo-Saxon saints such as Cuthbert and Wilfred). This may account for the disparaging remarks made by the hagiographer, Goscelin of St-Bertin, concerning the state of learning at Salisbury during Osmund's episcopacy. He had been part of Bishop Hereman's *familia*, but left Salisbury after quarrelling with Osmund: see 'The *Liber Confortatorius* of Goscelin of St. Bertin', ed. C. H. Talbot, *Studia Anselmiana*, fasc. xxxviii (*Analecta Monastica*, 3rd ser.) (Rome, 1955), 29, 82; *The Life of King Edward who rests at Westminster*, ed. F. Barlow (London, 1962), 100–1, 107 n. 4.

[33] For the *Liber graduum*, see W. Maskell, *Monumenta ritualia ecclesiae Anglicanae: The Occasional Offices of the Church of England According to the Old Use of Salisbury*, 2nd edn (Oxford, 1882), i. pp. clxxvi–clxxvii. For a full discussion of the text as it appears in Salisbury Cathedral, MS 162, see below, Ch. 5, and for a transcription of the text, see App. 3.

A similar thoroughness is demonstrated by the canons' collection of texts on computistics. They copied one large compendium of texts (now London, British Library, MS Cotton Vitellius A XII, fos. 4–71), and acquired another from elsewhere (Salisbury Cathedral, MS 158).[34] In the early twelfth century these were supplemented by two more texts—the *Epistola Cummiani* and Bede's letter to Plecguin, *De aetatibus saeculi* (London, BL, MS Cotton Vitellius A XII, fos. 79–86).

The canons also acquired multiple copies of some texts. In certain cases it is possible that a second copy of a text may have been copied inadvertently, when an exemplar containing a number of texts, including one or more texts already possessed by the canons, was copied in its entirety. However, in other cases it is clear that second copies were made intentionally, as when a manuscript produced at Salisbury itself acted as an exemplar for a second copy. For example, Salisbury Cathedral, MS 106 (a Group I manuscript) acted as the exemplar for three items in another Group I manuscript: Salisbury Cathedral, MS 169 (the items are Augustine, *Sermo* 37, an Easter sermon attributed to Augustine, and Augustine, *De octo quaestionibus Dulcitii*).

The breadth of the canons' interests is demonstrated by the number and character of the classical and secular texts they copied or acquired in the early twelfth century. These include not only texts which reflect earlier and contemporary teaching of the *artes* in the schools: for example, Remigius, Commentary on Martianus Capella (surviving on Salisbury Cathedral, MS 10 flyleaf), and Chalcidius on the *Timaeus* (surviving on Salisbury Cathedral, MS 110 flyleaf) but also the Comedies of Plautus (London, BL, MS Royal 15 C xi, fos. 113–94), Cicero, *Tusculan Disputations* (London, BL, MS Royal 15 C xi, fos. 1–58), and a compilation comprising Cicero, *De officiis*, extracts from Seneca, *De beneficiis*, and a *florilegium* of extracts from Aulus Gellius and Valerius Maximus (Cambridge, Trinity College, MS R.16.34). These were texts which had been popular among intellectual circles on the Continent in the ninth century, and which enjoyed renewed popularity in the eleventh and twelfth centuries. The Cicero, Seneca, Aulus Gellius, and Valerius Maximus texts were especially valued for their ethical and philosophical content, and for the eloquent manner in which universal truths were expressed: they were, for example, among the sources from which the *Florilegium Angelicum* was compiled in Orleans in the third quarter of the twelfth century.[35] However, the presence of such prose texts at an

---

[34] Salisbury Cathedral, MS 158 can be shown to have been acquired by the canons no later than the late 11th cent. since it contains annotations consisting of a **D.M.** *nota* mark written in a hand (probably that of scribe i) which annotated several Group I manuscripts in this manner.

[35] See R. H. Rouse and M. A. Rouse, 'The *Florilegium Angelicum*: Its Origin, Content and Influence', *Medieval Learning and Literature: Essays presented to Richard William Hunt*, ed. J. J. G. Alexander and M. T. Gibson (Oxford, 1976), 66–114.

English centre in the early twelfth century is very unusual. The Salisbury copies of these texts, and of the Comedies of Plautus, provide the earliest evidence for knowledge of them in England.

The impression derived from the Salisbury collection as a whole is that the canons' overriding concern was to acquire enough texts to provide a thorough basis of learning for their new foundation, and to equip them-selves as well as possible for their practical duties. The manuscripts of Groups I (late eleventh-century) and II (early twelfth-century) indicate the way in which they set about making this collection. The texts contained in the Group I manuscripts show that at first the canons' concern was to acquire a thorough collection of patristic texts; the texts contained in the Group II manuscripts show that the canons' need for patristic texts had become somewhat satisfied, and that their choice of texts became more eclectic, and also included a number of secular texts and texts by pagan authors.

When compared with contemporary manuscript collections at centres elsewhere in England, the Salisbury collection stands out as being distinctive in a number of respects. Such comparisons are difficult because the incidence of survival of manuscripts from the different English monastic and secular communities is uneven. However, for several centres enough evidence survives in manuscripts or in catalogues to give an impression of the character of their collections, which enables us to compare them with the Salisbury collection.[36]

The community at Salisbury appears to have been unusual amongst English communities (whether secular or monastic) in the late eleventh and early twelfth centuries in the number of copies of texts by all the major patristic authors which it acquired. By contrast, at Worcester, for example, the monks concentrated for the most part on collecting the works only of Gregory and Jerome.[37] The Salisbury collection stands out in particular for the number of *opuscula* of Augustine which it contains. The short texts of Augustine in some Group I manuscripts indicate that the canons obtained copies of such texts even before the community at Durham, which acquired copies of a great many patristic texts in the late eleventh century through the gift of the bishop, William of St Calais

[36] For recent surveys of the content of post-Conquest book collections, see Thomson, 'The Norman Conquest and English Libraries', and the general remarks in K. Waller, 'Rochester Cathedral Library: An English Book Collection based on Norman Models', *Les Mutations socio-culturelles au tournant des XIᵉ–XIIᵉ siècles. Colloque international du CNRS: Le Bec-Hellouin, 11–16 juillet 1982* (Paris, 1984), 237–50.

[37] See E. A. McIntyre, 'Early Twelfth-Century Worcester Cathedral Priory, with Special Reference to Some of the Manuscripts written there', D.Phil. thesis (Oxford University, 1978), 84–128.

(d. 1096).[38] Moreover, William donated copies only of Augustine's principal works, such as the *Enarrationes in psalmos, De civitate Dei*, the Letters, and the Homilies on St John's Gospel: Durham did not acquire copies of any of Augustine's short treatises on specific moral or doctrinal questions until the early or mid-twelfth century.[39] The Salisbury canons possessed the earliest extant English copies of over fifteen Augustine or Pseudo-Augustinian texts, and for at least five of these—*De beata vita, De duabus animabus* (Oxford, Bodl. Libr., MS Bodley 698), *Speculum* (Salisbury Cathedral, MS 35), *Quaestiones veteris et novi testamenti* (Salisbury Cathedral, MS 129), and *De genesi ad litteram imperfectus* (Salisbury Cathedral, MS 197 + London, BL, MS Royal App. 1) no other English copies survive from the late eleventh or twelfth centuries.[40] The Salisbury canons also possessed the earliest known, or sole-surviving English copies of several texts on the Bible and individual theological and pastoral topics, by authors such as Hilary of Poitiers, and the Irish Pseudo-Hilary. Their collection of classical prose texts was highly unusual for an English centre at this period. A mid-twelfth-century catalogue indicates that there was considerable interest in classical texts amongst the members of the community at Bury St Edmunds, but none of the prose works possessed at Salisbury are mentioned—the Bury monks appear to have concentrated almost entirely on poetical texts.[41]

The special characteristics of the composition of the Salisbury collection may reflect the different interests of the Salisbury canons, interests which derived, perhaps, from their special needs as canons.[42] But the presence of texts at Salisbury which do not appear to have been produced or acquired by centres elsewhere in England in the eleventh and twelfth centuries may also indicate that Salisbury had independent links with Continental centres which gave the community access to exemplars which were not available elsewhere in England.

[38] For a facsimile of a contemporary list of William of St Calais's donations, see New Palaeographical Society, *Facsimiles of Ancient Manuscripts, etc.*, ed. E. M. Thompson, G. F. Warner, F. G. Kenyon, and J. P. Gilson, 2nd ser. (London, 1913–30), Pl. 17.

[39] For early 12th-cent. manuscripts surviving from Durham, and the texts they contain, see R. A. B. Mynors, *Durham Cathedral Manuscripts* (Oxford, 1939), 46–63.

[40] For information concerning extant English copies of Augustine and Pseudo-Augustinian texts, I have relied upon the lists in Römer.

[41] See R. M. Thomson, 'The Library of Bury St Edmunds Abbey in the Eleventh and Twelfth Centuries', *Speculum*, 47 (1972), 632–3.

[42] It is unfortunate that, with the exception of Exeter, no book collections of significant size have survived from this period from any other English communities of canons: few books of this period have survived from St Paul's, London, or from St Peter's, York; the books of Lincoln Cathedral date, for the most part, from the first half of the 12th cent.: see R. M. Thomson, *Catalogue of the Manuscripts of Lincoln Cathedral Chapter Library* (Cambridge, 1989), xiv–xv.

3

SALISBURY AND THE TRANSMISSION OF LATIN LITERATURE

THE large number of manuscripts produced at Salisbury in the late eleventh and early twelfth centuries demonstrates the resources available at Salisbury for copying books: the presence of a large number of scribes, and the availability of an impressive number of exemplars. As N. R. Ker observed, this collection 'may be worth investigation, if we want to get as near as we can to the exemplars available for copying in England about the time of the Conquest and soon afterwards.'[1] An examination of the texts copied at Salisbury, and their relationships with manuscripts copied or acquired by other English centres should throw light on whence the Salisbury canons obtained their exemplars. Such an examination should indicate the extent to which they used as exemplars manuscripts imported from the Continent after the Conquest, or copies derived from them, or how far they could rely for exemplars on manuscripts already in England by the time of the Conquest. It should also provide a picture of the manner in which texts circulated in England in this period, and the part played by Salisbury in their transmission. Finally it should show how far the collection at Salisbury can provide an indication of what texts were available in England in the first fifty or sixty years after the Conquest, or to what extent the Salisbury collection was untypical of other English collections.

THE ACQUISITION OF EXEMPLARS

The acquisition of exemplars was potentially one of the most difficult of the problems facing an individual or community wishing to produce a collection of books. The obvious hurry in which Salisbury manuscripts were produced may have been occasioned not only by the urgent demand for texts but also by the urgency to return exemplars. The role of the head of a community or its patron was often crucial in obtaining exemplars. The *Gesta abbatum* of St Albans abbey emphasizes the close relationship between Abbot Paul and Lanfranc, before telling us that Paul had a number of books produced for his community, 'from

[1] Ker, *English Manuscripts*, 14.

exemplars supplied by Lanfranc'.[2] Herbert Losinga, bishop of Norwich (1100–19) repeatedly begged a certain Abbot Richard for exemplars.[3] When William of Malmesbury writes of the many books acquired for Salisbury during Osmund's episcopate, he may be referring to the acquisition of exemplars as well as the production of books.[4] And since, according to William, Osmund played a part in copying and binding books himself, it is more than likely that he would have been instrumental in helping to acquire exemplars. Bishop Roger too may have used his contacts on the Continent to procur exemplars for the second phase of copying at Salisbury in the early twelfth century.

MANUSCRIPTS COPIED FROM IMPORTED EXEMPLARS

As far as we can tell from the surviving manuscripts and booklists, and from studies of the sources for literature written in Anglo-Saxon England, many of the texts copied at Salisbury were either not present in England before the Conquest, or were not widely available. We can be more certain that this was the case when an imported manuscript can be shown to represent the archetype for all English copies of the texts it contains, and where all those copies were produced after the Conquest. So far, four such imported manuscripts have been identified. An examination of these manuscripts and the English copies derived from them should bring to light patterns of dissemination, and should also indicate the position held by Salisbury in the transmission of texts in England after the Conquest.

The most ancient of these imported manuscripts survives only as fragments, now London, BL, MS Add. 40165A (*CLA* 179).[5] These are the remains of a late fourth-century copy of the works of Cyprian, written in Africa in uncial script. By the end of the twelfth century the copy had been split up and used in the binding of a late twelfth-century English manuscript.[6] We have no evidence to show when the manuscript

---

[2] *Gesta abbatum monasterii sancti Albani*, ed. H. T. Riley, RS (London, 1867), i. 58, see R. M. Thomson, *Manuscripts from St Albans Abbey 1066–1235* (Woodbridge, Suffolk, 1982), i. 13.

[3] Cited ibid. 16.

[4] *GP* 184: 'librorum copia conquisita'.

[5] Facsimiles of three of the fragments are printed in New Palaeographical Society, *Facsimiles of Ancient MSS, etc.*, ed. E. M. Thompson, G. F. Warner, F. G. Kenyon, and J. P. Gilson, 2nd ser. (London, 1913–30), Pl. 101 (at which time the fragments were still in the possession of the Duke of Norfolk).

[6] This was a late 12th-cent. copy of a collection of exegetical and theological texts. Nothing is known of its origin and history before the 19th cent. when it was in the possession of Bernard Edward Howard, 12th duke of Norfolk (d. 1842): see British Museum, *Catalogue of Additions to the Manuscripts 1921–1925* (London, 1950), 64–6.

arrived in England, but from the evidence of the fragments of the five leaves which have survived, Maurice Bévenot showed that it contained a number of peculiar readings also found in ten other manuscripts, nine of which were copied in England after the Conquest.[7] This suggests that London, BL, MS Add. 40165A represents the archetype for a whole family of manuscripts copied in England after the Conquest. The copy made at Salisbury (London, BL, MS Royal 6 B xv) is the earliest of these manuscripts, and Bévenot considered it to be the best—in all probability copied directly from the fourth-century exemplar.[8]

R. A. B. Mynors demonstrated that seventeen extant English copies of Cassiodorus, *Institutiones*, Book I, and a well-defined corpus of bio-bibliographical texts are derived from a ninth-century Continental manuscript, now Hereford Cathedral, MS O.iii.2.[9] The Salisbury copy, Salisbury Cathedral, MS 88, may well be the earliest surviving copy, and, in Mynors's opinion, is the only extant copy to have been made directly from the imported exemplar. All the other English manuscripts, he suggested, were derived from the imported exemplar through an intermediary—Oxford, Bodl. Libr., MS Bodley 391, an early twelfth-century manuscript copied at St Augustine's, Canterbury, itself not copied directly from Hereford O.iii.2, but possibly at one stage removed.[10] He went on to suggest, somewhat cautiously, that 'the centre of the diffusion of this *corpus* of treatises throughout XIIth-century England is to be placed at Canterbury ... But this is to go farther than our evidence in such a case can ever warrant.'[11]

Another ninth-century Continental manuscript was imported to England, probably in the second half of the eleventh century. It was written in France, probably the Paris-Beauvais region, and is now London, BL, MS Add. 23944A.[12] The earliest English provenance we have for this manuscript is from the abbey of Burton-on-Trent at the end of the twelfth century. It contains two texts of Augustine, *De nuptiis et concupiscentia* and *Contra Julianum.* The association of these two texts in a number of English manuscripts suggested to N. R. Ker that they might all derive from this Continental manuscript. Closer examination of the texts showed this to be so. As in the case of the British Library

---

[7] M. Bévenot, *The Tradition of Manuscripts: A Study in the Transmission of St. Cyprian's Treatises* (Oxford, 1961), 9–15. This is his **E** family (ibid. 15). The only member of this family which does not appear to be of English origin is now Paris, BN, MS lat. 1656 (s.xii).

[8] Ibid.: see e.g. 61–5 (on the reading 'parentibus indictoaudientes'), esp. 62.

[9] *Cassiodori senatoris institutiones*, ed. R. A. B. Mynors (Oxford, 1937), xv–xvi, xxxix–xlix.

[10] Ibid.

[11] Ibid. xlix.

[12] For this identification, and for what follows, see Ker, *English Manuscripts*, 12–13, 54–7.

Cyprian and the Hereford Cassiodorus, the copy made at Salisbury (Salisbury Cathedral, MS 138, a Group I manuscript) is one of the earliest, if not the earliest, of the surviving English copies derived from the imported exemplar, and, moreover, it was made directly from it. In the early twelfth century, another copy was made at Salisbury (Salisbury Cathedral, MS 65), but this was made from Salisbury copy, rather than from the original exemplar. As Mynors had suggested for the Hereford Cassiodorus, Canterbury was instrumental in the diffusion of these two Augustine texts. Ker demonstrated that corrections were made to a copy probably produced at Canterbury (now Oxford, Bodl. Libr., MS Bodley 145) (Ker's **B¹**), and from this corrected copy were derived (though not directly), Oxford, Bodl. Libr., MS Bodley 134 (Ker's **B²**), copied at Rochester, and Hereford Cathedral, MS P.vi.2 (Ker's **H**), probably from Hereford. Later, Oxford, Bodl. Libr., MS Add. C.181 (Ker's **B³**), from Bury St Edmunds, was copied (possibly directly) from **B²**. Ker, like Mynors, allowed himself to speculate: 'It is tempting to suppose that one of the two copies of De nuptiis and Contra Julianum recorded in the medieval Christ Church, Canterbury, catalogue ... was the missing manuscript from which **H** and **B²** were copied, and that the other copy was **B¹** itself. But this is no more than a possibility.'[13] However, what is interesting for us, is that in every case cited so far, the Salisbury copy was made directly from the imported exemplar, rather than from a copy made at Christ Church, Canterbury. From this we may infer either that Salisbury obtained the imported manuscript before it passed on to Canterbury, or that, if the manuscript went first to Canterbury, the Christ Church scribes were willing to lend the Salisbury scribes this, their original exemplar, whilst they provided a copy they had produced to act as an exemplar for scribes at other centres. This might suggest that the Salisbury scribes had something of a reputation either for their ability to read different and sometimes ancient forms of script, or for the speed with which they could produce a copy from an exemplar.

The fourth surviving imported exemplar from which a large group of English manuscripts are derived is perhaps a special case, since, not only do we know where it was copied, when it was brought to England, whence it was obtained, and by whom but its dissemination was probably due to a deliberate policy. This manuscript contains Lanfranc's canon law collection: his abridgement and rearrangement of the Pseudo-Isidorian Decretals and Canons of Councils, which now survives as Cambridge, Trinity College, MS B.16.44.[14] A contemporary note in the manuscript tells us that it had been sent from Bec to Lanfranc at

[13] Ibid. 13 n. 2.

[14] Z. N. Brooke, *The English Church and the Papacy from the Conquest to the Reign of John*, 2nd edn (Cambridge, 1989), 59–83.

Canterbury. Z. N. Brooke showed that ten copies made in England in the late eleventh or twelfth centuries derive from this manuscript; six or possibly seven of them were associated with cathedrals.[15] Brooke suggested that the dissemination of this text may have been part of a deliberate policy to provide all cathedrals with an approved handbook of canon law.[16] In this instance, Canterbury was certainly the centre for the dissemination of the text. Unlike the other three cases, the Salisbury copy (Salisbury Cathedral, MS 78), was not made directly from the imported exemplar, but derives from it through a now no longer extant inter-mediary. In fact, no manuscripts survive which were copied directly from the imported exemplar. Brooke postulated that two copies had been made at Canterbury; from one of these copies derive two manuscripts: Cambridge, Peterhouse, MS 74, associated with Durham Cathedral Priory, and Cambridge, Corpus Christi College, MS 130, of unknown provenance. Most, if not all, of the remaining English manuscripts, including that made at Salisbury, derive from another copy.[17]

Although the transmission of Lanfranc's canon law collection is something of a special case, it does confirm the impression derived from the patterns of dissemination of the other three texts or groups of texts. It demonstrates the ease with which texts were disseminated after the Conquest, and the geographical extent to which they did so. Within a short space of time a single exemplar could be the means for the dissemination of a text across the whole of England.

These examples provide us with a paradigm which allows us to reconstruct the patterns of circulation of other texts in England after the Conquest for which the imported exemplars have not survived. Where the text contained in a group of manuscripts copied in England after the Conquest belongs to a distinct English tradition of that text, and where no pre-Conquest copies bearing witness to that same tradition survive, we may presume that they are derived from an exemplar which had either been imported after the Conquest, or which only became widely available for copying after the Conquest. Such reconstructions, of necessity, involve a certain amount of speculation because of the loss of manuscripts which provide vital links in the chain of transmission.

This sort of reconstruction also involves a considerable dependence on the work of editors. Unfortunately, as N. R. Ker observed, manu-scripts of interest to understanding the dissemination of a text are not always of interest to editors whose principal concern is to establish the text.[18] However, some editors have gone further than merely establishing

---

[15] Ibid. 59–83, 231–5, and also the updated bibliography on pp. xx–xxi, n. 2.
[16] Ibid. 78–80.
[17] Ibid. 231–5.
[18] Ker, *English Manuscripts*, 12.

their texts, and have noted groups of manuscripts which contain the same variant readings, among them, distinct English families. Even where editors have not gone this far, it is still possible to discover readings not recorded in the editions which are common to English manuscripts, and thus isolate a distinct English textual tradition. Therefore, I have, in some cases, supplemented the information supplied by editors with that derived from my own collations. These collations have been selective, and are only sufficient to bring to light common variant readings which indicate that the texts in two or more manuscripts are related; they cannot indicate the exact nature of the relationships between manuscripts of the same textual tradition.

J. E. Chisholm, in his edition of the Pseudo-Augustinian *Hypomnesticon*, admits to having taken to heart N. R. Ker's *caveats* concerning many editions of patristic texts.[19] In this edition he identifies a distinct English tradition of the text of the 4-*Responsio* version of the *Hypomnesticon*, which, he demonstrates, almost certainly derives from a manuscript imported from Normandy, although this manuscript has not survived.[20] He has identified a large number of English manuscripts which bear witness to this tradition, including over ten from the twelfth century alone, and has drawn some conclusions concerning the relationships between the different manuscripts of this tradition. The variant reading which Chisholm views as being most distinctive of the English family, appears in Continental manuscripts as 'gratia est heretice' (*Responsio* iv, 6). In English manuscripts this appears variously as 'gratia est ħ heretice'; 'gratia est hoc heretice'; 'gratia est haec heretice'; or (more rare), the Continental reading, 'gratia est heretice'. Chisholm argues that this diversity of readings arose from the fact that the manuscript which represented the archetype for the English family probably read 'gratia est autem heretice', in which 'autem' was abbreviated in the old insular form of ħ. This is the reading which appears in a late eleventh-century manuscript associated with St Albans: London, BL, MS Harley 865, and in a twelfth-century manuscript, Lincoln Cathedral, MS 134. In a late eleventh-century manuscript from St Augustine's, Canterbury (now Brussels, Bibliothèque Royale, MS 444–52), however, the scribe has mistakenly expanded the abbreviation as 'hoc'. The St Albans manuscript has also introduced an incorrect reading of its own, transcribing 'Paulo fideli magistro' (*Responsio* i. 2) as 'Paulo fidei magistro'. However, both the Lincoln manuscript and the St Augustine's manuscript have the correct 'Paulo fideli magistro' reading, and hence both probably derive not from the St Albans manuscript but from its exemplar. Chisholm

---

[19] *The Pseudo-Augustinian Hypomnesticon against the Pelagians and Celestians*, ed. J. E. Chisholm, ii, *Text edited from the Manuscripts* (Fribourg, 1980), 26 n. 1.

[20] Ibid. 24–42.

speculates that this exemplar might be the now lost *Codex* 53 of Christ
Church, Canterbury, a manuscript in which the *Hypomnesticon* was
preceded by the same texts as those found in the St Albans manuscript.
Chisholm adduces further evidence which points to this lost Christ
Church manuscript as representing the archetype of the English family of
manuscripts, or at least being very close to the imported Norman
exemplar which was, since these were the same contents as those in a
now lost twelfth-century Norman manuscript from the abbey of St
Évroul.[21] Two copies of the *Hypomnesticon* were made at Salisbury, both
in the early twelfth century: one is now divided between Salisbury
Cathedral, MS 197 and London, BL, MS Royal App. 1, and the other is
Salisbury Cathedral, MS 35. Both have the correct 'Paulo fideli magistro'
reading, but Salisbury 197 + Royal App. 1 has 'gratia est haec heretice',
whilst the slightly later Salisbury 35 has 'gratia est heretice'. Chisholm
demonstrates that the earlier copy almost certainly derives from a
manuscript which, like Brussels, Bibliothèque Royale, MS 444–52,
expanded the 'autem' abbreviation as 'hoc'. The Salisbury scribe, or the
scribe of his exemplar, tried to make sense from the nonsense 'gratia est
hoc heretice', and made 'hoc' agree with 'gratia', thus rendering it as
'haec'. We see this same solution in a twelfth-century manuscript
associated with Exeter, Oxford, Bodl. Libr., MS Bodley 149. The slightly
later Salisbury manuscript seems not to have been copied from the
earlier Salisbury copy (for example, it omits 'haec'), but, in all other
respects, it is very closely related to it. Was it, therefore, copied from the
same exemplar, an exemplar which read *hoc*, which the scribe omitted
because he could not make sense of it, or was it copied from a different
exemplar, possibly even another imported exemplar which had the
Continental reading of 'gratia est heretice'? This cannot yet be determined. As a result of the loss of the Évroul manuscript, the earliest
extant Norman copy is a twelfth-century manuscript, Rouen, Bibliothèque Municipale, MS 478. This copy has the reading 'gratia est
heretice', but in a number of other instances, diverges from the 'English'
readings in Salisbury 35. However, Chisholm notes that another twelfth-
century Continental manuscript, Paris, Bibliothèque Nationale, MS lat.
17398, which has the Continental 'gratia est heretice' reading, in all other
respects contains a text very similar to that of the English textual
tradition.[22] Salisbury 35 may, therefore, have been copied from another
imported exemplar similar to this copy.

A Norman exemplar almost certainly also lies behind the post-
Conquest English copies of Ambrose, *De mysteriis* and *De sacramentis*.
These copies share a number of readings which may be traced back to

[21] For the lost Évroul manuscript, see ibid. 25–6, esp. 25 nn. 1–3.
[22] Ibid. 37.

corrections attributed to Lanfranc.[23] Otto Faller, in his edition of these two Ambrose texts, identified a large family of manuscripts from both England and Western France which contain the readings identified by him as Lanfranc's emendations.[24] It is not clear from his edition whether all the English copies derive from a single imported exemplar, or whether more than one copy bearing witness to this tradition of the text was imported. In some of the English manuscripts, including that from Salisbury (Oxford, Bodl. Libr., MS Bodley 768), these two Ambrose texts appear together with a corpus of texts by or ascribed to Ambrose on the subjects of virginity and widowhood.[25] This collocation of texts appears to be peculiar to English manuscripts; it may represent the contents of a common imported exemplar.[26]

A corpus of Augustine texts also circulated together in England after the Conquest, probably because the texts were together in the common exemplar (now lost). This exemplar probably contained *De adulterinis coniugiis*, *De natura et origine animae*, the *Sermo arianorum* and Augustine's reply, *Contra sermonem Arianorum*, and *Contra adversarium legis et prophetorum*. It may also have contained *De mendacio*, *Contra mendacium*, *De cura pro mortuis gerenda*, and *De vera religione*.[27] No

[23] A late 11th- or 12th-century copy of these two Ambrose texts derived from the manuscript emended by Lanfranc survives as Le Mans, Bibliothèque Municipale, MS 15, fos. 123–41. On fo. 142 the scribe has copied from his exemplar the colophon 'Lanf. hucusque correxi', see Ambrose, *De sacramentis*, etc., ed. O. Faller, CSEL 73 (Vienna, 1955), 36*.

[24] Ibid. 36*, 45*–7*, esp. 47* n. 55. The manuscripts which bear witness to the Lanfranc corrections comprise Faller's *recensio* Y.

[25] This corpus comprises: *De virginibus*, *De viduis*, *De virginitate*, *Exhortatio virginitatis*, and *De lapsu virginis consecratae*.

[26] For a list of manuscripts containing Ambrose, *De mysteriis* and *De sacramentis*, see Faller, *De sacramentis*, viii–xviii. This list includes two manuscripts now in Paris which also contain the corpus of texts on virginity and widowhood together with the *De mysteriis* and *De sacramentis*: Paris, BN, MS lat. 1751 and Paris, Bibliothèque de l'Arsenal, MS 236. Both, however, are of English origin: the former is a late 11th-cent. manuscript written in English Caroline minuscule, probably from St Augustine's, Canterbury (see J. Vezin, 'Manuscrits des dixième et onzième siècles copiés en Angleterre en minuscule caroline et conservés à la Bibliothèque Nationale de Paris', *Humanisme actif: Mélanges d'art et de littérature offerts à Julien Cain* (Paris, 1968), ii. 295), the latter is a 12th-cent. manuscript, probably also of English origin since it was in England until the 18th cent. (see H. Martin, *Catalogue des manuscrits de la Bibliothèque de l'Arsenal* (Paris, 1885), i. 126–8, cf. 125).

[27] The extant manuscripts do not all contain every text in this corpus. The Salisbury copy (Salisbury Cathedral, MS 128) and a 12th-cent. manuscript of unknown origin, Eton College, MS 48, both contain *De adult. con.*, *De nat. et orig. an.*, *Serm. ar.*, *Contra serm. ar.*, and *Contra adv. legis et proph.*; Hereford Cathedral, MS P.i.5 (s.xii, from Gloucester) contains *De nat. et orig. an.*, *Serm. ar.*, *Contra serm. ar.*, and *Contra adv. legis et proph.*; Cambridge, Trinity College, MS B.3.33 (s.xii, from Christ Church, Canterbury) contains *De adult. con.*, *De mend.*, *Contra mend.*, *De cura pro mort. ger.*, *De vera relig.*, *De nat. et orig. an.*, *Serm. ar.*, *Contra serm. ar.*, *Contra adv. legis et proph.*; Oxford, Bodl. Libr., MS Bodley 387 (s.xii, from Rochester) contains the same contents as the Trinity manuscript except it lacks *De cura pro mort. ger.*, and *De vera relig.*; the first seven items of London, BL, MS Royal 5 A xiii (s.xii, from Worcester) are *De mend.*, *Contra mend.*, *De nat. et orig. an*,

pre-Conquest English copies survive of any of these texts, with the exception of the *De adulterinis coniugiis* (a tenth-century copy survives as Lambeth Palace, MS 149). It seems likely that the common exemplar for the English copies of this corpus of texts was a Continental manuscript imported after the Conquest, since similar, although not identical, groupings of texts occur in earlier Continental manuscripts and contemporary Norman manuscripts.[28] The sample collations I have made of the text of the *De natura et origine animae* in the English manuscripts which contain all or part of this corpus of texts, indicate that all of the English copies derive from a single imported exemplar. The English manuscripts share a number of readings not recorded in the printed edition.[29] They also all leave a gap of a couple of inches for a lacuna in the text of *De natura et origine animae*, II. v.[30] This gap may well reflect a lacuna or illegible passage in the imported exemplar.

Salisbury Cathedral, MS 128 is the earliest English representative of this corpus of texts, although it contains only five of the texts of the corpus: *De adulterinis coniugiis, De natura et origine animae, Sermo arianorum, Contra sermonem arianorum,* and *Contra adversarium legis et prophetarum*.[31] However, the process by which Salisbury 128 was copied, was a little more complicated than appears at first. The first item in the manuscript (*De adulterinis coniugiis*) had originally been copied independently from the other items, from an exemplar (London,

---

Serm. ar., Contra serm. ar., Contra adv. legis et proph., and *De cura pro mort. ger.*; Oxford, Bodl. Libr., MS Bodley 804 (s.xii, from Exeter) contains *Contra mend.,* and *De nat. et orig. an.,* I–III.

[28] Paris, BN, MS lat. 12207 (s.ix) contains *De nat. et orig. an., Serm. ar., Contra serm. ar., De adult. con., Epistola* 36, and *Contra adv. legis et proph.*; Paris, BN, MS lat. 12208 (s.xi, from Corbie) contains *De nat. et orig an.,* I–II; *De adult. con., Ep.* 36, and *Contra adv. legis et proph.*. A twelfth-century catalogue from Bec (Avranches, Bibliothèque Municipale, MS 159, fos. 1ᵛ–3, in H. Omont, *Catalogue générale des manuscrits des bibliothèques publiques de France: Departements,* ii, *Rouen,* etc. (Paris, 1888), 385–8), lists a manuscript which, in addition to other texts, contained *De mend., Contra mend., De cura pro mort. ger., De vera relig., De nat. et orig. an., Sermo ar., Contra serm. ar.,* and *Contra adv. legis et proph.* The only difference between the corpus of texts as it appears in this catalogue and that in the Trinity manuscript from Christ Church, Canterbury, is that in the former, the last two texts are separated by a copy of Augustine, *De utilitate credendi.*

[29] For example, *De nat. et orig. an.,* I. ii 'conquerer' instead of 'conquerar' (Augustine, *De natura et origine animae,* ed. C. F. Urba and J. Zycha, CSEL 60 (Vienna/Leipzig, 1913), 304, line 5); I. xiii 'lauacro' instead of 'sacramento' (ibid. 317, line 4).

[30] The manuscripts leave a gap between the words 'quae' and 'notos' (ibid. 342, line 24 and 343, line 1). This seems to reflect a reading found in five of the manuscripts collated by the editors of the printed edition, in which the passage 'quae denique presbyteros ... in contione quod' is omitted (ibid. 342, lines 25–343, line 1). The small gap in the English manuscripts probably represents the loss of only three words—'homines annosos scripsit'.

[31] The exemplar used by the Salisbury scribes may also have contained *De mendacio, Contra mendacium,* and *De cura pro mortuis gerenda,* but because Salisbury already possessed a copy of these items (Oxford, Bodl. Libr., MS Bodley 765), the scribes did not copy them a second time.

Lambeth Palace, MS 149) which did not contain the other texts of the corpus, and which bore witness to another textual tradition of the *De adulterinis coniugiis*. A little later, the Salisbury scribes obtained a manuscript which contained this text as part of the corpus of Augustine texts. They did not use this manuscript to make a copy of the *De adulterinis coniugiis*, since they already possessed a copy, but Group I scribe viii added to the manuscript which contained the existing Salisbury copy (Salisbury 128) four other texts of the corpus. In addition, Group I scribe i collated the text of the *De adulterinis coniugiis* in Salisbury 128 with that in the newly acquired manuscript. As a result of this collation, he discovered that the Salisbury copy contained numerous omissions. He therefore supplied the missing portions of text in its margins.

Sometimes it is possible to show that post-Conquest English manuscripts which appear to bear witness to the same tradition of the text, do not all derive from a common imported exemplar, but fall into two or more groups, each deriving from different, although related, exemplars. This can be seen in the post-Conquest transmission of the text of Ambrose, *De fide*. All of the late eleventh- and twelfth-century English manuscripts of this text belong to a family of manuscripts of which the earliest is a ninth-century manuscript from Mainz, now Munich, Clm 8113. This family is characterized by the reading at the beginning of Book III of *De fide*: 'Quondam, clementissime imperator'.[32] Moreover, the English manuscripts share a number of variant readings not found in Continental manuscripts which appears to suggest that there was a distinct English family.[33] However, so far as I have collated them, the late eleventh- and twelfth-century English manuscripts fall into two groups, each bearing witness to a slightly different textual tradition. In one group are two manuscripts from Christ Church, Canterbury (Oxford, Bodl. Libr., MS Bodley 827 is the earlier, and Cambridge, St John's College, MS 5 the later), and one from Rochester (London, BL, MS Royal 6 C iv). The second group comprises the copy made at Salisbury (Salisbury Cathedral, MS 140), Oxford, Bodl. Libr., MSS Bodley 739 (from Exeter), and Bodley 752 (from St Albans). The second group is distinguished from the first by a number of readings.[34] However, later in the twelfth century, the St Albans copy was collated with a manuscript from the Canterbury/Rochester tradition, and its readings were erased in favour

---

[32] Ambrose, *De fide*, ed. O. Faller, CSEL 78 (Vienna, 1962), 32*–3*.

[33] Faller (ibid. 33*–4*) takes Salisbury Cathedral, MS 140 as his representative of the English family. He collates it as **N**.

[34] For example, in I. iii (Faller, ibid. 5, line 21), where the Canterbury and Rochester copies read 'manu', the second group has 'manus' ; and in I. vii (ibid. 7, line 14), where the Canterbury and Rochester copies read 'ergo et Deus', the second group has 'ergo est Deus'.

of the readings of the first group.[35] The likelihood that the manuscripts from Salisbury, Exeter, and St Albans (in its unaltered form) all derive from an imported exemplar different from that used at Canterbury, is reinforced by the presence of a series of section headings not found in the Canterbury and Rochester copies.[36]

In many cases, however, it is much more obvious that the English copies of particular texts do not all derive from a common exemplar. The post-Conquest English copies of Augustine, *De agone christiano*, for example, fall into two distinct groups, each bearing witness to a different textual tradition. The two copies made at Salisbury (Salisbury Cathedral, MSS 63 and 35) both bear witness to the same tradition. In this tradition, the text is preceded by the relevant chapter from Augustine's *Retractationes*, and is accompanied by a set of *scholia*.[37] A copy bearing witness to this tradition of the text has also survived from Exeter (now Oxford, Bodl. Libr., MS Bodley 201). Other post-Conquest English copies of the *De agone christiano* (for example, Cambridge, Trinity College, MS B.3.32, from Christ Church, Canterbury, and Hereford Cathedral, MS P.i.3) bear witness to a different tradition of the text, a tradition also represented by Oxford, Trinity College, MS 4, an eleventh-century manuscript from the region of Angers or Tours.[38] This version of the text lacks the *scholia* present in the other version, and is not preceded by the relevant *retractatio*.

Sometimes two manuscripts bearing witness to two different textual traditions found their way to the same centre. For example, Cambridge, Corpus Christi College, MS 187 (copied at Christ Church, Canterbury in the late eleventh or early twelfth century) provides evidence that the Canterbury scribes gained access to two exemplars for the text of Rufinus's Latin version of Eusebius, *Historia ecclesiastica*. M. R. James noted that in this manuscript, a passage from book xi, xxiii–xxix originally read 'Post hoc reuulsum ceruisibus que apud illos sunt elementis cuius littere seu uocabuli', thus omitting a sizeable portion of

---

[35] For example, in the St Albans copy, the readings given in the previous note for the second group have been altered to agree with the Canterbury and Rochester copies: thus the 's' of 'manus' and the 's' of 'est' have been erased to give 'manu' and 'et'.

[36] These consist of some, but not all, of the section headings recorded by Faller in his edition. They include, for example, 'De Deo uno' (Faller, *De fide*, 8) but not 'Expositio fidei' (ibid. 6).

[37] The same *scholia* are also found in Munich, Clm 14492 (s.ix), Paris, BN, MS lat. 13365 (s.ix, from Corbie) and Bamberg, Staatsbibliothek, MS patr. 23 (B.III.13) (s.xi): see Augustine, *De agone christiano*, ed. J. Zycha, CSEL, 41 (Prague/Vienna/Leipzig, 1900), xvi–xvii.

[38] The *ex libris* inscription and table of contents on fo. 1 indicate that it was at St Augustine's Canterbury by the late 13th cent. It is possible that the manuscript was imported soon after the Conquest and acted as the common exemplar for the English copies which bear witness to this tradition of the text. However, I have not yet made sufficient collations to verify this possibility.

text from between 'ceruisibus' and 'que'.[39] James identified another twelfth-century English copy in which this portion of text was omitted: Cambridge, Corpus Christi College, MS 184 (from Rochester). G. F. Warner and J. P. Gilson also noted this omission in two more twelfth-century English manuscripts—London, BL, MSS Royal 13 B v (from St Albans) and Add. 21084 (of unknown origin or medieval provenance).[40] However, a little while after the Christ Church scribes had produced the manuscript which is now Cambridge, Corpus Christi College, MS 187, they acquired another manuscript of this text which brought the omission to their notice. Consequently they erased the words 'que apud illos sunt elementis', inserted a *signe de renvoi*, and supplied the missing text 'et depressum e medio ... que apud illos sunt elementis' on blank leaves at the end of the manuscript.[41]

Two manuscripts of the *Historia ecclesiastica* also made their way to Salisbury. Salisbury Cathedral, MS 139 was copied from an exemplar which did not have this lacuna. However, after the manuscript had been copied, it was collated with another witness to the text in which the passage had been omitted as in the copy first produced at Christ Church, Canterbury. The corrector of the Salisbury manuscript (Group II, scribe 9) not only recorded the variant readings but also drew attention to the passage in Salisbury 139 which had been omitted in the Canterbury manuscript, by placing a **b** over *ceruisibus* (fo. 109), and a **G** in the margin, and an identical pair of letters over *quę apud illos* (fo. 110ᵛ), and beside it in the margin.

When the Salisbury canons obtained a second manuscript of a text which bore witness to a textual tradition different from that in their existing copy, they sometimes used it as an exemplar for a second copy. Two textual traditions of Augustine, *De octo quaestionibus Dulcitii* circulated in England after the Conquest. The two traditions are easily isolated since each circulated with a different group of texts, probably reflecting the contents of an imported exemplar. At Salisbury, the canons produced copies bearing witness to each of these textual traditions, together with the texts associated with them.

One manuscript of the *De octo quaestionibus Dulcitii* reached Salisbury in the late eleventh century, and from it was copied Salisbury Cathedral, MS 106, fos. 59ᵛ–72ᵛ. In this Salisbury copy the text of the

---

[39] M. R. James, *A Descriptive Catalogue of the Manuscripts in the Library of Corpus Christi College, Cambridge* (Cambridge, 1912), i. 444–5. The omitted text is 'et depressum medio simul extrahitur ... velut unum ex ceteris litterarum': see Eusebius, *Die Kirchengeschichte*, ed. E. Schwartz, GCS 9 (Leipzig, 1908), ii. 1028–35.

[40] G. F. Warner and J. P. Gilson, *British Museum, Catalogue of Western Manuscripts in the Old Royal and King's Collections* (London, 1921), ii. 94; cf. entry for MS Royal 11 E vi, ibid. i. 359.

[41] James, *Corpus Christi College*, i. 445.

Octo quaestiones begins with a list of the eight questions posed, and follows two items attributed to Augustine: his *Sermo* 37, and a pseudonymous Easter sermon. Copies of the *Octo quaestiones,* together with these two sermons appear in two other English manuscripts: Hereford Cathedral, MS P.i.10, a late eleventh-century manuscript,[42] and Hereford Cathedral, MS P.i.6, a twelfth-century manuscript, probably from the West of England. The texts in these copies have many peculiar readings also present in the Salisbury copy, but they were not copied from it. The implication is that all these copies were made or derived from a common exemplar. Salisbury Cathedral 106 and Hereford P.i.10 are the two earliest extant English witnesses to the texts of all four items. In the late eleventh century the same four items in Salisbury Cathedral, MS 169 were copied from Salisbury 106.

A second manuscript which bore witness to a different tradition of the *De octo quaestionibus Dulcitii* reached Salisbury in the early twelfth century, and from it was copied Salisbury Cathedral, MS 109. This version lacks the preliminary list of questions present in the other version, and its text contains a number of readings different from those in the other two Salisbury manuscripts. A peculiarity of this version is that it is followed by the sixth *Responsio* of the Pseudo-Augustinian *Hypomnesticon,* copied without a new heading as if it were a part of the previous text. Chisholm noted that this occurred in an early twelfth-century manuscript from Durham, Durham Cathedral, MS B.IV.12, and in a number of other English manuscripts, although he did not know of the Salisbury copy.[43] The close relationship between all the copies of this version, and their probable dependence on a single imported exemplar is indicated also by the collocation of the *Octo quaestiones* and the sixth *Responsio* with the same group or groups of texts in all the surviving witnesses to this version. In the two earliest English witnesses to this version—Salisbury Cathedral, MS 109 and Durham Cathedral, MS B.IV.12—the *Octo quaestiones* and the sixth *Responsio* are collocated with three groups of texts which had each hitherto enjoyed a separate circulation.[44]

[42] Its origin is unknown, but a contemporary contents list on the verso of the flyleaf is in the hand of the main scribe of Domesday Book. For a suggested place of origin, based on this identification, see P. Chaplais, 'William of Saint-Calais and the Domesday Survey', in *Domesday Studies: Papers read at the Novocentenary Conference of the Royal Historical Society and the Institute of British Geographers, Winchester 1986,* ed. J. C. Holt (Woodbridge, Suffolk, 1987), 74. I am grateful to Mr Pierre Chaplais for allowing me to read a typescript of his paper prior to publication. In the mid-16th cent. the manuscript was in the possession of Sir John Prise who collected a large number of manuscripts from dissolved religious houses in the West of England, see N. R. Ker, 'Sir John Prise', *The Library,* 5: 10 (1955), 10, 15.

[43] Chisholm, *Hypomnesticon,* ii. 42–66, esp. 46–7.

[44] Durham B.IV.12 is a composite manuscript: fos. 1–38 and 121–87, which contain texts not found in Salisbury 109, are structurally independent of the rest of the manuscript, and may derive from other exemplars.

First, in these two manuscripts, and indeed in all of the English manuscripts which contain this version, the *Octo quaestiones* are preceded by Prosper, *De gratia et libero arbitrio,* and the group of Prosper texts known collectively as the *Responsiones Prosperi contra Pelagianos.* The *Octo quaestiones* also appear together with this group of texts and the sixth *Responsio* in three ninth-century Continental manuscripts: St Gall, Stiftsbibliothek, MS 29, Boulogne, Bibliothèque Municipale, MS 48, and Cologne, Erzbischöfliche Dombibliothek, MS Dom. 79, a manuscript which contains a text whose readings are closest to those found in the English representatives of the sixth *Responsio.*[45]

Secondly, in both Salisbury Cathedral 109 and Durham B.IV.12, following the Prosper and Augustinian texts, is a corpus of Christmas and Epiphany sermons which ultimately derive from a homiliary of which a more complete form has been identified in Worcester Cathedral, MS F 92.[46] This corpus of sermons together with the *Octo quaestiones,* the sixth *Responsio* of the *Hypomnesticon,* and the group of Prosper and Augustinian texts appear together in another twelfth-century English manuscript, now Hereford Cathedral, MS O.iii.1.

Thirdly, in both the Salisbury and Durham copies we find a further group of texts consisting of a corpus of Ambrose texts: his *Sermo* 64—a pseudonymous sermon (*Mirum satis*), *De misteriis, De Gedeon,* and *De apologia David.*[47] This group of texts, which represents the same textual traditions as those of the Salisbury and Durham manuscripts, is also found in two ninth-century Continental manuscripts: Rheims, Bibliothèque Municipale, MS 376, and London, BL, MS Add. 18332.[48]

Many more of the texts copied at Salisbury can be shown to be related to late eleventh- or twelfth-century manuscripts associated with other English centres. The examples I have cited bear witness to the remarkable extent and rapidity with which texts were disseminated in England after the Conquest. But they also indicate that the manner in which texts were transmitted and the position occupied by Salisbury in that transmission were rather more varied and complex than the paradigm provided by the Hereford Cassiodorus and the British Library Cyprian and Augustine had implied. Texts were sometimes transmitted through one common exemplar, sometimes through more than one. In some cases Canterbury acted as the centre for the dissemination of a particular text or group of texts throughout the country, but in other cases, it played a part in disseminating a particular tradition of a text to only a limited

---

[45] Chisholm, *Hypomnesticon,* ii. 42–5.

[46] See C. Lambot, 'La Tradition manuscrite des sermons de saint Augustin pour la Noël et l'Épiphanie', *Rev. bén.,* 77 (1967), 217–45, esp. 232–3, and 233 n. 1.

[47] In the Durham manuscript the final two items in this group are reversed.

[48] Faller, *De sacramentis,* 51*–2*.

number of centres, whilst other communities derived their copies from another textual tradition, in whose transmission Canterbury played no part.

Salisbury occupies various positions in the patterns of dissemination of different texts. Moreover, when two copies of the same text were copied at Salisbury, in some instances each copy was made from a different exemplar. For example, in the case of the 4-*Responsio* version of the Pseudo-Augustinian *Hypomnesticon*, one of the Salisbury copies may have derived from a copy made at Canterbury, while the other may have been transcribed directly from an exemplar imported from the Continent. But it would appear that when a particular text was disseminated through two different channels, each with its own archetype, the Salisbury copy does not bear witness to the archetype represented by the copy produced at Canterbury, and therefore the Salisbury scribes must have acquired their exemplar from a different source. This conclusion is confirmed by the number of texts copied at Salisbury which do not seem to have been either acquired by or copied at Canterbury (see below).

For a number of the texts whose transmission I have discussed in detail in this chapter, the Salisbury copies are the earliest or among the earliest extant copies produced at or acquired by English centres. This is also the case for the majority of the patristic *originalia* introduced to England in the late eleventh and early twelfth centuries. Salisbury produced the earliest or one of the earliest extant English copies of, for example, Jerome's commentaries on Isaiah and Jeremiah (Salisbury Cathedral, MSS 25 and 24), several opuscula of Ambrose (Oxford, Bodl. Libr., MSS Bodley 698, 768 and 835), Augustine on John's Gospel, *De Genesi ad litteram* and *Contra Faustum* (Salisbury Cathedral, MSS 67, 128 and 116), and Hilary on the Trinity and Matthew's Gospel (Salisbury Cathedral, MSS 4 and 124). Gregory the Great is the only one of the Fathers whose commentaries were not copied at Salisbury earlier than at other English centres.

From my collation of the texts in Salisbury manuscripts and those in manuscripts from other centres, I have not been able to demonstrate that Salisbury copies themselves acted as exemplars for copies associated with other centres. For the most part, the evidence seems to suggest that this was not the case, since the Salisbury copies often contain errors which I have not found reproduced in later manuscripts.

TEXTUAL TRADITIONS NOT REPRESENTED BY OTHER ENGLISH MANUSCRIPTS

Several texts copied at Salisbury bear witness to traditions otherwise unrepresented by other English manuscripts. The Salisbury copies of, for example, Augustine, *De mendacio, Contra mendacium,* and *De cura pro mortuis gerenda* (Oxford, Bodl. Libr., MS Bodley 765), do not bear witness to the textual traditions represented by Cambridge, Trinity College, MS B.3.33 and other twelfth-century English manuscripts.[49] Likewise, the Salisbury copy of Gregory, *Moralia in Iob* (Salisbury Cathedral, MS 33), now bound as one volume, was originally divided into two parts, with the break occurring after book xviii: a division common in Continental manuscripts but not otherwise found in English copies, in which a break is more usual after books x and xxii (in 3-volume copies), or after book xvi (in 2-volume copies).[50]

The Salisbury scribes produced a copy of the works of Cyprian which forms part of a distinctively English tradition: London, BL, MS Royal 6 B xv (see above), but, earlier, they had produced another copy of five of Cyprian's treatises (Salisbury Cathedral, MS 9, fos. 1–35), the text of which witnesses to a different tradition, one not otherwise recorded in England. Instead, the text of this copy is very closely related to that in two manuscripts from St Gall: St Gall, Stiftsbibliothek, MS 89 (*c.*900), collated by M. Bévenot as **G**, and MS 150 (s.xi), probably copied from **G**.[51] The close relationship between the text in these two copies and that in Salisbury 9 is further indicated by the fact that all three manuscripts contain the same series of Cyprian treatises in the same order, together with one of the *Orationes* of Gregory Nazianzenus.[52]

Another text copied at Salisbury which bears witness to a tradition not found in any other English manuscripts is the so-called 'Rule of Saint Augustine' (Salisbury Cathedral, MS 169, fos. 77ᵛ–81ᵛ). This is a copy of the version known as the *Praeceptum,* a version which was known elsewhere in England, but here it is in a form otherwise unrepresented by English manuscripts.[53] It forms part of L. Verheijen's Ω family, a tradition represented by a number of Continental manuscripts. However, the text

---

[49] For example, the text of the Salisbury copy of *De mendacio* appears to belong to a textual tradition represented by the manuscripts collated as **S** and **W**, in the printed edition, whereas the text of Cambridge, Trinity College, MS B.3.33, etc. contains the readings of **M**: see Augustine, *De mendacio,* ed. J. Zycha, CSEL 41 (Prague/Vienna/Leipzig, 1900), 412–66.

[50] N. R. Ker, 'The English Manuscripts of the Moralia of Gregory the Great', *Kunsthistorische Forschungen Otto Pächt zu seinem 70. Geburtstag,* ed. A. Rosenauer and G. Weber (Salzburg, 1972), 78–81.

[51] The two St Gall manuscripts and Salisbury Cathedral, MS 9 are the only extant witnesses to a distinct subgroup of Bévenot's **2Bb** group: see Bévenot, *Cyprian,* 14.

[52] The treatises are: *De dominica oratione, De patientia, De opere et eleemosinis, De mortalitate,* and *De ecclesiae unitate.* Gregory Nazianzenus, *Ad cives nazianzenos gravi timore perculsos* falls between the third and fourth treatises. In all three manuscripts it is given the title 'De Hieremiae prophetae dictis in presente imperatore'.

[53] Other 12th-cent. English manuscripts of the so-called 'Rule of Saint Augustine' contain the version known as the *Regula recepta,* accompanied by a version of the *Praeceptum* in which the text is preceded by the first phrase of the *Ordo monasterii*: see Augustine, *La Règle de Saint Augustin,* ed. L. Verheijen, i, *Tradition manuscrite* (Paris, 1967), 217–18.

of the Salisbury manuscript belongs to a particular subgroup of one branch of that tradition for which there is only one other witness: a late tenth-century manuscript from Bobbio, now Turin, Biblioteca Nazionale, MS G.V.7.[54] The text in both of these manuscripts differs in a number of ways from that in a coherent group of ten manuscripts of French origin, with which it is otherwise closely related.[55] For example, the text in both the Salisbury and Bobbio manuscripts has the incipit, 'Precipimus in monasterio constituti', whereas the text in the other ten manuscripts begins, 'Haec igitur sunt quae ut obseruetis praecipimus in monasterio constituti'.

These examples suggest that the Salisbury canons had independent Continental sources for exemplars untapped by other English centres. This impression is confirmed by the number of texts which survive from Salisbury for which there are no other extant late eleventh- or twelfth-century English copies. However, it must be acknowledged that a proportion of this total probably has been created by the accidents of survival. For example, Salisbury Cathedral, MS 129 is the only complete English copy of Pseudo-Augustine (Ambrosiaster), *Quaestiones cxxvii*, to have survived from the twelfth century or earlier; we only know that the text was present elsewhere in late Anglo-Saxon England from the chance survival of fragments of the exemplar for Salisbury Cathedral, MS 129, as flyleaves to Salisbury Cathedral, MS 37.[56] I know of no other surviving twelfth-century English copies, apart from the Salisbury ones, of Augustine, *De beata vita, De duabus animabus*, the shorter commentary on Genesis: the *De genesi ad litteram imperfectus liber*, and the *Speculum*.[57] But the fourteenth-century Franciscan catalogue, the *Registrum Anglie*, which lists patristic and other texts present in cathedrals and monasteries in England and Southern Scotland, records a number of locations besides Salisbury, as possessing copies of each of these texts—it is possible that at least some of these were twelfth-century copies which have since been lost or destroyed.[58]

---

[54] For these and the other manuscripts of the Ω family, see Verheijen, ibid. 245–55.

[55] One of these manuscripts is from Normandy: Rouen, Bibliothèque Municipale, MS 488 (s.xii, from Jumièges), and two are from neighbouring Maine and Anjou: Le Mans, Bibliothèque Municipale, MS 143 (s.xii, from the abbey of Saints-Vincent-et-Laurent), and Angers, Bibliothèque Municipale, MS 306 (s.xii, from the abbey of Saint-Aubin): Verheijen, ibid. 250.

[56] See Ker, 'Beginnings', 32 n. 2. These leaves are written in English Caroline minuscule.

[57] The Salisbury copies are Oxford, Bodl. Libr., MS Bodley 698, and Salisbury Cathedral, MSS 197 and 35 respectively.

[58] I have used the 15th-cent. copy of the *Registrum Anglie* in Oxford, Bodl. Libr., MS Tanner 165, fos. 101ᵛ–120ᵛ. A complete study of this text, including the identification of its references with surviving manuscripts, medieval library catalogues, etc. is being undertaken by R. H. and M. A. Rouse: see their 'The *Registrum Anglie*: the Franciscan "Union Catalogue" of British Libraries', in *Manuscripts at Oxford: An Exhibition in Memory of Richard William Hunt (1908–1979)*, ed. A. C. de la Mare and B. C. Barker-Benfield (Oxford, 1980), 55–6.

TEXTS SURVIVING ONLY FROM SALISBURY

But there are other texts for which Salisbury manuscripts contain the only extant English copies, and which, because of their rarity even on the Continent, we can assume with more confidence were not copied or acquired elsewhere in England in the late eleventh and twelfth centuries, or, indeed in the later Middle Ages.

Perhaps the most unusual of these texts is the *Rule of the Four Fathers*, contained in Salisbury Cathedral, MS 12. Not only was this a rare text by the twelfth century, but the text as it appears in Salisbury Cathedral, MS 12, belongs to a very unusual recension. This is A. de Vogüé's π recension,[59] for which he knew of only one witness: Paris, BN, MS lat. 12005 (*CLA* 633)—the important late sixth- or early seventh-century southern Italian manuscript which contains the earliest complete copy of the *Regula magistri* together with a number of other early monastic rules.[60] By the end of the seventh century the manuscript was at Corbie.[61]

The Salisbury scribes also made copies of a group of Irish exegetical texts for which there are no other extant English manuscript witnesses. Salisbury Cathedral, MS 115 contains a compendium of questions and answers on the books of the Old and New Testaments. This compendium is similar to many of the products of the teaching of Irish scholars in the early Middle Ages.[62] It is a highly disorganized text which reflects the fact that it was not composed so much as evolved through a process of compilation and adaptation. This Salisbury manuscript may be a hitherto unrecognized witness to the text of the so-called *Irish Reference Bible*: parts of the text correspond (apart from some minor variations) with that in Paris, BN, MS lat. 614 (Bischoff's Group IB).[63]

Salisbury Cathedral, MS 124 contains, in addition to Hilary of Poitiers, Commentary on St Matthew's Gospel, a commentary on the seven Catholic Epistles attributed in this manuscript to Hilary as well.[64] The

---

[59] *Les Règles des saints pères*, ed. A. de Vogüé (Paris, 1982), ii. 547–603.

[60] See *La Règle du Maître*, ed. F. Masai (Brussels, 1953), 59–60, and *La Règle du Maître*, ed. A. de Vogüé (Paris, 1964), i. 125–6.

[61] See *CLA* 633.

[62] For the characteristics of early medieval Irish exegesis, see Bischoff, 'Wendepunkte'.

[63] Ibid. 224 (231; 97). Extracts from BN, lat. 614 are printed in Stegmüller, nos. 10301–19. For further details, see below, App. 2.

[64] Hilary, Commentary on St Matthew's Gospel also appears to have been very rare in England. The *Registrum Anglie* (Oxford, Bodl. Libr., MS Tanner 165, fo. 108) lists only three locations apart from Salisbury: the Augustinian priories of Merton and Kenilworth and the Charterhouse of Witham. None of these copies have survived. As far as I am aware, Salisbury 124 contains the only extant English copy. Admittedly, for many texts, the *Registrum* fails to record locations which we know from other evidence possessed copies of these texts, but it is noteworthy that, for this text, not a single Benedictine house or cathedral, other than Salisbury, is listed.

rubric on fo. 3 (see Pl. 9*a*), and a twelfth-century contents list written on the flyleaf indicate that the commentary on the Catholic Epistles was considered to be the work of Hilary of Poitiers as well.[65] However, the text has been identified as a piece of late seventh- or early eighth-century Irish exegesis, the work of a scholar now designated 'the Irish Pseudo-Hilary'.[66] This piece of exegesis was known to Bede and had reached the Continent by the end of the eighth century.[67] Ælfric also quoted from it in a comment in Latin in his otherwise vernacular Ascension Day homily. However, the implication in Ælfric's citation, is that the text was hardly known, if at all, by his readers.[68] Salisbury Cathedral, MS 124 contains a version of this commentary very similar in form and content to that contained in a ninth-century manuscript (probably copied in the Naples region), Naples, Biblioteca Nazionale, MS Vindob. lat. 4. This manuscript was used by R. E. McNally for his edition of this commentary, and was, indeed, the only manuscript known to him which contained more than short extracts.[69] The text of the Salisbury manuscript does, however, contain a large number of readings different from those of the text of the Naples manuscript. Some of these readings may be the result of a scribe copying from an exemplar in insular script with insular abbreviations with which he was unfamiliar.[70]

A. Souter argued that the Salisbury copy of Pelagius, Commentary on the Pauline Epistles (Salisbury Cathedral, MS 5) was also copied directly from an early exemplar in insular script.[71] In support of this assertion, he noted that the Salisbury scribe had considerable difficulty in transcribing his exemplar. For example, frequent wrong word-division indicates that

---

[65] The *Registrum* also lists this text with the works of Hilary of Poitiers: Salisbury is the only location given.

[66] Bischoff, 'Wendepunkte', 270-2 (266-7; 141-2); *Tractatus Hilarii in septem epistolas canonicas*, ed. R. E. McNally, *Scriptores Hiberniae minores*, CCSL 108 B (Turnhout, 1973), i, pp. x-xvii.

[67] Glossator B of the Codex Fuldensis (Fulda, Landesbibliothek, MS Bonifatianus I), draws on this commentary. For his activity, and for his association with St Boniface, see M. B. Parkes, 'The Handwriting of St Boniface: A Reassessment of the Problems', *Beiträge zur Geschichte der Deutschen Sprache und Literatur*, 98 (1976), 172-9.

[68] On Ælfric's knowledge of Pseudo-Hilary, and on this point in particular, see J. E. Cross, 'More Sources for Two of Ælfric's *Catholic Homilies*', *Anglia*, 86 (1968), 77-8, and the opinions of Peter Clemoes cited there. Professor Cross also points out that Ælfric casts doubt on the ascription to Hilary.

[69] Bischoff ('Wendepunkte', 270 (266; 142)) and McNally (*Tractatus Hilarii*, 52) record the existence of extracts in Monte Cassino, Arch. della Badia, MS 384, p. 91 (s.x); a brief extract also precedes a copy of the text of the Epistles themselves in Karlsruhe, Badische Landesbibliothek, MS Augiensis CCXXII.

[70] For example, the frequent confusion of *quia, quoniam, quam* and *quod*, arising from the scribe's lack of familiarity with insular abbreviations beginning with the letter **q**; and the incorrect reading 'non' instead of 'nomen'.

[71] *Pelagius's Expositions of Thirteen Epistles of St Paul*, ed. A. Souter, Texts and Studies, 9 (1922), i. 283-6.

his exemplar had poor, if any, word-division; he often confused letter forms; numerous corruptions indicate that he was copying from an exemplar which included an abbreviation system which had become extinct by the early ninth century, sometimes he did not attempt to expand the abbreviations he found, but simply reproduced them in his copy. To make matters worse, several words in the exemplar were damaged or illegible; for these, the scribe carefully left a space of the correct length.[72] Souter assumed that the exemplar was an 'Anglo-Saxon manuscript of the end of the eighth or the beginning of the ninth century', the implication being that it had never left England. But it could equally have been a manuscript in insular script, either copied in Britain and exported to the Continent, or copied by insular scribes on the Continent. It is possible that the exemplars for all of these unusual Irish or insular exegetical works were acquired by the Salisbury canons from centres on the Continent which had been frequented by Irish scholars.[73]

For one Irish text, the copy made by Salisbury scribes is the only known extant witness. This is the *Epistola Cummiani*, a computistical treatise chiefly concerned with the controversy over the date of Easter.[74] It was copied, together with a copy of Bede, *De aetatibus saeculi*, in an originally independent booklet, now London, BL, MS Cotton Vitellius A XII, fos. 79–86. Although this is an insular text, it too may have been preserved in a Continental centre or centres frequented by Irish scholars, and then reintroduced to England (and possibly just Salisbury) after the Conquest.

CLASSICAL LATIN TEXTS

Thus far I have been concerned solely with Christian Latin texts. But the Salisbury scribes also produced an unusual collection of classical Latin texts: texts for which the Salisbury copies are either by far the earliest surviving English copies, or the only extant English copies. Perhaps the most interesting of these is London, BL, MS Royal 15 C xi, fos. 113–94, a copy of the first eight plays of the Palatine recension of the Comedies of Plautus.[75] The plays of Plautus do not seem to have enjoyed as much

---

[72] Ibid. 284–5.

[73] However, for evidence of textual links between the Irish Reference Bible and Old English literature, see J. E. Cross, 'Towards the Identification of Old English Literary Ideas—Old Workings and New Seams', in *Sources of Anglo-Saxon Culture*, ed. P. E. Szarmach (Kalamazoo, 1986), 79–83.

[74] *Cummian's Letter, De controversia Paschali and the De ratione conputandi*, ed. M. Walsh and D. Ó. Cróinín, Toronto Pontifical Institute of Medieval Studies, Studies and Texts, 86 (Toronto, 1988).

[75] For a study of this copy, see R. M. Thomson, 'British Library Royal 15 C. xi; A Manuscript of Plautus' Plays from Salisbury Cathedral (*c*.1100)', *Scriptorium*, 40 (1986), 82–7.

popularity as the plays of Terence, and medieval copies are not plentiful.[76] The Salisbury copy is now recognized to be of considerable textual interest, since the scribe of its exemplar 'was emending, to some extent, from a MS. significantly better than **B**, the oldest and best of the surviving Palatine MSS'.[77] R. M. Thomson suggests, somewhat cautiously, that this exemplar may have been produced in Germany in the tenth century. He also argues that this exemplar went on to be the source for other English manuscripts of the plays of Plautus, or *florilegia* compiled from them.[78]

London, BL, MS Royal 15 C xi, fos. 1–58, was also copied at Salisbury. It contains the earliest known English copy of Cicero, *Tusculan Disputations*. T. W. Dougan demonstrated that the text of this manuscript (collated by him as **E**) is most closely related to that in an eleventh-century manuscript from Gembloux: Brussels, Bibliothèque Royale, MS 5351 (collated as **B**).[79]

A third manuscript containing a number of classical Latin texts was also copied at Salisbury in the early twelfth century, and is now Cambridge, Trinity College, MS R.16.34. The immediate exemplar for this manuscript was almost certainly of Norman origin, or had reached Normandy by the second half of the eleventh century, since the Salisbury copy contains a summary of the provisions of one of the reforming synods of the Province of Rouen: the Synod of Lisieux of 1064 (incidentally, the only extant witness to the provisions of this synod).[80] These provisions were evidently copied by the Salisbury scribe from the same exemplar, since the text follows on immediately from the previous text without a break, new heading, or change of hand. The provisions may have been added in a convenient blank space in the exemplar. This Salisbury manuscript also contains the earliest known English copies of Cicero, *De officiis* (i–ii. iii. 9); extracts from Seneca, *De beneficiis*, and an anthology compiled from Valerius Maximus and Aulus Gellius. This anthology also survives in two twelfth-century French copies: Paris, BN, MS lat. 4952, and Vatican, Biblioteca Apostolica, MS lat. 3307, and in

[76] For the surviving manuscripts, and an examination of the transmission of Plautus' plays, see R. J. Tarrant in *Texts and Transmission: A Survey of the Latin Classics*, ed. L. D. Reynolds (Oxford, 1983), 302–7.

[77] Thomson, 'Royal 15 C. xi', 87.

[78] See ibid. and also, R. M. Thomson, 'A Thirteenth-Century Plautus Florilegium from Bury St. Edmunds Abbey', *Antichthon*, 8 (1974), 33–4.

[79] *Cicero Tusculanarum disputationum libri quinque*, ed. T. W. Dougan (Cambridge, 1905), i. pp. xxvii, xxxvii–xxxviii.

[80] L. Delisle, 'Canons du Concile tenu à Lisieux en 1064', *Journal des Savants*, 3: 66 (1901), 516–21; repr. in C. J. Hefele, *Histoire des Conciles*, tr. and ed. H. Leclercq (Paris, 1911), iv. 1420–3.

excerpts in two other manuscripts.[81] The anthology is of considerable textual importance for the text of Aulus Gellius, *Noctes Atticae*, since the extracts it contains come from both books i–vii and books ix–xx (which circulated separately in the early Middle Ages). Indeed, copies of this anthology are the earliest extant witnesses to the text of books i–vii. Furthermore, since the Salisbury copy is the earliest surviving witness to this anthology, it is, therefore, our earliest extant witness to the text of the first seven books of the *Noctes Atticae*.[82] However, a recent study of this anthology concluded, 'Unfortunately, none of the surviving whole manuscripts of books i–vii comes from the source from which the anthology was compiled, nor does the anthology's text of Valerius Maximus aid in revealing its place of origin.'[83] Another *florilegium* of extracts from both books i–vii and ix–xx of the *Noctes Atticae* was known to William of Malmesbury and to John of Salisbury: William's copy has survived as Oxford, Bodl. Libr., MS Rawlinson G. 139. However, the extracts in this *florilegium* are not the same as those in the Gellius/Maximus anthology contained in Cambridge, Trinity College, MS R.16.34.[84]

The large number of texts for which Salisbury provides us with the earliest or the only known English copies, or copies textually unrelated to other English manuscripts, demonstrates that there were direct links between Salisbury and centres on the Continent: links, moreover, which were strong enough to allow exemplars to be sent on the hazardous journey across the Channel. This is all the more surprising since the Salisbury canons, as a secular community, had no ready-made associations with Continental centres, such as those which existed between certain monastic houses. This fact also makes it more difficult for us to discover from whereabouts on the Continent the canons did acquire exemplars.

The manuscripts themselves give us some clues, but it is not possible to identify individual centres with any certainty. Cambridge, Trinity College, MS R.16.34 was certainly copied from an exemplar from a Norman centre, but it is not possible to determine which one. The

---

[81] For other witnesses to this anthology, and also for the transmission of Aulus Gellius, *Noctes Atticae*, see P. K. Marshall in Reynolds, *Texts and Transmission*, 176–80. See also, D. M. Schullian, 'The Anthology of Valerius Maximus and A. Gellius', *Classical Philology*, 32 (1937), 70–2.

[82] For a fuller discussion of the transmission of books 1–7, and for the position occupied by copies of this anthology in that transmission, see P. K. Marshall, J. Martin, and R. H. Rouse, 'Clare College MS. 26 and the Circulation of Aulus Gellius 1–7 in Medieval England and France', *Mediaeval Studies*, 42 (1980), 369–70.

[83] Ibid. 370.

[84] Ibid. 370–3.

exemplars for the Irish texts, and those copied or derived from insular centres, may well have been acquired from Continental centres which had had contacts with Irish scholars. Perhaps one of these centres was Laon, since we know that canons from Salisbury studied there, among them Bishop Roger's two nephews, Alexander and Nigel.[85] But unfortunately none of these texts have survived in manuscripts from Laon, and therefore this hypothesis cannot be substantiated. We also know, from other evidence, that the Salisbury canons obtained at least one manuscript from Le Mans. A copy of a letter from Bishop Hildebert of Le Mans to the dean of Salisbury, datable to before 1125, has survived in a late twelfth-century manuscript from St Augustine's, Canterbury (Lambeth Palace Library, MS 185).[86] In this letter, Hildebert tells the dean that he has enclosed a copy of two of his sermons and a letter, and promises to send more. The copy he sent to Salisbury has not survived.

For the most part, it is necessary to draw inferences from the relationships which can be established between copies of texts in Salisbury manuscripts and copies from other centres. These are very varied, and do not tend to point consistently to the same centre or area. In some cases, these relationships point to the great Carolingian centres. For example, the text of the Salisbury copy of the *Rule of the Four Fathers* (Salisbury Cathedral, MS 12) is related to that in a copy known to have been at Corbie (Paris, BN, MS lat. 12005); the copy of Hilary's commentary on St Matthew's Gospel (Salisbury Cathedral, MS 124) shares a number of readings with a manuscript from Lorsch (Vatican, Biblioteca Apostolica, MS Pal. lat. 167).[87] What is more difficult to show is whether such exemplars were obtained directly from these centres, or at one or more stages removed, either from manuscripts which had migrated to other centres nearer to Normandy and England or from copies derived from them. In the case of the *Rule of the Four Fathers*, it is difficult to argue for anything other than a direct link with Corbie, since Paris, lat. 12005, which was at Corbie from the end of the seventh century until the seventeenth century, is the only other extant witness to the recension of the text found in Salisbury 12. But in other cases, the manuscript evidence allows for intermediary copies from other centres nearer to Normandy and England. For example, a second Bobbio manuscript of the Ω text of the *Praeceptum* version of the so-called 'Rule of Saint Augustine' (now Vatican, Biblioteca Apostolica, MS lat. 5762) is very similar to the group of ten French manuscripts of that text, which indicates that a copy which contained a text closely related to it, migrated

---

[85] *Hermanni monachi de miraculis s. Mariae Laudunensis*, ii. xiii: *PL* 156. 982–3.

[86] A. Wilmart, 'Les Sermons d'Hildebert', *Rev. bén.*, 47 (1935), 34–6.

[87] Collated as **L** in *Hilaire de Poitiers sur Matthieu*, ed. J. Doignon, 2 vols. (Paris, 1978–9), esp. i. 46–7.

to France and represented the archetype for that group.[88] It is therefore possible that a manuscript which depended on the Bobbio manuscript with which the text of the Salisbury copy is most closely related (Turin, Biblioteca Nazionale, MS G.V.7) travelled north-west, and that the copy produced at Salisbury was derived from it. But, until intermediaries have been identified, such explanations remain speculative.

The Low Countries played an important role in the transmission of classical texts in the eleventh century.[89] Moreover, in the latter half of the eleventh century, the schools at Liège, in particular, had a reputation as a centre for classical learning:[90] Orderic Vitalis tells us that Odo, bishop of Bayeux, 'sent promising clerks to Liège and other cities where he knew that philosophic studies (*philosophorum studia*) flourished.'[91] Among these clerks were Thomas, later archbishop of York, his brother Samson, later bishop of Worcester, William of Rots, abbot of Fécamp, and Thurstan, abbot of Glastonbury. Perhaps Norman scholars such as these brought copies of classical texts from the Low Countries to Salisbury. The evidence of the text of the Salisbury copy of Cicero's *Tusculan Disputations* would seem to support such a suggestion, since, as seen above, the manuscript with which it is most closely related, is an eleventh-century manuscript associated with Gembloux.

It is also possible that the scholarly *clerici* who William of Malmesbury tells us were attracted to Bishop Osmund's circle brought books with them from the Continent.[92] For the most part, exemplars were probably acquired through personal requests between heads of houses, but texts were sometimes transmitted informally by travelling scholars. For example, a whole recension of the text of Augustine, *De libero arbitrio*, which probably originated in Tournai, may have derived from the copy bought, by chance, by Odo of Tournai from a passing monk in 1092.[93] In such cases, the origin or provenance of a manuscript with which a copy is very closely related, would not provide reliable evidence for the immediate source of the exemplar used by the scribe of that copy. It may

---

[88] Augustine, *Règle*, 245–55.

[89] For the acquisition of classical texts by Olbert, abbot of Gembloux and St James's Liège, see A. Boutemy, 'Un grand abbé du xie siècle: Olbert de Gembloux', *Annales de la Société archéologique de Namur*, 41 (1934), 43–85; and for the presence of classical texts at Lobbes, see F. Dolbeau, 'Un nouveau catalogue des manuscrits de Lobbes aux xie et xiie siècles', *Recherches augustiniennes*, 13 (1978), 3–36; 14 (1979), 191–248.

[90] B. Bischoff, 'Living with the Satirists', in *Classical Influences on European Culture AD 500–1500*, ed. R. R. Bolgar (Cambridge, 1971), 83–94; repr. in his collected papers, *Mittelalterliche Studien* (Stuttgart, 1981), iii. 260–70.

[91] Orderic Vitalis, *Historia ecclesiastica*, bk. viii, ed. M. Chibnall (Oxford, 1973), iv. 118–19.

[92] *GP* 184.

[93] For this recension, and for the abbey of St Martin, Tournai as a centre for the transmission of patristic texts, see W. M. Green, 'Mediaeval Recensions of Augustine', *Speculum*, 29 (1954), 531–4.

be that channels of transmission such as this explain some of the more unusual textual traditions to which some of the Salisbury manuscripts bear witness.

PRE-CONQUEST EXEMPLARS

From the evidence of surviving manuscripts we can see that some texts copied at Salisbury were already present in England at the time of the Conquest, either in manuscripts copied in England or in manuscripts imported from the Continent. However, we cannot assume that because a text was present at one centre in England, it would be available for copying at another. It is necessary, therefore, to demonstrate that a text copied at Salisbury was either made from an extant pre-Conquest manuscript, or shared an exemplar with an earlier manuscript from an English centre, or bears witness to the same textual tradition as that of a text contained in a manuscript present in England before the Conquest.

Two pre-Conquest manuscripts survive, which almost certainly acted as exemplars for Salisbury manuscripts: London, Lambeth Palace, MS 149 and Oxford, Bodl. Libr., MS Bodley 319. Both came from Exeter Cathedral, and were probably among the books donated by Leofric, bishop of Exeter to his community.[94] Lambeth 149 almost certainly acted as the exemplar for the copy of Augustine, *De adulterinis coniugiis* in Salisbury Cathedral, MS 128. As N. R. Ker observed, Lambeth 149 contains a highly defective version of the text, with many omissions.[95] Soon after they had made their copy from Lambeth 149, the Salisbury canons obtained another copy of the text, from which scribe i supplied the missing portions of text. As far as I have collated it, Bodley 319 seems to have been the exemplar for the Salisbury copy of Isidore, *De miraculis Christi* in London, BL, MS Royal 5 E xvi.

Since Lambeth 149 was at Salisbury in the late eleventh century, its text of Bede's commentary on the Apocalypse could have served as the exemplar for the Salisbury copy in Aberdeen, MS 216, but I have not yet been able to check this. Leofric also gave copies of Smaragdus, *Diadema monachorum* and Isidore, *Libri etymologiarum* to the Exeter Chapter, but since these copies have not survived it is not possible to determine whether they could have provided exemplars for Salisbury Cathedral, MSS 12 and 112.

In other instances it is possible to show that a Salisbury copy of a text

---

[94] E. M. Drage, 'Bishop Leofric and the Exeter Cathedral Chapter (1050–1072): A Reassessment of the Manuscript Evidence', D.Phil. thesis (Oxford University, 1978), 58, 57 respectively.

[95] Ker, 'Beginnings', 35.

was made from the same exemplar as that employed for a pre-Conquest manuscript. For example, Exeter Cathedral, MS 3507 (not listed in Leofric's donation list, therefore probably owned by the Chapter)[96] contains a series of computistical texts which appear with only minor changes in order in London, BL, MS Cotton Vitellius A XII, fos. 10ᵛ–65, part of a Group I manuscript from Salisbury. But, from his examination of the texts in the two manuscripts, N. R. Ker concluded that the Salisbury copy was not made from the Exeter one.[97] However, they may have shared a common exemplar.

Exeter Cathedral, MS 3507 and another Exeter book, Oxford, Bodl. Libr., MS Bodley 718, are in the hand of the scribe who copied the Sherborne Pontifical (now, Paris, BN, MS lat. 943).[98] Sherborne certainly co-operated with the Exeter community to provide them with exemplars, since the copy of Alfred's translation of Gregory, *Cura pastoralis* produced in the mid-eleventh century by Exeter scribes (Cambridge, University Library, MS Ii.2.4), has a preface which begins 'Aelfred kyning hateð gretan Wulfsige bisceop'. Wulfsige was bishop of Sherborne from 879×889 to (890×896)×900, and therefore the Exeter copy was almost certainly derived from the copy originally sent by Alfred to Sherborne.[99] But unfortunately we do not know whether the Sherborne Pontifical was actually produced at Sherborne; all that is known about the manuscript is that it was at Sherborne by the early eleventh century.[100] But if Exeter 3507, Bodley 718 and Paris, BN lat. 943 were copied at Sherborne, then Exeter 3507 may have been copied from a now lost manuscript which belonged to the community at Sherborne. However, since this hypothetical manuscript has not survived it is not possible to verify the simple explanation that it was borrowed from Sherborne by the Salisbury canons and served as the exemplar for the Salisbury manuscript which is now London, BL, MS Cotton Vitellius A XII, fos. 4–71.

More positive evidence exists which indicates that Salisbury manuscripts shared common exemplars with manuscripts made a little earlier at Worcester Cathedral Priory.[101] For example, B. Colgrave showed that

[96] Drage, *Leofric*, 273 n. 3.

[97] Ker, 'Beginnings', 38–9.

[98] Drage, *Leofric*, 273.

[99] Ibid. 269.

[100] N. R. Ker, *Catalogue of Manuscripts Containing Anglo-Saxon* (Oxford, 1957), no. 364: 'The additions on ff. 1ᵛ, 2, 170ᵛ ... show that the manuscript was at Sherborne by, at latest, the very beginning of the eleventh century, and it may well have been written there.'

[101] Because the last Anglo-Saxon bishop of Worcester, Wulfstan, remained bishop until his death in 1095, there are grounds for regarding late 11th-cent. Worcester manuscripts as representative of late-Anglo-Saxon traditions. But the possibility remains that manuscripts produced at Worcester after the Conquest were copied from recently imported Continental exemplars.

the text of the copy of Felix's *Life of Guthlac*, produced at Worcester in the late eleventh century,[102] is closely related to that in the copy made at Salisbury (now, Dublin, Trinity College, MS 174, fos. 73–85). However, he considered that the Salisbury copy was not made from the Worcester one, but that both were derived from the same exemplar.[103]

The large collection of saints' lives preserved in Salisbury Cathedral MSS 221 + 222 (Group I manuscripts)[104] was almost certainly copied from the same exemplar as that employed for the contemporary or slightly earlier Worcester copy (London, BL, MS Cotton Nero E I + Cambridge, Corpus Christi College, MS 9).[105] These two copies are of special importance since they are the earliest extant witnesses to this collection of saints' lives. Ælfric used as sources for his *Catholic Homilies* and *Lives of the Saints*, saints' lives which had close textual similarities with some of those in the Salisbury and Worcester copies.[106] It should, however, be emphasized that this evidence does not allow us to assume that Ælfric had access to a corpus of saints' lives analogous in size to that represented by the Salisbury and Worcester Passionals—the Salisbury and Worcester copies provide us with the earliest evidence of the presence in England of this or indeed any other analogous collection of saints' lives.

It is also possible to show that certain texts copied at Salisbury bear witness to Anglo-Saxon textual traditions, which suggests that the Salisbury canons had obtained their exemplars for these texts from another English centre or centres. For example, the Salisbury copies of the *Cosmographia*, attributed in medieval times to Aethicus (Salisbury Cathedral, MS 110), and of Amalarius, *Liber officialis* (Salisbury Cathedral, MS 154), are both witnesses to English textual traditions. The earliest surviving English copy of the *Cosmographia* is now Leiden,

[102] London, BL, MS Cotton Nero E I, fos. 185–96. P. H. Zettel observes that the *Life of Guthlac* is almost certainly an independent addition to the corpus of saints' lives contained in this manuscript, see 'Ælfric's Hagiographic Sources and the Latin Legendary Preserved in BL MS Cotton Nero E I + CCCC MS 9 and Other Manuscripts', D.Phil. thesis (Oxford University, 1979), 19 n. 46.

[103] *Felix's Life of Saint Guthlac*, ed. B. Colgrave (Cambridge, 1956), 50–1.

[104] Formerly, Oxford, Bodl. Libr., MSS Fell 4 and 1 respectively. These manuscripts were returned to Salisbury in 1985.

[105] A complete study of the relationship between these two copies has not yet been undertaken; but their dependence on a single exemplar seems assured from the studies made of individual lives in the collection: see, for example, H. Delehaye, 'Les Actes de s. Marcel le centurion', *Analecta Bollandiana*, 41 (1923), 257–87; and M. Esposito, 'On the Earliest Latin Life of St. Brigid of Kildare', *Proceedings of the Royal Irish Academy*, (C), 30 (1912), 307–26. E. A. McIntyre dates the Worcester copy to the second half of the 11th-cent., see 'Early Twelfth-Century Worcester Cathedral Priory with Special Reference to the Manuscripts Written There', D.Phil. thesis (Oxford University, 1978), 202, 204.

[106] P. H. Zettel, 'Saints' Lives in Old English: Latin Manuscripts and Vernacular Accounts: Ælfric', *Peritia*, 1 (1982), 17–37. A fuller account is given in Zettel, 'Ælfric's Hagiographic Sources'.

Bibliotheek der Rijksuniversiteit, MS Scaliger 69, copied at St Augustine's, Canterbury in the second half of the tenth century.[107] Shortly after, a copy of this manuscript was made at Worcester, now, London, BL, MS Cotton Vespasian B X.[108] The text in Salisbury 110 is very closely related to that in both of these manuscripts, but, as far as I have collated them, the Salisbury manuscript does not appear to have been copied from either of the other two.

The Salisbury copy of Amalarius, *Liber officialis* (Salisbury Cathedral, MS 154) contains a version of that text, called by Hanssens, *Retractatio I*, which circulated in England before the Conquest.[109] Three manuscripts of this version have survived from pre-Conquest English centres: Cambridge, Corpus Christi College, MS 192 (copied in Brittany, but which was at Christ Church, Canterbury by the mid-eleventh century);[110] Cambridge, Trinity College, MS B.11.2 (copied at St Augustine's, Canterbury in the second half of the tenth century, but at Exeter by the mid-eleventh); and Boulogne, Bibliothèque Municipale, MS 82, copied in tenth-century Anglo-Saxon square minuscule.[111] However, as N. R. Ker pointed out, Salisbury 154 contains an aberrant version of the *Retractatio I*, not found in any of the extant manuscripts known to have been in England before the Conquest, and not noted by Hanssens. The text has been significantly rearranged, and there are several additions.[112]

[107] See the facsimile edition of this manuscript, and the introduction by T. A. M. Bishop, *Aethici Istrici cosmographia Vergilio Salisburgensi rectius adscripta: Codex Leidensis Scaligeranus 69, Umbrae codicum occidentalium*, 10 (Amsterdam, 1966).

[108] Ibid. xvii. Bishop also notes that a mid-12th-cent. copy, Dublin, Trinity College, MS 371, from the library of Christ Church, Canterbury, is textually allied to Leiden, MS Scaliger 69. He speculates that this might be a copy of a lost Christ Church copy of *c*.1000, when a number of St Augustine's manuscripts seem to have been copied by Christ Church scribes. M. Lapidge has identified another manuscript which bears witness to the same tradition of the text as Scaliger 69: Vatican, Biblioteca Apostolica, MS Reginensis, lat. 1260, a manuscript from Fleury. He suggests that this manuscript may have acted as the exemplar (possibly via an intermediary) for Scaliger 69, see 'The Present State of Anglo-Latin Studies', in *Insular Latin Studies: Papers on Latin Texts and Manuscripts of the British Isles: 550–1066*, ed. M. Herren (Toronto, 1981), 57–8.

[109] For the characteristics of *Retractatio I*, see *Amalarii episcopi opera liturgica omnia*, ed. J. M. Hanssens, *Studi e testi*, 138 (1948), 162–9. This *retractatio* was not, however, confined to England. Of the seven copies of this *retractatio* listed by Hanssens, four are of Continental origin: ibid. 129.

[110] F. A. Rella, 'Continental Manuscripts Acquired for English Centers in the Tenth and Early Eleventh Centuries: A Preliminary Checklist', *Anglia*, 98 (1980), 110.

[111] Boulogne 82 is in the same hand as another 10th-cent. manuscript of English origin: Cambridge, Trinity College, MS B.16.3, a copy of Rhabanus Maurus, *De laude sanctae crucis*, see M. B. Parkes, 'A Fragment of an Early-Tenth-Century Anglo-Saxon Manuscript and its Significance', *ASE* 12 (1983), 137 n. 50.

[112] Ker, 'Beginnings', 46–7, sets out the principal differences. Although the preface *Postquam scripsi* was originally omitted, it was supplied soon after on blank leaves at the end of the manuscript by Group I scribe ii, whilst on blank leaves at the front, another Group I scribe, scribe iv, added the letter *Gloriosissime imperator* (Hanssens, *Amalarius*, *Studi e testi*, 139 (1948), 19–21), a part of the full text of the *Liber officialis* not usually associated with *Retractatio I*.

A Salisbury manuscript, London, BL, MS Royal 15 B xix, fos. 200–5, contains a series of Boniface riddles almost identical with that in a mid-eleventh-century manuscript from Canterbury (Cambridge, University Library, MS Gg.5.35), but there are enough substantial variant readings between the texts of the two manuscripts to indicate that neither was the Salisbury copy made from the Canterbury copy nor were both copies made from a common exemplar.[113] The same series of riddles appears in a tenth-century Continental manuscript, now Einsiedeln, Stiftsbibliothek, MS 302.[114] Both English manuscripts share readings with the Einsiedeln manuscript, and each English manuscript agrees independently with other readings in this manuscript.[115]

I have also observed relationships between texts copied at Salisbury and those in two manuscripts from other English centres which may have been produced before the Conquest: Cambridge, Trinity College, MS B.3.25 and London, BL, MS Harley 3080. Both are manuscripts written in English Caroline minuscule, but, since English Caroline minuscule continued to flourish at many centres well after the Conquest,[116] the possibility remains that both were copied after the Conquest. They might, therefore, not represent pre-Conquest English textual traditions, but have been copied from Continental exemplars imported after the Conquest.

Cambridge, Trinity College, MS B.3.25, an eleventh-century manu-script with a Christ Church, Canterbury provenance, contains a copy of Augustine, *De haeresibus*, which has an unusual incipit, 'Symoniaci a symone'.[117] F. Römer noted the same incipit in two early twelfth-century manuscripts: Durham Cathedral, MS B.IV.6 (from Durham Cathedral Priory), and London, BL, MS Royal 5 B xvi (from Rochester).[118] I have also noted the same incipit in an early twelfth-century copy of the text

[113] See the edition of Boniface, *Aenigmata*, ed. F. Glorie, *Variae collectiones aenigmatum Merovingicae aetatis*, CCSL 133 (Turnhout, 1968); London, BL, MS Royal 15 B xix, fos. 200–5 is collated as L², and Cambridge, U. L., MS Gg.5.35, as G. F. Glorie (p. 157) follows E. Dümmler (ed.), *Poetae latini aevi Carolini*, MGH (Berlin, 1881), i. 2, in ascribing the whole of London, BL, MS Royal 15 B xix to Rheims: Ker, however ('Beginnings', 25, 25 n. 1), demonstrated that fos. 200–5 were detached leaves from Salisbury 115.

[114] F. Glorie, *Aenigmata*, 154, collated as E.

[115] For evidence of links between England and Einsiedeln in the late tenth century, see M. B. Parkes, 'A Note on MS Vatican, Bibl. Apost., lat. 3363', in *Boethius, His Life, Thought and Influence*, ed. M. T. Gibson (Oxford, 1981), 426.

[116] See Ker, *English Manuscripts*, 22, 29–30, 34.

[117] R. W. Southern included this manuscript in his list of books surviving from the pre-Conquest library of Christ Church, Canterbury: see *St Anselm and His Biographer* (Oxford, 1963), 243 n. 1, but Ker did not list it among his list of pre-Conquest copies of the works of the four great Latin Fathers written in English Caroline minuscule (*English Manuscripts*, 8 n. 2).

[118] Römer, 99–100.

from Salisbury, Salisbury Cathedral, MS 165, fos. 108–19. As far as I have collated them, the texts of the three twelfth-century copies contain a number of the unusual readings found in the text of the Canterbury copy. The close relationship between the Canterbury copy and those from Durham and Rochester is more evident, since in all three manuscripts the *De haeresibus* is preceded by a copy of Augustine's *Confessiones*. However, this is not the case with the Salisbury manuscript. A copy of the *Confessiones* was produced at Salisbury (Salisbury Cathedral, MS 6), but from a different exemplar, since this copy was produced somewhat earlier than the Salisbury copy of the *De haeresibus*, and, moreover, it represents a different textual tradition from that represented by the Canterbury, Rochester, and Durham copies. However other mid- or late eleventh- and twelfth-century English copies of the *Confessiones* do represent the same textual tradition as that to which Salisbury 6 bears witness. Besides sharing a number of readings against the Canterbury, Durham, and Rochester copies, these manuscripts and the Salisbury copy also share a number of marginal subject headings.[119] From the appearance of script, London, BL, MS Harley 3080 is the earliest witness to this tradition.[120] Neither its medieval origin nor provenance are known. Other English manuscripts which bear witness to this tradition are Oxford, Bodl. Libr., MS Bodley 815 (s.xiex, from Exeter), Hereford Cathedral, MS O.iv.8 (s.xii), and London, BL, MS Royal 5 B xiv (s.xii, from Bath). From sample collations, and also from an examination of the marginal headings, it seems that none of the three earliest witnesses to this tradition (Harley 3080, Salisbury 6, and Bodley 815) were copied from each other, but that all three probably derive from the same exemplar. It should be observed that a copy of Augustine's *Confessiones* was not listed among the books donated by Leofric to the Exeter Chapter, nor copied by Exeter scribes active during his episcopacy. Bodley 815 seems, therefore, to have been the earliest copy of the text at Exeter. It is possible that, in the West Country at least, Augustine's *Confessiones* were not available in the late-Anglo-Saxon period until the appearance of the common exemplar for Harley 3080, Bodley 815 and Salisbury 6.

It is clear, then, that for a small proportion of the texts copied at Salisbury, exemplars were already available in England. It has also been possible to identify centres from which the Salisbury canons obtained

---

[119] Headings common to all the late-11th-cent. English copies of this tradition include: 'Gemitus Augustini', 'Unde Paulus ita uocetur', 'Fenea' and 'Euodius' (Salisbury 6, fos. 13, 31ᵛ, and 37ᵛ).

[120] Ker included this manuscript in his list of patristic manuscripts copied in English pre-Conquest Caroline minuscule, but as one of the manuscripts which may have been written either a little before or a little after the Conquest (*English Manuscripts*, 8 n. 2).

exemplars: Exeter, certainly, and probably Sherborne as well, if the common exemplar for Exeter 3507 and Cotton Vitellius A XII was a Sherborne manuscript. It is unfortunate that none of the manuscripts known to have been at Sherborne in the late eleventh century contain texts which were copied at Salisbury. For this reason, it is impossible to prove whether the Salisbury canons obtained other exemplars from Sherborne. We know that at least two books were transferred from Sherborne to Salisbury when the see was moved in 1075 (see below), and, therefore, it seems likely that exemplars were borrowed as well.

Sadly, there is also no correspondence between texts copied at Salisbury and the contents of books surviving from before the Conquest from other important centres in the South-West such as Glastonbury, Bath, and Malmesbury. Oxford, Trinity College, MS 28, a manuscript with a sixteenth-century Winchester provenance, which may have been copied before the Conquest, does contain two texts copied at Salisbury—Bede, *De tabernaculo* and Pseudo-Augustine, *De essentia divinitatis.*[121] However, this manuscript need not have had a West-Country origin or medieval provenance.[122] In any case, the texts of the Bede and the Pseudo-Augustine do not bear witness to the same textual traditions as those of the texts in the Salisbury manuscripts.

Some of the texts copied at Salisbury are also contained in manuscripts which were at Worcester at the time of the Conquest, or which were copied very shortly afterwards. However, as I have shown above, although manuscripts from Salisbury and Worcester can be shown to share common exemplars, or to belong to the same textual traditions, I have not yet discovered any instances of Worcester manuscripts acting as exemplars for Salisbury scribes.

The Salisbury canons did not automatically draw on manuscripts already in the country for use as exemplars since they acquired a Continental manuscript of Bede, *De temporum ratione* (Salisbury Cathedral, MS 158) rather than copy a manuscript already in England. C. W. Jones has demonstrated that several post-Conquest copies of Bede, *De temporum ratione* seem to have been derived from a Continental archetype brought to English schools connected with Fleury, possibly by Abbo in the early eleventh century. One such manuscript is London, BL, MS Cotton Vespasian B VI, which was written in Northern France *c.*850, and which had reached England by the early eleventh century.[123] However, the Salisbury canons did not produce a copy of this text, but

---

[121] The Salisbury copies are Salisbury 165, fos. 23–87, and Salisbury 165, fos. 88–93[v].

[122] See P. Chaplais, 'William of Saint-Calais', 73–4.

[123] Bede, *Opera de temporibus*, ed. C. W. Jones (Cambridge, Mass., 1943), 143, and also Bede, *De temporum ratione liber*, CCSL 123 B (Turnhout, 1977), 241.

acquired for themselves a Continental copy (Salisbury Cathedral, MS 158).

Nor did Salisbury use the copy of Paschasius, *De corpore et sanguine domine* made at Worcester in the second half of the tenth century (London, BL, MS Royal 8 B xi). Indeed this manuscript does not appear to have been used anywhere in England as an exemplar: the Salisbury copy (Salisbury Cathedral, MS 130), is one of several made in England after the Conquest which bear witness to a distinct English textual tradition, but the tenth-century Worcester copy is not a representative of this tradition.[124] And although the copy of Cassian, *Collationes* produced at Worcester in the late eleventh century (Oxford, Bodl. Libr., MS Hatton 23) and that produced at Salisbury (Salisbury Cathedral, MS 10) are the earliest extant English witnesses to this text, they probably represent different textual traditions, since Hatton 23 contains only the first ten *Collationes*, whereas the Salisbury copy contains in addition *Collationes* xiv, xv, xxiv, and xi.

SALISBURY MANUSCRIPTS NOT PRODUCED AT SALISBURY

Not all the books which can be shown to have been at Salisbury in the late eleventh and early twelfth centuries were copied there. A small number of books were acquired from other centres: four almost certainly from other English centres, and one possibly from the Continent. With one exception, they do not appear to have acted as exemplars for any of the books copied at Salisbury in this period, and therefore they were presumably acquired to form part of the community's collection. However, they too provide evidence of texts available in England before and after the Conquest, and may indicate the sources from whence the Salisbury canons also obtained exemplars.

At least two of these books were brought to Salisbury from Sherborne: a Pontifical (now London, BL, MS Cotton Tiberius C I),[125] and a copy of Alfred's translation of Gregory, *Cura pastoralis* (now Cambridge, Trinity College, MS R.5.22, fos. 72–158).[126] Both books contain texts associated with the role and duties of a bishop, and thus it is not surprising that,

---

[124] Paschasius Radbertus, *De corpore et sanguine domini*, ed. B. Paul, CCCM 16 (Turnhout, 1969), xiii–xvi. For the date and origin of London, BL MS Royal 8 B xi, see T. A. M. Bishop, *English Caroline Minuscule* (Oxford, 1971), 16.

[125] The oldest parts of this manuscript are in German hands of the mid-11th-cent., but N. R. Ker demonstrated that additions to the manuscript indicate that it had been at Sherborne, and was then transferred to Salisbury: see Ker, 'Three Old English Texts', 262–79.

[126] Identified by Ker, 'Salisbury Cathedral Manuscripts', 156.

when Bishop Hereman moved the see from Sherborne to Salisbury in 1075, he should have transferred these two books as well. It is possible that Hereman brought other books from Sherborne, or, like his contemporary Leofric, bishop of Exeter, owned a personal collection of books himself, which he then left to his community; but we have no positive evidence of this.

Two more manuscripts were acquired by Salisbury from as yet unidentified centres in England. The flyleaves to Salisbury Cathedral, MS 37 are the remains of a copy of Pseudo-Augustine (Ambrosiaster), *Quaestiones cxxvii*, written in English Caroline minuscule by a scribe whose hand I have not identified in any other Salisbury manuscript. The display script at the beginning of the list of *Quaestiones* on fo. 1 is not typical of Salisbury books either, which leads me to suspect that it was copied elsewhere in England. This copy may have reached Salisbury by the late eleventh century, since it seems to have acted as the exemplar for a Group I manuscript, Salisbury Cathedral, MS 129.[127]

Salisbury Cathedral, MS 101 was written on the Continent in the early tenth century, and contains three items: Isidore, *Quaestiones in vetus testamentum*; an epitome of Gregory, *Moralia in Iob*, known as the *Speculum Gregorii*, attributed to one Adalbert (possibly Adalbert of Metz, d. c. 969),[128] and Augustine, *Tractatus in epistolam Iohannis ad Parthos*. It was certainly at Salisbury by the early twelfth century since a portion of text missing from the *Quaestiones* of Isidore was supplied on an added leaf (fo. 32) by Group II scribe 10. Although this manuscript was written on the Continent, it was almost certainly acquired by the canons of Salisbury from an English centre since, soon after the manuscript had been produced, it had reached Christ Church, Canterbury, where it acted as the exemplar for Cambridge, Trinity College, MS B.4.27.[129]

Another manuscript of Continental origin, Salisbury Cathedral, MS 158, had reached Salisbury by the late eleventh century. (It contains **D.M.** *notae* in the hand of the annotator who marked many of the

---

[127] Unfortunately these flyleaves have been severely damaged by damp, and in many places it is impossible to read the text. However, Ker noted the poor separation of the words 'quae reseruata' in Salisbury Cathedral, MS 37, fol. 4/29 which, he suggested, may have caused the incorrect reading, 'quaere seruata', in Salisbury Cathedral, MS 129, fol. 6/21: see 'Beginnings', 32, esp. n. 2.

[128] M. Manitius, *Geschichte der lateinische Literatur des Mittelalters* (Munich, 1911), i. 100. The preface is printed in E. Martene and U. Durand, *Thesaurus novus Anecdotorum* (repr. New York, 1968), i. 84, with the incipit: 'Dilectissimo in Christo ac venerabili patri Harimano presbytero Adalberto humillimus levitarum sempiternam in Domino felicitatem'. For a summary of the different attempts to identify this Adalbert, see J. Dalstein in *Dictionnaire d'histoire et de géographie ecclésiastiques* (Paris, 1912), i. 443–4.

[129] I am grateful to Linda Brownrigg for informing me of the relationship between Salisbury Cathedral, MS 101 and Cambridge, Trinity College, MS B.4.27.

Salisbury books in the late eleventh century.) However the earlier provenance of the manuscript is obscure. It is a composite manuscript comprising a collection of computistical texts, including Bede, *De temporum ratione* (written in a ninth-century Continental Carolingian minuscule) and Helperic, *De computo* (written in an eleventh-century Continental hand).[130] But we have no evidence to show whether the Salisbury canons acquired the manuscript directly from the Continent or via another English centre.

These five books or fragments of books are the only manuscripts not produced at Salisbury which can be demonstrated to have been there in the late eleventh and early twelfth centuries. A number of other books or fragments dating from the first quarter of the twelfth century or earlier have also survived at Salisbury or have a Salisbury provenance. They too may shed light on the centres with which the Salisbury canons had contacts, and from which they may have obtained exemplars, but their evidence is less secure since we cannot be sure when they were acquired.

Of these manuscripts, three were certainly at Salisbury by the thirteenth or early fourteenth centuries. Salisbury Cathedral, MS 117 was at Salisbury in the thirteenth century, when it acted as the exemplar of Salisbury Cathedral, MS 100, fos. 89–141.[131] A thirteenth-century *ex libris* inscription indicates that Salisbury Cathedral, MS 160 was also there by this date. A third manuscript had been split up for use in bindings for Salisbury manuscripts by the late thirteenth or fourteenth centuries, and survives now as Salisbury Cathedral, MS 117, fos. 163–4; Oxford, Bodl. Libr., MS Lat. bib. C.8 (P) (removed from Oxford, Bodl. Libr., MS Bodley 516); and Tokyo, Professor T. Takamiya, MS 21 (formerly Cheltenham, Phillipps Collection, MS 36183, and then Geneva, Bodmer Collection).[132] Patrick Young's catalogue of 1622 or 1623 (now Salisbury Cathedral, MS 225) provides the earliest evidence of Salisbury ownership of eight more manuscripts: Salisbury Cathedral MSS 38, 89, 96, 133, 134, 172, 173, and 180 (Young, nos. 3, 22, 47, 71, 95, 74, 13, and 106 respectively).[133] Another manuscript, Oxford, Bodl. Libr.,

---

[130] C. W. Jones thought that this copy of Bede was produced in the West of England, see Bede, *Opera de temporibus*, 156–7, and also Bede, *De temporum ratione liber*, 253, but, for a different view, see R. W. Hunt, review of the former in *Medium Aevum*, 16 (1947), 63, esp. n. 2.

[131] Ker, 'Beginnings', 33.

[132] *CLA* 259. Lowe recorded that on one of the Takamiya (formerly Cheltenham/ Geneva) leaves, a late 13th- or early 14th-cent. hand has written: 'Iste lib' est de almario Sarr'.

[133] For Young's catalogue, and for identifications with extant manuscripts, see Ker, 'Salisbury Cathedral Manuscripts', 165–83. Two early manuscripts in Young's list can, however, be excluded from a tentative list of manuscripts at Salisbury in the late 11th and early 12th cents. Salisbury Cathedral, MS 157 (Young, no. 14), an 11th-cent. copy of several texts by Augustine and others, was probably only acquired by Salisbury late in the medieval period since it seems to have been in Normandy in the 13th cent. Salisbury

MS Bodley 516, was removed from Salisbury in about 1610 for the use of Thomas James, Bodley's Librarian.[134] Finally, fragments from one or two earlier books survive as flyleaves to a Group I manuscript, Salisbury Cathedral, MS 10. But this manuscript was rebound in the 1950s, and no evidence remains which might indicate whether these leaves formed part of a medieval binding.

Some or all of these manuscripts may have been acquired by the Salisbury canons early on. If so, at least half would have been acquired from other English centres. However, it is very difficult to establish any individual centre with any certainty. Even when one can demonstrate where a manuscript was produced, the place of origin need not have been the centre from which the Salisbury canons acquired it. For example, two of these manuscripts—Salisbury Cathedral, MSS 38 and 172 (copies of Aldhelm, *De virginitate* and Augustine, *Enchiridion*, respectively)—had been produced at Canterbury, possibly St Augustine's.[135] However, the Canterbury origins of these two manuscripts do not allow us to assume that Salisbury acquired them direct from Canterbury, since many of the manuscripts produced at St Augustine's and Christ Church Canterbury in the late tenth century were exported to a number of different English houses before the Norman Conquest.[136] Several were sent to Worcester,[137] others had reached Exeter by the mid-eleventh century.[138] Two more of these manuscripts had been produced in England before the Conquest but at as yet unidentified centres. The

Cathedral MS 150 (Young, no. 30), a late 10th-cent. Psalter, although almost certainly from the Salisbury area, was still in a Benedictine house in about 1300 when antiphons which are arranged for the Benedictine office (hence not applicable to the secular office at Salisbury) were added. Salisbury probably only acquired this manuscript after the Dissolution.

[134] Ker, 'Beginnings', 156–7.

[135] T. A. M. Bishop, whilst ascribing these two manuscripts to the scriptorium of St Augustine's, adds the cautionary note that these attributions depend 'on the doubtful evidence of mere aspect, and this ... has some resemblance to that of certain MSS provisionally attributed to Christ Church Canterbury': see his introduction to *Aethici Istrici cosmographia*, xx.

[136] Salisbury 38 has been annotated with a **K** (for *Kapitulum*), a *nota* mark found, for the most part, in manuscripts produced in Italy from the 1st to the 6th cent., but it is also found in an English manuscript with a South-West of England provenance, associated with Boniface (Oxford, Bodl. Libr., MS Douce 140). Its occurrence in this manuscript indicates a familiarity with Italian practice, a familiarity no doubt brought about by the close contacts between Wessex and Italy in the early 8th cent., see M. B. Parkes, 'St Boniface', 170, esp. n. 39. Later instances of the use of **K** with this sense are rare, but it is used with this sense in an 11th-cent. manuscript associated with Worcester, London, BL, MS Cotton Nero A I (see fos. 122ᵛ–63, reproduced in *A Wulfstan Manuscript Containing Institutes, Laws and Homilies: British Museum Cotton Nero A.I*, ed. H. R. Loyn, EEMF 17 (Copenhagen, 1971)).

[137] F. A. Rella, 'Some Aspects of the Indirect Transmission of Christian Latin Sources for Anglo-Saxon Prose from the Reign of Alfred to the Norman Conquest', B.Litt. thesis (Oxford University, 1977), 83.

[138] Drage, 'Leofric', 271.

Salisbury/Bodleian/Tokyo fragments originally formed part of a ninth-century copy of Deuteronomy and Numbers, probably produced in Mercia,[139] and Salisbury Cathedral, MS 134 is a copy of Remigius, Commentary on Sedulius, produced in England in the late tenth century.[140] Two further manuscripts, although produced on the Continent, would almost certainly have been acquired from English centres: Oxford, Bodl. Libr., MS Bodley 516 is a ninth-century miscellany of patristic and penitential texts, copied in northern Italy. It was in Brittany or Wales by the tenth century, and in England by the eleventh, when an Old English cryptogram was added on fo. 63^v.[141] Salisbury Cathedral, MS 173 (Augustine, *Soliloquia*, etc.), of Continental origin, was also in England by the mid-eleventh century when Old English scribbles were made on fos. 92^v and 142^v.[142]

The six remaining books or fragments were all produced on the Continent, and their Salisbury provenance is the earliest evidence of their presence in England. Three are ninth- or tenth-century manuscripts—Salisbury Cathedral, MSS 133 (produced at Tours, and possibly the earliest extant copy of Alcuin's Commentary on Ecclesiastes),[143] 96 (Gregory, *Dialogues*), and 180 (the Hebraicum and Gallicanum versions of the Psalter). They may have reached England before the Conquest, and hence may have been acquired from another English centre or centres. However, the remainder of these manuscripts or fragments are more likely to have been acquired directly from the Continent. Salisbury Cathedral, MS 89, a mid- or late-eleventh-century copy of the *Orationes* of Gregory Nazianzenus, also contains on the front fly-leaf a copy of the Anglo-Norman *Laudes regiae*. Both the copy of the Gregory and that of

[139] For a reassessment of the date and origin of these fragments, see J. J. Morrish, 'An Examination of Literacy and Learning in England in the Ninth Century', D.Phil. thesis (Oxford University, 1982), 86–125, esp. 90–1, 111.

[140] M. Lapidge tentatively identifies this manuscript with the 'Commentum Remigii super Sedulium' entered in a late 11th-cent. list of texts in Oxford, Bodl. Libr., MS Tanner 3, fos. 189^v–90, a manuscript with a Worcester provenance: see, 'Surviving Booklists from Anglo-Saxon England', *Learning and Literature in Anglo-Saxon England: Studies presented to Peter Clemoes on the Occasion of his Sixty-fifth Birthday*, ed. M. Lapidge and H. Gneuss (Cambridge, 1985), 69–72. However, the only evidence which can be adduced to support this identification is that the wording of the title given in the manuscript is the same as that in the list.

[141] Rella, 'Continental Manuscripts', 114.

[142] Ibid. 115.

[143] For the origin of Salisbury Cathedral, MS 133, see E. A. Lowe, 'A Manuscript of Alcuin in the Script of Tours', in *Classical and Medieval Studies in Honour of Edward Kennard Rand*, ed. L. W. Jones (New York, 1938), 191–3; repr. in Lowe's collected papers, *Palaeographical Papers 1907–1965*, ed. L. Bieler (Oxford, 1972), i. 342–4. Another manuscript probably copied at Tours in the early 9th cent., Oxford, Bodl. Libr., MS Bodley 218 (a copy of Bede on Luke), was certainly in England (possibly at Canterbury or Winchester) by the first half of the eleventh century, or earlier: see Rella, 'Continental Manuscripts', 113.

the *Laudes* can be ascribed to Fécamp in Normandy on the evidence of script, decoration and the inclusion of St Frodmundus, bishop of Coutances, in the acclamations of the *Laudes*.[144] Both the Norman origin of the manuscript, and the inclusion of the *Laudes* make it likely that it was imported not long after the Conquest.[145] Salisbury Cathedral, MS 160 is an anonymous Psalter commentary probably both composed and copied in northern France in the early twelfth century.[146] If it arrived at Salisbury soon after it was produced it is most likely to have been acquired by someone who had studied at the schools in northern France. Other books may have been brought to Salisbury by scholars who had travelled and studied abroad. The flyleaves to Salisbury Cathedral, MS 10 (a Group I manuscript) are fragments from early eleventh-century copies of the *Liber glossarum* (a 'dictionary-encyclopaedia' compiled at Corbie in the ninth century),[147] and Remigius, Commentary on Martianus Capella. Both were written in three columns in tiny informal Continental hands such as those found in other Continental manuscripts which contain texts associated with the schools. It is possible that the copy of the *Liber glossarum* was acquired from Corbie; it is a comparatively rare text, otherwise unknown in England, as far as we can tell from the evidence of manuscripts and booklists. This might, then, support the evidence of the textual affiliations of the copy of the *Rule of the Four Fathers* produced at Salisbury (Salisbury Cathedral, MS 12), that Corbie provided the Salisbury canons with exemplars.

The manuscripts acquired for Salisbury from elsewhere demonstrate that the canons had contacts with other centres in England and on the Continent. But they are less helpful in pin-pointing individual centres, and thus indicating from whence the canons may also have obtained exemplars. When manuscripts were obtained from elsewhere as exemplars, they were evidently almost always returned.

These manuscripts comprise a somewhat motley collection of texts which together present a marked contrast with the coherence of the content of the books produced at Salisbury. For the most part they are 'older' books, which indicates that they were not produced on commission for the community at Salisbury and also that they may have been *ad*

[144] F. Wormald, 'An Eleventh-Century Copy of the Norman *Laudes regiae*', *BIHR* 37 (1964), 73–4.

[145] On the chanting of the *Laudes regiae* in Normandy and England in the 11th and 12th centuries, see H. E. J. Cowdrey, 'The Anglo-Norman *Laudes regiae*', *Viator*, 12 (1981), 37–78. Cowdrey suggests that Bishop Osmund brought the manuscript from Normandy to Salisbury: ibid. 38, 48–9.

[146] For a full discussion of the date of the text contained in Salisbury Cathedral, MS 160, see below, Ch. 4.

[147] T. A. M. Bishop, 'The Prototype of the *Liber glossarum*', in *Medieval Scribes, Manuscripts and Libraries: Essays presented to N. R. Ker*, ed. M. B. Parkes and A. G. Watson (London, 1978), 69–86. Bishop did not know of this fragment from Salisbury.

hoc acquisitions. They, thus, reinforce the impression derived from the books produced at Salisbury that, from the start, the canons intended to produce themselves the manuscripts which would form their book collection, and not to commission them from elsewhere.

CONCLUSION

The evidence of textual relationships between texts copied at Salisbury and those in manuscripts associated with other centres, together with the manuscripts acquired by the canons from elsewhere, indicate that the suggestion that the collection of manuscripts formed at Salisbury may allow us 'to get as near as we can to the exemplars available for copying in England about the time of the Conquest and soon afterwards'[148] is more complex than it might seem at first sight. For many of the texts copied at Salisbury the scribes used exemplars which themselves, or copies derived from them, circulated throughout the country. But a number of texts were copied at Salisbury which seem to have been copied only there, or which were not copied elsewhere until much later. This is evidence which probably tells us more about the unusual interests of the Salisbury canons than the availability of those texts elsewhere: we cannot prove either way whether such texts were not copied elsewhere because they were not available, or simply because other centres were not interested in them. What this evidence does indicate, however, is Salisbury's remarkable independence from other English centres in the acquisition of exemplars, and that the Salisbury collection should not be seen as wholly representative of the kinds of collections made elsewhere in England in the century before or after the Conquest.

[148] Ker, *English Manuscripts*, 14.

4

INTELLECTUAL INTERESTS

THE content of the Salisbury canons' collection of books went far beyond what would have been required for purely spiritual purposes. The secular texts copied at Salisbury, or acquired from elsewhere, suggest scholarly activity. Furthermore, the number of biblical commentaries amongst the collection, and the character of some of them, indicate that the canons' interests in the text of the Bible were of a scholarly as well as a spiritual nature. In this chapter I shall examine the content of the texts which throw most light on the canons' intellectual interests, and I shall set those interests within the context of contemporary learning in England and on the Continent.

MAGISTRI SCHOLARUM

Several references to the presence of a *magister scholarum* at Salisbury during the twelfth century have survived.[1] In 1107, or soon after,[2] Hildebert, bishop of Le Mans, wrote to Roger, newly consecrated bishop of Salisbury, in response to Roger's request for him to recommend a suitable *magister scholarum*, and sent his own precentor, Guy of Étampes, warmly praising his learning ('in him you will find many masters').[3] Guy had studied first under Anselm of Laon,[4] and then had

---

[1] Much of the information concerning *magistri scholarum* at Salisbury and elsewhere in England in the late 11th and 12th cent. was compiled by Eleanor Rathbone in 'The Influence of Bishops and of Members of Cathedral Bodies in the Intellectual Life of England, 1066–1216', Ph.D. thesis (London University, 1935). See also K. Edwards, 'The Cathedral of Salisbury', *VCH, Wilts*, iii. 157–8, for problems of terminology, and also K. Edwards, *The English Secular Cathedrals in the Middle Ages*, 2nd edn (Manchester, 1967), 181–3. What follows is based upon their findings. For a complete list of *magistri scholarum* at Salisbury, see Greenway, *Fasti*, iv, list 4.

[2] Hildebert begins his letter by congratulating Roger on becoming bishop of Salisbury— Roger was consecrated in 1107.

[3] Hildebert of Le Mans, *Epistolae*, II. xii: *PL* 171. 219: 'Unus ex nostra Ecclesia excerptus est, cui et ad fructum scientia et ad exemplum mores exuberant. Unus ille tibi pro multis erit, quoniam in illo uno multos magistros invenies.' An account of Guy's life and career is given in *Actus pontificum Cenomannis in urbe degentium*, ed. G. Busson and A. Ledru, Archives historiques du Maine (Le Mans, 1901), ii. 422–42. He succeeded Hildebert as bishop of Le Mans in 1122; prior to that he had been a canon of Lincoln, precentor (*c.*1120) and *magister scholarum* of Le Mans, and archdeacon of Rouen (*c.*1123): see Greenway, *Fasti*, iv, list 4.   [4] *Actus pontificum*, 424.

undertaken scholarly activities in Paris: an exchange of verses between him and Peter Abelard is quoted in an anonymous gloss on Priscian—the gloss *Promisimus*.[5] He also appears to have lectured on dialectic, since an entry in a twelfth-century catalogue from the abbey of Bury St Edmunds lists 'Glose super dialecticam magistri Widonis de Stampis et episcopi Cenomannensis'.[6] It seems reasonable to assume that Guy was sent to Salisbury to do more than teach elementary grammar. But, unfortunately, we do not know anything about what he did teach: whether he lectured upon any of the *artes* or any of the higher studies. A *magister* Ailwinus, who may have acted as *magister scholarum*, occurs among the witnesses of a charter of Bishop Roger, datable to 1122 or a little earlier,[7] but we know nothing further about him or his duties. Other documentary evidence concerning the office of *magister scholarum* at Salisbury in the twelfth century is also unhelpful in telling us about what was taught. King Stephen gave the churches of Odiham, Liss, and Bentworth 'ad opus magistri scholae Sarum', but the duties of the *magister* are not defined.[8] The so-called *Institutio Osmundi*, now shown to be a product of the mid-twelfth century or later,[9] defines the duties of an *archischola*: to set and hear the lessons, to keep the chapter seal, to compose letters and documents, and to mark the readers' names upon the board.[10] The same document assigns additional but similar duties to the chancellor: he is to be ruler of the schools and corrector of the books.[11] Aside from the question of whether or not the *archischola* and the chancellor were one and the same person,[12] we are still not told what was taught. In the absence of explicit documentary evidence, the canons' books are our best source of information concerning the scholarly interests and activities of the community at Salisbury.

SECULAR STUDIES

The study of the liberal arts was the starting point for all scholarly

---

[5] Cited by R. W. Hunt, 'Studies on Priscian in the Twelfth Century: II', *Medieval and Renaissance Studies*, 2 (1950), 17, 41; repr. in his collected papers, *The History of Grammar in the Middle Ages*, ed. G. L. Bursill-Hall (Amsterdam, 1980), 55, 79.

[6] R. M. Thomson, 'The Library of Bury St Edmunds Abbey in the Eleventh and Twelfth Centuries', *Speculum*, 47 (1972), 635. The copy has not survived; no evidence is extant of the content of Guy's teaching on dialectic.

[7] E. J. Kealey, *Roger of Salisbury* (Berkeley, Calif., 1972), 92, 238.

[8] *Regesta regum Anglo-Normannorum 1066–1154*, iii, no. 789, probably datable to December 1139; printed in *Charters and Documents Illustrating the History of the Cathedral, City, and Diocese of Salisbury in the Twelfth and Thirteenth Centuries*, ed. W. R. Jones and W. D. Macray, RS (London, 1891), 8–9.

[9] Greenway, 'The False *Institutio*', 77–101.   [10] Ibid. 96.   [11] Ibid.

[12] See Edwards, 'The Cathedral of Salisbury', 157–8.

pursuits in the Middle Ages. Secular learning as an essential preliminary to sacred studies formed part of the programme of study advocated by Augustine in the *De doctrina christiana,* and set out in detail by Cassiodorus in the two books of his *Institutiones*: two texts which formed the principles for all subsequent early medieval programmes for study and learning.

From Carolingian times, education in the liberal arts centred on the study of a widely accepted canon of reading which comprised pagan and christian poets and grammarians, accompanied by commentaries and other handbooks and glossaries. By the tenth and eleventh centuries, several of these 'school books' (for example, Arator, *De actibus apostolis,* Sedulius, *Carmen paschale,* Prosper, *Epigrammata,* Boethius, *De consolatione philosophiae,* Martianus Capella, *De nuptiis philologiae et mercurii,* and the *Disticha Catonis*) were known and studied in England.[13]

The evidence that such texts were taught or studied at Salisbury in the late eleventh and early twelfth centuries is limited. No copies produced at Salisbury have survived, but the remains of a small number of copies produced elsewhere have survived in the cathedral library at Salisbury. Salisbury Cathedral, MS 134 contains a copy of Remigius, Commentary on Sedulius (one of the most widely read schoolbooks in Anglo-Saxon times),[14] which was produced in England in the late tenth century. However, there is no evidence to show when the copy came to Salisbury, let alone whether it was used for teaching purposes there.[15] Fragments of two books which were probably produced in the *milieux* of the Continental schools now survive as flyleaves to Salisbury Cathedral, MS 10.[16] One leaf is from a copy of Remigius, Commentary on Martianus Capella, the other is a fragment of the *Liber glossarum*: a dictionary–encyclopaedia which combined discussion of individual Latin and also some Hebrew and Greek words, with extracts from the works of both

---

[13] On such studies in Anglo-Saxon England, and a reassessment of the significance of Latin glosses in copies of these texts, see M. Lapidge, 'The Study of Latin Texts in Late Anglo-Saxon England: The Evidence of Latin Glosses', in *Latin and the Vernacular Languages in Early Medieval Britain,* ed. N. Brooks (Leicester, 1982), 99–140; G. R. Wieland, 'The Glossed Manuscript: Classbook or Library Book?', *ASE,* 14 (1985), 153–73.

[14] Lapidge, 'Latin Glosses', 113–16.

[15] This copy has been associated with an entry in a late 11th-cent. list of books (now, Oxford, Bodl. Libr., MS Tanner 3). The origin of this list is unknown, although the manuscript has a later Worcester origin: see M. Lapidge, 'Surviving Booklists from Anglo-Saxon England', in *Learning and Literature in Anglo-Saxon England: Studies presented to Peter Clemoes on the Occasion of his Sixty-fifth Birthday,* ed. M. Lapidge and H. Gneuss (Cambridge, 1985), 69–72.

[16] Salisbury Cathedral, MS 10 contains a copy of Cassian, *Collationes,* produced at Salisbury in the late 11th cent. The present binding is modern, and there is no evidence to indicate when the two fragments were first used as flyleaves to this volume.

pagan and Christian writers to cover the field of universal knowledge.[17] Both leaves are written in three columns in tiny Continental hands, probably of the early eleventh century.[18] As with the copy of Remigius, Commentary on Sedulius, neither of these two fragments reveal any indications that they were used for teaching purposes at Salisbury. It is possible that the copies from which these two fragments came were brought to Salisbury by someone who had studied in the Continental schools. The acquaintance of the Salisbury canons with the liberal arts teaching of the Continental schools is indicated by a fragment of a copy of Chalcidius, Commentary on the *Timaeus*, produced at Salisbury in the early twelfth century, now surviving as a flyleaf to Salisbury Cathedral, MS 110. The *Timaeus* only became popular as a school text on the Continent in the mid-eleventh century, and remained popular until the mid-twelfth century.[19] Again, it is not possible to tell whether this manuscript was used at Salisbury for teaching or for private study.

Although these somewhat fragmentary remains do not provide concrete evidence for the teaching of the liberal arts at Salisbury, they do indicate an acquaintance with the learning of the schools, and the Continental schools in particular. It is possible that they represent the interests of canons who had been to schools on the Continent, and who wished to continue their study of secular authors at Salisbury. We know of at least one Salisbury canon whose career followed this pattern— Hubald, archdeacon in the late eleventh and early twelfth centuries, who, according to William of Malmesbury, was well-learned in the liberal arts.[20] This impression is further supported by the number of classical texts copied at Salisbury in the early twelfth century, which did not form

[17] T. A. M. Bishop, 'The Prototype of the *Liber glossarum*', *Medieval Scribes, Manuscripts and Libraries: Essays Presented to N. R. Ker*, ed. M. B. Parkes and A. G. Watson (London, 1978), 69–86.

[18] Although not uncommon in the 5th cent. and earlier, a three-column format is very unusual in later manuscripts other than for parallel texts. It was, however, the format chosen by the designers of the prototype of the *Liber glossarum*: see T. A. M. Bishop, ibid. For other examples of books written in three columns, see B. Bischoff, *Latin Palaeography: Antiquity and the Middle Ages*, tr. D. Ó. Cróinín and D. Ganz (Cambridge, 1990), 27–8, esp. nn. 68–70. Oxford, Bodl. Libr., MS Laud lat. 49, an 11th-cent. Continental (southern German or south-east French) manuscript which contains several texts associated with the study of the trivium (for example, Cicero, *Topica* and *De inventione* together with the commentary of Victorinus), offers close parallels with the two leaves in Salisbury Cathedral, MS 10, not only in its three-column format but also the small hands in which it is written, and the type of texts it contains.

[19] M. T. Gibson, 'The Study of the "Timaeus" in the Eleventh and Twelfth Centuries', *Pensamiento*, 25 (1969), 183–94.

[20] *GP* 429: 'vir qui liberalium artium non exiguum experimentum cepisset'. For Hubald, see Greenway, *Fasti*, iv, list 6. Orderic Vitalis lists a number of analogous examples— Norman clerics who rose to prominence in English cathedral chapters and monasteries, who had first studied the classical *auctores* (*philosophi*) at Liège: *Historia ecclesiastica*, bk. VIII, ed. M. Chibnall (Oxford, 1973), iv. 118–19.

part of the early medieval curriculum but which indicate more advanced studies: Plautus, *Comoediae* (London, BL, MS Royal 15 C xi), Cicero, *Tusculan Disputations* (London, BL, MS Royal 15 C xi), parts of Cicero, *De officiis*, a *florilegium* of Aulus Gellius and Valerius Maximus, and extracts from Seneca, *De beneficiis* (Cambridge, Trinity College, MS R.16.34). The presence of such texts in England at this date is unusual, but on the Continent the study of the *artes* had engendered interest in these and other such texts in the course of the eleventh century.[21]

BIBLICAL STUDIES

In Augustine's and Cassiodorus's scheme of learning, the study of the *artes* was only a preliminary to higher study. But, in the tenth and first half of the eleventh centuries, whilst the study of the liberal arts flourished in several Continental schools, there was no corresponding advance in biblical scholarship. From her examination of the study of the Bible in the Middle Ages, Beryl Smalley concluded that there had been an interruption to biblical studies after the death of Remigius (*c*.908) until the mid-eleventh century: 'The Cluniac and other tenth-century religious reformers emphasized the liturgy at the expense of study. As the offices multiplied, *lectio divina* moved out of the cloister into the choir.... Meanwhile the masters, in the cathedral schools especially, were more interested in the arts and sciences than in theology.'[22]

More recently, Karl Leyser has drawn attention to evidence which would suggest that the tenth century was not altogether a period of stagnation in biblical studies.[23] Nevertheless, from the mid-eleventh century, scholars on the Continent focused their attention on the Bible with fresh vigour.[24]

The composition of the collection of books produced for the community at Salisbury provides evidence that the canons were well abreast

[21] See, for example, the list of pagan authors recommended by Haimeric in his *Ars lectoria*, written in the late 11th cent., a list which includes a number of other classical authors besides those who were lectured upon in the schools (ed. C. Thurot, 'Documents relatifs à l'histoire de la grammaire au moyen âge', *Academie des Inscriptions et Belles Lettres: Comptes rendus*, NS 6 (1870), 242–51). The list of authors is classified according to Haimeric's view of their relative merits. The authors he considered to be of the highest order were Terence, Virgil, Horace, Ovid, Sallust, Lucan, Statius, Juvenal, and Persius; next came Plautus, Ennius, Cicero, Varro, Boethius, Donatus, Priscian, Sergius, Varus, and Plato; third place was given to Cato, Homer, and Aesop.

[22] B. Smalley, *The Study of the Bible in the Middle Ages*, 3rd edn (Oxford, 1983), 44–5.

[23] K. Leyser, 'Liudprand of Cremona, Preacher and Homilist', in *The Bible in the Medieval World: Essays in Memory of Beryl Smalley*, ed. K. Walsh and D. Wood (Oxford, 1985), 43–60. See also, M. T. Gibson, 'The Twelfth-Century Glossed Bible', *Studia Patristica*, xxiii, ed. E. A. Livingstone (Leuven, 1989), 234–5.

[24] Gibson, ibid. 241–3; I. S. Robinson, 'The Bible in the Investiture Contest: The South German Gregorian Circle', in *The Bible in the Medieval World*, 61–84.

of these new developments in Continental biblical scholarship. For example, the content of the collection fulfilled to a striking extent the bibliographical requirements for sacred learning set out by Cassiodorus in the second book of the *Institutiones*. But two manuscripts acquired by the canons demonstrate their scholarly interest in biblical texts most clearly since both contain texts which were the products of contemporary Continental biblical scholarship: Oxford, Keble College, MS 22—a copy of the Pauline Epistles with glosses added, and Salisbury Cathedral, MS 160—an anonymous commentary on the Psalms and Canticles.

OXFORD, KEBLE COLLEGE, MS 22

Oxford, Keble College, MS 22 was copied at Salisbury in the late eleventh century. Like many of the Group I manuscripts it is a small, easily portable book, with just sufficient decoration to articulate the texts it contains. It contains a copy of the Pauline Epistles in the following order: Romans, 1, 2 Corinthians, Ephesians, Philippians, 1 Thessalonians, Colossians, 2 Thessalonians, 1, 2 Timothy, Titus, Philemon, and Hebrews.[25] Each of the epistles, with the exception of Romans, is preceded by the relevant Marcionite prologue. Romans was originally copied without its prologue, but a little later, Group I scribe iv copied the Pseudo-Jerome prologues to the epistles as a whole and to Romans into a new quire which was then appended to the front of the copy.

The layout and ruling indicate that the copy was designed from the outset to receive glosses (see Pl. 15). The text of the epistles themselves was copied by four collaborating scribes in a narrow column in the centre of each page with wide margins. The lines were ruled with plenty of space between each of them to enable interlinear glosses to be added. The margins were ruled with more narrowly spaced lines to receive the more lengthy glosses. The number of glosses which have been added varies from epistle to epistle and from page to page. A wide repertoire of *signes-de-renvoi* has been used to link text and gloss, although, with the exception of Group I scribe i, who sometimes used the letters of the alphabet in sequence,[26] there does not appear to be any system lying behind the sequence of symbols.[27]

[25] A contemporary note at the end of 1 Thessalonians indicates that 2 Thessalonians should have been copied at this point. Although the sequence Colossians, 1, 2 Thessalonians was the most common order, the sequence 1, 2 Thessalonians, Colossians was not uncommon in pre-13th-cent. manuscripts, see S. Berger, *Histoire de la Vulgate pendant les premières siècles du moyen âge* (Paris, 1893), 341–2.

[26] See, for example, fo. 6 (Pl. 15).

[27] On the development of the layout of glossed books of the Bible before the 12th cent., and the kinds of reference signs found in them, see Gibson, 'The Twelfth-Century Glossed Bible', 233–7.

It is clear that the glosses were added after the text of the epistles had been copied, since the scribe of the text is rarely the scribe of the accompanying gloss. But, although a number of different scribes added glosses, the evidence suggests that they were working as part of a single enterprise, and not in a somewhat *ad hoc* fashion. Even where different hands appear to have added glosses on the same page, I can find no evidence for different layers of glosses. On the contrary, there is evidence that the scribes were collaborating, and were working from the same exemplar. On a number of occasions, one scribe took over from another in mid-gloss. For example, in the final marginal gloss on fo. 6 'Nota apostolum inter romanos' (see Pl. 15), Group I scribe xiv took over from Group I scribe i in the middle of a sentence—scribe i copied as far as 'utrunque' at the end of the first line of the gloss, and scribe xiv began the second line 'statum'. There is also some evidence to suggest that some, if not all of the glosses were copied from the same exemplar as the text of the epistles. There are a number of instances where what must have been an interlinear correction of the epistle text in the exemplar, was mistaken for an interlinear gloss by the scribes of Keble 22. For example, the text of Hebrews 1: 6 (fo. 137^v) should read: 'in agnitione omnis operis boni', however, the scribe of the epistle text omitted the word 'operis'; the word was added by the glossator not in the form of a correction but as the first word of the interlinear gloss written above the word 'boni'.

The Sources and Content of the Glosses

(i) Patristic sources

The content of the glosses consists of both inherited material (derived from patristic and early medieval exegesis) and contemporary teaching on the books of the Bible. The substance of the commentaries which, in the twelfth century, became widely adopted as the standard work of reference on the books of the Bible—the *Gloss* (later called the *Glossa ordinaria*), was derived predominantly from patristic and early medieval exegesis.[28] By contrast, Keble 22 contains comparatively little patristic or early medieval material. Only twenty-four of the glosses cite patristic

---

[28] For the most recent study of the content and development of the *Glossa ordinaria*, see Gibson, 'The Twelfth-Century Glossed Bible', and the literature cited there. Her conclusions revise the picture of development presented in Smalley, *Study of the Bible*, 46–66.

authorities by name: fourteen cite Augustine,[29] nine Ambrose,[30] and one Jerome.[31]

Augustine did not write a commentary on the Pauline Epistles as a whole, but many of his texts contain exegesis on passages from St Paul. In the mid-ninth century these pieces of exegesis were excerpted and compiled to form a commentary on the Epistles. This *Collectaneum*, believed to have been the work of Florus, deacon of Lyons, enjoyed widespread popularity in the eleventh and twelfth centuries: it has been shown, for example, to have been the source for all the Augustine excerpts associated with Lanfranc's commentary on the Pauline Epistles.[32] It seems likely that it was also the source for the glosses in Keble 22 which cite Augustine, since they are all derived from passages of Augustine included in Florus's *Collectaneum*.

Ambrose also did not write a commentary on the Pauline Epistles, but during the medieval period a commentary circulated which was thought to be his—the commentary now called 'Ambrosiaster'. This commentary is the source for all the glosses in Keble 22 which are attributed to Ambrose.[33]

The single gloss in Keble 22 which cites Jerome, comments on the Epistle to the Romans as a whole, and is derived from the Prologue to Romans from Pelagius's commentary on the Pauline Epistles, which in the medieval period was widely believed to be that of Jerome.[34]

Many of the late eleventh- and twelfth-century copies of the Pauline Epistles with glosses, contain glosses which cite patristic authorities. These glosses consist of direct quotations (sometimes abbreviated), usually prefaced by the name of the authority written either in full, or in an abbreviated form. Nine of the glosses in Keble 22 cite the names of

[29] The glosses on Rom. 5: 13 (fo. 12ᵛ), Rom. 7: 8 (fo. 15), Rom. 11: 4 (fo. 22), Rom. 16: 25–7 (fo. 31ᵛ), 1 Cor. 11: 21 (fo. 48), 2 Cor. 1: 22 (fo. 61ᵛ), 2 Cor. 2: 16 (fo. 62ᵛ), 2 Cor. 12: 2 (fo. 76ᵛ), Eph. 5: 15 (fo. 96ᵛ), 2 Thess. 2: 11 (fo. 120ᵛ), 2 Thess. 3: 15 (fo. 121ᵛ), 2 Tim. 4: 14 (fo. 133ᵛ), and Heb. 1: 3 (fo. 139).

[30] Glosses on the beginning of Rom. (fo. 5), Rom. 1: 4 (fo. 5), Rom. 5: 13 (fo. 12ᵛ), Rom. 12: 3 (fo. 24), 2 Cor. 2: 13 (fo. 62ᵛ), 2 Cor. 5: 13 (fo. 66), Eph. 3: 18 (fo. 93), Eph. 5: 13 (fo. 96ᵛ) and 1 Tim. 2: 15 (fo. 124).

[31] Gloss on the beginning of Rom. (fo. 5).

[32] M. T. Gibson, 'Lanfranc's "Commentary on the Pauline Epistles"', *Journal of Theological Studies*, 22 (1971), 96–7.

[33] The 'Ambrose' glosses in Keble 22 thus differ from Lanfranc's commentary on the Pauline Epistles for which Ambrosiaster is the source for the 'Ambrose' glosses on only Romans and 1 and 2 Corinthians. In Lanfranc's commentary the source for Galatians-Philemon is the commentary of Theodore of Mopsuestia, and for Hebrews, Alcuin's paraphrase of the Latin version of John Chrysostom, see Gibson, 'Lanfranc's Commentary', 97–101. In Keble 22, the letter to the Hebrews contains no 'Ambrose' glosses.

[34] See *Pelagius's Expositions of Thirteen Epistles of St Paul*, ed. A. Souter, Texts and Studies, 9 (1922), i. 1–33.

patristic authorities in this form. One further gloss (on 2 Cor. 2: 13) consists of a quotation but is introduced with a phrase, 'Unde Ambrosius', followed by the quotation. Other glosses consist of excerpts from Ambrosiaster or Florus, but are given anonymously.[35] However the remaining glosses which cite patristic authorities do not consist of quotations but are condensed paraphrases or very brief summaries, possibly intended to act as *aides-memoire*. The form in which the name of the authority is cited is also different in these glosses: 'secundum Ambrosium',[36] 'secundum Augustinum',[37] 'secundum beatum Augustinum',[38] 'secundum istam sententiam beati Ambrosii',[39] 'Beatus Augustinus appositum ostendit',[40] or 'Beatus Augustinus exponit'.[41] Such citations seem to indicate that the reader was to use this manuscript in association with a copy of the commentaries of 'Ambrose' (i.e. Ambrosiaster) and 'Augustine' (i.e. Florus's *Collectaneum*).[42]

The content of several of the patristic citations are concerned with the literal understanding of the Pauline text. Two glosses, for example, juxtapose and contrast the interpretations of Ambrose and Augustine on specific passages, noting that the differences in their interpretations arise from their differing understanding of the literal meaning of the texts.[43]

(ii) Eleventh-century exegesis

The majority of the glosses in Keble 22 are not derived from patristic exegesis but reflect the contemporary exposition of masters in the

---

[35] For example, the gloss on Rom. 12: 1 (fo. 24), 'Post tractatum legis et fidei ad bonam uitam eos hortatur', is an excerpt from Ambrosiaster.

[36] The glosses on the beginning of Rom. (fo. 5), Rom. 5: 13 (fo. 12^v), 2 Cor. 5: 13 (fo. 66), Eph. 5: 13 (fo. 96^v), 1 Tim. 2: 15 (fo. 124).

[37] Glosses on Rom. 5: 13 (fo. 12^v), 2 Cor. 2: 16 (fo. 62^v), Eph. 5: 15 (fo. 96^v), 1 Tim. 2: 15 (fo. 124).

[38] Gloss on 2 Cor. 12: 2 (fo. 76^v).

[39] Gloss on Rom. 1: 4 (fo. 5).

[40] Gloss on Rom. 16: 25–7. A similar form of citing the name of Ambrose appears in the gloss on Rom. 12: 3, but in this case the scribe appears to have misunderstood his exemplar, thinking that 'Ambrosius aperte ostendit' was the form of citation, whereas 'aperte ostendit' is the first two words of the gloss itself—an extract from Ambrosiaster.

[41] Gloss on 2 Cor. 1: 22 (fo. 61^v).

[42] No copy of Florus's *Collectaneum* has yet been identified as being associated with Salisbury, but a copy of Ambrosiaster was made there in the late 11th cent. (now Oxford, Bodl. Libr., MS Bodley 756), and a copy of Pelagius (under the name of Jerome), was produced at Salisbury in the early 12th cent. (Salisbury Cathedral, MS 5).

[43] Glosses on Rom. 5: 13 (fo. 12^v) and 1 Tim. 2: 15 (fo. 124). The gloss on Rom. 5: 13 ('Usque ad legem enim peccatum erat in mundo'), for example, points out that the phrase 'usque ad' has two possible meanings: 'up until, and including' or 'up until, but not including', and he notes that Augustine and Ambrose differ in their choice of meaning, Augustine understanding it as being inclusive, and Ambrose, as exclusive: 'secundum Augustinum inclusiuum est, sicut si diceretur usque ad templum, et ita *usque ad legem*, intelligitur usque ad Cristum ... Uel, secundum Ambrosium, usque exclusiuum est, ut intelligamus de illis tantum qui fuerunt ante legem ...'.

schools. In two glosses the master is cited by name: the gloss on 2 Cor. 3: 18 (fo. 64) cites 'BER' and that on Eph. 4: 26 (fo. 95), 'BR' (both citations refer to Berengar of Tours).[44] A few of the anonymous glosses in Keble 22 are derived from Lanfranc's commentary on the Pauline Epistles:[45] for example, the gloss on Romans 3: 9 (Causati enim):

Quasi diceret, qui pares sumus precelsiores esse non possumus, nec hoc superius in hac epistola dicit, sed credendum est in sermone quem habebat eum dixisse.[46]

However, for the most part, the anonymous glosses in Keble 22 do not derive from any known commentary or master, although I have identified a group of these glosses in a twelfth-century glossed copy of the Pauline Epistles, Vatican, Biblioteca Apostolica, MS lat. 143.

The purpose of the majority of these anonymous glosses is to elucidate the letter of Paul's text. This could be in such simple ways as employing letters to help construe difficult sentences, or by giving a simple paraphrase. Other glosses go further and attempt to show the structure of the argument underlying Paul's often highly compressed prose, employing both the terminology and the techniques of rhetoric and logic.

The following gloss on Paul's letter to the Romans 8: 5–8 (Keble 22, fo. 16ᵛ), illustrates many of these techniques. The Pauline text itself reads:

Qui enim secundum carnem sunt, quę carnis sunt, sapiunt. Qui uero secundum spiritum, quę sunt spiritus, sentiunt. Nam prudentia carnis, mors est. Prudentia autem spiritus, uita et pax. Quoniam sapientia carnis inimica est Deo. Legi enim Dei non est subiecta. Nec enim potest. Qui autem in carne sunt, Deo placere non possunt.

The gloss on this passage in Keble 22 (fo. 16ᵛ) is as follows:

Probatio quod non secundum carnem ambulantes iustificantur: si illi qui sunt ambulantes secundum carnem non iustificantur, tunc illi, id est, a contrario. Sed isti non, extra. Probatio assumptionis, utrum illi qui ambulant secundum carnem iustificentur, non. *Qui secundum carnem sunt quae carnis sunt sapiunt* (Rom. 8: 5), propositio in libro. Sed qui sapiunt quę sunt carnis, non iustificantur, a pari. Et hoc probatio: si mortui sunt non iustificantur, extra, a repugnantibus. Et hoc probatio quod mortui sunt: si prudentia carnis mors est, tunc illi qui sapiunt quae sunt carnis mortui sunt, a causa, assumptio in libro—*nam prudentia carnis mors est* (Rom. 8: 6). Et hoc probatio: uere est mors, quia est inimica Deo, a toto, assumptio est in libro—*quoniam sapientia carnis inimica est Deo* (Rom. 8: 7). Et

---

[44] The former appears among a group of glosses ascribed to Berengar found in two 12th-cent. manuscripts: Vatican, Biblioteca Apostolica, MS lat. 143 (fo. 71ᵛ) and Berne, Burgerbibliothek, MS 334, ii: fos. 86–156 (fo. 112ᵛ): printed by B. Smalley in 'La Glossa Ordinaria: Quelques prédécesseurs d'Anselme de Laon', *RTAM* 9 (1937), 393; the latter, 'Explanatio quorsum dixerit irascendum', also occurs in Vat. lat. 143 (fo. 136), but Berengar's name is not cited.

[45] For this commentary, see Gibson, 'Lanfranc's Commentary', 86–116.

[46] Keble 22, fo. 9; *PL* 150, with minor differences.

hoc probatio: quia legi Dei non est subiecta, a toto, assumptio est in libro—*legi enim Dei non est subiecta* (Rom. 8: 7). Et hoc probatio a causa: quia non potest, assumptio—*nec enim potest* (Rom. 8: 7). Restat alia pars de spiritu. An ambulantes secundum spiritum iustificentur, propositio in libro—*Qui uero secundum spiritum, quę sunt spiritus sentiunt* (Rom. 8: 5). Sed qui senciunt quę sunt secundum spiritum, iustificantur. Et hoc probatio: quia sunt habentes uitam et pacem, ab effectu. Et hoc probatio, a causa: si prudentia spiritus est uita et pax, et qui senciunt quę sunt spiritus habent uitam et pacem, assumptio in libro— *prudentia autem spiritus uita et pax* (Rom. 8: 6). Probatio iterum quod sapientia carnis est inimica Deo, ab effectu: quia qui in carne sunt, Deo placere non possunt, assumptio—*qui autem in carne sunt Deo placere non possunt* (Rom. 8: 8).

The gloss begins by claiming that the proof for Paul's argument that they that do not live according to the flesh are justified, is a proof derived from contraries: if they that live according to the flesh are not justified, then they that do not live according to the flesh are justified. The remainder of the gloss sets out the arguments which prove the premise that they that live according to the flesh are not justified, and also the contrary premise, that they that do not live according to the flesh are justified.

In order to do this, the gloss employs the techniques and terminology of syllogistic argument: major and minor premises (*propositio* and *assumptio*), each with their proof (*probatio*).[47] In addition, the gloss employs the terminology of the topical differences in order to define the different kinds of argument being used for the proofs: it distinguishes extrinsic arguments (*extra*) from those intrinsic to the argument under discussion, and it defines these arguments as being derived from the whole (*a toto*), from equals (*a pari*), from contraries (*a contrario*), from contradictories (*a repugnantibus*), from the efficient cause (*a causa*), and from effect (*ab effectu*). Such terminology would have been familiar to a student schooled in the *artes*, and in particular in texts such as Cicero, *De inventione* and *Topica*, and Boethius, *De differentiis topicis*. The gloss also indicates when a premise has been explicitly stated in the Pauline text (*in libro*).

The gloss begins its line of argument with the major premise stated in the text (*propositio in libro*): *they that are according to the flesh mind the things that are of the flesh* (Rom. 8: 5). The gloss then puts forward a minor premise (*assumptio*), which is dependent on the major premise as an argument derived from equals (*a pari*): they that have wisdom of the things of the flesh are not justified (and therefore they that are according to the flesh are not justified). The proof (*probatio*) of the minor premise

---

[47] None of the glosses in Keble 22 employs the full syllogism since the *conclusio* is usually omitted.

is that if they are dead they are not justified—a statement drawn from outside the argument, i.e. extrinsic to it (*extra*), and an argument derived from contradictories (*a repugnantibus*).

The gloss continues the syllogistic argument with further premises and proofs:

If the wisdom of the flesh is death, then they that have wisdom of the things of the flesh are dead, an argument derived from the efficient cause (*a causa*), stated in the text as a minor premise—*for the wisdom of the flesh is death* (Rom. 8: 6).

The gloss then proves the proof of the premise that the wisdom of the flesh is death:

Because it is an enemy to God, an argument derived from the whole (*a toto*), stated by St Paul (*in libro*) as a minor premise—*because the wisdom of the flesh is an enemy to God* (Rom. 8: 7).

The gloss then proves the premise that knowledge of the flesh is hostile to God:

Because it is not subject to the law of God, an argument derived from the whole, stated by St Paul as a minor premise—*for it is not subject to the law of God* (Rom. 8: 7). The proof of this premise is an argument derived from the efficient cause: because it cannot be subject to the law of God, and this is stated as a minor premise—*neither can it be* (Rom. 8: 8).

The gloss then turns to prove that those who live according to the spirit are justified.

Major premise—*they that are according to the spirit mind the things that are of the spirit* (Rom. 8: 5). Minor premise—they that mind the things that are of the spirit are justified. This is the proof of the minor premise that they that mind the things that are of the spirit are justified: because they have life and peace, an argument derived from effect (*ab effectu*). This is the proof, an argument derived from the efficient cause: if the wisdom of the spirit is life and peace, then they that mind the things that are of the spirit have life and peace. This is expressed in the text as a minor premise—*but the wisdom of the spirit is life and peace* (Rom. 8: 6). Here is a further proof that the wisdom of the flesh is hostile to God, an argument derived from effect: because they that are in the flesh cannot please God. This is expressed in the text as a minor premise—*and they that are in the flesh cannot please God* (Rom. 8: 8).

Other glosses not only show the rhetorical structure of the argument but express it in the form of a dialogue, filling in what an opponent might have said to invite Paul's statements. Several glosses begin 'Quasi diceret' or simply 'Quasi'—('As if someone might say'). For example, in the gloss on Romans 2: 13 (Keble 22, fo. 7ᵛ) the glossator explains the verse 'For not the hearers of the law are just before God: but the doers of the law shall be justified' as a response to an opponent's challenge:

Quasi, Iudei non peribunt ut tu dicis, sed pocius, iustificabuntur quia audierunt legem. Ad hoc, *non enim* . . .

(As if someone might say 'Then the Jews will not perish as you say, but rather, they shall be justified because they have heard the law.' In answer to this, Paul says 'For not the hearers of the law are just before God, but the doers of the law shall be justified.'

In some instances the gloss points out where Paul himself has adopted the *pars aduersarii* (the opponent's part) for rhetorical effect.

The rhetorical terminology employed most frequently is that of the topical differences, but occasionally the glosses refer to rhetorical figures: for example, *endiadis*,[48] *antipophora*,[49] *aposiopesis*,[50] and *antonomasia*.[51]

The use of the term *in libro* ('in the book') to refer to what is stated in the text being commented upon—in this case the Pauline Epistles—may also be a practice borrowed from teaching on the *artes*.[52] The term is used to refer to the text being commented upon in commentaries on certain schools' texts: the Lotharingian scholar, Garlandus Composita (d. before 1086), refers in his *Dialectica*[53] to a *liber*, by which he probably means Boethius, *De topicis differentiis*,[54] and an anonymous eleventh- or twelfth-century commentary on the *Micrologus* of Guido of Arezzo, refers to Guido's treatise as *liber*.[55] G. Morin and B. Smalley (following Morin), noted the presence of this term in the commentary of Pseudo-Bede on the Psalms.[56] It is clear that in this commentary too, *liber* refers to the text of the Psalms, since the quotations from the *liber* are underlined, and are quotations from the Psalm being commented upon.

Other practices of teaching on the *artes* have left their mark in Keble

---

[48] e.g. 'sedis magnitudinis' in Hebrews 8: 1 is glossed 'endiadis' (fo. 147ᵛ), i.e. the use of two nouns instead of a noun + adjective.

[49] Rom. 8: 18, 'Existimo enim quod non sunt . . .' (fo. 17) is glossed 'antipofora', in order to indicate that Paul's statement refutes an objection by employing a contrary inference.

[50] e.g. Heb. 3: 11, 'si introibunt in requiem meam' (fo. 141ᵛ) is glossed 'aposiopesis'.

[51] e.g. Rom. 1: 18, 'impietatem et iniustitiam' (fo. 6) is glossed 'Impios uocat idolatros quorum quosdam ratione disputationis per creaturas creatorem cognoscentes, et cultum tantum sibi denegantes. Apostolus uocat iniustos, antonomasice.'

[52] The phrase is used several times in this way: for example, in the glosses on Rom. 2: 1 (fo. 7); Rom. 6: 16 (fo. 14); Rom. 8: 5 (fo. 16ᵛ); Heb. 7: 12 (fo. 146ᵛ), and Heb. 8: 7 (fo. 148).

[53] Ed. L. M. de Rijk (Assen, 1959). Garlandus was associated with the schools at Liège, and in 1084 was *magister scholarum* at Besançon: ibid. xxxviii–xlii.

[54] Ibid. xlvi–xlvii.

[55] e.g. 'Notandum vero quia *tonus* non definitur a libro': *Commentarius anonymus*, ed. P. C. Vivell, Sitzungsberichte der kaiserliche Akademie der Wissenschaften in Wien, phil.-hist. Klasse, 185/5 (Vienna, 1917), 17.

[56] G. Morin, 'Le Pseudo-Bède sur les Psaumes, et l'*opus super psalterium* de Maître Manegold de Lautenbach', *Rev. bén.*, 28 (1911), 336; B. Smalley, 'Gilbertus Universalis, Bishop of London (1128–34), and the Problem of the "Glossa Ordinaria"', *RTAM* 8 (1936), 47. Morin ascribed this commentary to Manegold of Lautenbach, but, for a more recent assessment of this ascription, see W. Hartmann, 'Psalmenkommentare aus der Zeit der Reform und der Frühscholastik', *Studi Gregoriani*, 9 (1972), 313–66.

22, such as the use of simple *schemata* which illustrate the whole and its parts. Oxford, Bodl. Libr., MS Laud lat. 49, an early eleventh-century manuscript (probably from France), which contains several texts of the *artes*, provides numerous examples of such *schemata* added in the margins as part of the scholarly apparatus.[57] Several such *schemata* also appear in the margins of Keble 22. For example, the text of Romans 8: 35, 'Who then shall separate us from the love of Christ? Shall tribulation? (*tribulatio*) Or distress? (*angustia*) Or famine? (*fames*) Or nakedness? (*nuditas*) Or danger? (*periculum*) Or persecution? (*persecutio*) Or the sword? (*gladius*)' is presented in schematic form on fo. 18ᵛ:

$$
\begin{array}{c}
\text{tribulatio} \\
\diagup \quad \diagdown \\
\text{periculum} \qquad \text{gladius}
\end{array}
$$

$$
\begin{array}{c}
\text{angustia} \\
\diagup \quad \diagdown \\
\text{fames} \qquad \text{nuditas}
\end{array}
$$

In these two *schemata* the list of things which might be thought to separate us from the love of Christ are divided into two *genera*: tribulation and distress. Danger and the sword are shown to be two species of tribulation, and famine and nakedness, two species of distress.[58] These *schemata* thus provide a diagrammatic representation of the interlinear glosses written above *fames an nuditas*—'a partibus angustiae', and above *periculum an gladius*—'partes tribulationis'.

It is also possible that the patristic citations presented in the form of a paraphrase introduced by the word 'secundum' followed by the name of the authority cited, may reflect the words of a master teaching in the schoolroom.

Although an important function of the anonymous glosses in Keble 22 is to elucidate the letter of the Pauline text, some of the glosses offer spiritual interpretation of a doctrinal or moral nature. For example, the gloss on 1 Cor. 11: 24 (fo. 48ᵛ) sets out the orthodox doctrine of the Eucharist, stating that the bread and wine on the altar, although retaining the appearance of bread and wine, in its fundamental nature is completely changed into the body and blood of Christ.[59]

---

[57] See esp. fos. 129ᵛ–30, part of Cicero, *De inventione*, with the commentary of Victorinus added as a marginal gloss.

[58] Other *schemata* occur on fos. 13ᵛ, 21, 25ᵛ, 61ᵛ, 139.

[59] 'Nota panem corpus Cristi fieri in altari, per uerba ipsius Cristi. In quo quidem Cristi corpore propter sumentium honorem, sapor panis et figura remanet, sed substantialis omnino mutata in corpus Cristi est panis natura. Idem et de sanguine credi oportet.'

Keble 22 and Vatican, Bibliotheca Apostolica, MS 143

A large number of the anonymous glosses in Keble 22 also occur in an early twelfth-century manuscript—Vatican, Biblioteca Apostolica, MS lat. 143, a manuscript produced in Italy, but otherwise of unknown origin and later provenance. This is also a copy of the Pauline Epistles, laid out in order to receive marginal and interlinear glosses. Both text and glosses are written by a single scribe. The manuscript is more heavily glossed than Keble 22: it contains more patristic citations, and also cites Lanfranc, Berengar, and Drogo. The manuscript has already received attention as an important witness to Lanfranc's commentary on the Pauline Epistles.[60]

The glosses in Vat. lat. 143 which correspond to those in Keble 22 form part of what appears to be a separate sequence of glosses which are written in the inner column ruled for glosses, whilst the glosses which correspond to the Lanfranc commentary are written in the upper margin and outer column. There is substantial, although by no means complete correspondence between the sequence of glosses in Vat. lat. 143 and the glosses in Keble 22. Both begin with the same gloss: 'Secundum Ieronimum intentio apostoli . . .', and both share a number of glosses which complement the Marcionite prologues to each epistle by commenting on the cirumstances which led to the epistle in question being written. A comparison of the glosses on Romans 11: 29–36, for example, reveals a correspondence of three glosses:[61]

Romans 11: 29 *Sine poenitentia.* Uere quia promisit patribus eos eligit,[62] quia *sine penitentia* et cetera. Uel uere erunt karissimi secundum electionem, quia *sine penitentia* (Vat. lat. 143, fo. 23ᵛ; Keble 22, fo. 23ᵛ).

Romans 11: 31 *misericordiam consequantur.* Uere karissimi, quia misericordiam consequentur, sed interponit similitudinem (Vat. lat. 143, fo. 24; Keble 22, fo. 23ᵛ).

Romans 11: 35 *aut quis prior.* Ut gentilis sic etiam Iudeus[63] nil prius dedit Deo, ut sibi[64] retribuatur[65] iustificatio, et ita utrunque reprimit de iustitia presumentem (Vat. lat. 143, fo. 24; Keble 22, fo. 24).

The *schemata* in the margins of Keble 22 also occur in Vat. lat. 143.

[60] For a description of the manuscript, see Smalley, 'Glossa Ordinaria', 384, and Gibson, 'Lanfranc's Commentary', 93–4. I am grateful to Margaret Gibson for lending me photostats of Vat. lat. 143 and Berne 334 (see below).

[61] I have transcribed the extracts from Vat. lat. 143; variant readings in Keble 22 are noted in the footnotes.

[62] eos eligit] elegit.

[63] Ut gentilis sic etiam iudeus] Ut iudeus sic etiam gentilis.

[64] sibi] omitted.

[65] retribuatur] retribuatur et.

Vat. lat. 143, like Keble 22, has some glosses which consist of paraphrases from patristic authorities, and which are introduced by the word
'secundum' followed by the name of the authority cited, but, as far as I
have been able to collate the two manuscripts, with the exception of the
opening gloss citing Jerome, they do not correspond with those in Keble
22. The term *liber* likewise is used in Vat. lat. 143, in the same manner
but in different glosses from those in Keble 22.[66]

The anonymous glosses in Vat. lat. 143 which do not correspond with
those in Keble 22, do, however, employ similar terminology and
techniques of argument. For example, compare the following glosses in
Keble 22 and Vat. lat. 143 on Romans 8: 18 'Existimo enim . . .'

Vat. lat. 143, fo. 16: 'Responsio antiphorie. Quasi aliquis diceret, "non oportet
conpati ut glorificemur quia maiora sunt tormenta quę irrogantur ab aduersariis,
quam cęlestis gloria quę promittitur nobis". "Absit", inquit, "*Existimo enim . . .*"'

Keble 22, fo. 17: 'Antipofora quod aliquis diceret, "non conpatiamur, quia
compassiones nostrę sunt condignę, id est, equiponderis cum illa gloria futura".
Ad hoc respondet, "non est uerum quod dicis. *Existimo enim . . .*"'

In this example both glosses interpret Paul's assertion (that our sufferings
in this world are not comparable to the glory which is to come) as a
response to the argument of an adversary. Both use the correct rhetorical
figure to define this response—*antipofora*, although their suggestions
differ as to what an adversary might have said to provoke Paul's
response: Vat. lat. 143 imagines that the adversary claimed that we ought
not to share Christ's sufferings, since our sufferings in this world are
greater than the promised glories of Heaven, whereas, in Keble 22, the
adversary is imagined to have said that our sufferings are equal to those
glories.

Similarities have already been noticed between the glosses in Vat. lat.
143 and another twelfth-century copy of the Pauline Epistles—Berne,
Burgerbibliothek, MS 334, ii (fos. 86–156).[67] The glosses in this manuscript are similar to those in Keble 22 in that they are derived from both
patristic and eleventh-century exegesis, and also contain simple
schemata. But, as far as I have been able to collate the two manuscripts, I
have been unable to find any glosses which are common to both.

Keble 22 and Eleventh-Century Pauline Exegesis

Close parallels with the content, terminology and techniques employed in
the anonymous glosses in both Keble 22 and Vat. lat. 143 can be found in

---

[66] e.g. in the gloss on Heb. 1: 5 (Vat. lat. 143, fo. 159ᵛ).
[67] Smalley, 'Glossa Ordinaria', 384–5.

Lanfranc's commentary on the Pauline Epistles. Several scholars are known to have produced commentaries on the Pauline Epistles, or to have expounded them in the second half of the eleventh century, but our most certain knowledge is of the exegetical work of Lanfranc of Bec. His commentary was quite widely known, as was his reputation as a teacher. In about 1060, Williram of Ebersberg, writing in south Germany, commented that many of his fellow-countrymen (*multi nostrorum*) were flocking to France to hear Lanfranc, a man once renowned for his teaching on dialectic, who had now turned his attention to biblical exegesis:

Unum in Francia comperi Lantfridum nomine, antea maxime ualentem in dialectica. Nunc ad ecclesiastica contulit studia, et in Epistolis Pauli et in Psalteris multorum sua subtilitate exacuisse ingenia; ad quem audiendum ... multi nostrorum conflu(unt).[68]

More important, Lanfranc gained a reputation for employing a new method in his biblical exegesis. A contemporary, Sigebert of Gembloux, noted that Lanfranc employed the techniques of dialectic (*propositio*, *assumptio*, and *conclusio*) in the study of the Pauline Epistles, whenever the opportunity presented itself:

Lanfrancus, dialecticus et Cantuarensis archiepiscopus, Paulum apostolum exposuit, et ubicunque opportunitas locorum occurrit, secundum leges dialecticae proponit, assumit, concludit.[69]

The text of his commentary bears this out. In her examination of Lanfranc's commentary, Margaret Gibson asserts 'Lanfranc ... brought to Pauline commentary a quite new concern for the forms of argument, for logical consistency and rhetorical effect ... (He) is interested in the order of St. Paul's argument, the point of formal proof or, less often, the syllogism that lies behind the proof ... There is nothing quite like this in earlier Pauline commentary. Even allowing for the occasional phrase in Ambrosiaster or Pelagius, this free use of words and methods from the texts of the *artes* is new.'[70] But Dr Gibson also points out that although Lanfranc was happy to employ such methods and terminology, he was careful to use them only to draw out the underlying structure of Paul's argument, not to take off into further theological speculation.

The anonymous glosses in Keble 22 and Vat. lat. 143 exhibit a similar unwillingness to employ the techniques and terminology of the *artes* for the purposes of theological speculation. Thus, although the content of the glosses go beyond the needs of someone interested merely in

---

[68] Quoted in Gibson, 'Lanfranc's Commentary', 86.
[69] *Liber de scriptoribus ecclesiasticis*: PL 160. 582–3.
[70] Gibson, 'Lanfranc's Commentary', 102–3.

personal, spiritual edification, I have not yet found any evidence in them which would suggest speculative thinking: the activity is scholarly, not scholastic.

If Lanfranc was the scholar responsible for introducing the techniques of the *artes* to Pauline exegesis, then it is possible that the glosses in Keble 22 and Vat. lat. 143 might represent the teaching of someone who had been taught by Lanfranc. But the glosses in Keble 22 are, for the most part, independent of Lanfranc's commentary. Moreover, although Lanfranc was the first to gain a reputation for applying rhetorical and dialectical techniques to the study of the sacred page, the techniques themselves were well known from commentaries on texts used in the study of the *artes*. Therefore, other teachers may have independently introduced such techniques to their teaching on the books of the Bible. This hypothesis is strengthened by the existence of Trier, Stadtbibliothek, MS 14, a copy of the Psalms with an anonymous marginal gloss which exhibits many of the rhetorical devices found in Lanfranc's commentary and in the glosses in Keble 22 and Vat. lat. 143.[71] This manuscript was made at Werden in the northern Rhineland, and, more important, dates from the mid-eleventh century: i.e., the period when Lanfranc himself was only just beginning to lecture on the Psalms and Pauline Epistles. Sadly only fragments have survived of biblical exegesis which can safely be attributed to Lanfranc's contemporaries, Berengar and Manegold of Lautenbach, but they too may have employed the techniques of the *artes* in their teaching on the books of the Bible.

The glosses in Keble 22, Vat. lat. 143, Trier 14 and Berne 334, in particular the group of glosses common to Keble 22 and Vat. lat. 143, and that common to Vat. lat. 143 and Berne 334, provide evidence that many different groups of glosses, not necessarily associated with the names of well-known teachers, such as Lanfranc, Berengar, Manegold, and Drogo, were copied, attained some popularity, and circulated throughout Europe in the late eleventh and early twelfth centuries.

Keble 22 is of particular importance since not only is it one of the earliest surviving copies from anywhere in Europe of a book of the Bible with glosses which reflect the new mode of biblical exegesis but also it demonstrates that an interest in such teaching was present in England before the end of the eleventh century.

Keble 22 and Biblical Studies at Salisbury

The glosses in Keble 22 do not in themselves indicate that the manuscript was used by a master at Salisbury for the purpose of teaching. It is possible that the book was used for private study. None the less, there is

[71] Gibson, 'The Twelfth-Century Glossed Bible', 241–3.

evidence which indicates that the book did receive scholarly attention at Salisbury in the late eleventh century.

The text of the Pauline Epistles has been carefully repunctuated. This appears to have been the activity of Group I scribe i, undertaken whilst he corrected the text itself: in every case the colour of the ink used for the new punctuation corresponds with that of the words which have been corrected. Scribe i's activity in adding or altering the punctuation had a complementary function to that of the glosses. Punctuation was added in order to aid the understanding of the text (see Pl. 15). It could not only aid the literal understanding of a *sententia* but could also impose a particular spiritual interpretation upon a *sententia*. M. B. Parkes has shown that scribe i added punctuation to the first seven verses of Paul's Epistle to the Romans in order to emphasize the three points of theological significance contained within that passage.[72] Dr Parkes has also shown that in some cases, scribe i repunctuated the text in the light of the accompanying gloss. For example, he repunctuated 1 Cor. 16: 13–14, 'Vigilate, state in fide, uiriliter agite, confortamini. Omnia uestra in caritate fiunt' (Keble 22, fo. 58ᵛ),[73] by turning the two verses, originally punctuated as separate *sententiae*, into a single *sententia*, by altering the final point after *confortamini* into a *punctus elevatus*. This was in accordance with the moral interpretation offered by the interlinear glosses: 'uiriliter agite' ('do manfully') is glossed 'et supra fidem bona opera insistite' ('and, beyond faith, apply yourself to good works'), and 'omnia uestra in caritate fiant' ('let all your deeds be done in charity') is glossed 'in eo sitis perseuerantes, et cum hec feceritis, non faciatis propter humanum fauorem' ('so that you may be resolute, and that, when you do these things, you will not be doing them for human favour').[74]

There is also evidence that the Salisbury canons studied the Pauline text and the accompanying glosses in Keble 22 in part for the theological content of the Epistles, especially that concerning the doctrine of the Eucharist. The gloss on 1 Corinthians 11: 24 (fo. 48ᵛ) which sets out the orthodox doctrine of the Eucharist was shortly afterwards supplemented by other texts concerning the Eucharist added by Group I scribe viii on blank leaves at the front of the volume. These additions consist of extracts from Paschasius, *De corpore et sanguine domini* (under the title *Sermo beati Augustini*), and from a Paschasian *catena* of proof-texts on the Eucharist, extracted from the works of the Fathers.[75] Both the gloss

---

[72] M. B. Parkes, 'Punctuation, or Pause and Effect', in *Medieval Eloquence: Studies in the Theory and Practice of Medieval Rhetoric*, ed. J. J. Murphy (Berkeley, Calif., 1978), 135–6.

[73] 'Watch ye: stand fast in the faith: do manfully and be strengthened. Let all your deeds be done in charity.'   [74] Parkes, 'Punctuation', 141–2.

[75] For this *catena*, see Ratramnus, *De corpore et sanguine domini*, ed. J. N. Bakhuizen van den Brink, 2nd edn (Amsterdam/London, 1974), 6–7, 29–32.

and the additions support the orthodox Eucharistic doctrine championed by Lanfranc: the gloss on 1 Corinthians 11: 24 sets out the Lanfrancian doctrine of the Eucharist, whilst the patristic *catena* added on fos. 3^v–4^v is derived from the same *catena* employed by Lanfranc.[76] In the early twelfth century the canons took their study of this topic one stage further. They copied both the full text of Paschasius's treatise and also the enlarged list of patristic proof-texts (known as the *Exaggeratio*) together with the brief treatise on the Eucharist by Heriger of Lobbes with which the *Exaggeratio* was commonly associated (Salisbury Cathedral, MSS 130 and 61 respectively; both are Group II manuscripts).

This choice of texts indicates the canons' concern, in the wake of the Berengarian controversy, to possess orthodox teaching on the subject of the Eucharist. Berengar's second recantation of 1079, which provided a definitive statement of the Church's doctrine on the Eucharist, was added by Group I scribe iv to the canons' copy of Lanfranc's canon law collection (Salisbury Cathedral, MS 78, fo. 97^v). It would seem that the canons were not interested in the controversy for itself; they did not copy Berengar's treatise, or any of those written in response to it. Nor is there any evidence that they entered into any speculative thinking on the subject. Their concern was to learn true doctrine, and to possess the authoritative biblical and patristic justification for it. The Pauline Epistles supplied the biblical authority, and Paschasius's treatise and the *Exaggeratio* demonstrated the overwhelming unanimity of the Fathers' teaching on this topic.

The additions made to Keble 22 and the texts copied in the early twelfth century to supplement those additions (Salisbury Cathedral, MSS 61 and 130) indicate the beginnings of a new development in biblical and theological studies: the transition from a study organized around the *ordo narrationis* of the Bible, towards a study organized by topic—in this case, the Eucharist. This new organization, however, had not yet become systematic; the Salisbury canons did not produce any copies of text books which could be compared to the *Summae* compiled in the twelfth century, and the traditional method of study, following the narrative of the individual books of the Bible with the help of patristic commentaries, had not yet been replaced. Although the canons were interested in theological questions to a level which went beyond that required merely for teaching the parochial clergy and laity, they do not appear to have become interested in scholastic theology—I have not yet found any evidence of speculative thinking. Nor did the canons exploit their study to produce original works of theology. The intent which lay behind their study seems to have been the desire to find answers to various

[76] For the patristic *catena* employed by Lanfranc, see M. T. Gibson, *Lanfranc of Bec* (Oxford, 1978), 83–4.

theological and moral questions, and to learn the doctrine which underlay and justified them. But for these answers they were content to rely on the authoritative teaching of the Fathers.

SALISBURY CATHEDRAL, MS 160

Whilst Keble 22 provides evidence that the canons were abreast of Continental biblical scholarship in the late eleventh century, another manuscript now at Salisbury—Salisbury Cathedral, MS 160—may indicate that the canons stayed in touch with developments in biblical scholarship on the Continent in the first half of the twelfth century. This manuscript contains an anonymous commentary on the Psalter and the first six weekly canticles,[77] which was probably composed during the first half of the twelfth century. The value of Salisbury 160 as evidence for the intellectual interests of the Salisbury canons is less assured than that of Keble 22, since it is not possible to show whether the book was produced at Salisbury, or, if produced elsewhere, when it was brought to Salisbury.[78] But it may well have been produced or acquired to act as a companion volume to Keble 22.

Salisbury 160, like Keble 22, is a small, easily portable book, with very little decoration, intended for personal scrutiny rather than for liturgical purposes. It is written throughout by a single scribe who employed an expert small 'academic' hand (see Pl. 16). Although many of the Salisbury scribes also employed such hands, I have not yet identified the hand of this scribe in any other Salisbury book. Such small hands are very difficult to date according to purely palaeographical criteria, but I would suggest that this hand is no later than the first half of the twelfth century, and could well be as early as the first quarter of the century: the relatively small number of abbreviations, the consistent employment of the ampersand instead of the tironian *nota* for 'et', and the fact that the parchment is ruled in dry-point, all indicate an early twelfth-century date. The script and general appearance of the book suggest an origin in the *milieu* of the schools of northern France.

The commentary contained in Salisbury 160 survives in a number of other twelfth-century copies, none of which are closely datable.[79] The text of the commentary has never been printed, and has received

---

[77] *Confitebor tibi* (Is. 12), *Ego dixi* (Is. 38: 10–20), *Exultavit cor meum* (1 Reg. 2: 1–10), *Cantemus domino* (Ex. 15: 1–19), *Domine audivi* (Hab. 3: 2–19), and *Audite coeli* (Deut. 32: 1–43).

[78] The earliest evidence for the presence of Salisbury 160 at Salisbury is a thirteenth-century *ex libris* inscription on fo. ii: *Liber ecclesie Sarr'*.

[79] For a list of manuscripts which contain this commentary, see Stegmüller, nos. 5337–40. Another copy is Oxford, Magdalen College, MS 207 (imperfect at the beginning).

relatively little scholarly attention.[80] However, Mme M.-Th. d'Alverny, from her examination of copies of the commentary in the Bibliothèque Nationale in Paris, has identified two redactions: a longer redaction, represented by the text in Paris, Bibliothèque Nationale, MS lat. 12006, and a shorter redaction, represented by the text in Paris, Bibliothèque Nationale, MS lat. 440.[81] The text in Salisbury 160 corresponds with that of the shorter redaction.

The authorship of the commentary, and its date of composition is uncertain. In a large number of the surviving copies, the name of the author is not given. The entry for Salisbury 160 in Patrick Young's catalogue records a tradition at Salisbury which ascribed the text to one Anselm.[82] Another copy (Paris, Bibliothèque Nationale, MS lat. 440) attributes the commentary to John of Rheims, prior of Saint-Evroul (d. 1125).[83] The most common attribution, however, is to one Ivo of Chartres,[84] and it is this attribution which has received general acceptance by modern scholars. Beryl Smalley distinguished this Ivo from the canonist, Ivo, bishop of Chartres (1090–1117), and identified him as a pupil of Gilbert de la Porrée, and contemporary of Peter Lombard and Robert of Melun.[85] This Ivo is known from several sources: he attended the Council of Rheims as a witness for Gilbert in 1148; is mentioned as a pupil of Gilbert's in a marginal note in the Chronicle of Robert of Auxerre for the year 1152, and is represented sitting at Gilbert's feet in a miniature in Valenciennes, Bibliothèque Municipale, MS 197.[86] Miss Smalley also identified this Ivo with the Ivo who attested charters of 1155–9 as dean of Chartres. This evidence would seem to place Ivo's scholarly activity, and the composition of the commentary in the 1140's.[87]

There is, however, other evidence which suggests that the commentary may have been composed as early as the first quarter of the twelfth

[80] The fullest treatment to date of the authorship and content of the commentary is B. Smalley, 'Master Ivo of Chartres', *EHR* 50 (1935), 680–6.

[81] This information is recorded in D. Van den Eynde, 'Literary Note on the Earliest Scholastic *Commentarii in Psalmos*', *Franciscan Studies*, 14 (1954), 128–9.

[82] See Ker, 'Salisbury Cathedral Manuscripts', 170, 177.

[83] Stegmüller, nos. 5337, 5340.

[84] Ibid. nos. 5337–40.

[85] Smalley, 'Master Ivo', 680–6.

[86] Ibid. 680–1.

[87] The glossed Psalter 'secundum magistrum Ivonem' mentioned in a mid-12th-cent. catalogue from Durham Cathedral Priory (now Durham, Cathedral Library, MS B.IV.24) may refer to a copy of this commentary (pr. *Catalogi veteres librorum ecclesiae cathedralis Dunelm.*, Surtees Society, vii (1838), 8 'Libri Laurentii Prioris'). The manuscript was given to the community at Durham by Lawrence, prior from 1149–53. If this was the same text, the reference provides a useful *terminus post quem non* for the composition of the text: see Smalley, 'Master Ivo', 681.

century, and therefore casts doubt on the identification with Ivo, pupil of Gilbert de la Porrée.

Miss Smalley identified extracts from the commentary attributed to Ivo in an anonymous commentary on the Psalms contained in London, BL, MS Royal 3 B xi.[88] The author or compiler of this commentary states that he used Augustine, 'et nobilium glosulas magistrorum Yvonis et Anselmi, Monogoldi atque Serlonis' (fo. 1ᵛ).[89] It may be of significance that this author places Ivo in the same company as at least two scholars not of the mid-twelfth century, but of the late eleventh and early twelfth centuries—Anselm of Laon and Manegold of Lautenbach.[90]

Moreover, Miss Smalley observed that the commentary attributed to Ivo revealed no influence of the commentary on the Psalms of his master Gilbert—the *media glosatura*, nor the literary forms of *quaestio* and *distinctio* which became employed in commentaries in the course of the twelfth century.[91] This would be surprising if this Ivo had been a pupil of Gilbert de la Porrée, and had studied in the Paris schools in the second quarter of the twelfth century. On the other hand, Miss Smalley did find evidence which indicated the influence of late eleventh-century exegesis, in particular, the commentary printed in the *Patrologia latina* as a spurious work of Bede (once thought to be the work of Manegold of Lautenbach),[92] and possibly also Lanfranc's lost commentary on the Psalms.[93] Further examination reveals that the commentary attributed to Ivo has similarities in form, content and terminology with a number of commentaries now thought to have been composed no later than the first quarter of the twelfth century:[94] the commentaries of Pseudo-Haimo,[95] Letbert of Lille,[96] Honorius Augustodunensis,[97] Pseudo-Remigius,[98] and

---

[88] Smalley, 'Master Ivo', 682–3.

[89] Ibid. 682.

[90] The Serlo referred to here has not yet been identified.

[91] Smalley, 'Master Ivo', 683.

[92] *PL* 477–1098. See Morin, 'Pseudo-Bède' and Hartmann, 'Psalmenkommentare'.

[93] Smalley, 'Glossa Ordinaria', 374–8.

[94] For these commentaries, see V. I. J. Flint, 'Some Notes on the Early Twelfth-Century Commentaries on the Psalms', *RTAM* 38 (1971), 80–8. This article challenges the conclusions of D. Van den Eynde ('Literary Note') who rejected the previous identifications of Pseudo-Haimo as Anselm of Laon, and Pseudo-Bede as Manegold, since he tried to show that both commentaries relied on the commentary of Letbert. He therefore argued that these commentaries reflected an explosion in exegetical activity in the second quarter of the twelfth century. He also noted close similarities between Letbert's commentary and that of Ivo. Accepting Miss Smalley's identification of Ivo as a pupil of Gilbert de la Porrée, he assumed that Ivo had borrowed from Letbert's commentary, and thus reinforced Miss Smalley's conclusion that Ivo's commentary was produced in the 1140s.

[95] *PL* 116. 191–696.

[96] The commentary on the first 75 Psalms is printed in *PL* 21. 641–960, under the name of Rufinus: see A. Wilmart, 'Le Commentaire sur les Psaumes imprimé sous le nom de Rufin', *Rev. bén.*, 31 (1914–19), 258–76.

[97] Portions of this commentary have been printed in *PL* 172. 269–312.

[98] *PL* 131. 133–844.

the commentary attributed to Bruno the Carthusian,[99] in addition to that of Pseudo-Bede.

A number of points of similarity have already been observed between the commentaries of Pseudo-Bede, Pseudo-Haimo, Letbert, Honorius, Pseudo-Remigius, and 'Bruno',[100] but it has proved very difficult to demonstrate the nature of the relationships between them all. As V. I. J. Flint has observed: 'The textual tradition of commentaries on the Psalms written in the early twelfth century is still extremely difficult to unravel. The ground is strewn with doubtful ascriptions and inadequately established dates.'[101] The nature of the relationships between these different commentaries is also complicated by the fact that at this period the written representation of a master's teaching did not necessarily circulate in the form of a commentary with an established text but could also be disseminated as groups of glosses which were liable to be rearranged and added to in the course of transmission. At the present state of our knowledge, therefore, it is possible to indicate the points of similarity between the commentary contained in Salisbury Cathedral, MS 160 and early twelfth-century Psalter commentaries, but not to demonstrate with any precision the nature of the relationships between them.

A comparison of the prologues to the Psalms illustrates some of the similarities between the commentary in Salisbury 160 and the early twelfth-century Psalter commentaries, and also indicates the complex nature of the relationships between them.

The content of these prologues was derived partly from inherited material (primarily the commentaries of Augustine and Cassiodorus, transmitted and sometimes adapted by Carolingian scholars), and partly from contemporary exegesis. In some instances the inherited material is quoted at length, but, for the most part, a single sentence or phrase is quoted and then elaborated upon. It is in these elaborations that we can observe points of similarity or difference between each of the commentaries.

For example, all of these commentaries define the word 'psaltery' from which the word 'Psalter' is derived. The commentary attributed to Bruno presents a definition wholly derived from a passage attributed to Jerome in Cassiodorus, *Expositio psalmorum*:[102] 'Psalterium est quoddam

---

[99] *PL* 152. 637–1420.

[100] For the similarities between the commentaries of Pseudo-Bede, Pseudo-Haimo, and Honorius, see Flint, 'Some Notes', and for the similarities between the commentaries attributed to Bruno the Carthusian and Gilbert the Universal, and that of Pseudo-Remigius, see Smalley, 'Gilbertus Universalis', 51–60.

[101] Flint, 'Some Notes', 80.

[102] Cf. Cassiodorus, *Expositio psalmorum*, praefatio, iv (CCSL 97. 11).

musicum instrumentum quod ex superiori cavitate resonat.'[103] All the
other commentaries, however, expand this description of the psaltery
and expound its significance. They observe, for example, that the
psaltery has ten strings which they interpret as signifying the ten
commandments. Pseudo-Haimo, Letbert, Pseudo-Bede, and Pseudo-
Remigius present broadly similar interpretations, but there is a
particularly close similarity between the commentaries of Pseudo-Haimo
and Letbert:

(Pseudo-Haimo) Hoc autem opus ab illo instrumento hac significatione
Psalterium vocatum est, quia sicut illud instrumentum decem chordas habens, et
superius concavum unde resonat: ita haec prophetia resonat, semper loquendo de
superioribus ... Decem vero chordae illius psalterii, decem legis praecepta
significant. Quae omnia praecepta bene implet, qui ea quae in Psalterio leguntur
exsequitur.[104]

(Letbert) Sicut hoc instrumentum decem chordas habet, et superius est concavum
unde resonat: ita haec prophetia resonat de superioribus, quae nos instruit de
spiritualibus ... Decem vero chordae psalterii, decem praecepta legis significant:
quae omnia bene implet, qui ea exequitur, quae in psalterio scripta decantantur.[105]

(Pseudo-Bede) Vocatur vero liber iste Psalterium hac similitudine, quia sicut illud
musicum instrumentum de superiori parte reddit sonum, ita liber iste de supernis
sonat: id est, super coelestia et divina nobis demonstrat, quia docet nos quae de
Christi humanitate vel divina natura fideles scire oportet. Docet etiam decem
principalia praecepta per decem chordas musici instrumenti significata, in quibus
omne Novum et Vetus Testamentum comprehenditur.[106]

(Pseudo-Remigius) Psalterium, ut diximus, musicum instrumentum est, triangu-
latum, habens decem chordas super se extensas; quod inferius percussum, dulcem
sonum desuper reddit ... In decem chordis, decem verba legis accipimus.[107]

Honorius and the author of the commentary contained in Salisbury 160
also discuss the significance of the ten strings of the psaltery, but both
expand this discussion still further. Honorius adds a Christological
element: he compares the psaltery to the body of Christ, and adds that
the ten precepts of the law, signified by the ten strings of the psaltery, are
delivered through Christ. The author of the commentary in Salisbury 160
extends the tropological (moral) significance, claiming that we cannot
sing God's praises without endeavouring to possess true faith and all the
other virtues which together comprise the new law, prefigured in the ten
precepts of the old law:

(Honorius) Psalterium, quod Christum et Ecclesiam concinit, forma sua corpus
Christi exprimit. Dum enim inferius percutitur, superius resonat: et corpus Christi
dum ligno crucis suspenditur, divinitas per miracula resonat ... Decem chordae,

---

[103] *PL* 152. 637.   [104] *PL* 116. 195–6.   [105] *PL* 21. 644.
[106] *PL* 93. 481.   [107] *PL* 131. 147.

quae in Psalterio extenduntur, sunt decem praecepta legis, quae per Christum traduntur.[108]

(Salisbury 160) Psalterium enim est quoddam musicum instrumentum, concauum lignum in superiori parte habens, et cordas decem, quę cordę inferius repercussę, sonum superius emittunt. Et hoc figurat nobis quod laudes Dei canere non possumus, nisi per decem cordas: id est, per decem ueteris legis pręcepta, quę decem pręcepta spiritualiter accepta continent in se quicquid habetur in lege noua. Et noua lex nichil aliud est quam fidei ueritas, et morum honestas; quasi diceret: non possumus laudes Dei psallere, nisi ueram fidem et ceteras uirtutes studuerimus habere.[109]

Another example taken from the prologues of these early twelfth-century commentaries presents a different pattern of relationships. All seven commentaries note that the book of Psalms is also called the book of hymns, and that the individual psalms are called hymns. In this instance, it is Pseudo-Haimo rather than 'Bruno' who offers the least 'developed' commentary: 'Hymni vocantur singuli psalmi: hymnus enim est laus Dei cum cantico.'[110] The other commentators define the word 'hymnus' more closely as being the praise of God written in metre. The definitions of Pseudo-Remigius and the commentary attributed to Bruno are very similar, and both quote a verse from Arator:

(Pseudo-Remigius) *Hymnorum*, id est laudum Dei. Hymnus est laus Dei metrice composita. Hinc Arator: *Psalterium lyrici composuere pedes.*[111]

(Attrib. Bruno) Ideoque merito liber iste apud Hebraeos Liber hymnorum dicitur, id est Dei laudum. Hymni vero laudes Dei metrice factae proprie dicitur, psalmi autem lyrico metro compositi fuerunt; ut Arator ait: *Psalterium lyrici composuere pedes.*[112]

Honorius, Pseudo-Bede, Letbert, and the author of the commentary in Salisbury 160 take the subject one step further, and observe that, although the Psalms had been written in metre in the original Hebrew, in the course of translating the Psalms from the Hebrew, it had not proved possible to preserve the metre. Honorius, for example, writes thus:

Titulus libri hujus est liber hymnorum: hymnus est laus Dei metrice composita. Omnes quippe psalmi in Hebraea lingua certo metro decurrunt: sed hoc translatores propter simplices minime servare curarunt.[113]

Pseudo-Bede and Letbert add, employing very similar wording, that, even though the Latin version of the Psalter is not in strict metre, we may nevertheless still call it the book of hymns, since the most important part of the definition of a hymn—the praise of God—still applies:

---

[108] *PL* 172. 271–2.   [109] Salisbury 160, fo. 1ᵛ.   [110] *PL* 116. 193.
[111] *PL* 131. 148.   [112] *PL* 152. 638.   [113] *PL* 172. 270–1.

(Pseudo-Bede) Intitulatur autem hic liber apud omnes tam Hebraeos quam
Graecos atque Latinos, totius respectu, *liber hymnorum* ... Hymnus est proprie
laus Dei, metrice scripta. Constat enim totum Psalterium in Hebraeo metrice
compositum. Unde proprie in Hebraeo dicitur liber hymnorum. Apud nos vero,
et fortasse apud Graecos, non servat, impediente translatione, metrum. Dicitur
tamen apud nos recte liber hymnorum, quia licet non teneat metrum, tenet tamen
id quod est praecipuum, scilicet quod in omni parte tam apud nos quam apud
Hebraeos laude Dei est conspicuum.[114]

(Letbert) Ideo titulus ejus est, *Liber hymnorum*: quia totum istud opus pertinet
ad laudem Dei ... Dicunt et quidam quod hymnus proprie dicitur, laus Dei
metrice composita. Unde proprie in Hebraeo dicitur *Liber hymnorum*, quia ibi
totum psalterium est metrice scriptum. Dicitur etiam apud nos recte *Liber
hymnorum*, quia licet, impediente translatione, non teneat metrum, tenet tamen
quod praecipuum est: scilicet quod in omni parte apud nos, sicut et apud
Hebraeos, laudem Dei significat, quod perspicuum est.[115]

The commentary contained in Salisbury 160 offers two passages on this
subject, both of which note the loss of the metrical character of the
Psalms through the process of translation. However, the second of the
two passages, in its use of the word *lirico* instead of *metrice*, has
similarities with the treatment of this passage by Pseudo-Remigius and
'Bruno':

Psalmus uero est ymnus, uel laus Dei. Dicuntur autem ymni quod laudem metrice
in sua lingua cantant. Nam ymnus est laus, cuiusque metri ratione conposita.
Quod autem metri rationem non seruauerunt, utique translationis causa factum
est, quoniam interpres non potuit in aliam linguam ipsos psalmos transferens,
legem metri seruare.[116]

Liber ymnorum ideo intitulatur, quia totum istud opus ad laudem Dei pertinet, et
lirico carmine est conpositum. Ynnus (*sic*) enim dicitur laus Dei, lirico carmine
conposita: sed tamen apud nos lirico carmine non distinguitur, et hoe propter
translationes. In primis enim de Hebreo in Grecum, postea a beato Iheronimo de
Greco in Latinum fuit translatum.[117]

The commentary contained in Salisbury 160 not only shares common
subject matter (and sometimes phraseology) with these early twelfth-
century commentaries but also a common set of technical terms: *titulus,
materia, intentio,* and *pars philosophiae.* Such terms derive ultimately
from late-antique commentaries; this particular set of terms derives from
Boethius's commentary on the *Isagoge* of Porphyry, a *schema* designed
originally for introductions to philosophical texts.[118] From the late

---

[114] *PL* 93. 480–1.   [115] *PL* 21. 644.   [116] Salisbury 160, fo. 1.
[117] Salisbury 160, fo. 1ᵛ.
[118] R. W. Hunt's type C prologue: see 'The Introductions to the "Artes" in the Twelfth
Century', *Studia mediaevalia in honorem admodum reverendi patris Raymundi Josephi
Martin* (Bruges, [1948]), 85–112, esp., 94–7; repr. in his collected papers, *The History of
Grammar in the Middle Ages,* ed. G. L. Bursill-Hall (Amsterdam, 1980), 117–44, esp. 126–9.

eleventh century various *schemata* composed of these and other terms came to be employed in the introductions to literary texts (the *accessus ad auctores*).[119] By the early twelfth century such terminology was being employed in commentaries on biblical texts, in particular, the Psalter.

For the most part, the early twelfth-century commentators employed such terms only in the prologue to the Psalter as a whole, and made no more than a spasmodic use of a few terms, in particular *titulus, materia,* and *intentio,* in the short prologues which precede the verse by verse commentary on the individual Psalms; this is also the case with the commentary contained in Salisbury 160.[120] Not all of the early twelfth-century commentators on the Psalter used all of these terms, even in their prologues to the Psalter as a whole. For example, the term 'pars philosophiae' is not used by either Pseudo-Bede or Pseudo-Haimo; 'Bruno' and Honorius discuss whether the Psalms should be considered as pertaining to physics, ethics or logic but do not employ the actual term 'pars philosophiae'. See, for example, Honorius's discussion:

Philosophia est amor sapientiae; philo quippe *amor,* sophia dicitur *sapientia:* haec dividitur in tres partes, in physicam, ethicam et logicam; id est in naturalem, moralem, rationalem ... Ad physicam pertinet Genesis, quae de naturis loquitur; Epistolae Pauli ad ethicam pertinent, quae de moribus tractant: Psalterium ad logicam, quae et theorica dicitur, eo quod de ratione divinae scientiae memorat.[121]

Pseudo-Remigius uses the term 'pars philosophiae' in relation to the books of the Bible, but does not specify to which *pars* the book of Psalms belongs. However, the author of the commentary contained in Salisbury Cathedral, MS 160 and Letbert both employ the term and assign part of the book of Psalms to ethics, and part to physics:

(Salisbury Cathedral, MS 160) Solet queri cui parti philosophię supponatur. Ad quod istud respondemus, secundum hoc quod tractat de moribus ethice supponitur; secundum hoc uero quod tractat de natura ipsius diuinitatis phisice potest supponi.[122]

(Letbert) Quaeritur a quibusdam, cui parti philosophiae supponatur. Quibus

[119] Ibid.; see also, R. B. C. Huygens, *Accessus ad auctores: Bernard d'Utrecht; Conrad d'Hirsau* (Leiden, 1970), and A. J. Minnis, *Medieval Theory of Authorship: Scholastic Literary Attitudes in the Later Middle Ages* (Andover, 1988), 13–28; 40–58.

[120] I know of only one early 12th-cent. commentary which consistently employs the terms *titulus, materia, modus,* and *intentio* in each of the prologues to the individual psalms: a commentary entitled *Tituli in psalterium,* contained in Oxford, Bodl. Libr., MS Bodley 781, and also used as part of the Latin apparatus in the Eadwine Psalter (Cambridge, Trinity College, MS R.17.1. On this commentary, see M. T. Gibson, 'The Latin Apparatus', in *The Eadwine Psalter,* ed. M. T. Gibson, T. A. Heslop and R. W. Pfaff (forthcoming).

[121] *PL* 172.270.

[122] Salisbury 160, fo. 2.

respondendum est, secundum quod agit de moribus, Ethicae: secundum quod tractat de natura, Physicae potest supponi.[123]

The commentary contained in Salisbury 160 also exhibits another characteristic found in some biblical commentaries from the end of the eleventh century—a tendency, especially in passages of moral interpretation, to include allusions to contemporary circumstances, or illustrations which would be familiar to a contemporary audience. For example, Augustine in his commentary on Psalm 1: 1, 'Et in cathedra pestilentiae sedit' ('nor sat in the chair of pestilence') interpreted *pestilentia* as a disease which spreads to all, or almost all: 'Pestilentia est enim morbus late peruagatus, et omnes aut paene omnes inuoluens.'[124] Pseudo-Haimo based his interpretation of 'pestilentia' on Augustine's but made his description a little more detailed, by referring to the spread of disease from one animal to many others: 'Pestilentia quidem infirmitas est, quae ab uno animali ad plura, sive ad omnia transit.'[125] The commentary contained in Salisbury 160 adds an even more specific detail, and likens 'pestilentia' to the kind of disease which infects a herd of pigs: when one is infected, all the others, or almost all of them are infected: 'Pestilentia est quidam morbus qui solet intrare greges porcorum, quo morbo uno corrupto, corrumpuntur omnes alii aut pęne omnes.'[126]

References to monks and clergy figure large in such passages of moral interpretation: as, for example, in the interpretation of Psalm 106 given in Salisbury 160. This Psalm describes four groups of people who have been redeemed, and who should give thanks to God for their redemption. The commentary in Salisbury 160 interprets these four groups of people as having been subject to four different kinds of temptation. The third group of people, described in verses 17–22, it interprets as having been subject to the temptation of *accidia* (weariness of the spirit), a temptation which it associates particularly with the monastic life:

anima eorum abominata est, omnem escam spiritualem, id est, exosam habuit, et orationem, et lectionem, et bonam operationem, tanto tedio et fastidio oppressi fuere. Istud maxime est in claustralibus.[127]

The fourth group of people, described in verses 23–30, are those who face danger in ruling those placed under them, and these are the *pręlati* who are liable to be unduly elated or cast down by the good behaviour or short comings of those in their care:

quia pręlati, cum uident subditos in tranquillitate et bene operari, *ascendunt usque ad cęlos* (Ps. 106: 26): id est, tantum presumunt de subditis, quod reputant eos cęlos, id est cęlestes, et iam in uirtutibus perfectos, et ita presumendo

---

[123] *PL* 21. 644.   [124] CCSL 38. 1.   [125] *PL* 116. 198.
[126] Salisbury 160, fo. 2.   [127] Salisbury 160, fo. 156ᵛ.

temptantur. Non dictum est hoc de omnibus pręlatis sed de sanctissimis uiris, qui pro caritate pręsunt non pro terrenis diuitiis, qui cum apostolo possunt dicere: *quis infirmatur et ego non infirmor*? (2 Cor. 11:29) Et cum uident eos in uitia cadere, descendunt usque ad abyssos (Ps. 106: 26): id est, ita desperant de salute eorum, ac si essent ita profundissimi in uitiis, quod nunquam resipiscere possent.[128]

Bernhard Bischoff has noted this moralizing tendency in other biblical commentaries from the late eleventh and twelfth centuries and has compared it with a similar tendency in late eleventh- and early twelfth-century commentaries on classical authors, in particular the satirists.[129]

If the commentary contained in Salisbury 160 was composed in the first quarter of the twelfth century, and the manuscript itself was produced not long after (as the palaeographical evidence would seem to indicate), then it would have been possible for the copy to have arrived at Salisbury in the early part of the twelfth century. Unfortunately this hypothesis cannot be proved. But the speculation that the commentary may have been used by the Salisbury canons as a companion volume to the glosses on the Pauline Epistles contained in Oxford, Keble College, MS 22 is given weight not only by the similarity between the appearance of the two manuscripts but also by common characteristics in their content: an absence of lengthy quotations from the Fathers; a lack of anything which might suggest speculative thinking, and an emphasis on moral as opposed to allegorical interpretation.

The glosses in Keble 22 and the commentary in Salisbury 160 (if we may use it as evidence) demonstrate that the scholarly interests of the Salisbury canons derive from the teaching of masters in the schools of northern France in the late eleventh and early twelfth centuries—the period before biblical exegesis and theology had assumed a speculative character. The Salisbury canons' collection of patristic texts provides further evidence in support of this assertion. From the evidence of the numbers of commentaries which were copied at Salisbury for particular books of the Bible, the books which aroused most interest at Salisbury were Genesis, the Psalms, St Matthew's Gospel, and the Pauline Epistles. These were the books which received most attention in the schools.

---

[128] Salisbury 160, fo. 157. See also, Smalley, 'Master Ivo', 684.

[129] B. Bischoff, 'Living with the Satirists', in *Classical Influences on European Culture, AD 500–1500*, ed. R. R. Bolgar (Cambridge, 1971), 83–94, esp. 89–90 and 90 n. 1; repr. in his collected papers, *Mittelalterliche Studien* (Stuttgart, 1981), iii. 260–70, esp. 266 and 266 n. 14. His findings go against Miss Smalley's earlier suggestion ('Master Ivo', 683), that the moralizing tendency exhibited by the commentary attributed to Ivo, and also the introduction of vernacular words, are exceptional in commentaries earlier than the second quarter of the 12th cent.

Furthermore, the patristic texts copied at Salisbury, in particular the shorter treatises of Augustine, were those which provided the principal patristic sources for the numerous glosses, commentaries and *sententiae* which emanated from the schools.

The glosses, commentaries, and *sententiae* which were produced by those who had attended or taught at the Continental schools in the late eleventh and early twelfth centuries are considered to have been a response to the moral and doctrinal concerns which preoccupied clergy and scholars in the wake of the Gregorian reform.[130] Dom Jean Leclercq has defined these activities more closely, as the emergence of a new pastoral theology which included both questions of Christian morality and the doctrines which underlay and justified it.[131] He distinguishes this pastoral theology from both the spiritual 'monastic' theology, and the speculative, scholastic theology which emerged in the twelfth century. Since the intellectual activities of the canons of Salisbury, reflected by the texts they copied, correspond in many respects to those of the Continental schools, they may indicate the emergence of this new pastoral theology at Salisbury too in the late eleventh and early twelfth centuries.

[130] See, for instance, V. I. J. Flint, 'The "School of Laon": A Reconsideration', *RTAM* 43 (1976), 89–110.

[131] J. Leclercq, 'The Renewal of Theology', in *Renaissance and Renewal in the Twelfth Century*, ed. R. L. Benson and G. Constable (Oxford, 1982), 79.

5

THE RELIGIOUS LIFE

WE do not possess any detailed or explicit expression of the religious aims and attitudes held by the Salisbury canons in the first century after their establishment. Bishop Osmund stated in his foundation charter that his endowments for the canons had been made 'illis viventibus canonice', but neither here nor elsewhere did he spell out what he meant by the phrase.[1] Presumably no formal expression of his intentions was required while he was still alive, but even in the decades after his death the Salisbury canons did not draw up regulations concerning their practice of the religious life, nor did they adopt an existing rule. Before long, they had become known as 'secular canons', a somewhat contradictory term used increasingly from the beginning of the twelfth century to distinguish those canons who did not adopt a rule from those who did.[2]

Very little is known of the religious aims and practices of secular canons, and the ways in which, or the extent to which they differed from those of the regular orders. The twelfth century was a period in which monks and regular canons were prolific in composing or compiling works of spiritual direction for themselves, but few such works survive from the same period for secular canons. Rather more abundant are derogatory accounts of the worldliness of the secular clergy; by the end of the twelfth century, if not earlier, the image of the secular canon as of the world, worldly, had become something of a commonplace. However, in the early twelfth century and before, it would have been difficult to draw a firm distinction between the religious attitudes and practices of those canons who lived the full common life and adopted a rule, and those who did not. As some studies of eleventh- and early twelfth-century spirituality have shown, it is easier to identify the underlying similarities between the different orders of monks and canons, both regular and secular, than to distinguish the differences.[3]

---

[1] For the full text of the charter, see Greenway, 'The False *Institutio*', 98–100.

[2] K. Edwards, *The English Secular Cathedrals in the Middle Ages*, 2nd edn (Manchester, 1967), 1–20.

[3] See, for example, C. N. L. Brooke, 'Monk and Canon: Some Patterns in the Religious Life of the Twelfth Century', in *Monks, Hermits, and the Ascetic Tradition*, ed. W. J. Sheils, Studies in Church History, 22 (Oxford, 1985), 109–29, and the references cited there. Because of the nature of the evidence, secular canons have not received as much attention in this context as the regular orders. For a study which seeks to reinstate the seculars, see

The content of the Salisbury manuscripts, together with annotations added to them, are our best evidence of the religious aims and attitudes of the Salisbury canons. They enable us to determine whether their religious aims and attitudes do indeed display underlying similarities with those of the regular orders.

TEXTS OF SPIRITUAL AND MORAL EDIFICATION COPIED AT SALISBURY

When one examines the content of the Salisbury book collection from the point of view of texts of spiritual advice and edification, its general similarity with monastic book collections very quickly becomes apparent. A large number of the texts copied for the Salisbury canons in the first phase of book production in the late eleventh century express or promote the ideals, aims, and practices of the religious life. Among them are several of the standard texts of early medieval monasticism, such as Cassian, *Collationes*,[4] Smaragdus, *Diadema monachorum*,[5] and the *Sermones ad monachos* of Caesarius and Eusebius 'Gallicanus'.[6] These are texts one would expect to find in any monastic library; copies of them or compilations of extracts survive from several English monastic book collections formed both before and after the Norman Conquest.

The predominance of monastic texts amongst the texts of spiritual guidance acquired by the Salisbury canons should not surprise us. It is, in part, a reflection of the fact that during the early Middle Ages, Western spirituality had been dominated by the monastic ideal, hence almost all texts of spiritual and moral guidance had been addressed to monks. None the less it is important to recognize that such texts were evidently valued and used by the Salisbury canons, in spite of the sometimes explicitly monastic spirituality which they promote. The copy of the *Sermones ad monachos* of Caesarius and Eusebius 'Gallicanus' is one of the most heavily annotated of all the Salisbury books.

But there is also evidence that the canons felt that such texts were not wholly adequate for their needs, since, in the early twelfth century, they appear to have sought out more unusual texts which express the ideals and purpose of the religious life. Among the texts they acquired were two

L. Musset, 'Recherches sur les communautés de clercs séculiers en Normandie au xiᵉ siècle', *Bulletin de la Société des Antiquaires de Normandie*, 55 (1961, for 1959–60), 5–38. For the spirituality of regular canons, see C. W. Bynum, 'The Spirituality of Regular Canons in the Twelfth Century', in *Jesus as Mother: Studies in the Spirituality of the High Middle Ages* (Berkeley, Calif., 1982), 22–58.

4 Salisbury Cathedral, MS 10. This copy contains *Collationes*, i–x, xiv–xv, xxiv, and xi.
5 Salisbury Cathedral, MS 12, fos. 1–56.
6 Oxford, Bodl. Libr., MS Bodley 392.

early medieval rules: the *Praeceptum* (part of the so-called 'Rule of St Augustine'),[7] and the *Rule of the Four Fathers*.[8] Both texts were copied in the early twelfth century, as part of the second phase of book production at Salisbury. At this time, the Augustinian rule was becoming increasingly popular on the Continent as the rule to be adopted by canons who wished to live the full common life, but very few copies are extant from England in the early twelfth century.[9] The *Rule of the Four Fathers* had become a rather less popular text; I know of no other English copy. It is a rule composed in the early fifth century by those who presided over the early community at Lerins, writing under the Egyptian pseudonyms of Macarius, Serapion, Paphnutius, and another Macarius.[10] Not only were these two texts uncommon in England at this time, but, as shown above (Chapter 3), the Salisbury copies each bear witness to a tradition of the text for which only one other witness survives: in the case of the Augustine, a tenth-century manuscript from Bobbio, and in that of the *Rule of the Four Fathers*, a late sixth- or early seventh-century manuscript of southern Italian origin which from the end of the seventh century was at Corbie. It is unlikely that these manuscripts acted as the exemplars for the Salisbury copies, but it seems clear that the Salisbury canons must have gone to some trouble to acquire exemplars, and that, therefore, the texts were far from being chance acquisitions.

These two rules may well have been of particular interest to the Salisbury canons because whilst both advocate the common life and advise on the manner in which it should be conducted, they are concerned more with precepts than with specific regulations on the ordering of each day. Neither rule, for example, contains the detailed liturgical requirements which, from the ninth century, had become associated with the Benedictine rule and which were an important constituent of the rule of Chrodegang. The Salisbury canons could practise the general precepts of each rule, without adopting the rule itself. In this context, it is significant that the canons copied the *Praeceptum* and not the other principal constituent of the Augustinian rule, the *Ordo monasterii*, which is more specific in its prescriptions.

The book collection of the Salisbury canons indicates that they, like other religious communities, both of monks and of canons, looked for spiritual advice to the writings of the Fathers and to the literature of early medieval monasticism. But, in common with other religious communities

[7] Salisbury Cathedral, MS 169, fos. 77ᵛ–81ᵛ.

[8] Salisbury Cathedral, MS 12, fos. 59–60.

[9] For a list of extant manuscripts of the Augustinian rule in British libraries, see Römer, 160–3.

[10] For the importance of this text in the early medieval period, and its relation to the *Regula magistri* and the *Rule of St Benedict*, see *Les Règles des saints pères*, ed. A. de Vogüé, 2 vols. (Paris, 1982).

at this time, they also sought new texts of spiritual advice. Two such texts survive from Salisbury: an anonymously compiled ascetic *florilegium* copied at Salisbury in the early twelfth century, and a text composed at Salisbury at about the same time, the *Meditationes* of Godwin the cantor. While neither provides an overall synthesis for the practice of the religious life, both provide valuable evidence of the religious values and attitudes of the Salisbury canons.

The central concern of both texts is the attainment of a life of apostolic perfection, an ideal which was at the heart of the late eleventh- and early twelfth-century reform movement, but is one not normally associated with canons who did not adopt the full common life. The texts set out to demonstrate, one implicitly, the other explicitly, that the attainment of perfection is possible not only for those who live the full common life but also for those who do not.

THE SCALA VIRTUTUM

Salisbury Cathedral, MS 162, fos. 19–27, an originally independent booklet copied at Salisbury in the early twelfth century, contains an ascetic *florilegium*—a compilation of biblical and patristic *sententiae* concerned with personal discipline. I know of no other manuscript which contains the complete *florilegium* as it exists in this copy.[11] It lacks a formal title, but I shall refer to it as the *Scala virtutum.* Neither the compiler nor the date and place of origin is known. The short prologue with which the text begins provides no information concerning the compiler or the intended audience. It merely expresses the aims commonly presented by the compilers of ascetic *florilegia* in their prologues or letters of introduction: the mass of sacred writings is too great for most to read and learn, therefore the compiler, with great toil, has drawn together these florets for whoever wishes to use them.[12]

Thereafter, the text is presented without any formal divisions, but its content falls into three parts, each part deriving from a different source. The first part consists of *sententiae* which describe or promote the virtues, and these, for the most part, derive from the *Liber scintillarum* of Defensor of Ligugé.[13] The second part complements the first by providing a discussion of the vices, followed by a short account of the

---

[11] For the text of this *florilegium* as it appears in Salisbury Cathedral, MS 162, see App. 3.

[12] For the characteristics of prologues to ascetic *florilegia*, see H.-M. Rochais, 'Contribution à l'histoire des florilèges ascétiques du haut moyen âge latin: Le "Liber scintillarum"', *Rev. bén.*, 63 (1953), 264–5.

[13] Defensor, *Liber scintillarum*, ed. H.-M. Rochais, CCSL 117 (Turnhout, 1957).

canonical hours, derived from Cassian, *De institutis coenobiorum*.[14] The *florilegium* ends with a miscellany of *sententiae* concerning simoniacal and schismatic clergy, taken from Deusdedit, *Libellus contra invasores et symoniacos et reliquos scismaticos*.[15] It is possible that each of the three groups of *sententiae* may represent different stages in the compilation of the text, or the work of different compilers. I know of no other copy of the complete compilation, but at least twelve copies are extant of the first part of the *florilegium*, of which the Salisbury copy is by far the earliest.[16] I have not yet found any other copies of the prologue or either of the two other parts.

The first part of the *florilegium* is the most organized in its structure. It consists of a compilation of biblical and patristic *sententiae* arranged as a list of thirty steps leading to perfection, using the image of Jacob's ladder. Each step promotes a particular moral precept or practice, by defining it, and giving examples of how to practise it. The principal source of the *sententiae* is the *Liber scintillarum*, itself an ascetic florilegium compiled at the end of the seventh century by Defensor of Ligugé. The *Liber scintillarum* was a popular quarry for medieval writers composing works of spiritual advice and exhortation,[17] and, from the tenth century, copies of the *Liber scintillarum* survive in which the text has been significantly rearranged and modified.[18] This process of adaptation became more common and more drastic in the eleventh century when *sententiae* from the *Liber scintillarum* were extracted and recompiled in many different forms: for example, as collections of personal edification.[19] The first part of the *Scala virtutum* is a hitherto unrecognized compilation.[20] The extreme selectivity and the extent to which the compiler has rearranged

[14] Cassian, *De institutis coenobiorum*, ed. M. Petschenig, CSEL 17 (Vienna, 1888).

[15] Deusdedit, *Libellus contra invasores et symoniacos et reliquos scismaticos*, ed. E. Sackur, *Libelli de lite imperatorum et pontificum*, ii, MGH (Hanover, 1892), 291–365. The extracts in Salisbury Cathedral, MS 162 come from Sackur's 'A' text.

[16] Salisbury Cathedral, MS 162, s.xii in; Vatican, Biblioteca Apostolica, MS lat. 10807, s.xiii; Bordeaux, Bibliothèque Municipale, MS 35, s.xiii-xiv; Paris, BN, MS lat. 3645, s.xv; Paris, BN, MS lat. 8207, s.xv; Munich, Clm 11730, s.xv; Cambridge, Corpus Christi College, MS 194, s.xv; Cambridge, Peterhouse, MS 114, s.xv; London, BL, MS Add. 34807, s.xv; London, BL, MS Cotton Julius B VII, s.xv; Oxford, Bodl. Libr., MS Bodley 731, s.xv; Oxford, Bodl. Libr., MS Rawlinson Liturg. e. 42, s.xv. I am grateful to Mr Richard Hamer for references to Vat. lat. 10807, Bordeaux 35 and Paris, BN lat. 8207.

[17] Rochais, 'L'Histoire des florilèges', 267–8.

[18] The earliest of such copies seems to be Bamberg, Staatsbibliothek, MS Patr. 134, in which the copyist has rearranged the order of the chapters and has added some sentences of his own, see Rochais, ibid. 269.

[19] Ibid. 269–70.

[20] M. W. Bloomfield, B.-G. Guyot, D. R. Howard, and T. B. Kabealo (eds.), include Salisbury 162 in their *Incipits of Latin Works on the Virtues and Vices, 1100–1500 AD* (Cambridge, Mass., 1979), no. 5360, but they were unable to identify the text. They suggested that it might be a Latin translation of the *Scala paradisi* of Iohannes Climacus.

and modified the *sententiae* lead me to suspect that it was compiled in the latter part of the eleventh century.

The compiler selected *sententiae* from only twenty-six of the eighty-one chapters of the *Liber scintillarum*, and although some of the steps of the ladder are composed exclusively from *sententiae* from Defensor, no step employs more than seven *sententiae* from any one chapter. This represents a considerable reduction: many of the chapters in the *Liber scintillarum* contain over twenty *sententiae*, and one chapter, chapter xviii, contains 111. The order of subjects in the ladder is also very different from that in the *Liber scintillarum*. Although the organization of subjects within the framework of the ladder is not systematic, nor is there a clear logical or psychological progression from one step to the next, there has been some conscious organization by grouping together virtues on related topics which were scattered in the *Liber scintillarum*. For example, steps 20–2 are three precepts concerned with different forms of discretion and judgement: *silentium moderatum, consilium bonum*, and *iudicium rectum*—topics which are scattered in the *Liber scintillarum* as chapters xvi, lxv, and lxxvi respectively.

The extent to which the ladder of virtues differs from the *Liber scintillarum* might suggest that it was derived from it only indirectly. But I have not been able to identify a probable intermediary.

The *Liber scintillarum* had been compiled for monks, and until the twelfth century was transmitted almost exclusively in monastic *milieux*.[21] As I indicated above, it would not have been unusual for the Salisbury canons to have looked to a monastic text for spiritual and moral edification. However, the compiler's principles of selection, and the alterations and additions he made, have had the effect of modifying the essentially monastic emphasis of Defensor's *florilegium*. His intention would seem to have been to direct his ladder of virtues more specifically towards a non-monastic audience.

He was careful not to choose *sententiae* which promote virtues associated with the contemplative life. He did not, for example, use any *sententiae* from xl, *De monachis*. He also avoided *sententiae* which express or explore interior or contemplative aspects of a virtue. Instead, he preferred those *sententiae* which present a practical illustration or application of the virtue. For example, it is the practical aspects of the virtue, humility, which are illustrated rather than the contemplative.

[21] Rochais concluded from surviving manuscripts and catalogue entries that even in the 12th cent.: 'Le *Liber scintillarum* reste donc une lecture des moines; les nouveaux ordres l'accueillent aussi et les chanoines mêmes lui font place dans leur bibliothèque. Mais il n'apparaît guère chez les séculiers' ('L'Histoire des florilèges', 270–1). In a list compiled from medieval catalogues, Rochais records the presence of a copy of the *Liber scintillarum* at Salisbury, see 'Les Manuscrits du "Liber scintillarum"', *Scriptorium*, 4 (1950), 307 (no. 25). However, this is a mis-attribution—for Salisbury read Salzburg.

Humility is to be promoted primarily as a virtue to be exercised towards other men: it is to be shown in every thought, action and word, whatever one is doing; it is forgiving your brother even before he sins against you.[22] Wherever possible, the compiler chose to begin each step with a *sententia* from the Gospels which gives a practical illustration of the virtue to which that step is devoted. For example, the seventh step, *indulgentia* is given practical exemplification with a passage from Matthew 5: 23–4:

Indulgentia: id est, si offeres munus tuum ad altare, et ibi recordatus fueris quam frater tuus habet aliquid aduersum te, relinque ibi munus tuum ante altare, et uade reconciliari prius fratri tuo, et tunc ueniens offeres munus tuum.[23]

The principles which underlay the compiler's selection of *sententiae* from the *Liber scintillarum* also appear to have influenced his choice of additional matter. Instead of adding passages of meditation, as was the habit of some monastic compilers of *florilegia*, the compiler has added *sententiae* which merely serve to multiply examples or provide further advice of a wholly practical nature, often drawing upon the Gospels. For example, in the ninth step, *oratio*, after a *sententia* from the *Liber scintillarum*, the compiler adds that one should pray for everyone: for oneself, for all catholic people, friends and neighbours, enemies and persecutors, echoing Matt. 5:44, 'pray for them that persecute and calumniate you': 'Oratio debet esse pro uobismetipsis, pro omni populo catholico, pro amicis uel proximis, pro inimicis, et persequentibus uos.'[24]

Many of the steps of the *Scala virtutum* contain similar *sententiae* which are not derived from the *Liber scintillarum*. Three of the steps are on subjects for which there are no chapters or *sententiae* at all in the *Liber scintillarum*: steps 18 (hospitality), 24 (visiting the sick), and 25 (frequenting the shrines of the saints and holy places). The practice of the Christian virtues through the performance of good works, although not excluded from the monastic way of life, was considered especially appropriate for those who lived outside the cloister. The biblical passage from which the compiler has constructed his steps on hospitality and visiting the sick—Matt. 25: 31–46—is a passage which does not appear at all in the *Liber scintillarum*, but was one which formed the basis for the promotion of the corporal works of mercy among the laity in the later Middle Ages.[25]

---

[22] *Liber scintillarum*, iv, 51.

[23] Ibid. v. 1; Salisbury 162, fo. 19ᵛ.

[24] Salisbury 162, fo. 20.

[25] In its promotion of the practice of the Christian virtues, the *Scala virtutum* anticipates trends in English vernacular homiletic literature in the 12th and 13th cent., in which the performance of good works is given an increasingly prominent place, by contrast with the homiletic literature of the 10th and 11th cents.: see K. Greenfield, 'Changing Emphases in English Vernacular Homiletic Literature, 960–1225', *Journal of Medieval History*, 7 (1981), 283–97.

Such emphasis on the practical aspects of the virtues would not alone permit us to interpret the *Scala virtutum* as a text intended for a non-monastic audience. But the compiler made other modifications and additions which explicitly extend the intended audience to those who were not monks, and imply that the search for perfection was open to all. In ten steps, the compiler added references to *omnis cristianus*, or *omnis homo*, or *cristianus homo* (steps 3, 9, 13, 15, 16, 19, 20, 21, and 22). In step 29, *uoluntas bona*, the implied inclusive nature of the intended audience is spelled out in full in a passage not derived from the *Liber scintillarum*, and, in all likelihood, written by the compiler himself, in which he asserts that good will is a virtue which may be practised by all: babes and sucklings, young men and old, men and women, rich and poor:

uere omnes hoc gradus, infantes et lactantes, iuuenes et senes, uiri et feminę, omnisque aetatis hominis sępe ascensuros nouimus. Hunc itaque gradum, id est bonam uoluntatem, pauper et pauperrimus habere potest, sicut et diues et potentissimus.[26]

The compiler concludes his description of the ladder of virtues by interpreting the two sides of the ladder as the eucharist and the memory of *sanctę abrenuntiationis* (in other words, baptism), without which all the steps of the ladder are ascended in vain. In other words, there is no point in performing good works, if one does not receive the sacraments as well.[27]

The account of the ladder of virtues is followed by a second group of *sententiae*, extracted from Cassian, *De institutis coenobiorum*. These *sententiae* were almost certainly compiled as an accompaniment to the first part of the *florilegium*, rather than as a separate unit, even if they represent the work of a different compiler. Not only does their content complement that of the ladder of virtues by providing a discussion of the eight principal vices and remedies by which each might be avoided, but the principles which lay behind their selection, and the modifications made to them are very similar to those employed by the compiler of the ladder of virtues.

The compiler of the second part of the *florilegium* was just as selective in his approach to his source as the compiler of the spiritual ladder was in his use of the *Liber scintillarum*, if not more so. His description of the eight principal vices reduces eight books from the *De institutis coenobiorum* to eight short paragraphs. He too preferred precise

---

[26] Salisbury 162, fo. 23.
[27] I have not yet found this interpretation of the two sides of the ladder in any other account of a spiritual ladder.

descriptions and definitions, and avoided the more contemplative passages in his source. He also favoured similar themes: for example, the evangelical precept that any observance is worthless if the intention which lay behind it is wrong. Compare the concluding *sententia* of step 12, *abstinentia*, which asserts that one gains nothing from subduing the flesh with abstinence if one does not free the mind from faults, 'Nichil enim prodest carnem abstinentia affligere si mentem a uitiis non emendamus',[28] with a similarly worded *sententia* expressing the same message (that it profits one nothing to possess no money if one still desires it) employed in the discussion of conflict against the vice *philargiria* (the love of money): 'nichil prodest pecunias non habere si uoluntas manet possidendi.'[29] *Sententiae* such as these would seem to represent an attempt to prevent the *florilegium* from becoming a mere catalogue of virtuous practices and observances to be performed and vices to be avoided.

The compiler of the second part of the *Scala virtutum* also avoided *sententiae* which were appropriate only for monks, and chose instead passages of more general application. Likewise, he modified the wording of certain passages to make them applicable to a wider audience than monks alone. For example, where Cassian wrote 'Itaque monachus ad perfectionem tendens et agonem spiritalem legitime cupiens decertare ab omni irae furorisque uitio alienus exsistat',[30] the compiler removed the word *monachus* (monk), and substituted the more neutral term 'quis' (anyone): 'si quis enim ad perfectionem tendens . . .'.[31]

The ladder of virtues and the compilation of *sententiae* from the *De institutis coenobiorum* represent a coherent work of spiritual and moral edification appropriate for anyone wishing to live a Christian life of perfection. But the third group of *sententiae* which comprise the *florilegium* as it exists in Salisbury Cathedral, MS 162, does not at first sight appear to belong to the same work, since the subject matter is rather different. These *sententiae* are concerned with canon law; all but the last two *sententiae* are concerned with schismatic and heretical clergy, and in particular with the validity of sacraments administered by such clergy. They derive from the second chapter of the shorter version of Cardinal Deusdedit's *Libellus contra invasores et symoniacos et reliquos scismaticos*—a compilation of *auctoritates* made in 1097 to support the

---

[28] Salisbury 162, fo. 20ᵛ. Cf. *Liber scintillarum*, x. 61, where Defensor attributed it to Caesarius; the source is, in fact, Eusebius 'Gallicanus'.

[29] Cf. Cassian, *De institutis*, vii. xxi; Salisbury 162, fo. 24ᵛ.

[30] Ibid. viii. v.

[31] Salisbury 162, fo. 24ᵛ. Likewise, in the struggle against the sixth vice, *accedia* (weariness of the spirit), where Cassian refers to 'monasterii claustris' (x. v), the compiler substitutes 'loco'.

argument that sacraments administered by schismatics or simoniacs are invalid.[32]

In the Salisbury copy they follow straight on from the preceding *sententiae* without a change of hand or ink, new heading, or any other indication that they might form a separate work or represent additions. It is possible that these *sententiae* from Deusdedit's *Libellus* were not originally intended to form part of the *florilegium*, but that they had been added by chance to the exemplar used by the Salisbury scribes. But irrespective of whether the *sententiae* from the *Libellus* first became associated with the *Scala virtutum* intentionally, or by chance, the Salisbury scribes may have copied these *sententiae* deliberately, because they considered them to be of relevance to the preceding groups of *sententiae*.

The interpretation of the two sides of the spiritual ladder in the *Scala virtutum* had emphasized the importance of receiving the sacraments, and therefore also, by implication, the essential role performed by the clergy who administered them. Christians might ascend each of the rungs in the ladder of perfection through their own efforts, but they required the clergy to administer the sacraments to them. The question of the proper administration of those sacraments, and the validity of sacraments administered by clergy who had defiled their orders through schism or heresy, was therefore crucially important.

Neither the discussion of the vices nor the final group of *sententiae* appear to have attained any popularity in this form. But the ladder of virtues occurs little altered in several manuscripts, both English and Continental, dating from the later Middle Ages. Its success almost certainly derived from the ever growing popularity of the image of Jacob's ladder as a vehicle for works of spiritual advice and exhortation.[33]

Although we cannot be certain that the *Scala virtutum* originated at Salisbury, there is strong evidence that it was Salisbury which actively promoted its use as a devotional text, by incorporating it as a formal part of the Use of Sarum. In three English fifteenth-century manuscripts (London, BL, MS Cotton Julius B VII, Oxford, Bodl. Libr., MSS Bodley 731 and Rawlinson Liturg.e.42) the ladder of virtues is found in association with the Sarum *Martyrologium*. In this context it was intended to perform an analogous function to that of the Benedictine

---

[32] Ed. E. Sackur in *Libelli de lite imperatorum et pontificum*, ii, MGH (Hanover, 1892), 291–365. The extracts in Salisbury Cathedral, MS 162 derive from Sackur's 'A' text.

[33] For a survey of spiritual ladders in Medieval literature, see É. Bertaud and A. Rayez, 'Échelle spirituelle', *Dictionnaire de spiritualité*, fasc. xxv (Paris, 1958), 62–86.

rule for monks: a text to be read in chapter after Prime.[34] The rubric in one manuscript explicitly associates this practice with Salisbury: 'Liber de gradibus uirtutum a sancto Ambrosio ordinatus qui legitur ad primam in ecclesia Sarum.'[35] The rubric in another copy explains how it was to be read:

Incipit liber de gradibus uirtutum, a sancto Ambrosio ordinatus, quibus ad celeste Ierusalem item ad patriam angelorum supernam itinere recte ascenditur ab omni perseuerante, et potest legi ad primam post martilogium, itaque quando luna est prima legatur primus gradus scale ... cum luna secunda, secundus gradus, et sic semper usque ad aliam lunam primam et tunc reincipatur.[36]

Thus, as a single section of the Benedictine rule was read each day, so a single step from the ladder of virtues would be read each day: one step for each day of the month. Unfortunately we lack evidence which might indicate whether the ladder of virtues performed this function at Salisbury as early as the twelfth century.

THE *MEDITATIONES GODWINI CANTORIS*

The message implied in the *Scala virtutum* is that the ascent to perfection is something not confined to those who follow the monastic life, but is open to all. This same message is promoted more explicitly in a second text of which the Salisbury origin is more assured. This is the *Meditationes Godwini*, a text written at Salisbury some time in the first third of the twelfth century by the precentor, Godwin,[37] although it has

---

[34] Oxford, Bodl. Libr., MS Bodley 731, fos. 63ᵛ–64. For this text in the context of the Sarum Use, see W. Maskell, *Monumenta ritualia ecclesiae Anglicanae: The Occasional Offices of the Church of England According to the Old Use of Salisbury*, 2nd edn (Oxford, 1882), i. pp. clxxvi–clxxvii. The rubric in BL, Add. 34807 also associates this text with Sarum Use.

[35] London, BL, MS Add. 34807 (s.xv). The ascription to Ambrose occurs in the three English 15th-cent. copies in which the text follows on from the Martyrologium. Only one other manuscript attempts to identify the compiler: Bordeaux, Bibliothèque Municipale, MS 35 (s.xiii-xiv), which attributes the compilation to Augustine.

[36] Oxford, Bodl. Libr., MS Bodley 731, fos. 63ᵛ–64. This rubric complicates the picture a little since it implies that the ladder of virtues itself was not always used at Salisbury cathedral, and, in its place, a text referred to as 'Haymo' was read: 'Tamen in ecclesia Sarum legitur Hamo, sed qui illum non habet potest legere gradus scale uirtutum a sancto Ambrosio compositur.' I have not been able to identify this text; the reference may be to the English Franciscan friar, Haymo of Faversham (d. 1244).

[37] Godwin was precentor at Salisbury some time during the first third of the 12th cent. The inscription on his tomb records that he was ordained by Archbishop Anselm (1093–1109): see the 'Report on the Excavation of the Cathedral Church of Old Sarum in 1913', *Proceedings of the Society of Antiquaries of London*, 2: 26 (1913–14), 113. He was certainly precentor at Salisbury by c.1122, since he is named as such in the witness list of a charter of that date of Bishop Roger of Salisbury (see, E. J. Kealey, *Roger of Salisbury* (Berkeley/London, 1972), 238–9).

not survived in a copy made at or for Salisbury.[38] The heading in the only extant copy, 'Meditaciones Godwini cantoris Salesberie ad Rainilvam reclusam' seems to indicate that Godwin wrote his text for an anchoress: indeed, the first sentence of the work is addressed to 'Cristiana', but elsewhere in the text the author refers frequently to 'fratres' which suggests that he intended his work to have a wider audience.

The text is presented as a commentary on the Beatitudes. It is divided into two parts: the first entitled *Meditationes*, and the other, *Sermo*, although there is little difference in form, style or content between the two. The *Meditationes* consists of a commentary on the first beatitude, and the *Sermo* is a commentary on the remaining seven (the title *Meditationes* merely indicates that the commentary on the first beatitude is more lengthy and discursive than that on the other seven). Unlike the *Scala virtutum* which is scarcely more than *catenae* of biblical and patristic *sententiae*, Godwin's text depends very little upon inherited material. His principal sources are biblical, in particular the Gospel of St Matthew and the Epistles of Paul.

Godwin used his commentary as a vehicle to present what is essentially an apology for those who do not adopt the common life. It stands as a response to those reformers who advocated a return to what they conceived to be a life of apostolic perfection: a life modelled on a literal interpretation of Christ's words to the rich young man in Matthew 19: 21–2, and the ideal of the Christian community in Jerusalem in Acts 4: 32. When the rich young man asked Christ how he might become perfect, Christ replied: 'If thou wilt be perfect, go, sell what thou hast and give it to the poor and thou shalt have treasure in heaven. And come follow me.' This was the teaching adopted by the community at Jerusalem which 'had but one heart and soul. Neither did anyone say that aught of the things which he possessed was his own; but all things were common unto them.' Thus, the life of apostolic perfection promoted by the late eleventh- and early twelfth-century reformers was one which entailed the rejection of all private property and which advocated the holding of all goods in common.

The *Meditationes Godwini* sets out an alternative (and rather more pragmatic) plan for a life of apostolic perfection, appropriate for those who do not wish to give up their private possessions, and who engage in secular affairs. Its emphasis on the practical is similar to that of the *Scala virtutum*, but the tone with which it is written, and the literary devices

---

[38] It has survived in only one manuscript: Oxford, Bodl. Libr., MS Digby 96, a 12th-cent. manuscript of unknown origin. As the editor of the catalogue of Digby manuscripts in the Bodleian Library points out, this copy may well have been the copy noted by Leland at Abingdon (see *J. Lelandi antiquarii de rebus Britannicis collectanea*, ed. T. Hearnius (Oxford, 1715), iii. 57).

employed are very different. The *Scala virtutum* presents merely an organized series of *sententiae* which together form a plan by which any Christian might achieve perfection; there is no attempt to compare it with any other form of Christian life, or to justify it. Godwin's text, however, is overtly apologetic in tone, and he employed a wide range of literary and rhetorical devices to assist in the presentation of his arguments. He made frequent recourse to rhetorical questions. In his interpretation of Matthew 19: 24, that it is easier for a camel to pass through the eye of a needle than for a rich man to enter the kingdom of Heaven, he asks whether this was intended to mean that all rich men were to be excluded from the kingdom of Heaven, and answers himself, 'Of course not': 'Quid ergo? Nunquid dominus omnem diuitem a regno cęlorum hac sententia intendit excludere? Absit.'[39] On several occasions the argument is heightened with apostrophe. After quoting Paul's pragmatic teaching on celibacy and marriage, 'it is better to marry than to be burnt (1 Cor. 7: 9)' and 'for fear of fornication, let every man have his own wife (1 Cor. 7: 2)', Godwin exclaims 'O wisdom of the doctor of the Church', and praises Paul for enjoining all to struggle against fornication, even though not all can aspire to virginity and celibacy: 'O prudentia doctoris ęcclesię! Ecce dum non potest omnes animare ut sint uirgines, aut saltem post solutionem continentes, omnes contestantur ne sint fornicatores.'[40] The text also displays some knowledge of the techniques of rhetoric employed in late eleventh- and early twelfth-century biblical commentaries and glosses, such as drawing out the structure of the argument underlying a particular passage. This technique is used to interpret the meaning of the Lord's prayer:

Adueniat regnum tuum subintelligi potest: sicut in cęlo et in terra nostra. Quomodo? *Fiat uoluntas tua sicut in cęlo et in terra* bona, scilicet per uerbum, sine quo fieri nec intelligi potest, eius qui in cęlo est uoluntas Patris. Unde apte subiungitur, *Panem nostrum . . .*[41]

(*Thy kingdom come* can be understood further to mean on our earth, as it is in Heaven. How can it? *Thy* good *will be done on earth as it is in Heaven,* in other words, through his word who is the will of the Father in Heaven, without which nothing can be done or understood. Whence it appropriately goes on to say, *give us this day our daily bread . . .*)

But perhaps the sharpest weapon in Godwin's polemic is his attempt to beat the reformers at their own game by adopting their phrases and favourite *auctoritates* in his own defence. Thus he frequently refers to the *vita* or *forma apostolice perfectionis* which the apologists of the full

---

[39] Oxford, Bodl. Libr., MS Digby 96, fo. 9ᵛ.

[40] Ibid. fo. 13ᵛ. Godwin does not make it clear whether he is here referring to married laity or whether he is condoning clerical marriage.

[41] Digby 96, fo. 54.

common life asserted was possible only for them, and he turns to his own advantage the reformers' favourite texts: the story of the rich young man and the description of the community at Jerusalem. He does this by ridiculing an exclusively literal interpretation and by offering as an alternative, a moral one. He points out that if such passages are taken literally they conflict with other passages of the New Testament. He takes the example of a sentence at the end of the story of the rich young man, which states that everyone who has left house or brothers or sisters or father or mother or children or lands for Christ's sake will receive a hundredfold and inherit eternal life (Matt. 19: 29). Godwin begins by admitting the case of the reformers, agreeing that this text permits those who wish to be perfect to sell everything they possess, and give it to the poor, leaving behind their brothers and sisters, father and mother:

Ergo forte hac auctoritate domini licet unicuique ut sit perfectus, domum et agros et omnia que possidet uendere, et pauperibus erogare; licet fratres et sorores, patrem et matrem et seipsum relinquere, et Cristo artius adherere.[42]

But he goes on to pour scorn on the notion that this text permitted a married man to leave his wife and children in order to become a monk or hermit: 'sed numquid licet ei, qui alligatus est coniugio uxorem et filios relinquere, et monasterium aut heremum ad sumendum habitum religionis ire . . .? Absit.'[43] And he cites other passages from the New Testament in support of this, for example, 1 Cor. 7: 10: 'But to them that are married, not I, but the Lord, commandeth that the wife depart not from her husband.'[44] Godwin then counters the argument that those in the married state cannot therefore follow a life of apostolic perfection, by resorting to moral interpretation, supported by the teaching of St Paul. He claims that there are two ways of abandoning the things of this world and following Christ: in thought and in practice.[45] Therefore, those in the married state or those who own property can follow the *spirit* of Christ's teaching (for example, living as if they owned no property, in other

[42] Digby 96, fo. 12.

[43] Ibid., fo. 12. C. N. L. Brooke (*The Medieval Idea of Marriage* (Oxford, 1989), 44–5, 44 n. 12) points out that there is a confusion in the relevant biblical passages (Luke 18: 28–30; Mark 10: 28–30 and Matt. 19: 27–9) concerning whether one is permitted to leave a wife in order to follow Christ. Luke 18: 29–30, for example, states 'Who said unto them: Amen, I say to you, there is no man that hath left house or parent or brethren or wife or children, for the kingdom of God's sake, who shall not receive much more in this present time, and in the world to come life everlasting'. In the Vulgate, all three passages mention 'wife', and thus would run counter to Godwin's argument, but in the Greek, the word 'wife' is omitted from Matthew and Mark.

[44] Ibid., fo. 12ᵛ.

[45] 'Duo profecto ea que sunt huius mundi relinquendi, et duo sequendi et imitandi crucem Cristi sunt genera, unum scilicet in mente, et aliud simul aperta operatione.' Ibid. fo. 13.

words, not yearning after greater riches), and in this way it is possible for them to follow a life of apostolic perfection:

Habent ... diuites et uxores habentes remedium quo predictam formam apostolicam omnia relinquendi quodammodo ualeant imitari, si uidelicet iuxta apostolici consilium habentes tanquam non habentes sunt, nichil scilicet affectu possidentes nec aliena concupiscentes. Si qui habent uxores, et relinquere non possunt, tanquam non habentes sint: id est, si habent amore prolis, non ardore libidinis . . .[46]

He returns to this theme at the end of the *Meditationes*, and presents a moral interpretation of what it means to leave brother, sister, father, wife, children, and fields, interpreting brothers and sisters as the confederation of the vices in one consanguinity, the father as the devil, the mother the flesh, and so on.[47]

Godwin, like the compiler or compilers of the *Scala virtutum*, emphasizes the pastoral commonplace that intentions are as important as, if not more so than, the actions and observances behind which they lie.[48] But for him the precept forms an essential part of his argument. It is not the form of life one adopts which determines whether or to what extent one is achieving apostolic perfection, but the spirit in which one lives that life. Seen in this light, Godwin's main text, 'Blessed are the poor in spirit', acquires a special significance: in Matthew's Gospel, Christ does not say 'blessed are the poor', but 'blessed are the poor in spirit'.[49] The obvious implication is that there is no benefit in renouncing all one's property if one does so in a spirit of pride: a somewhat thinly veiled criticism of some advocates of the full common life.

At the heart of Godwin's argument lies an attack upon the view that there is a hierarchy of perfection within the Christian life based upon the form of life adopted. This was the opinion held, for example, by a Continental contemporary, the author of the *De vita vera apostolica*.[50] This author presents a wholly literal interpretation of the story of the rich

---

[46] Ibid., fo. 13.

[47] 'Si fratres et sorores, id est una consanguinitate uitiorum confederatos, et ob hoc unius gehenne coheredes, abnegas. Si preterea patrem—diabolum, et uxorem—carnem, et paruulos eorum, id est male conceptos affectus allidendos ad petram respuis. Si denuo agros, id est laboriosam nimiam curam mundi alium, relinquis, ut Cristo adhereas et Cristo ex his que possides pauperibus succurrendo seruias, centuplum accipies, et uitam ęternam possidebis.' Ibid., fo. 29.

[48] For example, 'Sunt enim nonnulli, tam uiri quam femine, qui inuiti corporis continentiam sub aliena custodia seruant, corpore integri sed mente corrupta. Vnde et pulchre dominus noluit dicere, "Beati mundo et integro corpore", sed potius, "Beati mundo corde". Nouit enim quia non quemquam integritas corporis beatum efficit, nisi de consensu mentis': ibid., fo. 49–49ᵛ.

[49] But cf. Luke 6: 20, in a very similar passage, 'Blessed are the poor, because thine is the kingdom of God'. Godwin chose to ignore this version of the Beatitudes.

[50] *PL* 170. 609–64, where it is attributed to Rupert of Deutz.

young man, and, with the support of a moral interpretation of a passage from St Paul which points out that the different celestial bodies radiate different levels of brightness, uses it to assert a hierarchy of perfection: monks at the top, then canons, and the laity at the bottom.⁵¹ Godwin counters such an interpretation with the Pauline doctrine of variety: the Church is one body but has many members, none of which can claim a superiority.⁵² He explains the different forms of religious life in historical terms: each form of religious life emerging in response to changing circumstances and needs. Even monasticism, he points out, is a modification of a stricter form of life.⁵³ He argues that secular canons possess personal property in order to support their special needs as pastors, and since such property is being used for the common good it should be regarded as no different from the property held in common by those communities who live the full common life.⁵⁴

Godwin's rejection of the notion of a hierarchy of perfection based upon the form of religious life adopted, displays similarities with the views of another, Continental contemporary, the anonymous author of the *Libellus de diversis ordinibus et professionibus qui sunt in aecclesia*.⁵⁵ This author, probably a canon regular, has been commended by his

---

⁵¹ 'Cum igitur constet Jesum toties in Evangelio clamare nullum posse ejus perfectum discipulum esse, nisi qui vult omnibus quae possidet renuntiare, et sequens illum crucem portare, id autem probatum sit ratione et auctoritate, dignius et perfectius monachos qui suum student propositum, ut ipsos apostolos, consummare, potes sanum consilium dare omnibus volentibus huic mundo renuntiare, et ad perfectionem, ut veri Christi discipuli, pertingere, ut se debeant ad monasticam vitam contrahere. Sicut *alia* est enim *claritas solis, alia claritas lunae; et stella differt a stella in claritate* (1 Cor. 15: 41), ita alia est claritas monachi, alia est claritas canonici, alia claritas laici. Unde qui vivit ut bonus laicus facit bene, melius qui est canonicus, peroptime qui est monachus.' *PL* 170. 663–4.

⁵² 'Multis modis adhuc ex sanctorum patrum scriptis potui ostendere quomodo inter se ordines ęcclesię uideantur differre, sed multo utilius iudico breuiter demonstrare quomodo omnia membra Cristi ad perfectam formam ęuangelice institutionis, mecum et sancte multitudinis credentium quibus erant omnia communia possint pro suo modulo aspirare. Si enim uerba apostoli diligenter attendimus, euidenter omnes remedium inuenimus, quo utramque propositam formam quodam modo imitari possimus. Ait enim scribens uniuersę ęcclesię romanę, *Sicut enim in uno corpore multa membra habemus, omnia autem membra non eundem actum habent: ita multi unum corpus sumus in Cristo, singuli autem alter alterius membra* (Rom. 12: 4–5).' Oxford, Bodl. Libr., MS Digby 96, fo. 23–23ᵛ.

⁵³ 'Optimum enim in monasteriis refugium inuenire possunt, qui heremi inediam et nuditatem et laborem manuum ferre nequeunt.' Ibid., fo. 19.

⁵⁴ 'Illi uidelicet qui ea que de ęcclesia possident non in conmessationem et ebrietatem, non in pretiosarum uestium uanitatem, non in turpis lucri multiplicationem, sed in necessitates potius fidelium domesticorum, et in usus pauperum, et opus rerum ęcclesiaticarum fideliter administrant, qui *unitatem spiritus in uinculo pacis* iuxta predictam sanctam formam *solliciti seruant* (Eph. 4: 3), et predicant, qui in ecclesie ministerio tamquam apostolico gradui succedentes sancte et pie ministrant ... Quid interest siue hec propria siue illa communia dicantur, si tamen hec que dicuntur propria clericorum, communia pro ratione temporum inueniantur et pauperum, et illa que dicuntur communia monachorum, ipso usu cotidie inueniantur propria singulorum?' Ibid., fo. 21.

⁵⁵ Ed. G. Constable and B. Smith (Oxford, 1972). This text, like Godwin's, survives only in one manuscript.

modern editors for his perception that 'the fundamental distinction was not between the orders of hermits, monks, and canons but between the strict, moderate, and lax groups within each order, and that the fundamental similarity, therefore, was between the similar tendencies in each order'.[56] This author did not exclude secular canons from his survey of the religious orders, and his comments concerning the similarity between the similar tendencies in each order was intended to include the seculars. His assertions are well supported by the evidence from Salisbury. The texts of spiritual and moral edification copied and composed there provide ample testimony that the Salisbury canons looked to the same sources for inspiration and guidance in their practice of the religious life as those used by monastic communities, and that the search for a life of apostolic perfection was as much a concern for them as it was for those more usually identified with the reform movements of the late eleventh and early twelfth centuries.

THE PRACTICE OF THE RELIGIOUS LIFE

Many aspects of the scholarly activities of the Salisbury canons can be interpreted as a practical application of their approach to the religious life. Their biblical studies indicate a particular concern for questions of morality and discipline, and the patristic literature they acquired to support such studies displays a predilection for tracts and treaties by Augustine which deal with specific questions which might arise in the practice of the Christian life by monks, canons, and the laity.[57] In this context, two issues stand out as being of particular interest to them: the regular reception of the sacraments in the practice of the Christian life, and a deeper concern to establish the validity of the orders of the clergy who were to administer them.[58]

---

[56] Ibid. xxiii.

[57] Such interests do not distinguish the Salisbury canons' practice of the religious life from that of the monastic orders. Those conservatives and reformers who attempted to distinguish between the monastic and canonical orders on the grounds that the former pursued the *vita contemplativa* and the latter the *vita activa*, were taking what was rapidly becoming an outdated standpoint: see G. Constable, *Monastic Tithes From their Origins to the Twelfth Century* (Cambridge, 1964), 136–97. Jerome's statement, 'sed alia ... Monachorum est causa, alia Clericorum. Clerici pascunt oves: ego pascor' (*Epistola xiv: ad Heliodorum: PL* 22. 352), no longer held good either in practice, or increasingly in the generally perceived ordering of Christian society. Monastic and clerical orders were becoming merged, and Christian society was becoming viewed as divided into just two orders: the clergy and the laity.

[58] Their interest in these two issues can be viewed as an early witness to a trend which took firm hold in the twelfth century: a sharpening of the distinction between the clergy and the laity, and associated with this, the placing of a greater emphasis on the mass and the other sacraments: see C. R. Cheney, *From Becket to Langton: English Church Government 1170–1213* (Manchester, 1956), 104–5.

There is evidence at Salisbury not only of an interest in the theological questions surrounding the doctrine of the Eucharist, a subject of widespread concern in the eleventh century, but also of a more practical emphasis on the central importance of the sacraments for all who live the Christian life. This emphasis is evident in the *Scala virtutum* in the interpretation of the two sides of the ladder of virtues as the sacraments, without which the rungs of the ladder are ascended in vain. Essentially the same message is promoted in another Salisbury book made a little earlier than the copy of the *Scala virtutum*: a glossed copy of the Pauline Epistles.[59] A gloss on Ephesians 13.18 ('You may be able to comprehend, with all the saints, what is the breadth and length and height and depth') offers an interpretation which expands upon that of Augustine, *De videndo Deo* (*Epistola* 147), xiv.[60] It follows Augustine's allegorical interpretation of the verse, as referring to the Cross, and then explains the moral sense: the breadth is the breadth of the Cross from right to left, which signifies love of God and love of neighbour; the length is the distance from Christ's feet to his head, which shows that love should not be something temporary; the height is the part of the Cross above Christ's head, which signifies that love is not confined to this world alone but lasts throughout eternity. Finally (a passage not derived from *De videndo Deo*, xiv), depth signifies the sacraments of the Church, and is added because width, length and height (i.e. eternal love of God and neighbour) profit nothing unless performed in conjunction with the sacraments.[61]

Associated with a greater emphasis on the sacraments came a concern to establish the validity of the orders of the clergy who were to administer them, and an interest in all aspects of clerical discipline. Such concerns were at the forefront of the reform movements of the eleventh and early twelfth centuries: questions of clerical discipline had been at the centre of the reform movement implemented, for example, in the Church in Normandy in the mid-eleventh-century synods of the Province of Rouen.[62] The Salisbury book collection is an important witness to the

---

[59] Oxford, Keble College, MS 22.

[60] *PL* 33.611.

[61] 'Quę sit latitudo et quid significet? Latitudo crucis Cristi dextra et sinistra. Quid longitudo? A pedibus usque ad caput Cristi. Quid sublimitas? Supra caput. Quid profundum? Sub pedibus. Dextra et sinistra, dilectionem Dei et proximi. Et ne dilectio sit ad horam, oportet ut addatur longanimitas. Et ne dilectio et longanimitas habeantur pro temporalibus, addenda est sublimitas, id est ut pro eterna uita sint. Sed quia illa tria nil prosint, nisi fiant in sacramentis ęcclesię, id est in baptismo etc., ideo addendum est profundum, quia sacramenta ęcclesię significat.' Keble 22, fo. 93.

[62] R. Foreville, 'The Synod of the Province of Rouen in the Eleventh and Twelfth Centuries', in *Church and Government in the Middle Ages: Essays Presented to C. R. Cheney on his Seventieth Birthday*, ed. C. N. L. Brooke, D. E. Luscombe, G. H. Martin, and D. Owen (Cambridge, 1976), 19–39, esp. 27–30.

introduction of such reforms to England.[63] The Salisbury canons' interest in such matters is evident not only in the third group of *sententiae* which form the *Scala virtutum* (discussed above) but also in other canon law texts which they acquired. It is an early twelfth-century Salisbury manuscript which contains our only surviving witness to the canons promulgated in 1064 at the Synod of Lisieux, one of the most important of the reforming synods of the Province of Rouen.[64] The Salisbury copy of Lanfranc's abbreviation of the pseudo-Isidorian Decretals and Canons of Councils also indicates a special interest in questions concerning the clergy.[65] One of the scribes who collaborated to produce books for Salisbury in the late eleventh century (Group I, scribe i), added a series of just over 300 subject headings in the margins of the manuscript. These marginal headings do not form a comprehensive subject index, but draw attention to passages of special interest to the annotator. About a third of them refer to matters of clerical discipline; a quarter of these are placed beside canons on the subject of clerical continence.

Unfortunately we do not know whether or how the interests revealed by the scribal and scholarly activities of the Salisbury canons were translated into the practical instruction of the local clergy and laity. For example, we lack evidence which would indicate whether the Salisbury canons or the clerics associated with Salisbury used texts such as the *Scala virtutum* and the *Meditationes Godwini* to deliver the precepts expressed in them to a wider audience. Neither text provides a systematic presentation of the pastoral office, or a programme of instruction for the clergy or laity. The earliest such manuals of pastoral instruction for the parochial clergy to have been produced in England are associated with the pastoral reform of the early thirteenth century, a reform movement which received formal expression at the fourth Lateran Council (1215).[66] Yet it is interesting to note that in this period as well, through the legislation of Bishop Richard Poore and the pastoral manuals of his archdeacon, Thomas Chobham, the diocese of Salisbury was in the

---

[63] For a study of the effect of one aspect of this reform movement elsewhere in England, see C. N. L. Brooke, 'Gregorian Reform in Action: Clerical Marriage in England, 1050–1200', *Cambridge Historical Journal*, 12 (1956), 1–21; repr. in his collected papers, *Medieval Church and Society* (London, 1971), 69–99.

[64] Cambridge, Trinity College, MS R.16.34. On this synod, see R. Foreville, 'Synod of the Province of Rouen', 29–30. The text of the canons is printed in L. Delisle, 'Canons du Concile tenu à Lisieux en 1064', *Journal des Savants*, 3: 66 (1901), 516–21, repr. in C. J. Hefele, *Histoire des Conciles*, tr. and ed. H. Leclercq (Paris, 1911), iv. 1420–3.

[65] Salisbury Cathedral, MS 78.

[66] For these pastoral manuals, see P. Michaud-Quantin, *Sommes de casuistique et manuels de confession au moyen âge (xii-xvi siècles)*, Analecta mediaevalia Namurcensia, xiii (Louvain, 1962), esp. 15–33.

forefront of pastoral reform in England.[67] Chobham's *Summa confessorum*, one of the most influential of the pastoral manuals produced in England, may even predate the Lateran Council,[68] whilst Poore's statutes represent the earliest, and most widely influential legislation which attempted to apply the Council's injunctions concerning pastoral reform to English pastoral conditions and needs.[69] Poore's statutes are concerned primarily with the conduct and training of priests, and their tenor is decidedly practical. It was Poore's expressed intention that they should be used not only for reference purposes but also as a handbook in the exercise of the pastoral care:

ut sacerdotes, ipsas frequenter habentes pre oculis, in ministeriis et dispensationibus sacramentorum sint instructiores et in fide (recta) catholica bene vivendo firmiores.[70]

It is tempting to speculate that the pragmatism reflected in Poore's statutes and Chobham's *Summa confessorum* may have owed something to the practical character of the scholarly interests of the early cathedral chapter at Salisbury.

THE 'D.M.' ANNOTATOR

Although we lack direct evidence that the Salisbury canons themselves engaged in pastoral activity, the Salisbury books do demonstrate that at least one scribe and scholar at Salisbury put his scholarly interests to practical use in his activity as an annotator.

His annotations consist of *nota* marks in the form 'D.M.' added in the margins of twenty-five of the Salisbury books.[71] Nota marks in the form

[67] See V. A. Gillespie, 'The Literary Form of the Middle English Pastoral Manual with Particular Reference to the *Speculum christiani* and Some Related texts', D.Phil. thesis (Oxford University, 1981), 9–12, 98–102.

[68] Ibid. 98–102.

[69] C. R. Cheney, *English Synodalia of the Thirteenth Century* (Oxford, 1941), 51–89; reissued with a new introduction (Oxford, 1968). See also, C. R. Cheney, 'The Earliest English Diocesan Statutes', *EHR* 75 (1960), 1–29; repr. with an additional note in *The English Church and its Laws 12th-14th Centuries* (London, 1982). For the texts, see *Councils and Synods*, ii. ed. F. M. Powicke and C. R. Cheney, i. 57–96.

[70] *Councils and Synods*, ii. i. 96.

[71] They occur in the following manuscripts (I have recorded the text or texts in which the annotations occur): Aberdeen University Library, MS 216 (Bede on the Apocalypse; Victorinus on the Apocalypse); Oxford, Bodl. Libr., MSS Bodley 392 (Sermons of Caesarius and Eusebius 'Gallicanus'), Bodley 444 (Isidore, *De ortu et obitu patrum*), Bodley 756 (Ambrosiaster on the Pauline Epistles), Bodley 765 (Augustine, *De mendacio*, *Contra mendacium*, *De cura pro mortuis gerenda*; Cyprian on the Lord's Prayer; Ambrose, *Epistola* 140), Bodley 768 (Ambrose, *De viduis*, *De virginitate*, *Exhortatio virginitatis*, *De lapsu virginis consecratae*, *De mysteriis*, *De sacramentis*), Bodley 835 (Ambrose, *De benedictionibus patriarcharum*, *De paenitentia*, *De excessu fratris*), Rawlinson C. 723

'D.M.' or 'd.m.' appear not uncommonly in twelfth-century books from centres elsewhere in England and also in other twelfth-century Salisbury manuscripts in a number of different hands. However, the work of this particular Salisbury annotator is unusual and worthy of special attention because of the extent of his activity, both in terms of the number of books he annotated and also the extent to which many of the individual texts have been annotated.

All the annotations of this Salisbury scribe occur in books produced for Salisbury in the late eleventh century as part of the first phase of scribal activity, with just two exceptions: Salisbury Cathedral, MS 158, an imported book, and Salisbury Cathedral, MS 198, probably one of the earliest of the Group II books. Because Salisbury Cathedral, MS 198 is the only Group II book to have been marked by this annotator, it seems likely that he undertook his annotating activity before most of the Group II books had been produced. It is difficult to identify any scribe on the basis of just two letters, but there is evidence to suggest that his work may be more closely identified as being that of one of the Group I scribes: the scribe-corrector, scribe i. N. R. Ker put forward this suggestion on the grounds that the books he annotated were, for the most part, the books in which this hand occurs as a corrector.[72] Ker also observed that the forms of the letters **D** and **M** are similar to those letter forms in the hand of scribe i, although he warned that these two letters alone are not sufficient to identify the hand. There is, however, further evidence which supports Ker's tentative suggestion. In Salisbury Cathedral, MS 198, in one place the annotation is expanded to 'D. Memoria'; and although none of the distinctive letter forms of scribe i's hand is present, the handwriting does look similar to that of scribe i. Furthermore, a close examination of the annotations in those books corrected by scribe i, the colour of the ink of both the annotations and the corrections is always the same, which suggests that both annotation

(Jerome on Ezekiel); Salisbury Cathedral, MSS 10 (Cassian, *Collationes*), 24 (Jerome on Jeremaiah), 25 (Jerome on Isaiah), 37 (Bede on Luke), 67 (Augustine on the Gospel of John), 78 (Lanfranc's abbreviation of the pseudo-Isidorian Decretals and Canons of Councils), 88 (Augustine, *Retractationes*), 106 (Augustine, *De doctrina christiana, Sermo 37, De octo quaestionibus Dulcitii*), 128 (Augustine, *De adulterinis coniugiis, De natura et origine animae*), 129 (Pseudo-Augustine (Ambrosiaster), *Quaestiones cxxvii*), 135 (Isidore, *Quaestiones super vetus testamentum*), 140 (Ambrose, *De fide, De spiritu sancto*), 154 (Amalarius, *Liber officialis*), 158 (Bede, *De temporum ratione*), 159 (Origen on Exodus and Leviticus), 165 (Pseudo-Methodius, *Revelationes*; Bede, *De tabernaculo*), 198 (Augustine, *Epistola 147, De fide et symbolo, Sermo 180, De agone christiano, Epistola 130, Epistola ad diversos, Sermo 291, De urbis excidio, Epistola 127*, eight sermons, *Epistola 228. vii, Ad inquisitiones Ianuarii, De cura pro mortuis gerenda*). For a specimen of these annotations, see Pl. 2.

[72] Ker, 'Beginnings', 33. Dr M. B. Parkes independently formed the same opinion (personal communication).

and correction were executed at the same time by the same scribe. This is seen most clearly in Oxford, Bodleian Library, MS Bodley 756, in which both the corrections of scribe i and the **D.M.** annotations are in the same distinctive pale reddish brown ink. Furthermore, we have positive evidence that scribe i did make annotations, since it was he who added the marginal subject headings in the Salisbury copy of Lanfranc's canon law collection (Salisbury Cathedral, MS 78), a manuscript in which the **D.M.** annotations also occur.

For the most part, the annotator added the **D.M.** annotations to copies of patristic *originalia*. In this context, such annotations had a specific function: to identify *sententiae* as *auctoritates*—texts which could be excerpted from their immediate context within the works of an *auctor*, and employed elsewhere as authoritative in their own right.[73] This specific function is also implied by the particular *notae* employed by the Salisbury annotator: **D.M.** standing for *dignum memoria*—worthy of memory.[74] To consign something to memory meant more than a purely mental exercise to the medieval reader; it implied the will to put what had been memorized into practice. The phrase 'dignum memoria' is remarkably similar to that used in the definition of an *auctoritas* given by Hugutio of Pisa in his *Magnae derivationes*: 'Auctoritas: id est sententia digna imitatione',[75] by which he meant imitation not only in literature but also in life. The activity of consigning *sententiae* to memory was part of a spiritual process, as well as an intellectual one, a process closely associated with the activities of *lectio* and *meditatio*. The reading of sacred texts as a spiritual activity involved meditating upon them; meditation meant to learn by heart, and in its turn, to learn by heart implied the will to put what had been learned into practice.

But such activity could have further implications. The practice of what had been consigned to memory could involve not only living it in one's own life but teaching it to others. Several of the passages noted by the annotator exhort priests and clerics to use their learning in order to teach others. For example, in the copy of Lanfranc's canon law collection the annotator noted the following passage:

Ignorantia, mater cunctorum errorum maxime in sacerdotibus dei uitanda est, qui docendi officium in populis susceperunt. Sacerdotes enim legere sanctas scripturas frequenter admonet Paulus apostolus, dicens ad Timotheum, 'Intende

---

[73] For this definition of *auctoritates*, and for their function, see M.-D. Chenu, *Introduction à l'étude de s. Thomas d'Aquin* (Paris, 1954), 109–13.

[74] The annotation is written out in full in a 12th-cent. manuscript from elsewhere in England, Oxford, University College, MS 191, fos. 115 and 121, see N. R. Ker, 'Salisbury Cathedral Manuscripts', 154 n. 3.

[75] Quoted by M. B. Parkes, 'The Influence of the Concepts of *Ordinatio* and *Compilatio* on the Development of the Book', in *Medieval Learning and Literature: Essays Presented to Richard William Hunt*, ed. J. J. G. Alexander and M. T. Gibson (Oxford, 1976), 116, n.1.

lectioni, exhortationi, doctrine' (1 Tim. 4: 13); semper mane in his. Sciant igitur sacerdotes scripturas sanctas et canones meditentur, ut omne opus eorum in predicatione et doctrina consistat, atque edificent cunctos tam fidei scientia quam operum disciplina.[76]

It may be that the annotator was marking such passages only for his own benefit, but it is possible that he was also directing the attention of others at Salisbury to them.

The annotator's activity indicates a process of selection, but it does not appear to have been systematic. I have not been able to discover any one criterion which accounts for all of his choices of *sententiae.* Nevertheless, certain preferences and special interests emerge.

An interest in pastoral problems and pastoral activity appears to lie behind the noting of many *sententiae.* For example, in a copy of Ambrosiaster's commentary on the Pauline Epistles the annotator notes Paul's exhortations to teachers to instruct the people in the faith, and to the faithful to carry out good works; and his instructions on specific moral questions, such as marriage, adultery and divorce. A concern to discover patristic teaching on difficult moral questions is particularly evident in the annotations added to a copy of Augustine, *De adulterinis coniugiis,* a closely argued text which expounds the various Gospel and Pauline passages concerned with the circumstances under which separation may be permissible, but that remarriage after separation is not permissible, whatever the circumstances. In the following passage (from the beginning of 1. vii), the annotator has noted each of the stages in the argument.

D.M. Porro beatus apostolus, immo per apostolum dominus, quia mulierem non permittit a uiro non fornicante discedere, restat ut eam prohibeat, si discesserit, nubere, quam permittit a fornicante discedere. De qua enim dicitur: si a uiro discesserit, non nubat (cf. 1 Cor. 7: 11); ea conditione discedere permittitur, ut non nubat. Si ergo elegerit non nubere, non est cur prohibeatur discedere.

D.M. Sicut illa de qua dicitur: Si se non continent, nubant (1 Cor. 7: 9), hac utique conditione non continere permittetur, ut tamen nubat. Si ergo elegerit nubere, cogi non potest continere.

D.M. Sicut ergo ista incontinens compellitur nubere, ut possit quod non continet non esse damnabile, sic a uiro illa discedens, innupta conpellitur permanere, ut possit quod discedit non esse culpabile.

D.M. Culpabiliter autem a uiro non fornicante discedit, etiam si innupta permanserit.[77]

The first two annotations note the analogy made between the case of a woman who is allowed to depart from her husband on the grounds of

[76] Salisbury Cathedral, MS 78, fo. 144ᵛ.
[77] Salisbury Cathedral, MS 128, fo. 7.

adultery if she does not remarry, with the case of a woman who is allowed to give up the practice of continence on condition that she does marry. The third annotation marks the *sententia* which sums up this analogy. The fourth annotation marks a new stage in the argument: a woman who leaves her husband without the grounds of adultery is doing wrong, even if she does not remarry.

In copies of commentaries on books of the Bible, it is passages of tropological rather than allegorical or mystical interpretation which have been noted, as, for example, in the following passage from Jerome's commentary on Ezekiel: 7–9:

Et introduxit me ad hostium atrii, et uidi, et ecce foramen unum in pariete; et dixit ad me: Fili hominis, fode parietem; et cum per fodissem parietem, apparuit ostium unum. Et dixit ad me: Ingredere, et uide abominationes pessimas quas isti faciunt hic. Hoc quod transtuli: *Et uidi, et ecce foramen unum in pariete*, in Septuaginta non habetur. Et quia omnia quasi in imagine picturaque monstrantur, unum in pariete foramen uidisse se dicit, iubereque sibi ut illud perfodiat, et amplius faciat, quo uidelicet aperto foramine latius possit intrare et uidere quę foris positus uidere non poterat.

D.M. Per quod ostenditur, tam in ęcclesiis quam in singulis nobis, per parua uitia maiora monstrari, et quasi per quędam foramina ad abominationes maximas perueniri: *Ex fructibus* enim *arbor agnoscitur*, et *ex abundantia cordis os loquitur.* Pro signo est interioris hominis uerborum potentia,

D.M. quomodo libidinosum qui sua callide celat uitia, interdum turpis sermo demonstrat, et auaritiam latentem intrinsecus paruulę rei cupido significat: minoribus enim maiora monstrantur, uultuque et oculis dissimulari non potest conscientia dum luxuriosa et lasciuia mens lucet in facie, et secreta cordis motu corporis et gestibus indicantur.[78]

This passage contains Jerome's commentary on Ezekiel's account of his vision of the abominations in the temple, and the instruction to Ezekiel to dig through to the door in the wall on order to see the abominations within. The annotator notes Jerome's tropological explanation: first, the general point, that the small faults that one can see on the outside are an indication of greater faults lying within; and then the annotator notes the passage which gives more specific examples, for example: desire for a little thing indicates hidden avarice within.

An emphasis on moral teaching is particularly evident in the annotations added to a copy of the sermons of Caesarius and Eusebius 'Gallicanus' (Oxford, Bodl. Libr., MS Bodley 392): a manuscript which is one of the most heavily annotated of all the Salisbury books. Several of these sermons are addressed to monks, but the *sententiae* chosen by the annotator are, for the most part, concerned with points of practical morality and discipline, appropriate for all forms of Christian life,

---

[78] Oxford, Bodl. Libr., MS Rawlinson C. 723, fo. 25ᵛ.

religious or lay (the sorts of themes which recur in the *Scala virtutum* and the *Meditationes Godwini*), rather than the contemplative or mystical aspects associated with monastic spirituality. For example, in the following passage from Eusebius 'Gallicanus', *Homilia* xxxix (one of his *Sermones ad monachos*), the annotator notes several *sententiae* all on the theme that ascetic observances or poverty are of no value of themselves, unless they are performed in the right spirit.

D.M. Et ideo hunc sibi specialiter modum religiosus debet imponere: ut tantum habeat quantum necessitas poscit, non quantum cupiditas concupiscit. Habendi enim amor, nisi ad integrum resecetur, ardentior est in paruis et plus torquet in minimis;

D.M. et, nisi ex corde pauper sis atque affectu, paupertas ipsa non uirtus sed miseria iudicanda est. Nouerimus itaque, fratres, nichil prodesse si carnem nostram ieiuniis ac uigiliis affligamus, et mentem nostram non emendemus aut quę interiora sunt non curemus.

D.M. Quid prodest afflictio corporalis, si linguam nequitiis et obtrectationibus polluamus? Nonne omnes labores nostri in nichilum rediguntur? nonne opus nostrum uelut fumus atque umbra euanescit et uelut stupę fauilla in nichilum redigitur? O quanti et quam diuturni labores subito pereunt! quanta bona frequenter, iam adquisita ac reposita, de manu rapiuntur, dum id, quod adquirere studemus, custodire negligimus!

D.M. Quapropter gratis nobis de cruce et corporis afflictione blandimur, si exterior homo noster sanctis laboribus exercetur, et a passionibus non curatur interior; sic est: quomodo si aliquis statuam faciat a foris auream ab intus luteam; uel quomodo si domus, magnifica arte constructa, a foris pulcherrimis coloribus depicta uideatur, et ab intus serpentibus atque scorpionibus plena sit.

D.M. Quid prodest quod affligis corpus tuum, quando nichil proficit cor tuum? Valde dura et nimis dolenda conditio: omni intentione studium laboris impendere, et fructum non recipere post laborem.

D.M. Ieiunare, et uigilare, et mores non corrigere, sic est: quomodo si aliquis extra uineam aut circa uineam extirpet et colat, uineam autem ipsam desertam atque incultam derelinquat, ut spinas ac tribulos germinet, quę insistente cultore iocundissimos ex se fructus proferrre potuisset.[79]

It is possible that some of the annotations might have had a further practical application, by identifying suitable material for sermons. Several of the annotations mark *sententiae* which introduce *exempla* (stories which give practical illustrations of points of moral teaching). For example, in a copy of the *Collationes* of Cassian, the annotator noted five *exempla* in *Collatio* ii, which illustrate the need for discretion and moderation in the practice of asceticism.

The identity of the annotator cannot be established with any certainty. N. R. Ker suggested that the scribe might be Bishop Osmund,[80] and

---

[79] Oxford, Bodl. Libr., MS Bodley 392, fo. 7.
[80] 'Beginnings', 33–4.

certainly the concerns displayed by the annotations would have been exercised by any conscientious bishop who sought to follow the ideals expressed in the *Cura pastoralis* of Gregory the Great. But an alternative, and perhaps more likely, candidate, is an archdeacon, the official whose responsibility it was to carry out the bishop's will regarding clerical discipline in the diocese.[81] The first few decades after the Norman Conquest are marked by a rapid proliferation of such officials.[82]

The names of four archdeacons from Salisbury are known from the late eleventh century (the period associated with the first phase of book production, during which scribe i was active): Gunter of Le Mans, Robert, Everard of Calne, and Hubald.[83] Gunter may be discounted, since by 1085 he had become abbot of Thorney, having already been a monk of Battle Abbey.[84] It is also unlikely that the scribe annotator is Everard of Calne, since he was still associated with Salisbury in 1115, and possibly until his election as bishop of Norwich soon after 13 March 1121.[85] If he was scribe i, then it is odd that he did not take part at all in the second phase of scribal activity which took place in the first couple of decades of the twelfth century. Nothing is known of the archdeacon Robert, except that his name occurs in connection with a church in Berkshire on 14 March 1089.

Archdeacon Hubald stands out as the most likely candidate. The dates for which he is associated with Salisbury correspond with the period of scribe i's activity.[86] He also possessed the relevant intellectual skills indicated by the correcting and annotating activity of this scribe.[87] He had almost certainly studied in the schools of northern France, since William of Malmesbury tells us that he was 'vir qui liberalium artium non

[81] For the duties of archdeacons in the post-Conquest period until the end of the reign of Henry I, see M. Brett, *The English Church under Henry I* (Oxford, 1975), 204–9.

[82] For evidence concerning the presence of archdeacons in England before the Conquest, and for their introduction to England after 1066, see C. N. L. Brooke, 'The Archdeacon and the Norman Conquest', in *Tradition and Change: Essays in Honour of Marjorie Chibnall*, ed. D. Greenway, C. Holdsworth, and J. Sayers (Cambridge, 1985), 1–19.

[83] Greenway, *Fasti*, iv, list 6.

[84] D. Knowles, C. N. L. Brooke, and V. C. M. London (eds.), *The Heads of Religious Houses: England and Wales 940–1216* (Cambridge, 1972), 74.

[85] *Regesta regum Anglo-Normannorum 1066–1154*, ii, ed. C. Johnson and H. A. Cronne (Oxford, 1956), nos. 981 and 1089; *Fasti Ecclesiae Anglicanae 1066–1300, ii: Monastic Cathedrals*, ed. D. Greenway (London, 1971), 55–6.

[86] He was archdeacon at some time between 1078 × 99—during Osmund's pontificate, see William of Malmesbury, *GP* 429–31. Eadmer refers to him as archdeacon in relation to Wilton in 1100: *Historia novorum in Anglia*, ed. M. Rule, RS (London, 1884), 123. However, the date of his death is uncertain. It is possible that he, like Everard of Calne, may have been present at Salisbury for much of the first quarter of the 12th cent., in which case, the same objections might apply as for Everard. He had certainly died by *c.*1122.

[87] For the scholarly abilities and interests demonstrated by scribe i's activities as a corrector, see above, Ch. 1.

exiguum experimentum cepisset', although his powers of communication were hindered by a bad stammer: 'pro titubantia oris parum eas audientibus expediret.'[88] It is tempting to speculate that Hubald compensated for his difficulties in oral expression with his ability with the quill, acting not only as scribe but also as director of book-production, corrector, and annotator.

[88] *GP* 429.

CONCLUSION

THE book collection of the Salisbury canons is an early and somewhat unusual witness to the so-called twelfth-century renaissance. It provides us with the earliest English examples of several important elements in this renaissance: a renewed interest in the works of the patristic and classical *auctores*, the consultation of such works for reference purposes, and a more ratiocinative scrutiny of the text of Scripture. Many of the patristic texts and all of the classical texts copied at Salisbury in this period are the earliest English copies to have survived. Moreover, Salisbury provides us with some of the earliest manuscript evidence from anywhere in Europe, of the new methods which were being applied to the study of the Bible: Oxford, Keble College, MS 22 is one of the earliest extant copies of the Pauline Epistles which contains glosses reflecting the application of the techniques of grammar, rhetoric, and logic to the study of the sacred page; whilst Salisbury Cathedral, MS 160 is one of the earliest extant copies of a Psalter commentary which employs the literary *accessus* in its prologue.

On the Continent such studies and interests stimulated further developments in methods of scholarship. *Auctoritates* culled from the works of the Fathers or the works of classical Antiquity were compiled into vast systematic compendia or *summae*, organized by topic to facilitate reference. Questions of theology or doctrine which emerged from the study of the sacred page were taken out of their context within the *ordo narrationis* of the Bible, and were studied as independent topics. The techniques of logic were employed no longer merely to aid the understanding of the structure of the argument presented by an *auctor* concerning a particular question but also to speculate further upon the question itself.

There is little evidence, however, that developments in scholastic method were so advanced at Salisbury during the twelfth century. The canons seem to have preserved the traditional method of study, following the *ordo narrationis* of the Bible. There is no evidence that their interest in individual theological problems led them to compile *summae* of *auctoritates* extracted from their immediate context within the works of the patristic and classical *auctores*, and rearranged by topic. I have not yet found any evidence which would indicate speculative thinking: the canons appear to have continued to rely upon the works of the Fathers for authoritative answers to doctrinal questions. The difference between the scholarly activities of the Salisbury canons and those of scholars on the Continent, seems to have been one of attitude rather than aptitude. The Salisbury canons appear to have been men of practical interests and abilities. The applications of their intellectual skills were more characteristic of pastors and administrators than of speculative thinkers.

None the less, intellectual interests and activities at Salisbury were more akin to those of the twelfth-century schools of northern France than those of the indigenous English intellectual tradition. For example, R. W. Southern has shown that one of England's most important contributions to the twelfth-century renaissance was in the sphere of historical writing,[1] but there is no evidence of an interest in history at Salisbury: Salisbury, as a post-Conquest foundation, had no history of its own to write about, nor ancient rights to defend.

In some respects the achievements of the early community at Salisbury formed an important legacy for pastors and scholars of the thirteenth century. It may be no coincidence that the earliest evidence of pastoral reform in England in the thirteenth century, comes from Salisbury, in the shape of the *Statutes* of Bishop Richard Poore, and the pastoral manuals of Thomas Chobham. I have speculated that something of the spirit of pragmatism of the early community (exhibited, for example, by the *Meditationes* of Godwin), had lived on at Salisbury to influence Richard Poore and Thomas Chobham in their writings.

More tangible evidence of the legacy of the early community to the community at Salisbury in the thirteenth century is provided by the book collection itself. When, in the early thirteenth century, the cathedral community moved from Old Sarum to its present site, the book collection was transferred as well. Annotations added to the margins of the books bear witness to the usefulness of the collection to scholars at Salisbury in the later Middle Ages. (For an example, see Pl. 8: the marginal annotations in this early twelfth-century copy of Rufinus on the Apostles' Creed are in a thirteenth-century hand.) The thirteenth century witnessed a renewed interest in patristic *originalia* (i.e. the works of the Fathers in full and in their immediate proper context).[2] This interest engendered throughout Europe a new spate of copying the works of the Fathers. Volumes were compiled which contained as many texts of a single author as possible, often constructed from independent booklets each containing one or more texts of that author.[3] Small handwriting and

---

[1] R. W. Southern, 'The Place of England in the Twelfth Century Renaissance', *History*, 45 (1960), 201–16; repr. with some alterations in his collected papers, *Medieval Humanism* (Oxford, 1970), 158–80.

[2] See J. de Ghellinck, '"Originale" et "Originalia"', *Bulletin du Cange*, 14 (1939), 95–105.

[3] M. B. Parkes, 'The Influence of the Concepts of *Ordinatio* and *Compilatio* on the Development of the Book', in *Medieval Learning and Literature: Essays Presented to Richard William Hunt*, ed. J. J. G. Alexander and M. T. Gibson (Oxford, 1976), 123–4.

numerous abbreviations enabled these volumes to be small enough to be used for personal study and reference purposes.

Yet the Salisbury canons of the thirteenth century had little need to supplement or replace the book collection formed by the cathedral community in the late eleventh and early twelfth centuries.[4] Indeed, the copies of the Fathers produced by the first community at Salisbury, in particular the volumes containing collections of Augustine's shorter treatises, in their composition, format, size of handwriting, and numerous abbreviations, are perhaps more comparable with the compendia of patristic *originalia* produced in the thirteenth century than with the stately volumes of patristic texts produced elsewhere in England in the late eleventh and twelfth centuries.

During the thirteenth century Salisbury Cathedral's reputation flourished: the organization of its chapter and the pattern of its liturgy were widely imitated and adopted elsewhere in England. Closely linked to the growing fame of the cathedral church itself, was the promotion of the founder of the first formal community there—Bishop Osmund. As early as the second half of the twelfth century, the name of Osmund was being associated with newly established practices at Salisbury, and the first (unsuccessful) process of canonization of Osmund was initiated by Richard Poore in 1228.[5] But, although tradition has falsely attributed to Osmund and the early community at Old Sarum much that only emerged during the twelfth and early thirteenth centuries, such attributions acknowledge the debt owed by the cathedral and chapter at Salisbury to their founder. The books produced by Osmund and the first canons of Salisbury Cathedral survive as our best witness to that legacy.

[4] The medieval book collection which remains at Salisbury contains only two thirteenth-century compendia of patristic texts (Salisbury Cathedral, MSS 66 and 100).

[5] Greenway, 'The False *Institutio*', 93–4.

APPENDIX 1

GROUP I MANUSCRIPTS: TEXTS AND SCRIBES

1. Aberdeen, University Library, MS 216 (fo. 1) Bede on the Apocalypse (*Clavis*, 1363);[1] (fo. 28) Jerome's recension of Victorinus on the Apocalypse (*Clavis*, 80)[2]
     Scribe i (fo. 36/1–11; corrections); scribe x (fos. 1–35ᵛ)

2. Dublin, Trinity College, MS 174, fos. 1–44ᵛ, 52–6, 95–103ᵛ,[3] (fo. 1) Miracula s. Andreae, auct. Gregorio Turonensis (*BHL* 430); (fo. 9) Passio s. Andreae (*BHL* 429); (fo. 10) Laudatio s. Lucae (*BHL* 4973, preceded by *BHL* 4973d); (fo. 12ᵛ) Vita et Passio s. Barnabae (*BHL* 985); (fo. 16) 'Sermo s. Augustini de s. Vincentio' (Augustine, *Sermo* 276: *PL* 38. 1255–7); (fo. 16ᵛ) 'Item alius sermo. Vincentii martiris sancti fortissimam et gloriosissimam passionem . . .'; (fo. 17) Revelatio s. Stephani (*BHL* 7854); (fo. 19ᵛ) Passio ss. Euphemiae et Sostenis ac Victoris (*BHL* 2708); (fo. 21) Passio martyrum Didimi et Theodorae virginis (*BHL* 8072); (fo. 22ᵛ) Passio s. Luceiae virginis (*BHL* 4980c); (fo. 23ᵛ) Passio ss. Spei et Fidei et Caritatis et matris earum Sapientiae (*BHL* 2970); (fo. 26) Passio s. Teclae (cf. *BHL* 8020a); (fo. 30) Passio s. Afrae (cf. *BHL* 109); (fo. 32ᵛ) Vita et conversatio s. Eupraxiae (*BHL* 2718); (fo. 41ᵛ) Passio ss. Victoris et Coronae (*BHL* 8561); (fo. 43ᵛ) Passio s. Crispinae (*BHL* 1989); (fo. 44) Passio Theodotae et filiorum eius (*BHL* 8096); (fo. 52) Miracula s. Nicholai (*BHL* 6190); (fo. 95) 'Sermo s. Augustini in natale s. Stephani protomartyris' (Augustine, Sermo *app.* 217: *PL* 39. 2147–9); (fo. 96) 'Cuius supra de eodem martire' (Augustine, *Sermo* 316: *PL* 38. 1431–4; (fo. 97) 'Item sermo de eodem martire' (Augustine, *Sermo* 382: *PL* 39. 1684–6); (fos. 98ᵛ–103ᵛ) 'Item sermo s. Augustini de s. Stephano. Quotienscumque caritatem uestram secundum preceptum domini . . .' (Caesarius, *Sermo* ccxx)[4]
     Scribe ii (fo. 54ʳ⁻ᵛ, fos. 95–103ᵛ), scribe v (fos. 1–11/6, fos. 12ᵛ–17/25, fos. 19ᵛ/ 33–28ᵛ/28), and two unidentified hands

3. London, BL, MS Cotton Tiberius C I, Additions to a Pontifical:[5] (fo. 93) Order of benediction of a monk; (fo. 111ᵛ) Canons promulgated after the Battle of Hastings;[6] (fo. 112ᵛ) Orders of benediction of an abbot, consecration of a virgin,

---

[1] Begins imperfectly in the Preface 'in preceptis habemus ut percepta talenta . . .' (*PL* 93. 133).
[2] This copy, like the three later English copies noted by J. Haussleiter, belongs to the CB version of the text: *Victorini episcopi Petavionensis opera*, CSEL 49 (Vienna/Leipzig, 1916), lxix–lxxii.
[3] A composite manuscript made up of a number of booklets. Some booklets are in the hands of Group I scribes, others are in the hands of Group II scribes. Group II scribes also made additions to booklets begun by Group I scribes.   [4] CCSL 104. 871–3.
[5] For these additions, see Ker, 'Three Old English Texts', 262–79.
[6] See *Councils and Synods with Other Documents Relating to the English Church I*, ed. D. Whitelock, M. Brett, and C. N. L. Brooke (Oxford, 1981), ii. 583–4.

and benediction of an abbess; (fo. 116ᵛ) Three prayers and a form of benediction at the enthronement of a bishop

Scribe i (fos. 112ᵛ–13ᵛ: rubrics); scribe iii (fos. 112ᵛ/11–116ᵛ/11: text); scribe iv (fos. 111ᵛ/22–112ᵛ/7; fos. 113ᵛ–16ᵛ: rubrics; fos. 116ᵛ/14–117: text and rubrics); scribe v (fos. 93/18–95)

4. London, BL, MS Cotton Vitellius A XII, fos. 4–71[7] (fo. 4ᵛ) *Dialogus Egberti*;[8] (fo. 8) Abbo of Fleury, *De differentia circuli et sperae*;[9] (fo. 10ᵛ) 'Incipit prologus Rabani peritissimi viri ad Gildam magistrum suum, sed opus est Gilde ...' (Rhabanus, *De computo*);[10] (fo. 40ᵛ) Misc. scientific texts:[11] (i) (fo. 40ᵛ) 'Versus de xii mensibus anni. Id circo certis ...' (ii) (fo. 41) 'Tetrasticon autenticum, de singulis mensibus. Hic iani mensis ...' (iii) (fo. 41ᵛ) 'Versus de singulis mensibus. Primus Romanas ordiris ... (iv) (fo. 41ᵛ) 'Versus de mensibus et signis xii. Dira patet iani ...' (v) (fo. 42) 'Versus de duodecim signis. Primus adest Aries ... ludere pisces' (vi) (fo. 42) 'Versus de cursu anni. Bissena mensium uertigine ...' (vii) (fo. 42ᵛ) 'De octo tramitibus circuli decennouennalis. Linea Criste tuos ...' (viii) (fo. 42ᵛ) 'Versus de septem dierum uo(ca)bulis. Prima dies Phẹbi ... (ix) (fo. 42ᵛ) 'De septem miraculis manu factis. Primum capitolium Romẹ saluum ... tam mirabilis ediaicii.' (x) (fo. 43) 'De duobus uerticibus mundi. Duo sunt extremi ...' (xi) (fo. 44) 'De diebus egyptiacis. Hos dies maxime obseruare debemus ... sed isti tres per omnia obseruandi sunt.' (xii) (fo. 44ᵛ) 'Incipit ordo librorum catholicorum in circulo anni legendorum. In prima in lxx ponunt eptaticum ... usque in lxxam.' (xiii) (fo. 44ᵛ) 'De uocibus litterarum. Omnes uero litterẹ a similitudine uocis caracteres acceperunt. A. Subhiato ore ... dum exprimitur imitatur.' (xiv) (fo. 45) Greek and Hebrew alphabets with interpretations, 'A alfa, agricola ... T Tau, errauit uel consummauit' (xv) (fo. 45ᵛ) A list of numbers with the Greek words for them, written in three columns 'A mia. i ... Ψ Niacusin. dccc; Chile ... Christus. xps; Alfa ... Eneacoses' (xvi) (fo. 45ᵛ) 'Si uis scire concurrentes ... In septimo decimo anno epactẹ xv concurrentes ii' (xvii) (fo. 46) 'De sex etatibus hominis. Prima infantia, vii annos tenet ... quẹ millum certum numerum annorum tenet'; (fo. 46) 'Incipit liber Gilde peritissimi de natura rerum. Domino et filio [ ] salutem. Dum te prestantem ... Finiunt expositiones numero quadraginta nouem.' (Isidore, *De natura rerum*: *Clavis*, 1188); (fo. 63ᵛ) 'Tres filii Noe diuiserunt orbem ... Iaphet in europa', followed by an Isidorian world diagram; (fo. 64ʳ⁻ᵛ) '℥ Ascorpione ... Signa in quibus singuli planetarum

---

[7] The items on fos. 10ᵛ–65 occur, with minor differences in order, in Exeter Cathedral, MS 3507, see Ker, *MMBL* (Oxford, 1977), ii. 813–14.

[8] *Councils and Ecclesiastical Documents relating to Great Britain and Ireland*, ed. A. W. Haddan and W. Stubbs (Oxford, 1871), iii. 403–13. This manuscript is the only extant witness to the text.

[9] See A. van de Vyver, 'Les Œvres inédites d'Abbon de Fleury'. *Rev. bén.*, 47 (1935), 140–1.

[10] CCCM 44. 199–321. For this manuscript, see ibid. 194.

[11] For nos. i–iii, v–viii, see H. Walther, *Initia carminum ac versuum medii aevi posterioris latinorum*, Carmina Medii Aevi Posterioris Latina, 1 (Göttingen, 1959), nos. 8654, 7988a, 14678, 14646, 2187, 10329, 14566; for nos. iii, v, vi, viii, see *Anthologia latina, Pars prior: Carmina in codicibus scripta*, ed. A. Riese (Leipzig, 1906), ii. nos. 639, cf. 615, 680, 488; for no. x see L. Thorndike and P. Kibre, *A Catalogue of Incipits of Mediaeval Scientific Writings in Latin*, 2nd edn (London, 1963), col. 473, cf. A. van de Vyver, 'Les Œvres inédites', 140.

morentur scies . . . ad quas sol numquam accedit'; (fo. 65) Three runic alphabets;[12] (fos. 65ᵛ–71) Calendar[13]

Scribe viii (fos. 4ᵛ–71)

5. London, BL, MS Royal 5 E xvi (fo. 1) Pseudo-Augustine, *De unitate sanctae Trinitatis* (*Clavis*, 379);[14] (fo. 1ᵛ) A compendium of extracts in dialogue format from Isidore, *De differentiis* and *Libri etymologiarum*, 'Inter Deum et dominum quid interest? Responsio. Hoc interest, ut in Dei appellatione patrem . . . Uictimę uero sacrificia.' (fo. 19ᵛ) Isidore, *De miraculis Christi* (*Clavis*, 1198)[15]

Scribe ii (rubrics); text in an unidentified hand

6. London, BL, MS Royal 5 E xix, fos. 1–20 (fo. 1) Isidore, *Liber synonymorum* (*Clavis*, 1203); (fo. 18ᵛ) Two homilies (i) 'Non est graue Theodore cadere luctantem . . .'[16] (ii) (fo. 19ᵛ) 'Fratres karissimi habemus a domino Deo nostro exemplum uerę humilitatis . . .'[17]

Scribe i (fo. 18ᵛ/12–22; fos. 19/30–37; fo. 19ᵛ/34–20ᵛ); scribe iii (fo. 6/4–37); scribe iv (fos. 18ᵛ/22–19/18; fo. 19ᵛ/1–33); scribe vi (fo. 19/19–30); scribe vii (fos. 1–6/4; fos. 6ᵛ–18ᵛ/10)

7. London, BL, MS Royal 5 E xix, fos. 21–36, Twelve homilies from the Homiliary of St-Père de Chartres (nos. 76, 1, 2, end of 27 (folio missing), 77, 29, 34, 36, 39 (beginning only), 37, 52, 53).[18]

Scribe i (fos. 21ᵛ–23/17; fo. 25ᵛ–26; fo. 28ᵛ/18–32; fos. 34/15–35/20); scribe vii (fo. 21; fos. 23/18–25; fos. 26ᵛ–28ᵛ/17; fos. 29–34/14; fos. 35/20–36ᵛ)

8. London, BL, MS Royal 5 E xix, fos. 37–52 (fo. 37) Alcuin on the Song of Songs (*PL* 100. 641–64); (fo. 46) An anonymous commentary on the Song of Songs, 'Incipit Sirasirin, id est canticum canticorum Salamon. Tribus nominibus uocatus est Salamon, id est pacificus; edida, id est dilectus . . . Dixit Cristus, et quia talis ut dixi futura'

Scribe i (corrections); scribe xi (fos. 37–52ᵛ)

9. London, BL, MS Royal 5 F xviii (fo. 1) Tertullian, *Apologeticum* (*Clavis*, 3);[19]

---

[12] See R. Derolez, *Runica manuscripta: The English Tradition* (Bruges, 1954), 222–37.

[13] No. 7 in F. Wormald, *English Kalendars Before AD 1100*, Henry Bradshaw Society, 72 (London, 1934), see also, Ker, 'Beginnings', 39.

[14] A defective copy, which begins 'in superna et perfecta Trinitate . . .' (*PL* 42. 1211). An entry for this manuscript in Patrick Young's catalogue (no. 23) indicates that this copy originally carried the title 'Isidorus a semetipso ad semetipsum' and had the incipit, 'Cum me peruigil cura fecisset . . .': see Ker, 'Salisbury Cathedral Manuscripts', 168, 173.

[15] Also known as the *De fide catholica*.

[16] Ker ('Beginnings', 42) lists seven other manuscript witnesses to this text.

[17] Another copy was added in the second half of the eleventh century to London, BL, MS Cotton Tiberius C I (fos. 172–3ᵛ), a pontifical transferred from Sherborne to Salisbury after 1075.

[18] See A. Barré, *Les Homéliaires Carolingiens de l'école d'Auxerre*, Studi e testi, 225 (1962), 18–24; see also, J. E. Cross, *Cambridge Pembroke College MS. 25: A Carolingian Sermonary used by Anglo-Saxon Preachers*, King's College London Medieval Studies, 1 (London, 1987), 17–43.

[19] A defective copy. It lacks two leaves at the beginning (caps i–ii '. . . lateat in occulto, quae': CCSL 1. 85–9), one leaf after fo. 4 (cap. vii 'aut arbitrio suspicionis' . . . ix 'non esse perspiceretis': ibid. 100–5), one leaf after fo. 12 (cap. xxi 'de humilitate, sequebatur . . . si uera est ista': ibid. 125–8), and one leaf after fo. 20 (cap. xxxvi 'ad uelamentum sui' . . . xxxviii 'dignitatis ardore frigentibus': ibid. 147–9).

(fo. 29ᵛ) Pseudo-Methodius, *Revelationes*, 'Sciendum namque est fratres karissimi quomodo in principio Deus creauit cęlum et terram . . .'[20]

Scribe ii (fos. 29ᵛ–32); Group II, scribe 2 (fos. 1–29)

10. London, BL, MS Royal 8 B xiv, fos. 154–6ᵛ, Fragment of a commentary on the Song of Songs (2: 1–5: 10), 'hoc est decus mundi ipse et lilium conuallium . . . Vel certe candidus in uirginitate, et rubicundus per passionem. Caput eius. Caput'

Scribe vi (fos. 154–6ᵛ)

11. London, BL, MS Royal 15 C xi, fos. 113–194[21] (fo. 113) Plautus, *Comoediae*;[22] (fo. 194ᵛ) Isidore, *Libri etymologiarum*, 1. xxi (on the critical signs of the grammarians: *PL* 82. 96–8)

Scribe ii (fos. 113–90ᵛ); (fos. 193–4ᵛ); Group II, scribe 1 (fos. 191–2ᵛ)

12. Oxford, Bodl. Libr., MS Bodley 392, Homilies by Eusebius 'Gallicanus' and Caesarius Arelatensis:[23] (fo. 1) Eusebius 'Gallicanus', *Homiliae* xxxvi–xliii, xlv, xii, xiv–xxiv, ix, x, xxxiv; (fo. 48ᵛ) Caesarius, *Homilia* ccxxxiii; (fo. 50ᵛ) Homily attrib. to Caesarius, 'Ad locum hunc, karissimi . . .';[24] (fo. 52) Caesarius, *Homilia* ccxxxvi; (fo. 53ᵛ) Eusebius 'Gallicanus', *Homilia* xliv;[25] (fo. 55) Caesarius, *Homiliae* ccxxxvi, iv; (fo. 58ᵛ) Anonymous homily, 'Tria sunt sub omnipotentis Dei manu habitacula . . .'[26]

Scribe i (corrections); scribe iv (fos. 1–16/10; fos. 16ᵛ–19/2; fos. 19ᵛ–24ᵛ/25; fos. 25ᵛ–7ᵛ/8; fos. 27ᵛ/11–62ᵛ), and two unidentified hands.

13. Oxford, Bodl. Libr., MS Bodley 444, fos. 1–27 (fo. 1ᵛ) Isidore, *Allegoriae* (*Clavis*, 1190), (fo. 10ᵛ) *Prooemia* (*Clavis*, 1192), (fo. 17ᵛ) *De ortu et obitu patrum* (*Clavis*, 1191)

Scribe i (corrections; glosses); scribe iv (fos. 1ᵛ–27)

[20] This copy bears the heading: 'In Cristi nomine incipit liber Bemethodi episcopi aeclesię Pateren(s)is et martiris Cristi quem de hebreo et greco in latinum transferre curauit, id est de principio seculi, et interregna gentium, et finem seculorum. Quem illustrissimus uirorum beatus Hieronimus in suis opusculis collaudauit.' It contains a substantial number of readings which differ from those in another copy of this text produced at Salisbury in the late eleventh century—Salisbury Cathedral, MS 165, fos. 11–22 (see below), and also from the text printed by M. de la Bigne, *Maxima bibliotheca veterum patrum* (Lyon, 1677), iii. 727–34.

[21] The first few leaves are severely damaged by damp.

[22] The first eight plays of the Palatine recension: *Amphitruo, Asinaria, Aulularia, Captivi, Curculio, Casina, Cistellaria, Epidicus*, see R. J. Tarrant, in *Texts and Transmission: A Survey of the Latin Classics*, ed. L. D. Reynolds (Oxford, 1983), 302–7, and R. M. Thomson, 'British Library, Royal 15 C.xi; a Manuscript of Plautus' Plays from Salisbury Cathedral (c.1100)', *Scriptorium*, 40 (1986), 82–7. On fo. 194 is the following verse colophon: Exemplar mendum tandem me compulit ipsum | Cunctantem nimium Plautum exemplarier istum, | Ne graspicus mendis proprias idiota repertis | Adderet, et liber hic falso patre, falsior esset.

[23] Eusebius 'Gallicanus', *Collectio homiliarum*, ed. F. Glorie, 3 vols, CCSL 101–101 B (Turnhout, 1970–1), and *Sancti Caesarii Arelatensis sermones*, ed. G. Morin, 2 vols, CCSL 103–4 (Turnhout, 1953).

[24] Caesarius, *Sermones*, CCSL 104. 955.

[25] A note on fo. 53ᵛ in the hand of Group I scribe i indicates that this homily should follow homily no. xliii on fo. 14ᵛ, where there is a corresponding note.

[26] Morin, *Caesarius*, CCSL 104. 989.

14. Oxford, Bodl. Libr., MS Bodley 756, Ambrosiaster, Commentary on the Pauline Epistles (*Clavis*, 184)

Scribe i (fo. 1/1–4, and corrections); scribe v (fos. 70/22–88/7; fos. 91–2/37; fos. 92ᵛ–135/1; fo. 135/26–135ᵛ; fo. 136/19–136ᵛ/21; fos. 137–42ᵛ); scribe vii (fos. 88/8–90ᵛ; fo. 135/1–25; fo. 136/1–18; fo. 136ᵛ/22–48); scribe ix (fo. 92/37–47); scribe x (fos. 1/5–70/21)

15. Oxford, Bodl., Libr., MS Bodley 765, fos. 1–9, Augustine, *Sermones* 351 and 393 (*PL*, xxxix, 1535–49, 1713–15)

Scribe iii (fo. 1/1–16; fos. 1/19–9ᵛ); scribe viii (fo. 1/16–19)

16. Oxford, Bodl. Libr., MS 765, fos. 10–77²⁷ (fo. 10) Augustine, *De mendacio* (*Clavis*, 303), (fo. 27) *Contra mendacium* (*Clavis*, 304), (fo. 45ᵛ) *De cura pro mortuis gerenda* (*Clavis*, 307), (fo. 55) Cyprian, *De oratione dominica* (*Clavis*, 43), (fo. 64) Ambrose, *Epistola* 63 (*Clavis*, 160)

Scribe i (corrections); scribe iii (fos. 10–45ᵛ; fo. 46/26–46ᵛ/6; fos. 46ᵛ/11–47/13; fo. 47/25–47ᵛ; fos. 48/22–49/4; fos. 49/15–77); scribe xiv (fo. 46/1–26; fo. 46ᵛ/7–10; fo. 47/14–25; fo. 48/1–21; fo. 49/4–15)

17. Oxford, Bodl. Libr., MS 768 (fo. 1) Ambrose, *De virginibus*²⁸ (*Clavis*, 145), (fo. 17ᵛ) *De viduis* (*Clavis*, 146), (fo. 26) *De virginitate*²⁹ (*Clavis*, 147), (fo. 38) Ambrose, *Exhortatio virginitatis* (*Clavis*, 149);³⁰ (fo. 47ᵛ) Pseudo-Ambrose, *De lapsu virginis consecratae* (*Clavis*, 651); (fo. 52) Ambrose, *De mysteriis* (*Clavis*, 155), (fo. 57) *De sacramentis* (*Clavis*, 154)

Scribe i (corrections); scribe xv (fos. 1–69)

18. Oxford, Bodl. Libr., MS Bodley 835 (fo. 1) Ambrose, *De Ioseph patriarcha* (*Clavis*, 131), (fo. 15ᵛ) *De patriarchis* (*Clavis*, 132), (fo. 26ᵛ) *De paenitentia* (*Clavis*, 156), (fo. 49) *De excessu fratris* (*Clavis*, 157)

Scribe i (corrections); scribe ii (fos. 1–14; fos. 19ᵛ/13–30/13; fos. 30ᵛ/15–34/5); scribe xv (fos. 14ᵛ–19ᵛ/12), and two unidentified hands

19. Oxford, Bodl. Libr., MS Rawlinson C. 723, Jerome, Commentary on Ezekiel (Books I–VI)³¹ (*Clavis*, 587)

Scribe i (corrections); scribe vii (fos. 1–81ᵛ)

20. Oxford, Keble College, MS 22, Pauline Epistles with prologues and glosses added (fo. 5) Romans; (fo. 31ᵛ) 1 Cor. with prologue (Stegmüller, 684); (fo. 59) 2 Cor. with prologues (Stegmüller, 700 and 'De pressura que ei facta est . . .'); (fo. 79ᵛ) Gal. with prologue (Stegmüller, 707); (fo. 89) Eph. with prologue (Stegmüller, 715); (fo. 99) Philipp. with prologue (Stegmüller, 728); (fo. 106ᵛ) 1 Thess. with prologue (Stegmüller, 747); (fo. 112ᵛ) Coloss. with prologue (Stegmüller, 736); (fo. 112) 2 Thess. with prologue (Stegmüller, 752); (fo. 122) 1 Tim. with prologue (Stegmüller, 765); (fo. 129) 2 Tim. with prologue (Stegmüller, 772); (fo. 134) Titus

---

²⁷ Contemporary quire signatures indicate that fos. 10–77 were originally bound independently of fos. 1–9.

²⁸ Entitled 'De uirginitate' in this copy.

²⁹ Entitled 'De uirginibus' in this copy.

³⁰ Ascribed to Augustine in this copy.

³¹ CCSL 75. 3–273.

with prologue (Stegmüller, 780); (fo. 137) Philem. with prologue (Stegmüller, 783); (fo. 138ᵛ) Heb. with prologue (Stegmüller, 793).

Scribe i (fos. 45ᵛ–6, and corrections); scribe iv (fo. 5; fos. 7/2–9ᵛ; fos. 10/13–33ᵛ; fos. 34ᵛ–7; fos. 38–45; fos. 46ᵛ–159ᵛ); scribe viii (fos. 5ᵛ–7; fo. 10/1–13); scribe ix (fo. 34; fo. 37ᵛ); glosses by scribes i, xiv, and at least one unidentified hand

Fos. 1–4ᵛ contain additions: (fo. 1) Prologues to Romans (Stegmüller, 651, 670, 674); (fos. 3–4ᵛ) Extracts on the Eucharist (i) (fo. 3) 'Sermo beati Augustini. Vtrum sub figura an sub ueritate hoc mistici calcis fiat sacramentum . . .';[32] (ii) (fo. 3ᵛ) 'Hilarius in libro de Trinitate. Eos inquirens . . . cum uiuat ipse per patrem';[33] (fo. 4) 'Sicut uerus est Dei filius . . . diuine eius substancie in illo participaris alimento.'[34]

Scribe iv copied the prologue to Romans; scribe viii copied the items on fos. 3–4ᵛ

Pl. 15

21. Salisbury Cathedral, MS 6, Augustine, *Confessiones* (with *Retractatio* ii. vi) (*Clavis*, 251)

Scribe i (corrections); scribe ii (fos. 1–71)

22. Salisbury Cathedral, MS 9[35] (fo. 1) Cyprian, *De dominica oratione* (*Clavis*, 43), *De bono patientiae* (*Clavis*, 48), *De opere et eleemosinis* (*Clavis*, 47); (fo. 19) Gregory Nazianzenus, *De Hieremiae prophetae*;[36] (fo. 22ᵛ) Cyprian, *De mortalitate* (*Clavis*, 44), *De catholicae ecclesiae unitate* (*Clavis*, 41); (fo. 37) Caesarius, *Epistola* 2, 'Incipit exortatio sancti Cesarii. Vereor, uenerabiles in Cristo filii . . . Uigeatis [ ] uenerabilis filii explicit.';[37] (fo. 41ᵛ) Pseudo-Isidore (Sisbertus Toletanus) *Lamentum paenitentiae* (*Clavis*, 1533); (fo. 44ᵛ) 'Item uersus beati Isidori. [ ] de morte sunt redempti . . . quos dilexit [ ]undo elegit'; (fo. 44ᵛ) '[ ]bro gloria hilaritate felicitate et sapientia domini . . . ueraciter uerus homo appareat mundo';[38] (fo. 47) 'De sepu[l]chro]. Non inmerito mouet eos qui simplicia . . . et erit sepulchrum eius gloriosum'; (fo. 47ᵛ) '[De] diuersis locis. [Betle]em ciuitas Dauid, in dorsum sita est . . . ecclesiam circumdata est'; (fo. 48ᵛ) '[De] tempore natiuitatis Cristi et eius miraculis. [Natiu]itas Cristi secundum carnem quomodo, et quo tempore . . . sed non exclusus. Qui uiuit et regnat in secula [seculorum]';[39] (fo. 49) 'De columba quę supra Cristum descendit. .i. In hac

---

[32] Extracts from Paschasius, *De corpore et sanguine domini*: CCCM 16, iv, 4–44; ix, 4–15; xii, 4–22, 56–62; xiii, 11–15, 25–9; xv, 13–42. These extracts under the name of Augustine occur in a number of 12th-cent. manuscripts, for example: Avranches, Bibliothèque Municipale, MS 84, Cambridge, Trinity College, MS O.7.9, Edinburgh, National Library of Scotland, Adv. MS, 18.4.3, and London, B.L., MS Arundel 180.

[33] Extracts from Hilary, *De Trinitate*, viii (*PL* 10. 246–7, 249).

[34] Ambrose, *De sacramentis*, vi. 1. 1–4 (CSEL 73. 72–3). These extracts from Hilary and Ambrose are derived from the '*Exaggeratio*': an extended Paschasian catena of Eucharistic proof texts, see Ratramnus, *De corpore et sanguine domini*, ed. J. N. Bakhuizen van den Brink, 2nd edn (Amsterdam/London, 1974), 6–7, 29–32. The full text of the *Exaggeratio* occurs in a Group II manuscript: Salisbury Cathedral, MS 61.

[35] This manuscript has been severely damaged by damp.

[36] CSEL 46. 193–206.

[37] *PL* 67. 1128–35, printed here as a sermon addressed to women.

[38] A text in dialogue format on Psalm 95: 11.

[39] A text in dialogue format.

namque columba hęc interroganda sunt ... Cur in columba specialiter pro innocentia et [ ] simplicitate eius';[40] (fo. 49ᵛ) 'Item de eius natura. [ ]aturis columbę secundum spiritalem ... Apte igitur ut septiformis in specie columbę. [ ] habentis discenderit'; (fo. 49ᵛ) 'Expositio fidei catolicę [ ] Hieronimi. [Credimus] in Deum patrem omnipotentem cunctorum uisibilium ... se esse comprobauit' (the Pelagian *Libellus fidei ad Innocentium papam*: *Clavis*, 731); (fo. 51) 'Incipit explanatio sex die[rum in] quibus creauit Deus cęlum et terram e dictis A[mbrosii] et Au[gustini]. In principio creauit Deus cęlum et terram. Istud capitulum omnium librorum caput est ... per aduentum fuisse saluatoris';[41] (fo. 58) 'De inspiratione homin[is]. Formauit igitur dominus Deus hominem de limo terr[ę] ... calificat frigidam, animam sanctificat, et p[ ] inluminat cor';[42] (fo. 59) Questions and answers on various biblical topics: 'De genealogia Io[b]. [Iob] filius Sare de Bosra... qui post abiectionem cornui [ ]onem regni promeruit'; 'Item de Iob alio loco. [ ]uerunt inquit Abraham dicentes, accepit Melcha ... que ibi continentur in hebreis [ ]us non habetur'; 'De stella que apparuit supra dominum. [Quaeren]dum est si stella quę apparuit ... maior hominibus pro diuinitate'; 'De Lazaro et Diuit[e]. [ ] Lazari et Diuitis quantę quęstiones ... hic liber euangelium nominatur'; 'De baptismo [ ]. Baptismi genera quod sunt in ueteri et nouo testamento ... sancti baptizantur'; 'De illo latrone Agustinus dic[it]. Quidem quod in Luca latroni saluator dicit ... Sed ego quod ab auctore inueni. libentissimae d[ ].'

Scribe ii (fo. 7/19–39), and an unidentified hand

23. Salisbury Cathedral, MS 10, Cassian, *Collationes* i–x, xiv, xv, xxiv, and xi (*Clavis*, 512)

Scribe i (fo. 7/7–14; fo. 8ᵛ/29–32; fo. 14/1–7; fo. 49/9–12; fo. 49/30–2; fo. 81ᵛ/ 1–3; fos. 83ᵛ–4; corrections); scribe iii (fos. 3–6, and over 20 other stints); scribe vi (fos. 6ᵛ–7/5; fo. 8ᵛ/9–29; fo. 22/1–6; fo. 25ᵛ/8–32; fo. 33/8–14; fo. 34/4–8; fo. 83; fos. 84ᵛ–5ᵛ/22; fo. 108/19–33; fo. 111/2–33); scribe viii (fo. 21/12–18; fo. 22/16–32; fo. 22ᵛ/26–32; fo. 23/18–23; fo. 23ᵛ/3; fo. 24/1–18; fo. 25/23–32), and at least four unidentified hands

Pl. 5

24. Salisbury Cathedral, MS 12 (fos. 1–56), Smaragdus, *Diadema monachorum* (*PL* 102. 593–690)

Scribe iv (fos. 1–56/10)

25. Salisbury Cathedral, MS 24, Jerome, Commentary on Jeremiah (*Clavis*, 586)

Scribe iii (fo. 82); scribe v (fos. 1–56ᵛ; fo. 57/14–58ᵛ/17; fo. 59/1–35; fo. 59/39– 81ᵛ); scribe vii (fo. 58ᵛ/18–41; fo. 59/36–8), and an unidentified hand

26. Salisbury Cathedral, MS 25, Jerome, Commentary on Isaiah (*Clavis*, 584)

Scribe i (fo. 8/1–3, and corrections); scribe viii (fos. 176ᵛ–203); scribe xi (fos. 161/23–165/20); scribe xiii (fos. 2–7ᵛ; fos. 8/4–78ᵛ; fos. 79–161/22)

27. Salisbury Cathedral, MS 33, Gregory, *Moralia in Iob* (*Clavis*, 1708)[43]

---

[40] A text in dialogue format.
[41] This text shares material with Pseudo-Bede, *De sex dierum creatione*: *PL* 93. 207–34.
[42] Ibid.
[43] Fos. 1–66ᵛ were substituted in the second half of the 12th cent.

Scribe ii (fos. 67–196; fo. 313va/4–41); scribe iii (fos. 274–313va/3; fos. 314–75^v; fo. 376va; fo. 377^a/1–36; fos. 377va/13–378va/5; fo. 379–379va/21; fo. 380–380va; fos. 453–97); scribe iv (fos. 258–73^v); scribe v (fos. 196^v–244^b/19; fos. 244^v–57); scribe vi (fo. 376; fo. 376vb; fo. 377^a/37–377va/12; fo. 378va/6–378vb/41; fo. 379va/22–379vb/41; fo. 381–436^b/29; fos. 436^v–7; fos. 438–52^v); scribe viii (fo. 244^b/19–41); scribe xiv (fo. 436^b/30–7; fo. 437^v)

28. Salisbury Cathedral, MS 37, Bede, Commentary on Luke (*Clavis*, 1356)
Scribe i (corrections); scribe x (fos. 133/6–164), and at least one unidentified hand

29. Salisbury Cathedral, MS 63 (fo. 1) Augustine, *De agone christiano* (*Clavis*, 296) (with *Retractatio* II. iii), (fo. 7) *De disciplina christiana* (*Clavis*, 310), (fo. 10) *Sermo app.* 252 (*PL* 39. 2210–12); (fo. 10^v) Theodulf of Orleans, *De processione Spiritus sancti* (*PL* 105. 242–76); (fo. 20) Augustine, *De utilitate credendi* (*Clavis*, 316), (fo. 28^v) *De gratia novi testamenti* (*Epistola* 140: *PL* 33. 538–77), (fo. 40^v) *De natura boni* (*Clavis*, 323) (with *Retractatio* II. ix); (fo. 46^v) Pseudo-Augustine (Quoduultdeus) *Adversus quinque haereses* (*Clavis*, 410)
Scribe i (fos. 10^v/37–14^v/35; fos. 15–18; fos. 18^v/34–19^v/22; fos. 20–4/32; fo. 24^v/1–5; fos. 24^v/25–25^v/32; fo. 26/1–45; fos. 26^v/15–28/45; fo. 28^v/23–45; fos. 29/30–31/12; fos. 31^v/11–32/23; fos. 32^v/14–33^v/13; fos. 33^v/30–37^v/24; fos. 38/18–39^v/45; fos. 40^v–41/45; fos. 41^v/14–45/31; fos. 46–50/21; fo. 50/34–45; fos. 50^{v}17–2/32, and corrections); scribe ii (fos. 1–10^v/2; fo. 10^v/12–36); scribe iii (fo. 24^v/5–24; fo. 25^v/32–45; fo. 26^v/1–15; fo. 32^v/1–13; fo. 38/1–17; fo. 41^v/1–14; fo. 45/32–45^v/6; fo. 50^v/1–16); scribe iv (fo. 18^v/1–33; fo. 19^v/22–45); scribe vi (fo. 37^v/25–45; fo. 45^v/7–45); scribe vii (fo. 10^v/3–12); scribe ix (fo. 14^v/36–44; fo. 24/32–45), and an unidentified hand

30. Salisbury Cathedral, MS 67, Augustine, Homilies on St John's Gospel (*Clavis*, 278)[44]
Scribe i (corrections); scribe ii (fos. 25–185; fos. 190–204^b/8; fos. 204^v–10^v; fos. 215^v–16^a; fos. 217^v–218^b/25; fos. 219vb/20–221^v; fos. 223^b–24va/12; fo. 225^b/25–225vb); scribe xvii (fo. 204^b/9–40), and an unidentified hand

31. Salisbury Cathedral, MS 78, Lanfranc's abbreviation of Pseudo-Isidore, Decretals and Canons of Councils[45]
Scribe i (fo. 89/27–43; glosses and corrections); scribe ii (fos. 2^v–97^v/20, except for six short stints); scribe iv (fos. 1–2; fo. 97^v/21–42); scribe v (fos. 98^v–182), and at least one unidentified hand
Pl. 3

32. Salisbury Cathedral, MS 88 (fo. 1) Jerome, *De viris inlustribus* (*Clavis*, 616); (fo. 18) *Decretum Gelasianum de libris recipiendis et non recipiendis*, 'Post propheticas . . .';[46] (fo. 20) Gennadius, *De viris inlustribus* (*Clavis*, 957); (fo. 31^v) Isidore, *De viris inlustribus* (*Clavis*, 1206); (fo. 34^v) Augustine, *Retractationes*

---

[44] Fos. 1–24 and 227–9 were substituted in the 13th cent.
[45] See Z. N. Brooke, *The English Church and the Papacy from the Conquest to the Reign of John*, 2nd edn (Cambridge, 1989), 57–83, 231–5.
[46] (Pseudo-Gelasius), ed. E. von Dobschütz, *Texte und Untersuchungen zur Geschichte der altchristlichen Literatur*, 38/iv (Leipzig, 1912), 7–13.

(*Clavis*, 250); (fo. 71ᵛ) Cassiodorus, *Institutiones divinarum litterarum*, bk. I;[47] (fo. 94ᵛ) Isidore, *Prooemia* (*Clavis*, 1192), (fo. 101ᵛ) *De ecclesiasticis officiis*, 1. xi ('Hii sunt autem libri ueteris testamenti ...') –xii ('... postulata sequentia prenotabo.') (*PL* 33. 746–50), (fo. 103) *De ortu et obitu patrum* (*Clavis*, 1191), (fo. 113) *Allegoriae* (*Clavis*, 1190); (fo. 121ᵛ) Note on the historical interpretation of the Bible, 'Disponere ita debemus ut Terentius dicit ...'[48]

Scribe i (corrections); scribe ii (fos. 1–15; fos. 16–125), and an unidentified hand

33. Salisbury Cathedral, MS 106 (fo. 1) Augustine, *De doctrina christiana* (*Clavis*, 263), (fo. 41ᵛ) *De quantitate animae* (*Clavis*, 257), (fo. 59ᵛ) *Sermo* 37 (*PL* 38. 221–35); (fo. 64ᵛ) Part of an Easter sermon attributed to Augustine, 'Fertur autem phisici natum leonis ... Nouum quidem est miraculum resurrectio saluatoris ... de sepulchro leuauit' (*PL*, Suppl. 2, 1202–4); (fo. 65) Augustine, *De octo quaestionibus Dulcitii* (*Clavis*, 291), (fo. 75) *De libero arbitrio* (*Clavis*, 260), (fo. 110ᵛ) *De natura boni* (*Clavis*, 323), (fo. 113) *De vera religione* (*Clavis*, 264), (fo. 133) *De disciplina christiana* (*Clavis*, 310)

Scribe i (fo. 120/20–40, and corrections); scribe iii (fos. 1–72ᵛ); scribe vi (fos. 75–120/19; fos. 120ᵛ–36)

34. Salisbury Cathedral, MSS 109, 114, 128 flyleaves, fragments of a copy of Augustine, *De genesi ad litteram*

Scribe i (MS 128, fo. 4ᵛ/1–5); scribe ii (MS 128, fo. 4ᵛ/22–4); scribe xiii (MS 109, fos. 1–8; MS 114, fos. 2–5ᵛ; MS 128, fos. 1–4; fo. 4ᵛ/6–21; fos. 4ᵛ/25–41)

35. Salisbury Cathederal, MS 114, Augustine, *De genesi ad litteram* (*Clavis*, 266)

Scribe iii (fos. 6–122)

36. Salisbury Cathedral, MS 119, Freculphus, *Chronicon*, bk. 1 (*PL* 106. 917–1116)

Scribe i (fo. 1/1–6; fo. 1ᵛ/6–33; fo. 5/15–34, and corrections); scribe iv (fo. 51/25–34; fo. 53/8–34), and three unidentified hands

37. Salisbury Cathedral, MS 120, Freculphus, *Chronicon*, bk. 1 (*PL* 106. 917–1116)[49]

Scribe ii (fo. 89ᵛ/1–11); scribe iv (fo. 89ᵛ/22–98); scribe vii (fos. 36–8ᵛ), and at least two unidentified hands

38. Salisbury Cathedral, MS 128 (fo. 5) Augustine, *De adulterinis coniugiis* (*Clavis*, 302), (fo. 25) *De natura et origine animae* (*Clavis*, 345); (fo. 66) *Sermo Arianorum* (*Clavis*, 701); (fo. 68ᵛ) Augustine, *Contra sermonem Arianorum* (*Clavis*, 702), (fo. 81ᵛ) *Contra adversarium legis et prophetarum* (*Clavis*, 326)

Scribe i (fos. 16ᵛ/20–17/1; fo. 17ᵛ/1; fo. 18ᵛ/6–20; fo. 19ᵛ/1–10; fo. 21ᵛ/15–33; fo. 24ᵛ/1–14, and corrections); scribe iii (fos. 5–16/16; fo. 16/19–16ᵛ/4; fo. 16ᵛ/17–19; fo. 17/1–32; fo. 17ᵛ/2–19; fo. 18–18ᵛ/5; fos. 18ᵛ/21–19; fos. 19ᵛ/11–21ᵛ/14; fos. 22–4; fos. 24ᵛ/15–25/28); scribe v (fo. 16ᵛ/5–17); scribe viii (fos. 25/28–116), and one unidentified hand

---

[47] On this copy and others related to it, see *Cassiodori senatoris institutiones*, ed. R. A. B. Mynors (Oxford, 1937), xv–xvi, xxxix–xlix.

[48] Pr. in Mynors, *Cassiodorus*, as a footnote to p. xv.

[49] Lacks the verses in *PL* 106. 919–20, and which are present in Salisbury 119.

39. Salisbury Cathedral, MS 129, Pseudo-Augustine (Ambrosiaster), *Quaestiones cxxvii*[50]

Scribe i (corrections); scribe v (fos. 1–111)

40. Salisbury Cathedral, MS 135, fos. 1–24, Treatise on the significance of rites and observances of the Church, 'Signorum usus a ueteri testamento sumptus est ... (fo. 1) Primum sacerdotale uestimentum ephot, solis pontificibus deputatur ... (fo. 3ᵛ) Episcopus de sacrario progrediens ecclesiam a leua ingreditur ... (fo. 7) Legitur in ecclesiastica historia quod Nabuchodonosor ... (fo. 15) Quoniam quod Dauid prophetauit, apostolus cuncorditer predicauit.' (fo. 17) 'Domus dominica methonomice dicitur aecclesia ... Postea pontifex benedicat ipsum altare.'[51]

Scribe ii (fos. 9ᵛ/12–22ᵛ/10), and two unidentified hands

41. Salisbury Cathedral, MS 135, fos. 25–59, An unfinished copy of Isidore, *Quaestiones in vetus testamentum* (as far as *In genesim*, xxvii 'Effusus es autem, sicut aqua, peccando in Cristo': *PL* 83. 207–77)

Scribe i (corrections); scribe ii (fos. 25–59)

42. Salisbury Cathedral, MS 138 (fo. 3ᵛ) Augustine, *Epistola* 200 (*PL* 33. 925–6), (fo. 3ᵛ) *De nuptiis et concupiscentia* (*Clavis*, 350), (fo. 10) *Epistola* 207 (*PL* 33. 949–50), (fo. 10) *Contra Iulianum* (*Clavis*, 351)

Scribe i (fo. 3ᵛ/1–5; fo. 33ᵛ/37–41; fo. 34/6–14); scribe iii (fos. 3ᵛ/6–16ᵛ/42; fos. 17–21ᵛ/17; fos. 21ᵛ/35–32ᵛ/36); scribe vi (fo. 21ᵛ/18–34); scribe vii (fo. 16ᵛ/43–48); scribe xii (fos. 32ᵛ/37–33ᵛ/34); scribe xiii (fo. 33ᵛ/35–7; fos. 33ᵛ/42–34/6; fos. 34/15–65)

43. Salisbury Cathedral, MS 140 (fo. 3) Ambrose, *De fide* (*Clavis*, 150), (fo. 54) *De spiritu sancto* (*Clavis*, 151), (fo. 88) *De incarnatione dominicae sacramento* (*Clavis*, 152)

Scribe i (fo. 3/1–14, and corrections); scribe iii (fos. 3/15–44/34; fos. 44ᵛ–96ᵛ); scribe vi (fo. 44/35–41)

44. Salisbury Cathedral, MS 140, flyleaves, Fragments of an unfinished copy of Berengaudus on the Apocalypse[52]

Scribe i (fo. 1/1–7); scribe xi (fos. 1/7–2ᵛ/30)

45. Salisbury Cathedral, MS 154, Amalarius, *Liber officialis*[53]

Scribe i (p. 39/5–16, glosses, and corrections); scribe ii (additions on pp. 158–

---

[50] The *recensio posterior*: see *Pseudo-Augustini quaestiones veteris et novi testamenti cxxvii*, ed. A. Souter, CSEL 50 (Vienna/Leipzig, 1908), xxxiii.

[51] These texts form part of a *Summa de divinis officiis*, parts of which are also found in Exeter Cathedral, MS 3525, pp. 121–74; Cambridge, Fitzwilliam Museum, MS McLean 101, fos. 169–74ᵛ; London, BL, MS Cotton Nero A I, fos. 106–8ᵛ, and Lambeth Palace, MS 1229, nos. 14 and 15 (two detached bifolia, probably from Lambeth Palace, MS 372), see Ker, *MMBL*, ii. 835.

[52] The scribe breaks off at '... Vt cum scandare coeperit' (*PL* 17. 770–1).

[53] An aberrant version of *Retractatio* I. For this *Retractatio*, see J. M. Hanssens, *Amalarii episcopi opera liturgica omnia, Studi e testi*, 138 (1948), i. 162–9, and for the ways in which Salisbury Cathedral, MS 154 differs from it, see Ker, 'Beginnings', 46–7. Group I scribes made the following additions to this copy; (p. 2) *Praefatio* (Hanssens, *Studi e testi*, 139, ii. 19–21); (p. 4) 'Hec tria genera distinguntur ... nocturnalia officia celebrantur' (ibid. 470–1); (p. 158) *Prooemium* (ibid. 13–18).

62); scribe iii (pp. 5–39/4; 39/17–50/14; 50/20–157); scribe iv (additions on pp. 2–4), and an unidentified hand
Pl. 2

46. Salisbury Cathedral, MS 162, flyleaves, Fragments of a copy of Berengaudus on the Apocalypse[54]
Scribe xvii (fos. 1–2; fos. 29–30)

47. Salisbury Cathedral, MS 165, fos. 1–10, Pseudo-Augustine (Vigilius Thapsensis), *Contra Felicianum* (*Clavis*, 808)
Scribe iv (fo. 1–1ᵛ/16); scribe ix (fos. 1ᵛ/17–6ᵛ); scribe xii (fos. 7–10)

48. Salisbury Cathedral, MS 165, fos. 11–22, Pseudo-Methodius, *Revelationes*, *inc.* 'Liber Methodii incipit. Sciendum namque quomodo exeuntes Adam quidem et Euam de paradiso uirgines fuisse . . .'[55]
Scribe i (heading on fo. 11); scribe xii (fos. 11–20ᵛ) (fos. 21–2 are blank)

49. Salisbury Cathedral, MS 165, fos. 23–87,[56] Bede, *De tabernaculo* (*Clavis*, 1345)
Scribe i (fo. 23/1–6, and corrections); scribe xii (fos. 23/6–71; fos. 77–86) (fo. 87 is blank); fos. 72–6ᵛ were supplied subsequently by Group II scribe 10; Group II scribes 9 and 10 also made corrections
Pl. 1*a*

50. Salisbury Cathedral, MS 165, fos. 122–78 (fo. 122) Alcuin, *De fide sanctae et individuae Trinitatis* (*PL* 101. 11–58), (fo. 153ᵛ) *De Trinitate ad Fredegisum quaestiones xxviii* (*PL* 101. 57–64), (fo. 157) *De animae ratione liber ad Eulalium* (*PL* 101. 639–47); (fo. 163ᵛ) Pseudo-Augustine (Gennadius), *De ecclesiasticis dogmatibus* (*Clavis*, 958); (fo. 172) *Decretum Gelasianum de libris recipiendis et non recipiendis*, 'Post propheticas . . .';[57] (fo. 175) Pseudo-Jerome, *De duodecim scriptoribus* (*PL* 23. 723–6); (fo. 176ᵛ) Two Eucharistic miracle stories (i) 'Quomodo presbiter Plecgis dominicum corpus in forma pueri a domino sibi demonstrari impetrauit. Quidam presbiter fuit religiosus ualde, Plecgis nomine . . . in eadem re quam exterius uisu conspexerat.'[58] (ii) 'De puero iudeo quem proprius pater pro susceptione corporis et sanguinis Cristi in fornacem ardentem proiecit. Iudei cuiusdam uitrarii filius . . . Agnitam ergo infans fidem catholicam credidit. In nomine Patris et Filii et Spiritus sancti, una cum genetrice sua. Deo gratias.'[59]

[54] From a different copy from that represented by the flyleaves to Salisbury Cathedral, MS 140. The fragments include parts of *Visiones* iv and v. For the full text, see *PL* 17. 765–970.

[55] Another copy was made at Salisbury in the late 11th cent.—London, B.L., MS Royal 5 F xviii, fos. 29ᵛ–32 (see above).

[56] Fos. 72–6 were subsequently supplied by Group II scribe 10.

[57] Von Dobschütz (ed.), *Texte und Untersuchungen*, 38/iv, 7–13.

[58] This version derives from Paschasius, *Liber de corpore et sanguine domini*, bk. iv: CCCM 16. 89–91.

[59] A miracle story, derived ultimately from Evagrius, which circulated widely during the Middle Ages in a number of different versions. It was incorporated in collections of miracles of the Virgin, and also circulated independently. See, for example, P. Carter, 'An Edition of William of Malmesbury's Treatise on the Miracles of the Virgin Mary', D.Phil. thesis (Oxford University, 1959), ii. 520–30, esp. 523 n. 1. The version represented in this copy is close to that in Paschasius, *Liber de corpore et sanguine domini*, bk. ix: CCCM 16. 60–61.

Scribe ii (fos. 122–78^v/13)
Pl. 1*b*

51. Salisbury Cathedral, MS 168 (fo. 2) Augustine, *De diversis quaestionibus lxxxviii* (*Clavis*, 290); (fo. 76) Pseudo-Augustine, *De duodecim abusivis saeculi* (*Clavis*, 1106); (fo. 85^v) Bede, *De die iudicii* (*Clavis*, 1370)

Scribe i (fo. 1–1^v/4; fos. 62^v–3; fo. 65^v/1–15; fo. 66/1–13; fos. 67^v–8/11; fo. 68^v–77); scribe ii (fo. 21/10–26; fo. 22/22–26; fo. 22^v/13–26; fo. 24–24^v/2; fo. 25/10–26; fo. 28/8–26; fo. 29^v/12–21; fo. 30/10–15; fos. 30^v/20–31/1; fo. 33^v/20–6; fos. 42–49^v); scribe iv (fo. 36^{r-v}); scribe vi (fo. 62; fo. 63^v–5; fo. 65^v/15–26; fos. 66/14–67; fos. 77^v–87); scribe ix (fos. 1^v/5–41^v, except for small stints by scribes ii, iv, xi, and unidentified hands); scribe xi (fo. 14/8–14), and four unidentified hands
Pl. 4

52. Salisbury Cathedral, MS 169 (fo. 1) Augustine, *Sermones* 351 and 393 (*PL* 39. 1535–49, 1713–15); (fo. 11) Pseudo-Augustine, *Dialogus quaestionum lxv* (*Clavis*, 373 n.), (fo. 26) (Vigilius Thapsensis) *Contra Felicianum* (*Clavis*, 808); (fo. 39) Augustine, *De disciplina christiana* (*Clavis*, 310), (fo. 45) *Sermo* 37 (*PL* 38. 221–35);[60] (fo. 54^v) Part of an Easter sermon attributed to Augustine;[61] (fo. 55^v) Augustine, *De octo quaestionibus Dulcitii* (*Clavis*, 291), (fo. 68) *Epistola* 130 (*PL* 33. 493–507)

Scribe iv (fos. 1–10; fos. 12^v–21; fos. 21/24–43/13; fo. 34/17–54/11; fos. 54^v–67; fos. 70–2; fos. 73^v–77/13); scribe vi (fos. 67^v–9), and two unidentified hands

53. Salisbury Cathedral, MS 179, Summer part of the Homiliary of Paul the Deacon

Scribe i (fos. 53^v/10–55/41; fo. 69^v–70/43; fo. 70^v/1–30; fos. 73^v/31–74/20; fo. 74^v/1–27; fo. 94/43–94^v); scribe iii (fo. 91^v/11–15); scribe v (fos. 1–2^v; fo. 5/21–5^v; fo. 70/43–49; fos. 70^v/31–73^v/31; fo. 74/20–49; fos. 74^v/28–88); scribe vi (fos. 3–5/20; fos. 46^v/27–49); scribe x (fos. 50–3^v/9; fos. 55/41–69; fos. 89–94), and at least two unidentified hands

54. Salisbury Cathedral, MS 221,[62] Passional (January–June): (fo. 1) Passio s. Martinae virginis (*BHL* 5588); (fo. 9) Vita s. Basilii episcopi, auct. Pseudo-Amphilochio (cf. *BHL* 1023); (fo. 22) Vita s. Genovefae virginis (*BHL* 3336); (fo. 28^v) Passio s. Theogenis martyris (*BHL* 8107); (fo. 30^v) Passio s. Luciani martyris (*BHL* 5010); (fo. 34) Passio ss. martyrum Iuliani et Basilissae (cf. *BHL* 4532); (fo. 47^v) Vita s. Hilarii episcopi, auct. Fortunato (*BHL* 3885 + *PL* 10. 549–52); (fo. 52^v) Passio s. Felicis martyris (*BHL* 2894); (fo. 54) Passio s. Felicis presbyteri

[60] *Sermo* 37, the Easter sermon and the *De octo quaestionibus Dulcitii* were copied either from Salisbury Cathedral, MS 106, or from the same exemplar used for that copy.

[61] See above, Salisbury 106.

[62] Formerly Oxford, Bodl. Libr., MS Fell 4. Salisbury Cathedral, MS 221 and its companion volume, Salisbury Cathedral, MS 222, were probably copied from the same exemplar as a Passional from Worcester, now London, BL, MS Cotton Nero E I and Cambridge, Corpus Christi College, MS 9. For a comparison of the contents of the Salisbury and Worcester Passionals, and for fuller details concerning the texts as they appear in these manuscripts, see P. H. Zettel, 'Ælfric's Hagiographic Sources and the Latin Legendary Preserved in BL MS Cotton Nero E i + CCCC MS 9 and Other Manuscripts', D.Phil. thesis (Oxford University, 1979), esp. 15–34.

(*BHL* 2885); (fo. 55) Passio s. Marcelli papae (*BHL* 5235); (fo. 59) Passio s. Marcelli martyris (*BHL* 5253); (fo. 59ᵛ) Vita vel visio s. Fursei presbiteri (*BHL* 3210); (fo. 66ᵛ) Vita s. Sulpitii episcopi (*BHL* 7928); (fo. 69) Passio ss. martyrum Speusippi, Eleusippi et Meleusippi, auct. Warnahario (*BHL* 7829); (fo. 74) Passio ss. martyrum Sebastiani et sociorum, perperam adscripta s. Ambrosio (*BHL* 7543); (fo. 93) Passio s. Agnetis virginis, auct. Pseudo-Ambrosio (*BHL* 156); (fo. 97) Passio ss. martyrum Fructuosi episcopi, Augurii et Eulogii diaconorum (*BHL* 3200); (fo. 98ᵛ) Passio s. Patrocli martyris (*BHL* 6520); (fo. 101) Passio s. Vincentii diaconi (*BHL* 8628, cf. 8630–1, 8634); (fo. 105) Passio s. Potiti martyris (*BHL* 6908); (fo. 109) Passio s. Asclae martyris (*BHL* 722); (fo. 110ᵛ) Passio s. Babylae martyris (*BHL* 891); (fo. 114) Passio s. Polycarpi episcopi (Epistula ecclesiae Smyrnensis) (*BHL* 6870); (fo. 117ᵛ) Passio ss. martyrum Thyrsi, Leucii, Callinici et sociorum (*BHL* 8280); (fo. 128) Vita s. Brigidae virginis, auct. Cogitoso (*BHL* 1457); (fo. 136ᵛ) Passio s. Triphonis martyris (*BHL* 8338); (fo. 142ᵛ) Passio s. Agathae virginis (cf. *BHL* 134); (fo. 145ᵛ) Vita s. Amandi episcopi, auct. Baudemundo (*BHL* 332);[63] (fo. 151) Passio s. Valentini martyris (*BHL* 8460); (fo. 153ᵛ) Passio s. Iulianae virginis (*BHL* 4522); (fo. 157ᵛ) Historia s. Theophili, interprete Paulo diac. Neapolitano (*BHL* 8121); (fo. 162ᵛ) Vita s. Albini episcopi, auct. Fortunato (cf. *BHL* 234); (fo. 165ᵛ) Passio ss. martyrum Felicitatis et Perpetuae (*BHL* 6633);[64] (fo. 170) Passio ss. quadraginta martyrum (cf. *BHL* 7538); (fo. 173) Vita s. Gregorii papae, auct. Paulo diac. (*BHL* 3639); (fo. 178) Confessio s. Patricii episcopi (*BHL* 6492); (fo. 184) Epistula s. Patricii ad cristianos Corotici Tyranni subditos (*BHL* 6493); (fo. 186) Passio s. Theodoriti presbyteri (*BHL* 8074); (fo. 188ᵛ) Passio s. Theodosiae paenitentis (*BHL* 8090); (fo. 195ᵛ) Vita s. Mariae Ægyptiacae virginis, adscripta Sophronio ep. Hieros., interprete Paulo diac. Neapolitano) (*BHL* 5415); (fo. 205ᵛ) Vita s. Ambrosii episcopi, auct. Paulino (*BHL* 377); (fo. 216) Passio ss. Eleutherii episcopi et Antiae matris eius (*BHL* 2451); (fo. 218ᵛ) Passio ss. Georgii martyris, auct. Pseudo-Passecrate (cf. *BHL* 3373–4); (fo. 221) Passio s. Marci evangelistae (*BHL* 5276); (fo. 225) Inventio et Passio ss. martyrum Geruasii et Protasii, auct. Pseudo-Ambrosio (cf. *BHL* 3514); (fo. 226ᵛ) Passio s. Iacobi minoris apostoli (*BHL* 4093); (fo. 227ᵛ) Vita s. Philippi apostoli (*BHL* 6814); (fo. 228) Inventio sanctae crucis (*BHL* 4169); (fo. 231ᵛ) Passio ss. martyrum Alexandri, Euentii et Theoduli (*BHL* 266); (fo. 236) Passio s. Quiriaci martyris (cf. *BHL* 7024); (fo. 239) Passio ss. martyrum Gordiani et Epimachi (*BHL* 3612); (fo. 240ᵛ) Passio s. Pancratii martyris (*BHL* 6423); (fo. 241ᵛ) Gesta ss. martyrum Nerei et Achillei (*BHL* 6058); (fo. 244ᵛ) Rescriptum Marcelli (*BHL* 6060); (fo. 245ᵛ) Vita ss. Petronillae et Feliculae (*BHL* 6061); (fo. 246) Passio s. Nicomedis martyris (*BHL* 6062); (fo. 246ᵛ) Passio ss. martyrum Nerei et Achillei (*BHL* 6063); (fo. 246ᵛ) Passio ss. martyrum Eutychetis, Victorini et Maronis (*BHL* 6064); (fo. 247ᵛ) Passio ss. martyrum Domitillae et sociorum (*BHL* 6066); (fo. 248ᵛ) Passio s. Torpetis martyris (*BHL* 8307); (fo. 251ᵛ) Vita s. Pudentianae virginis, auct. Pseudo-Pastore presb. (*BHL* 6991); (fo. 252ᵛ) Vita s. Germani episcopi, auct. Venantio Fortunato (*BHL* 3468); (fo. 263ᵛ) Passio s. Cononis martyris (*BHL* 1912); (fo. 264ᵛ) Passio

---

[63] Without the prologue listed in *BHL*.
[64] Without the prologue listed in *BHL*.

ss. martyrum Marcellini et Petri (*BHL* 5231); (fo. 267) Passio s. Erasmi episcopi (*BHL* 2580); (fo. 270ᵛ) Passio s. Bonefatii martyris (*BHL* 1413); (fo. 273) Vita s. Medardi episcopi, perperam adscripta Fortunato (cf. *BHL* 5864); (fo. 275) Passio ss. martyrum Primi et Feliciani (*BHL* 6922)[65]

Scribe i (fo. 223/2–16, and corrections); scribe iii (fos. 1–159ᵛ/26; fos. 160–223/2); scribe vi (fos. 225–243/30; fos. 243ᵛ–62/5; fos. 262ᵛ–77ᵛ); scribe ix (fo. 159ᵛ/27–31); scribe xvi (fo. 262/6–36), and one unidentified hand

55. Salisbury Cathedral, MS 222,[66] Passional: July–December (fo. 2) Passio s. Symphorosae cum septem filiis, falso adscripta Iulio Africano (*BHL* 7971); (fo. 2ᵛ) Translation of St Martin of Tours (*BHL* 5623); (fo. 3) Passio ss. martyrum Viti, Modesti et Crescentiae (*BHL* 8712); (fo. 6ᵛ) Passio ss. martyrum Gallicani, Iohannis et Pauli (*BHL* 3236, 3238); (fo. 9ᵛ) Passio s. Petri apostoli (cf. *BHL* 6664); (fo. 16) Passio s. Pauli apostoli (cf. *BHL* 6574, cf. *BHL* 6570); (fo. 22ᵛ) Passio ss. martyrum Processi et Martiniani (*BHL* 6947); (fo. 24) Passio s. Felicitatis cum septem filiis (*BHL* 2853); (fo. 25) Passio ss. martyrum Rufinae et Secundae (*BHL* 7359); (fo. 26ᵛ) Vita s. Praxedis virginis (*BHL* 6920); (fo. 27ᵛ) Passio s. Apollinaris episcopi (*BHL* 623); (fo. 33) Passio s. Iacobi maioris apostoli (*BHL* 4057); (fo. 35ᵛ) Passio ss. septem dormientium (*BHL* 2316); (fo. 41ᵛ) Passio s. Pantaleonis martyris (*BHL* 6437); (fo. 46ᵛ) Passio ss. martyrum Simplicii, Faustini et Beatricis (*BHL* 7790); (fo. 47ᵛ) Passio s. Felicis (*BHL* 2857); (fo. 48) Passio s. Stephani papae (*BHL* 7845); (fo. 53) Vita s. Cassiani episcopi (*BHL* 1632); (fo. 57) Passio ss. martyrum Polychronii, Parmenii, Abdon et Sennen, Sixti, Laurentii et Hippolyti (*BHL* 6884, 6, 7801, 4754, 3961); (fo. 67) Passio s. Donati episcopi (*BHL* 2291); (fo. 71ᵛ) Vita s. Gaugerici episcopi (cf. *BHL* 3287); (fo. 75) Passio s. Eupli diaconi (*BHL* 2729); (fo. 76) Passio s. Eusebii presbyteri (*BHL* 2740); (fo. 77) Passio s. Agapiti martyris (*BHL* 125); (fo. 79) Passio s. Symphoriani martyris (*BHL* 7967); (fo. 81ᵛ) Vita s. Audoeni episcopi (*BHL* 750); (fo. 84ᵛ) Passio s. Bartholomaei apostoli (*BHL* 1002); (fo. 89) Passio s. Genesii martyris, adscripta Paulino episcopo (*BHL* 3304); (fo. 89ᵛ) Miracula, adscripta Hilario episcopo Arelatensi (*BHL* 3307); (fo. 91) Vita s. Augustini episcopi, auct. Possidio (*BHL* 785); (fo. 110ᵛ) Vita s. Sabinae virginis (*BHL* 7408); (fo. 114) Passio s. Seraphiae virginis (*BHL* 7586); (fo. 117ᵛ) Passio s. Sabinae martyris (*BHL* 7407); (fo. 118) Vita s. Bertini abbatis (Pars media vitae ss. Audomari, Bertini et Winnoci) (cf. *BHL* 763); (fo. 121ᵛ) Passio s. Hadriani martyris (*BHL* 3744); (fo. 130) Vita s. Audomari episcopi (cf. (*BHL* 765); (fo. 136ᵛ) Passio s. Hyacinthi martyris (*BHL* 4053); (fo. 137) Passio s. Cornelii papae (*BHL* 1958); (fo. 138) Acta s. Cypriani episcopi (cf. *BHL* 2038); (fo. 139) Passio s. Euphemiae virginis (cf. *BHL* 2708); (fo. 144) Passio ss. martyrum Luciae et Geminiani (*BHL* 4985); (fo. 150) Vita s. Lamberti episcopi (cf. *BHL* 4677); (fo. 156ᵛ) Passio s.

---

[65] Ends incomplete '. . . corpora eorum proicerunt'. Two further lives may also have been lost from the end of this volume, since the numbering jumps from lx (Passio ss. Primi et Feliciani), at the end of Salisbury Cathedral, MS 221, to lxiii (Passio s. Symphorosae) at the beginning of the companion volume, Salisbury Cathedral, MS 222. The missing two lives are probably the Passio ss. martyrum Getulii, Cerealis et sociorum (cf. *BHL* 3524) and the Passio ss. martyrum Basilidis et sociorum (*BHL* 1019), see Zettel, 'Ælfric's Hagiographic Sources', 21–2.

[66] Formerly Oxford, Bodl. Libr., MS Fell 1.

Matthaei apostoli (*BHL* 5690); (fo. 162ᵛ) Passio s. Mauritii et sociorum, auct. Eucherio episcopo Lugdunensi (retractata) (cf. *BHL* 5743); (fo. 166ᵛ) Passio s. Firmini episcopi (*BHL* 3002); (fo. 171) Acta s. Cypriani episcopi (cf. *BHL* 2038); (fo. 171ᵛ) Acta ss. martyrum Cypriani et Iustiniae: Conversio (*BHL* 2047); (fo. 174ᵛ) Passio ss. martyrum Cypriani et Iustinae (*BHL* 2047); (fos. 175ᵛ–9) Passio ss. martyrum Cosmae et Damiani (*BHL* 1970); (fo. 179) Dedicatio ecclesiae s. Michaelis archangeli: Apparitio Michaelis in Monte Gargano (*BHL* 5948); (fo. 180ᵛ) Vita s. Hieronimi presbyteri, perperam adscripta Gennadio (*BHL* 3869); (fo. 184ᵛ) Vita s. Remigii episcopi, auct. Hincmaro (*BHL* 7152–9); (fo. 236) Vita s. Vedasti episcopi (cf. *BHL* 8508);[67] (fo. 242) Sermo auct. Alcuino (*BHL* 8509): (fo. 243ᵛ) Passio s. Piatonis martyris (cf. *BHL* 6846); (fo. 247) Gesta et passio s. Leodegarii (cf. *BHL* 4853); (fo. 262) Passio ss. martyrum Dionysii, Rustici et Eleutherii (*BHL* 2175); (fo. 277ᵛ) Passio ss. martyrum Sergii et Bacchi (*BHL* 7599); (fo. 283ᵛ) Vita s. Richarii abbatis, auct. Alcuino (*BHL* 7224)[68]

Scribe i (corrections); scribe iii (fo. 75ᵛ/29–33; fo. 288ʳ⁻ᵛ); scribe v (fos. 1–75ᵛ/28; fos. 77–85ᵛ/10; fo. 125ᵛ; fo. 150/8–36; fo. 152ᵛ/12–36; fo. 154/4–36; fo. 155ᵛ/25–36; fos. 157ᵛ/24–158ᵛ; fo. 168/12–36); scribe vi (fos. 184–286ᵛ/4; fo. 286ᵛ/18–32), scribe xvi (fo. 76ʳ⁻ᵛ; fos. 121–5; fos. 126–50/8; fos. 150ᵛ–2ᵛ/12; fos. 153–4/4; fos. 154ᵛ–5ᵛ/24; fos. 156–7ᵛ/24; fos. 159–68/12; fos. 168ᵛ–9; fos. 169ᵛ/11–183ᵛ), and two unidentified hands

---

[67] Without the prologue listed in *BHL*.

[68] A contemporary list of contents on fo. 184 indicates that the *vitae* or *passiones* of the following saints originally formed part of this volume: Callistus, Crispin and Crispinian, Simon and Jude, Quentin, Caesarius, Eustace, Hucbert, Winnoc, 'Quattuor coronati', Theodore, Martin, Menna, Briccius, Anianus, Cecilia, Longinus, Clement, Trudo, Chrysogonus, Saturninus, Andrew, Chrysanthus and Daria, Elegius, Sabinus, Eulalia, Faustinus and Victor, Luceia, Thomas, Anastasia, Eugenie, Marinus, John the Evangelist, Maximus, Lucia, Judoc, Christina, Maurus, Benedict and Scholastica, 'Exaltatio sancti crucis', Silvester, Columba, Wandregesil, 'Epistula Pseudo-Hieronimi ad Paulam et Eustocium de assumptione sanctae Dei genetricis semperque uirginis Mariae'; for the texts represented by this list, see Zettel, 'Ælfric's Hagiographic Sources', 28–34.

APPENDIX 2

GROUP II MANUSCRIPTS:
TEXTS AND SCRIBES

1. Cambridge, Trinity College, MS R.16.34 (fo. 1) *Florilegium* of extracts from Aulus Gellius, *Noctes Atticae* and Valerius Maximus, *Factorum et dictorum memorabilium libri*;[1] (fo. 23) Anonymous poem, 'Nec Veneris nec tu uini tenearis amore . . .';[2] (fo. 23) Extracts from Seneca, *De beneficiis* (from bks. I, iii; II, vii, xvi, xxvii; III, xxiii, xxvii; IV, xxxvii, VII, xxi); (fo. 26ᵛ) Provisions of the Council of Lisieux (AD 1064);[3] (fo. 27) Cicero, *De officiis*, I–II. iii, ix[4]

Scribe 4 (fos. 1–31ᵛ; fos. 32ᵛ–44), and an unidentified hand

2. Dublin, Trinity College, MS 174, fos. 45–52; 56ᵛ–94ᵛ, 104–20ᵛ,[5] (fo. 45) Vita s. Paterni, auct. Fortunato (*BHL* 6477); (fo. 50) Vita b. Ægidii, edita a Fulberto episcopo (*BHL* 93); (fo. 56ᵛ) Passio s. Iuliani, 'Beatus itaque Iulianus romana generositate clarissimus lingua facundus . . . pater eius Anastasius cum omni familia credidit et baptismi gratiam consecutus numero fidelium applicatus est' (cf. *BHL* 4546d); (fo. 58) Sermo Radbodi episcopi Ultraiectensis in natale s. Seruatii Tungrensis episcopi (*BHL* 7614); (fo. 60) Vita s. Leonardi (*BHL* 4862); (fo. 64) Passio ss. Iuliani et Basilissae (*BHL* 4529);[6] (fo. 72ᵛ) Passio s. Bathildis (*BHL* 905, imperfect); (fo. 73) Vita s. Guthlaci, auct. Felicis (*BHL* 3723); (fo. 85) Sermo adscriptus s. Athanasio in imagine Berytensi Cristi crucifixi (*BHL* 4230, imperfect); (fo. 86) Vita s. Amelbergae (*BHL* 323); (fo. 104) Passio s. Cypriani (*BHL* 2041); (fo. 107) Passio ss. Rufini et Walerii (*BHL* 7374); (fo. 114ᵛ) Gaudentius Brixiensis, *Tractatus* XV (*De Machabeis*) (*Clavis*, 215); (fo. 116) Passio s. Achatii (*BHL* 20)[7]

Scribe 10 (fos. 50–2); scribe 14 (fos. 58–61/3); scribe 15 (fos. 116/29–120ᵛ), and at least two unidentified hands

---

[1] Begins imperfectly in a story of Lais: 'omni gratia celebres erant' (Gellius, I. viii). For this *florilegium*, see D. M. Schullian, 'The Anthology of Valerius Maximus and A. Gellius', *Classical Philology*, 32 (1937), 70–2, and also L. D. Reynolds (ed.), *Texts and Transmission: A Survey of the Latin Classics* (Oxford, 1983), 177.

[2] *Anthologia latina, Pars prior: Carmina in codicibus scripta*, ed. A. Riese (Leipzig, 1906), ii, no. 633 (omitting lines 11–14).

[3] Pr. in L. Delisle, 'Canons du Concile tenu à Lisieux en 1064', *Journal des Savants*, 3: 66 (1901), 516–21; repr. in C. J. Hefele, *Histoire des Conciles*, tr. and ed. H. Leclercq (1911), iv. 1420–23.

[4] Ends 'si quando ea que dixi pugnare inter se uiderentur honestatis pars confecta est quam tibi' (ed. H. A. Holden, 8th edn (Cambridge, 1899), 63–4).

[5] A composite manuscript made up of a number of booklets. Some booklets are in the hands of Group I scribes, others are in the hands of Group II scribes. Group II scribes also made additions to booklets begun by Group I scribes.

[6] Omits the prologue listed in *BHL*.

[7] Lacks the letter of Anastasius; ends as *BHL* 21.

3. London, BL, MS Cotton Tiberius C. I, fo. 202ᵛ (addition to a Pontifical), Prayer, 'O sempiterne Deus edificator et custos Ierusalem . . .'
    Scribe 4 (fo. 202ᵛ)

4. London, BL, MS Cotton Vitellius A XII, fos. 79–86 (fo. 79) *Epistola Cummiani*;[8] (fo. 83) Bede, *Epistola ad Pleguinam de aetatibus saeculi* (*Clavis*, 2319)
    Scribe 11 (fos. 79–86ᵛ)

5. London, BL, MS Royal 5 F xviii[9] (fo. 1) Tertullian, *Apologeticum* (*Clavis*, 3); (fo. 29ᵛ) Pseudo-Methodius, *Revelationes*
    Scribe 2 (fos. 1–29); Group I scribe ii (fos. 29ᵛ–32)

6. London, BL, MS Royal 6 B xv, Cyprian, *Opera*: (fo. 2) *Ad Donatum* (*Clavis*, 38), (fo. 4ᵛ) *De habitu virginum* (*Clavis*, 40), (fo. 9) *De lapsis* (*Clavis*, 42), (fo. 16) *De catholicae ecclesiae unitate* (*Clavis*, 41), (fo. 21ᵛ) *De dominica oratione* (*Clavis*, 43), (fo. 28ᵛ) *De mortalitate* (*Clavis*, 44), (fo. 33) *De opere et eleemosinis* (*Clavis*, 47), (fo. 39) *Ad Demetrianum* (*Clavis*, 46), (fo. 44) *De bono patientiae* (*Clavis*, 48), (fo. 49) *De zelo et livore* (*Clavis*, 49), (fo. 52ᵛ) *Ad Fortunatum* (*Clavis*, 45), (fo. 60) *Ad Quirinum* (*Clavis*, 39), (fo. 89ᵛ) *Epistolae* lv, lxxiv, lxix, xl, lxvii, lxiv, ii, lx, lvii, lix, lii, xlv, xliv, li, xiii, xliii, lxv, i, lxi, xlvi, lxvi, iv (*Clavis*, 50), (fo. 122ᵛ) *Quod idola dii non sint* (*Clavis*, 57), (fo. 124) *Epistolae* lvi, iii, lxxii, lviii, lxiii, vi, lxxvi, lxxiii, lxxi, (fo. 138) *Sententiae episcoporum de haereticis baptizandis* (*Clavis*, 56), (fo. 141ᵛ) *Epistolae* xxviii, xxxvii, xxxviii, xxxix, lxx, (fo. 144ᵛ) Sermon attrib. to Cyprian, *De aleatoribus* (*Clavis*, 60), (fo. 147) Sermon attrib. to Cyprian, *De laude martyrii* (*Clavis*, 58), (fo. 152) *Epistolae* lxxix, xx, xxxii
    Scribe 3 (fos. 2–122ᵛ); scribe 7 (fos. 123–52ᵛ); scribe 10 (corrections)

London, BL, MS Royal 15 B xix, fos. 200–5: see below, Salisbury Cathedral, MS 115

7. London, BL, MS Royal 15 C xi, fos. 1–58, Cicero, *Tusculan Disputations*[10]
    Scribe 8 (fo. 9ᵛ/3–38); scribe 9 (fos. 31–58; corrections); scribe 12 (fos. 1–9ᵛ/3; fos. 10–30ᵛ)

8. London, BL, MS 15 C xi, fos. 113–94[11] (fo. 113) Plautus, *Comoediae* (fo. 194ᵛ) Isidore, *Libri etymologiarum*, I. xxi
    Scribe 1 (fos. 191–2ᵛ); Group I scribe ii (fos. 113–90ᵛ; fos. 193–4ᵛ)

9. Oxford, Bodl. Libr., MS Bodley 698 (fo. 1) Ambrose, *De Isaac vel anima* (*Clavis*, 128), (fo. 10ᵛ) *De fuga saeculi* (*Clavis*, 133), (fo. 18) *De Iacob et vita beata* (*Clavis*, 130); (fo. 31ᵛ) 'De consecratione ecclesiarum liber';[12] (fo. 40ᵛ) Augustine,

---

[8] The only extant witness to the text: see *Cummian's Letter, De Controversia Paschali and the De ratione conputandi*, ed. M. Walsh and D. Ó. Cróinín, Studies and Texts, Pontifical Institute of Medieval Studies, 86 (Toronto, 1988), 51–2.

[9] For the contents of this manuscript, see above, App. 1.

[10] Begins imperfectly: 'ornateque dicere. In quam exercitationem ita nos studiose operam dedimus . . .' (ed. T. W. Dougan (Cambridge, 1905), i. 11).

[11] For the contents of this manuscript, see above, App. 1.

[12] *PL* 131. 845–66, where it is ascribed to Remigius.

De beata vita (*Clavis*, 254),[13] (fo. 46) *De duabus animabus* (*Clavis*, 317);[14] (fo. 50) Pseudo-Augustine (Quodvultdeus), *De quattuor virtutibus caritatis*,[15] (fo. 52) *De tempore barbarico* (*Clavis*, 411),[16] (fo. 55ᵛ) *De quarta feria tractatus* (*Clavis*, 406), (fo. 59) *De tempore barbarico*[17]

Scribe 17 (fos. 1–63)

10. Salisbury Cathedral, MS 4 (fo. 1) Hilary, *De Trinitate* (*Clavis*, 433),[18] (fo. 111ᵛ) *De synodis* (*Clavis*, 434)[19]

Scribe 6 (fos. 1–127); scribe 10 (corrections)

11. Salisbury Cathedral, MS 5, Pelagius, Commentary on the Pauline Epistles (*Clavis*, 728)[20]

Scribe 8 (fos. 1–118); scribe 10 (corrections)

12. Salisbury Cathedral, MS 7, Isidore, *Libri sententiarum* (*Clavis*, 1199)[21]

Scribe 13 (fos. 1–39)

13. Salisbury Cathedral, MS 9, fos. 60ᵛ–81 (additions to a Group I manuscript), A monastic *florilegium*: (fo. 60ᵛ) Pseudo-Jerome, *Epistola* 42, *Ad Oceanum de vita clericorum* (*Clavis*, 633); (fo. 62) 'Senten[tiae] Isidori super levi[ticum]. Inter hec etiam iubetur . . .';[22] (fo. 62ᵛ) '[De] circumcisione. [Post]quam consummati sunt dies octo ait euangelium . . . Opus unius cuius [　] regnis probauit'; (fo. 63) 'Incipit sermo sancti Cesari[i　] super salmi, Vouete et reddite [　]. Quis quod potest uoueat et reddat . . .';[23] (fo. 64ᵛ) Caesarius, *Sermo* ccxxxviii;[24] (fo. 65ᵛ) 'Incipit admonitio sancti [Augus]tini de penitentia' (i.e. Caesarius, *Sermo* lxiii);[25] (fo. 66ᵛ) 'De epistola beati Gregorii directa ad Secundino Dei seruo de lapsu. [N]am tua sanctitas inde nobis requisiuit . . . qui peccatores sanguine suo redi[mere uenit] Cristus dominus noster';[26] (fo. 67) Caesarius, *Sermo* xviii;[27] (fo. 68ᵛ) '[De] qualitate anime [　]. [　] itaque imago id est interior homo . . . uel diligite aliquid. uel [　]'; (fo. 68ᵛ) '[Sancti] Cypriani dicta [　] fratres in mundo agitur, quam pugna

---

[13] Ends imperfectly at the bottom of fo. 45ᵛ: 'tam iocunde ageretur' (*PL* 32. 967).

[14] Begins imperfectly at the top of fo. 46: 'sentiuntur ista luce . . .' (*PL* 42. 98); ends: '. . . uel magis credere cogebamur.' (*PL* 42. 111).

[15] CCSL 60. 367–78.

[16] Ibid. 423–37.

[17] A second copy, with different readings from those of fos. 52–5ᵛ.

[18] Begins imperfectly in bk. ii: 'sensus incertus est. Ergo non preceptis . . .' (*PL* 10. 54).

[19] Ends imperfectly near the end: 'uidi carnes carnibus similes: sed post michi' (*PL* 10. 542).

[20] Ascribed in this copy to Jerome. On this manuscript, see *Pelagius's Expositions of Thirteen Epistles of St Paul: Introduction*, ed. A. Souter, Texts and Studies, 9 (1922), i. 283–6.

[21] Damaged at the end, now ends at iii. lxi: 'quia, quantumlibet breue sit temporis spatium, tamen': *PL* 83. 735.

[22] Isidore, *Quaestiones in vetus testamentum; In leviticum*, xiii, 'De sacerdotibus qui non offerunt sacrificium' (*PL* 83. 332–3).

[23] See *Sancti Caesarii Arelatensis sermones*, ed. G. Morin, CCSL 104 (Turnhout, 1953), ii. 983.

[24] CCSL 104. 949–53.

[25] CCSL 103. 272–4.

[26] See *Gregorii I papae registrum epistolarum*, ed. L. M. Hartmann, MGH, *Epistolae*, ii (Berlin, 1899), ii. 146–7 n.*.

[27] CCSL 103. 82–6.

aduersus [ ] cotidie geritur ... Domine da mihi hic modo pacientiam [ ]'; (fo. 68ᵛ) Caesarius, *Sermo* ccxxv;²⁸ (fo. 70) 'Item alia in natale omnium sanctorum martyrum et confessorum.' (Pseudo-Augustine, *Sermo* 209: *PL* 39. 2135–7); (fo. 72) 'Dicta beati Effrem diaconi de die iudicii. Venite benedicti atque dilectissimi fratres exortationem meam suscipite ...';²⁹ (fo. 72ᵛ) [Ser]mo sancti Isidori de his quia delictum post lacrimas redeunt. [I]nrisor est, non pęnitens, qui adhuc agit quod pęnitet ... retro acta negligo et adhuc pęnitenda [committo]';³⁰ (fo. 72ᵛ) 'De his qui hebrietatem diligunt. [Inter] cetera carissimi quę uobis precipimus ... Uides ergo quia mendacium mors est, ueritas [ ] dominus noster Iesus Cristus saluator mundi. Qui uiuit ...'; (fo. 73) 'Sermo [ ] Moysi. Timor domini effugiat omnem maliciam ... uirtutes has potest saluari per gratiam domini nostri Iesu Cristi, qui uiuit ...'; (fo. 73ᵛ) 'Sermo de misericordia. Misericordia fratres peccatorum remedia ... dicaturus erit. Qui in Trinitate unus Deus uiuit...';³¹ (fo. 74) 'Sermo sancti Augus[tini de muliere] deprehensa in adulterio' (Pseudo-Fulgentius, *Sermo* ix);³² (fo. 75) 'Sententia apostoli. Omne peccatum quodcumque fecerit homo extra corpus ... habet autem in se passionem'; (fo. 75) 'Admonitio Ieronimi de esu corporali. Primum igitur si tamen stomachi firmitas patitur ... Hęc est consilium monachi et salus animę qui [ ]'; (fo. 75) 'De carne superbię sermo. Ad te manum meam extendo, quem sentio in tim[ore] ... Humiliata est caro nostra qui potens erat in terram et animam humilem exaltauit. Ipsi honor et gloria in secula seculorum';³³ (fo. 76ᵛ) 'Collatio beati Pathnucii abbatis de penitentia. [Post] illam namque generalem baptismi gratiam ... hoc est spiritalia dona [atque uirtutes]';³⁴ (fo. 77ᵛ) 'De monachis [ ]. [ ] quisque munere locum uirtutis culminis ... uincamus mundum in caritatis uinculo'; (fo. 78) 'De quattuor temporibus anni. Annus uertens tempora ...'; (fo. 78) 'Oportet enim nos timere uerbum domini... Ita debemus et nos nostro [ ] nostrum. Cui est gloria cum Deo patre et sancto Spiritui per infinita [ ]'; (fo. 79) 'Expositio de oratione d⟨ominica⟩. Pater noster qui es in celis, supplicatio fidelium ad Deum patrem ... liberare dignetur incessanter cum deprecari [ ]';³⁵ (fo. 79ᵛ) 'Expositio simboli. [Simbo]lum greca lingua dicitur, quod latine interpretatur conlatio, siue [ ] Conlatio quod duodecim apostoli duodecim uersibus ... secundum opera eorum recepturos finit. Amen.'; (fo. 80ᵛ) 'Sermo de caritate. Caritas grece, latine autem dilectio dicitur. Quę caritas in duobus precep[ ] dilectionem uidelicet Dei et

²⁸ CCSL 104. 888–92.

²⁹ Extracts from Ephraim Syrus, *De die iudicii* (*Clavis*, 1143). Salisbury 131, fos. 27–9ᵛ (see below), contains the full text.

³⁰ *Libri sententiarum*, ii. xvi: *PL* 83. 619.

³¹ A variant text of one partially printed by W. Becker, 'The Latin Manuscript Sources of the Old English Translations of the Sermon *Remedia Peccatorum*', *Medium Ævum*, 45 (1976), 147–8. An extended version of this text is found in a Group I manuscript, Salisbury 179, fos. 46ʳ⁻ᵛ, within an augmented version of the Homiliary of Paul the Deacon.

³² The text is in *PL* 65. 868–9, but with variant readings.

³³ *Tractatus de carne superba*, ed. R. Était, 'L'Ancienne collection de sermons attribués à saint Augustin *De Quattuor Virtutibus Caritatis*', *Rev. bén.*, 95 (1985), 55–9.

³⁴ Cassian, *Collationes*, xx. viii; *PL* 49. 1159–65.

³⁵ M. W. Bloomfield, B.-G. Guyot, D. R. Howard and T. B. Kabealo, *Incipits of Latin Works on the Virtues and Vices, 1100–1500 AD* (Cambridge, Mass., 1979), no. 9186.

proximi consistit ... in concordia fidei cum uniuersali ecclesia a catholica [ ]biliter conseruanda est.'
Scribe 10 (fos. 65ᵛ/21–81); scribe 13 (fos. 60ᵛ–5ᵛ/21)

14. Salisbury Cathedral, MS 11, Pseudo-Clement, tr. Rufinus, *Recognitiones* (cf. *Clavis*, 198n.)[36]
Scribe 1 (fos. 1–41/27); scribe 4 (fos. 72–103ᵛ); scribe 10 (corrections), and an unidentified hand

15. Salisbury Cathedral, MS 12, fos. 56–60[37] (fo. 56) Eutropius, *De districtione monachorum* (*Clavis*, 1096); (fo. 59) *Rule of the Four Fathers*[38]
Scribe 2 (fos. 56/15–60ᵛ)

16. Salisbury Cathedral, MS 35 (fo. 3) Augustine, *Speculum* (*Clavis*, 272); (fo. 51) Pseudo-Augustine, *Hypomnesticon* (*Responsiones* i–iv) (*Clavis*, 381), (fo. 67) Pseudo-Augustine (Quodvultdeus) *De cataclismo* (*Clavis*, 407), (fo. 69ᵛ) *De cantico novo* (*Clavis*, 405), (fo. 72ᵛ) Pseudo-Augustine (Vigilius Thapsensis) *Contra Felicianum* (*Clavis*, 808); (fo. 79) Augustine, *De symbolo*, i–iv (tracts ii–iv, Pseudo-Augustine, i.e. Quodvultdeus) (*Clavis*, 309, 401–3); (fo. 99) Augustine, *De agone christiano* (with *Retractatio* ii. iii) (*Clavis*, 296), (fo. 106) *Sermones*[39] 393, 58, (fo. 108ᵛ) 'Incipit sermo sancti Augustini de misterio crucis. Qui enim cognouit, inquit, latitudinem et longitudinem ... ubi pax illa est que omnem intellectum.' (an extract from *Epistola* 147),[40] (fo. 109) *Sermones* 387, *app.* 271, *app.* 270, 178, 167, 40, *app.* 287, *app.* 105, *app.* 252, 168, 11, *app.* 315, 39, 383, 339, 16, *app.* 53, 333, 388, 353, (fo. 134) 'Sermo sancti Augustini de capitulo psalmi L, id est de peccato David. Quotienscumque fratres karissimi aliquos ex filiis nostris . . .;[41] (fo. 134ᵛ) 'Responsiones Nicholai papę ad consulta Bulgarorum ad fidem conuersorum. lxx. Consulendum decernitis utrum presbiterum habentem uxorem debeatis sustentare et honorare ... quia non statim qui accusatur, reus est; sed qui conuincitur, criminosus';[42] (fo. 135) 'De regula Gangrensis concilii. Capitula iiii. Quicunque decernit a sacerdote qui uxorem habet quod non oporteat esse ministrantem de oblatione accipere, anathema sit.'
Scribe 17 (fos. 122–3ᵛ; fo. 124ᵛᵇ/23–44; fos. 125ᵃ/22–135); scribe 18 (fos. 1–121ᵛ), and scribe 19 (fo. 124–124ᵛᵇ/22; fos. 124ᵛᵇ/44–125ᵃ/21)

17. Salisbury Cathedral, MS 57, Augustine, *Enarrationes in psalmos i–l* (*Clavis*, 283)

---

[36] Ed. B. Rehm, GCS 51 (Berlin, 1965). On this manuscript and its textual affiliations, see ibid. lxxii–lxxviii.

[37] Additions to a Group I manuscript.

[38] The text is that of A. de Vogüé's π recension, see *Les Règles des saints pères* (Paris, 1982), ii. 547–603. This copy now ends imperfectly: 'ut personarum acceptio ne apud' (Macharius, 5, 11: De Vogüé, 598). The entry for this manuscript in Patrick Young's catalogue of 1622 (no. 156), indicates that it also once contained a 'Catalogus librorum Augustini', probably that of Possidius: see Ker, 'Salisbury Cathedral Manuscripts', 172, 178.

[39] *PL* 38–9.

[40] *PL* 33. 611.

[41] *Bibliotheca Casinensis* (Monte Cassino, 1873), i. 114–16. This copy ends, 'Dicam hoc ipsum si potuero planius. Dauid nullum sibi' (ibid. 115).

[42] Pope Nicholas I, *Epistola* xcvii. lxx–lxxi: *PL* 119. 1006–7.

Scribe 8 (fo. 22va/1–30; fo. 22vb/15–29; fo. 37^{b}/21–30; fo. 40^{b}/29–42; fo. 42vb/21–42); scribe 10 (corrections); scribe 12 (fo. 7^{b}/25–36; fo. 12^{b}/10–42; fo. 13^{b}/16–42; fo. 14va/6–14vb/2; fo. 15va/2–15vb/42; fo. 22vb/1–14; fo. 25vb), and at least two unidentified hands, one of whom copied the bulk of the manuscript

18. Salisbury Cathedral, MS 58, Augustine, *Enarrationes in psalmos l–c* (*Clavis*, 283)

Scribe 7 (fo. 14vb/20–42); scribe 8 (fo. 19^{b}/18–30); scribe 9 (corrections); scribe 12 (fos. 1–5; he may also have written much of the rest of the manuscript, but the hand deteriorates to such an extent that positive identification is impossible), and at least one unidentified hand

19. Salisbury Cathedral, MS 59, Cassiodorus, *Expositio psalmorum ci–cl* (*Clavis*, 900)

Scribe 14 (fos. 55vb/11–56^{a}/6; fos. 164^{b}/19–194va/14; fos. 194vb–196^{a}/27; fos. 196^{a}/41–217^{b}/37; fo. 217va/2–30; fo. 217vb/18–27; fo. 218^{a}/10–24; fo. 218^{b}/1–35; fo. 218va/1–9; fo. 218va/35–218vb/2; fo. 218vb/11–22; fos. 218vb/31–219^{a}/20; fo. 219^{a}/36–219^{b}/37; fo. 219va/10–219vb/3; fo. 220^{a}/5–220^{b}/41; fos. 220va/20–221^{a}/34; fos. 221^{b}/14–222vb; fo. 223^{b}; fos. 223vb–224^{v}); scribe 15 (fos. 2–12^{a}/27; fos. 12^{a}/38–51^{b}/32; fos. 51^{v}–55vb/10; fos. 56^{a}/7–71^{b}/31; fos. 71^{v}–74vb/31; fos. 75–115vb/26; fos. 116–164^{b}/19); scribe 18 (fo. 74vb/32–42), and at least three unidentified hands

Pls. 12, 13

20. Salisbury Cathedral, MS 61, fos. 1–10 (fo. 1) Augustine, *Sermones* 65, 53, 277, 330 (*PL* 38. 426–30, 364–72, 1259–68, 1456–9); (fo. 10) 'Sermo sancti Augustini de misericordia. Audite itaque omnes qui estis in populo, et neglegentes aliquando cognoscite … ut misericordes misericordiam consequantur.'[43]

Scribe 3 (fos. 1–10)

21. Salisbury Cathedral, MS 61, fos. 11–20 (fo. 11^{v}) Augustine, *Epistola* 36 (*PL* 33. 136–51); (fo. 15^{v}) Pseudo-Augustine (Ambrosius Autpertus) *De conflictu vitiorum et virtutum*, 'Apostolica uox clamat …' (*PL* 40. 1091–1106); (fo. 19^{v}) A *catena* of short excerpts from Augustine, 'Augustinus in libro de ciuitate Dei. Qui in ecclesia Cristi morbidum … heretici sunt. Augustinus in libro de fide et operibus. Decimas et primitias et cetera bona ecclesie … in quo omnia ineffabiliter et non temporaliter dixit.'

Scribe 3 (rubrics); text in an unidentified hand

22. Salisbury Cathedral, MS 61, fos. 21–30, Augustine, *De natura boni* (with *Retractatio* ii. ix) (*Clavis*, 323)

Scribe 3 (fos. 21–30) (fo. 30^{v} is blank)

23. Salisbury Cathedral, MS 61, fos. 31–52 (fo. 31) Heriger, *De corpore et sanguine domini* with the enlarged Paschasian *catena* of Eucharistic proof texts (the *Exaggeratio*);[44] (fo. 42) Arnobius and Serapion, *Conflictus de Deo trino et uno* (*Clavis*, 239)

---

[43] Römer, 372.
[44] See Ratramnus, *De corpore et sanguine domini*, ed. J. N. Bakhuizen van den Brink, 2nd edn (Amsterdam/London, 1974), 6–7, 29–32.

Scribe 3 (fos. 31–34/38; fos. 34ᵛ–43ᵛ/7); scribe 7 (fo. 34/38–41; fos. 43ᵛ/8–52)
Pl. 7

24. Salisbury Cathedral, MS 64 (fo. 1) Augustine, *De baptismo contra Donatistas* (*Clavis*, 332), (fo. 61) *De spiritu et littera* (*Clavis*, 343), (fo. 81) *De pastoribus* (*Sermo* 46: *PL* 38. 270–95), (fo. 92ᵛ) *De ovibus* (*Sermo* 47: *PL* 38. 295–316), (fo. 102ᵛ) *De peccatorum meritis et remissione et de baptismo parvulorum* (*Clavis*, 342), (fo. 141ᵛ) *De unico baptismo* (*Clavis*, 336)
  Scribe 3 (fos. 1–80); scribe 6 (fos. 81–150)
  Pl. 6*a–b*

25. Salisbury Cathedral, MS 65 (fo. 1) Augustine, *Epistola* 200 (*PL* 33. 925–6), (fo. 1) *De nuptiis et concupiscentia* (*Clavis*, 350), (fo. 22) *Epistola* 207 (*PL* 33. 949–50), (fo. 22) *Contra Iulianum* (*Clavis*, 351)
  Scribe 7 (fos. 1–22ᵛ/17; fos. 23–115); scribe 8 (fos. 22ᵛ/18–40); scribe 10 (corrections)

26. Salisbury Cathedral, MS 101, fo. 32, a single leaf containing a missing portion of text supplied to a tenth-century Continental copy of Isidore, *Quaestiones in vetus testamentum* (*In exodum*, lii: *PL* 83. 313–34)
  Scribe 10 (fo. 32)

27. Salisbury Cathedral, MS 109 (fo. 9) Prosper, *De gratia et libero arbitrio* (*Clavis*, 516), (fo. 15ᵛ) *Pro Augustino responsiones ad capitula obiectionum Gallorum calumniantium* (*Clavis*, 520), (fo. 24) *Pro Augustino responsiones ad capitula obiectionum Vincentianarum* (*Clavis*, 521), (fo. 29) *Pro Augustino responsiones ad excerpta Genuensium* (*Clavis*, 522); (fo. 36) Augustine, *De octo quaestionibus Dulcitii* (*Clavis*, 291); (fo. 49ᵛ) Pseudo-Augustine, *Hypomnesticon* (*Responsio* vi) (*Clavis*, 381); (fo. 56) A corpus of Christmas and Epiphany sermons by Augustine, Eusebius and Origen;[45] (fo. 70) Pseudo-Ambrose, *Sermo* 46, 'Mirum satis . . .' (*Clavis*, 555), (fo. 74) *De mysteriis* (*Clavis*, 155), (fo. 81) *De Gedeon*, 'Hierobohal cum sub arbore . . .'[46] (fo. 83ᵛ) *De apologia prophetae David* (*Clavis*, 135)
  Scribe 6 (fos. 9–99)

28. Salisbury Cathedral, MS 110, Aethicus, *Cosmographia*[47]
  Scribe 8 (fo. 25ᵛ/8–18); scribe 10 (corrections); scribe 12 (fos. 2–25ᵛ/7; fos. 25ᵛ/19–37)
  Pl. 9*b*

29. Salisbury Cathedral, MS 110, flyleaf, a fragment from a copy of Chalcidius, Commentary on the *Timaeus*: 'moderatione. Deinde ait delegisse . . . monstrare naturam leges immutabilis'[48]
  Scribe 8 (fo. 1ʳ⁻ᵛ)

---

[45] See C. Lambot, 'La Tradition manuscrite des sermons de saint Augustin pour la Noël et l'Épiphanie', *Rev. bén.*, 77 (1967), 217–45, esp. 232–3, 233 n. 1.

[46] See O. Faller, ed., Ambrose, *De Spiritu sancto*, CSEL 79 (Vienna, 1964), 42*.

[47] See T. A. M. Bishop, ed., *Aethici Istrici cosmographia Vergilio Salisburgensis rectius adscripta: Codex Leidensis Scaligeranus 69, Umbrae codicum occidentalium*, x (Amsterdam, 1966), xvi–xvii.

[48] Caps cxl–cxlvii: *Timaeus a Calcidio translatus commentarioque instructus*, ed. J. H. Waszink, *Plato Latinus*, iv (London/Leiden, 1962), 181–4.

30. Salisbury Cathedral, MS 112, Isidore, *Libri etymologiarum* (*Clavis*, 1186)
Scribe 6 (fos. 1–151ᵛ); scribe 10 (corrections)

31. Salisbury Cathedral, MS 115+London, BL, MS Royal 15 B xix, fos. 200–5[49]
(Salisbury Cathedral, MS 115, fo. 1) Extracts from Gregory, *Moralia in Iob*, xviii.
i. 'Quibus modus loquitur Deus hominibus. Sciendum sumopere est quia duobus
modis locutio diuina distinguitur, cum aut per semetipsum dominus loquitur ...
quę infra se uentura sunt, uideant.'[50] (fo. 1ᵛ) 'Augustinus in examenon (*sic*) de
loquacite domini acute dicit. Vocauit Deus lucem diem et tenebras noctem. Quia
in uerbo sibi coeterno id est incommutabilis sapientię ... Facilius tamen
intelligitur quid dicitur simul, que quod prius atque posterius.' (fo. 2) A
compendium in dialogue format derived from Pseudo-Augustine, *Dialogus
quaestionum lxv* (*Clavis*, 373 n.) and Eucherius, *Instructiones* (*Clavis*, 489), 'In
nomine Dei Patris et Filii et Spiritus sancti incipit liber questionum sancti
Augustini. Licet multi et probatissimi ... Dic age. Prima interrogatio de Trinitate.
In primis quęro a te utrum Deus Trinitas sit, et quibus testimoniis ad probas nosse
desidero. Responsio. Principium geneseos euidenter ostendit ... ut inuenias
legem ut teneas dum inueneris non mittas. Explicit liber s. Sucherii (*sic*.) episcopi
ecclesię Lugdunensis prouincię Hispanię numero tres de diuersis creaturis quę in
ceteris libris habentur creatorem omnium rerum dominum Deum omnipotentem
in secula seculorum, Amen.' (fo. 15) *Decretum Gelesianum de libris recipiendis et
non recipiendis*, 'Incipit de spiritu septiformi qui in Cristo requiescit ... Passio
Cyrici et Iulitę apocrypha';[51] (fo. 17) Agnellus, *Epistula de ratione fidei ad
Arminium* (*Clavis*, 949);[52] (fo. 17ᵛ) Faustus, *De ratione fidei* (*Clavis*, 964); (fo. 18ᵛ)
Questions and answers on the subject of the Trinity, incorporating a commentary
on the Creed, 'De Trinitate interrogatio. Quomodo credis? Responsio. Credo
Patrem et Filium et Spiritum sanctum. Quomodo credis in Patre? Responsio.
Credo in Patrem omnipotentem ingenitum ante omnia subsistentem ... una
coeternitas certissime credenda est. Iteramus itaque simbolum. Dilectissimi ea
quę paulo ante eiusdem simplicitatem docuimus ... Erit opus iusticię et pax
cultus iusticię, silentium et securitas usque in sempiternum.'; (fo. 19ᵛ) 'Tractatus
sancti Augustini de euuangelio. Quod nos hortatus est dominus noster in
euuangelio ...';[53] (fo. 20) Questions and answers on the Old and New Testaments
(Genesis–Apocalypse), citing Jerome, Augustine, Gregory Nazianzenus, Gregory
the Great, Ambrose, Isidore, Cassiodorus, Cassian, Junilius and Eucherius:[54] (fo.
20) 'Incipit pauca problesmata de enigmata ex tomis canonum. Vetus

---

[49] London, BL, MS Royal 15 B xix, fos. 200–5 are detached leaves from Salisbury
Cathedral, MS 115, see Ker, 'Beginnings', 25.

[50] CCSL 143 B. 1396–401.

[51] *Das Decretum Gelesianum de libris recipiendis et non recipiendis*, ed. E. von
Dobschütz, *Texte und Untersuchungen zur Geschichte der altchristlichen Literatur*, 38/iv
(Leipzig, 1912), 3–13.

[52] Ends, 'Deus omnipotens hoc habere non potest?' (*PL* 68. 384).

[53] Morin, *Caesarius*, i–ii, CCSL 103–4, pp. lxxxv, 983.

[54] It appears to be a hitherto unrecognized copy of the Irish exegetical compilation
known as *The Irish Reference Bible*, see B. Bischoff, 'Wendepunkte', esp., 223–30 (231–6;
74–160). Parts of the text in Salisbury 115 correspond with Bischoff's version IB, as
represented by Paris, BN lat. 614A, extracts from which are printed in Stegmüller, nos.
10301–19: Salisbury 115, fos. 20–36 'Incipit pauca problesmata ... Rabbi ubi habitus',

testamentum ideo dicitur, quia ueniente nouo cessauit. De quo apostolus meminit ... (fo. 20) De ordine canonis apud hebreos et grecos et latinos secundum Hieronimus. Primus ordo legis in quinque libris accipitur quorum primus est bresit, quid est genesis ... (fo. 20ᵛ) In principio creauit Deus cęlum et terram. Terra autem erat inanis et uacua et spiritus Dei ferebatur super aquas. Interrogatio. In quo loco cępit Moyses scribere et in qua lingua, et ubi est initium legis in v libris Moyses? Responsio. Sic soluit Augustinus. In Egypto scripsit genesis ... (fo. 35) Incipit de euangelio. Interrogandum est quis qui euangelium scripserint? Respondetur quattuor uiri, id est Marcus, Matheus, Lucas, Iohannes. Interrogatio. Quo nomine proprio uel appellatiuo uocatur ... (fo. 36) De Matheo euangelio. Matheus ideo carnalem geneologiam ... (fo. 42ᵛ) Reliqueo duas litteras primam et ultimam sibi uindicat Cristus. Ipse enim principium ipse et finis dicens. Ego sum alfa et omega concurrentibus inter se alfa et omega. (London, BL, MS 15 B xix, fos. 200–5) (fo. 200) Symphosius, *Aenigmata*;[55] (fo. 204), Boniface, *Aenigmata de virtutibus*, v. ii, iii, vi, i. iv, vii–ix, x (part)[56]

Scribe 16 (fos. 35–8/40; fos. 38ᵛ–42ᵛ), and at least one unidentified hand
Pl. 14

32. Salisbury Cathedral, MS 116, Augustine, *Contra Faustum Manichaeum* (*Clavis*, 321)
Scribe 3 (fos. 1–191)

33. Salisbury Cathedral, MS 118[57] (fo. 1) Augustine, *De magistro* (*Clavis*, 259), (fo. 23) Extracts from *Confessiones*, Book xi, 'Confiteor tibi domine ignora[re me adhuc quid] sit tempus ... presens de futuris expectat [ ]'; (fo. 24) Epitome of Possidius, *Vita sancti Augustini*, 'Beatus Augustinus ex prouintia Africana ciuitate Tagathensi ... et cum uixisset annos septuaginta sex, in clericatu autem uel episcopatu annos ferme quadraginta complesset, migrauit ad dominum. Et libros mille dictauit et scriptsit, ut uersus de eo scripti testantur. (fo. 24ᵛ) Mentitur qui te totum legisse fatetur ... Si Augustinus adest sufficit ipse tibi';[58] (fo. 24ᵛ) Augustine, *De decem chordis* (*Sermo* 9: *PL* 38. 75–91)
Scribe 2 (fos. 1–2/24; fos. 2ᵛ–39); scribe 5 (fo. 2/25–30)

34. Salisbury Cathedral, MS 124 (fo. 3) Hilary on Matthew (*Clavis*, 430); (fo. 42ᵛ) Irish Pseudo-Hilary on the seven Catholic Epistles[59]
Scribe 9 (fo. 3; fos. 5/7–49ᵛ); scribe 10 (fos. 3ᵛ–5/6)
Pl. 9*a*

correspond with Paris 614A, fos. 3ᵛ–40ᵛ; Salisbury 115, fos. 36–7ᵛ correspond with Paris 614A, fos. 71ᵛ–5. See also, J. E. Cross, 'Hiberno-Latin Commentaries in Salisbury Manuscripts before 1125', *Hiberno-Latin Newsletter*, 3 (1989), 8, which cites these identifications in greater detail.

55 Ed. F. Glorie, *Variae collectiones aenigmatum merovingicae aetatis*, CCSL 133 A (Turnhout, 1968).
56 Id. CCSL 133 (Turnhout, 1968).
57 This manuscript has been damaged by damp, and is illegible in many places.
58 Ed. C. H. Beeson, '*Versus Isidori*', *Isidor-Studien*, ii (Munich, 1913), 159–60.
59 The text is similar to that in Naples, Biblioteca Nazionale, MS Vindob. lat. 4, used by R. E. McNally in his edition, *Tractatus Hilarii in septem epistolas canonicas, Scriptores Hiberniae minores*, i. CCSL 108 B (Turnhout, 1973). The Salisbury copy is damaged, and now ends at the beginning of the commentary on 1 Peter 1: 4 'In hereditatem in' (ibid. 78).

35. Salisbury Cathedral, MS 125, 'Item de libro differentiarum beati Ysidori. Inter animam et spiritum hoc doctores ... et pari iudicio dampnabuntur in ignem aeternum.[60] (fo. 1ᵛ) 'Incipit prefatio. Plurima sunt et paene innumerabilia in diuinis libris ... (fo. 2) 'Incipit capitula. i. De duobus testamenti, hoc est legis et euangelii, et de gemino precepto caritatis, et de tribus maximis uirtutibus, id est fide, spe et caritate' (The capitula list comprises 86 chapters); (fo. 4) 'De eo quod omnipotens Deus post naturalem legem quam primo homini ade cum eum creasset in sensu inseruit ...'.[61]

Scribe 5 (fos. 1–57/13; fos. 57ᵛ–66ᵛ/4; fos. 66ᵛ/14–80ᵛ), and two unidentified hands

36. Salisbury Cathedral, MS 130 (fo. 1) Paschasius, *De corpore et sanguine domini*;[62] (fo. 34) Paulinus of Aquileia, *Liber exhortationis*[63]

Scribe 5 (fos. 1–49ᵛ); scribe 10 (corrections)

37. Salisbury Cathedral, MS 131 (fo. 1) Sermons of Ephraim Syrus, in Latin (*Clavis*, 1143),[64] (fo. 1) *De compunctione cordis*, (fo. 15ᵛ) *De die iudicii et de resurrectione*, (fo. 19) *De beatitudine animae*, (fo. 21) *De paenitentia*, (fo. 25) *De luctaminibus*, (fo. 27) *De die iudicii*

Scribe 1 (fos. 26–9ᵛ); scribe 3 (fos. 1–8ᵛ; fos. 17–20ᵛ; fo. 25ʳ⁻ᵛ); an unidentified hand (s.xii¹) subsequently supplied fos. 9–16 (a complete quire), and a second unidentified hand (s.xii¹) supplied fos. 21–3ᵛ (a quire of four leaves, fo. 24 blank)

38. Salisbury Cathedral, MS 136, Bede, Commentary on Samuel (*Clavis*, 1346)[65]

Scribe 6 (fos. 1–78ᵛ)

39. Salisbury Cathedral, MS 137, Jerome, Commentary on Matthew (*Clavis*, 590)[66]

Scribe 18 (fos. 25ᵛ–34; fo. 34ᵛᵃ/13–34ᵛᵇ/6; fos. 35–36ᵃ/12; fo. 36ᵇ–36ᵛᵇ/17; fo. 37–37ᵛᵇ/35; fos. 38ᵛᵇ/10–39ᵛᵇ/16); scribe 19 (fos. 1ᵇ/20–17ᵛᵇ/6; fo. 34ᵛᵃ/1–12; fo. 34ᵛᵇ/7–29; fo. 36ᵃ/12–39; fo. 36ᵛᵇ/18–39; fos. 37ᵛᵇ/36–38ᵛᵇ/9; fos. 39ᵛᵇ/16–48ᵛ), and at least two unidentified hands. The handwriting on fos. 49–57 is no longer visible because of damage caused by damp.

40. Salisbury Cathedral, MS 139, Eusebius, tr. Rufinus, *Historia ecclesiastica*[67]

---

[60] *Isidore, De differentiis*, ii. xxx: (*PL* 83. 84).

[61] The end of the manuscript is damaged, and the text now ends in the middle of 85, 'perpetuam ultionem, per semetipsum in euangelio'. This is a hitherto unrecognized copy of Pseudo-Isidore, *Liber de variis quaestionibus adversus Iudaeos*, ed. P. A. C. Vega and A. E. Anspach (Escorial, 1940). For the authorship of this text, see J. N. Hillgarth, 'The position of Isidorian Studies: A Critical Review of the Literature, 1936–1975', *Studi medievali*, 3: 24 (1983), 843–4.

[62] CCCM 16.

[63] Ends imperfectly in lvii: 'imposita[m h]umeris suis reportauit ad' (*PL* 99. 265).

[64] A. Siegmund, *Die Überlieferung der griechischen christlichen Literatur in der lateinischen Kirche bis zum zwölften Jahrhundert* (Munich, 1949), 67–71, and also, T. H. Bestul, 'Ephraim the Syrian and Old English Poetry', *Anglia*, 99 (1981), 8 n. 28; 11 nn. 37–8.

[65] Several leaves at the beginning and end of the manuscript are damaged.

[66] Several leaves at the end of the manuscript are damaged.

[67] Begins imperfectly in i. xiii. 18: 'regnum Dei. Post hec autem abgarus ...' (Eusebius, *Die Kirchengeschichte*, ed. E. Schwartz, GCS 9 (Leipzig, 1903), i. 95).

Scribe 3 (fos. 1–87ᵛ; fos. 90–3ᵛ; fos. 104–5ᵛ; fos. 107–2); scribe 9 (fos. 88–89ᵛ; fo. 106ʳ⁻ᵛ; corrections); scribe 10 (fos. 94–103ᵛ)

41. Salisbury Cathedral, MS 162, fos. 3–18, Rufinus, *De symbolo* (*Clavis*, 196)
Scribe 8 (fos. 3–17) (fo. 18 is blank)
Pl. 8

42. Salisbury Cathedral, MS 162, fos. 19–27, *Scala virtutum*, 'In nomine sanctę Trinitatis. Scripturarum diuinarum mole quisquis affatim nequit potiri . . .'[68]
Scribe 7 (fos. 26ᵛ–27); scribe 11 (fos. 19–25/6; fos. 25ᵛ–26); scribe 12 (fo. 25/6–34)
Pl. 10

43. Salisbury Cathedral, MS 165, fos. 88–107 (fo. 88) Augustine, *De presentia Dei* (Epistola 187: *PL* 33. 832–48), (fo. 94) Pseudo-Augustine (Pelagius), *De vita christiana* (*Clavis*, 730), (fo. 102ᵛ) *Ad inquisitiones Ianuarii*, i (*Epistola* 54: *PL* 33. 199–204)
Scribe 10 (fos. 88–104ᵛ) (fos. 105–7 are blank)

44. Salisbury Cathedral, MS 165, fo. 178ᵛ, note on the works of the six days of Creation[69]
Scribe 7 (fo. 178ᵛ/14–22)

45. Salisbury Cathedral, MS 169 (fos. 77ᵛ–91),[70] (fo. 77ᵛ) *Regula Augustini* (the *Praeceptum*), 'Precipimus in monasterio constituti . . .';[71] (fo. 81ᵛ) Bede, Commentary on Tobit (*Clavis*, 1350)
Scribe 2 (fos. 77ᵛ–91)

46. Salisbury Cathedral, MS 197 + London, BL, MS Royal App. 1 (Salisbury Cathedral, MS 197, fo. 1) 'Liber Aurelii Augustini de origine animę. Dominum Deum nostrum qui nos uocauit . . . (i.e. *Epistola* 166: *PL* 33. 720–33), (fo. 5ᵛ) *De immortalitate animae* (*Clavis*, 256); (fos. 10–24ᵛ + London, BL, MS Royal App. 1, fos. 1–2ᵛ) Pseudo-Augustine, *Hypomnesticon* (*Responsiones* i–iv) (*Clavis*, 381); (London, BL, MS Royal App. 1, fo. 2ᵛ) Jerome, *Altercatio Luciferiani et Orthodoxi* (*Clavis*, 608); (fo. 10) 'Augustinus contra Pascentium hereticum' (i.e. Possidius, *Vita s. Augustini*, xvii: *PL* 32. 47–8), (fo. 10ᵛ) Augustine, *Epistolae* 238–

---

[68] An ascetic *florilegium* in the form of a ladder of virtues and a discussion of the vices, composed of extracts from Defensor, *Liber scintillarum*, together with a discussion of the vices extracted from Cassian, *De institutis coenobiorum*, and extracts from Deusdedit, *Libellus contra invasores et symoniacos*. For the full text of this *florilegium*, see App. 3.

[69] An addition to a Group I manuscript. The text is as follows: 'Prima die vii opera fecit Deus, id est, materiam informem, angelos, lucem, cęlos superiores, terram, aquam, atque aerem. Secunda die, firmamentum solum. Tercia die quattuor: materiam, semina, sationes, atque plantaria. Quarta die tria: solem, lunam et stellas. Quinta die tria: pisces et reptilia aquarum et uolatilia. Sexta die quattuor: bestias, pecudes, reptilia terrę et hominem. Et facta sunt omnia xxii genera in diebus sex. Et xxii generationes sunt ab Adam usque ad Iacob, ex cuius nascitur omnes gens Israel; et xxii libri sunt ueteris testamenti usque ad Hester, et xxii litterarum sunt elementa quibus constat diuinę legis doctrina.' A similarly worded passage occurs in another early 12th-cent. Salisbury manuscript—Salisbury 115, fo. 20.

[70] An addition to a Group I manuscript.

[71] The text contained in this manuscript belongs to a subgroup of L. Verheijen's Ω family, see *La Règle de saint Augustin*, i, *Tradition manuscrite* (Paris, 1967), 245–55.

241, *Ad Pascentium* (*PL* 33. 1038–52), (London, BL, MS Royal App. 1, fo. 15ᵛ+Salisbury Cathedral, MS 197, fos. 25–32ᵛ) Augustine, *De genesi ad litteram imperfectus liber* (*Clavis*, 268), (Salisbury Cathedral, MS 197, fo. 33) *De opere monachorum* (with *Retractatio* ii. xxi) (*Clavis*, 305), (fo. 45) *Epistola* 259 (*PL* 33. 1073–5), (fo. 45ᵛ) *De vita et moribus clericorum* i–ii (*sermones* 355–6: *PL* 39. 1568–81); (fo. 50) Sermon, 'Quod nos hortatur dominus in euangelio fratres karissimi agere debemus . . .';[72] (fo. 50ᵛ) Augustine, *Sermo* 97 (*PL* 38. 589–91); (fo. 51ᵛ) 'Fortasse quis dicat de prioris dominicę predicatione . . . Quid quęris uiuentem cum mortuis?'; (fo. 52) Extract from Possidius, *Vita s. Augustini*, xxx, 'Interea reticendum minime est . . . Isto modo rescriptum est ad eundem ab eodem' (*PL* 32. 59–60); (fo. 52ᵛ) Augustine, *Epistola* 228 (*PL* 33. 1013–19); (fo. 54ᵛ) *Epistola* 3 (*PL* 33. 63–6)

Scribe 3 (MS 197, fos. 1–13ᵛ; fos. 14/13–54ᵛ; MS Royal App. 1, fos. 1–15); scribe 10 (MS 197, fos. 55–6; corrections), and an unidentified hand

47. Salisbury Cathedral, MS 198 (fo. 1) Augustine, *Epistola* 147 (*PL* 33. 596–622), (fo. 17ᵛ) *De fide et symbolo* (with *Retractatio* i. xvii) (*Clavis*, 293), (fo. 25ᵛ) *Sermo* 180 (*PL* 38. 972–9), (fo. 30) *De agone christiano* (with *Retractatio* ii. iii) (*Clavis*, 296), (fo. 40ᵛ) *Epistola* 130 (*PL* 33. 494–507); (fo. 49) 'Epistola ad diuersos . . . Audistis apostoli sermonem . . .';[73] (fo. 50ᵛ) Augustine, *Sermo* 391 (*PL* 39. 1706–9), (fo. 53) *De urbis excidio* (*Clavis*, 312), (fo. 57ᵛ) *Epistola* 127 (*PL* 33. 483–7); (fo. 60ᵛ) '[De] libello uite sancti Augustini inter caetera et ad locum. Preterea cum quodam Pascentio . . . spatium occuparet.' (Possidius, *Vita s. Augustini*, xvii: *PL* 32. 47–8); (fo. 61ᵛ) Augustine, *Sermones* 259 (*PL* 38. 1196–201), 350, 346, 347, 348 (*PL* 39. 1533–5, 1522–4, 1524–6, 1526–9); (fo. 70) 'Incipit tractatus de fide. Hoc dicimus et hoc docemus . . . sed etiam cum delectatione faciamus.';[74] (fo. 71ᵛ) Augustine, *Sermones* 389+390 (*PL* 39. 1701–6), 351 (*PL* 39. 1535–49), (fo. 83) *Epistola* 228, vii, 'Quod autem ad eos attinet . . . sine impietate non possunt.' (*PL* 33. 1016), (fo. 83ᵛ) *Ad inquisitiones Ianuarii*, i–ii (*Epistolae* 54–5: *PL* 33. 200–23) (with *Retractatio* ii. xx), (fo. 96ᵛ) *De cura pro mortuis gerenda* (with *Retractatio* ii. lxiv) (*Clavis*, 307), (fo. 106ᵛ) 'Aug. in libro confessionum. Non ego inmunditiam . . . meruit improbari.' (Extr. from *Confessiones*, x. xxxi: *PL* 32. 799.)

Scribe 3 (fos. 1–107)

48. Salisbury Cathedral, MS 221,[75] fos. 223–4ᵛ (an addition to a Group I manuscript) *Vita sancti Blasii* (*BHL* 1370)

Scribe 14 (fos. 223–4ᵛ)

49. Salisbury Cathedral, MS 223[76]+Salisbury Cathedral, MS 222, fo. 1, (Salisbury Cathedral, MS 223, fo. 1) Vita s. Bonefatii, auct. Willibaldo (*BHL* 1400);[77] (fo. 4) Vita s. Ammonis (*PL* 21. 407–8); (fo. 4ᵛ) Miracula s. Gertrudis (*BHL* 3495); (fo. 7) Confessio s. Patricii (*BHL* 6492); (fo. 13) Vita s. Iohannis

---

[72] Morin, *Caesarius*, i–ii, CCSL 103–4, lxxxv, 983.
[73] Römer, 372.
[74] Ibid. 378–9.
[75] Formerly, Oxford, Bodl. Libr., MS Fell 4.
[76] Formerly, Oxford, Bodl. Libr., MS Fell 3.
[77] Damaged at the beginning. Now begins 'Hugoberti' (*PL* 89. 622, line 3).

Penariensis (*BHL* 4420); (fo. 13ᵛ) Passio s. Theodoriti presbyteri (*BHL* 8074) ; (fo. 19ᵛ) 'Conceptio sanctae Marię. [H]ęc ergo Maria prima inter feminas hoc constituit in corde suo ... Nunc igitur mores pensate et opera cogitationis considerate ut sine fine post modum retributionem reddat Ihesus Cristus unigenitus Patris qui cum ...'; (fo. 20) Passio s. Polychronii (*BHL* 6884); (fo. 21) Passio s. Torpetis (*BHL* 8307); (fo. 23ᵛ) Passio s. Cononis (*BHL* 1912); (fo. 24ᵛ) Passio s. Dioscori (*BHL* 2203e); (fo. 25ᵛ) 'Sermo sancti Leonis pape in natale sancti Iohannis baptistae.' (Augustine, *Sermo App.* 196, *PL* 39. 2111–13); (fo. 27) Passio s. Iulii (*BHL* 4555); (fo. 28) Passio s. Iuliani (*BHL* 4540); (fo. 28ᵛ) Passio s. Archadii (*BHL* 658); (fo. 29ᵛ) Passio s. Maximiliani (*BHL* 5813); (fo. 30) Passio s. Epipodii (*BHL* 2574); (fo. 31) Passio s. Maximi (*BHL* 5829); (fo. 31ᵛ) Apparitio Michaeli archangeli in Monte Tumba (*BHL* 5951); (fo. 34) Vita s. Wilfridi, auct. Eddio Stephano (*BHL* 8889); (fo. 57) Vita et miracula s. Cuthberti, auct. Beda (*BHL* 2021)+(fo. 76) Bede, *Historia Ecclesiastica*, iv. xxxi–xxxii and (fo. 77) 'Quicunque historiis ... a quo etiam sumpsistis primordia'; (fo. 77) Passio s. Ursini (*BHL* 8414+8411); (fo. 81ᵛ) Passio s. Concordii (*BHL* 1906); (fo. 82) 'Passio sancte Zoe. [B]eatissima Zoe cum apostolorum natale agebatur ... domum suam fecit ecclesiam. Cui omnes opes suas ad cristianorum requiem derelinquens, fecit ipsam ecclesiam heredem in Cristo. Cui est honor ...' (final part of *BHL* 7543: *PL* 17. 1052–8)); (fo. 84) Laudatio s. Honorati, auct. Hilario ep. Arelatensi (*BHL* 3975); (fo. 91) Passio s. Sabiniani (*BHL* 7438); (fo. 93) Passio s. Alexis (*BHL* 286); (fo. 95) Passio s. Theodori (*BHL* 8079); (fo. 99) Passio s. Salvii episcopi (*BHL* 7472); (fo. 102) Passio s. Fidis (*BHL* 2930), (fo. 103ᵛ) '[S]ancta et benedicta Fides preciosa et martir gloriosa, honor cęli decus paradisi ... consortio coniuncti, tecum feliciter ęternare mereamur in cęlis, amen.' (cf. *BHL* 2940), (fo. 104) 'Sanctissimo atque hominum doctissimo Fulberto Car[ ]notano episcopo ... (fo. 112) Reuersio tertia Bernardi ad sanctam Fidem et quod Witbertus illuminatus iam obiisset Anno igitur ab incarnatione domini millesimo uicesimo ... ante sacram [i]maginem dependens sudarium.' (extracts from Bernardus Andegavensis, *Miracula S. Fidis* (*BHL* 2942), with interpolations), (Salisbury 222, fo. 1) (begins imperfectly) 'malignitatis suę spiritus ... spiritus odorem ęternitatis beatę et leticiam beatitudinis sempiternae.' (Cf. *BHL* 2930).

Scribe 14 (fos. 1–26ᵛ/14; fos. 26ᵛ/19–33/36; fos. 34–48; fos. 48ᵛ/9–51ᵇⁱˢ/35; fos. 51ᵇⁱˢ ᵛ–54/17; fos. 54/32–79/2; fos. 100–1ᵛ); scribe 15 (fo. 33/37–33ᵛ; fos. 79/2–92ᵛ; fos. 95/15–97); scribe 16 (fo. 48ᵛ/1–8; fo. 51ᵇⁱˢ/35–39; fo. 103ᵃ/36–42); scribe 17 (fo. 54/18–31); scribe 18 (fos. 93–95/14; fos. 98–9ᵛ; fos. 102–3ᵃ/35; fos. 103ᵛ–20+Salisbury Cathedral, MS 222, fo. 1), and one unidentified hand Pl. 11

APPENDIX 3

THE SCALA VIRTUTUM

INTRODUCTION

THE TEXT

The text given here represents a transcription of Salisbury Cathedral, MS 162, fos. 19–27. These folios form a separate booklet written at Salisbury in the early twelfth century by three Group II scribes, working in collaboration. Scribe 7 copied fos. 26ᵛ–27; scribe 11 copied fos. 19–26, apart from fo. 25, lines 6–34 which were copied by scribe 12. Each scribe corrected his own work.

I have adopted modern conventions of word separation, punctuation and capitals, but I have retained the orthography of the manuscript (including scribal inconsistencies). Abbreviations have been expanded silently, following, as far as possible, the orthographical conventions practised by the Salisbury scribes (e.g. *Cristus* for *Xps*). The tironian *nota* for *et* and the ampersand are both reproduced as *et*. Scribal errors (other than orthographical peculiarities and inconsistencies) have been corrected, and the manuscript readings recorded in the textual footnotes. Errors corrected by the scribes themselves are also recorded in the textual footnotes. Words or letters illegible in the manuscript are supplied within square brackets. Other editorial matter (e.g. folio nos.) is entered between round brackets.

SOURCES

Footnotes refer only to the three principal texts from which the *florilegium* is derived. The references are to the following editions: Defensor of Ligugé, *Liber scintillarum*, ed. H.-M. Rochais, CCSL, 117 (Turnhout, 1957); Cassian, *De institutis coenobiorum et de octo principalium vitiorum remediis*, ed. M. Petschenig, CSEL, 117 (Prague/Vienna/Leipzig, 1888), and Deusdedit, *Libellus contra invasores et symoniacos et reliquos scismaticos*, ed. E. Sackur, *Libelli de lite imperatorum et pontificum*, ii, MGH (Hanover, 1892), 292–365.

SCALA VIRTUTUM

(Fo. 19) In nomine sanctę Trinitatis. Scripturarum diuinarum mole quisquis affatim nequit potiri quodam priuilegio his elucubratissimis flosculis medullitus se uelit condiri. Ne nos tenebrę fratres comprehendant, dum lucem habemus currere sanctis gradibus satagamus, ne hereditatem promissam culpa nostri quod absit amittamus.

Primus gradus est sacratissimę scalę fides recta cum operibus iustistię. Id est, ut in Patrem et Filium et in Spiritum sanctum perfecte credat. In sancta Trinitate unum Deum cognoscat, in uno Deo sanctam Trinitatem nouerit coeternum et coequalem Dei Filium Deo Patri et Deo Spiritui sancto. Quia qui incredulus est Filio Dei non uidebit uitam, sed ira Dei manet super eum.[1]

Secundus gradus est spes firma in Deum. Id est, ut unusquisque spem suam in Deo ponat; de omni re, de presentibus atque de futuris bonis, spem habeat quicquid boni uel cogitet uel faciat a Deo sibi remunerandi, et spem habeat indulgentię peccatorum si se ueraciter ad Deum conuertat per pęnitentiam. Desperatio autem peior est omni peccato, quia auget peccatum.[2]

Tertius gradus est maxime necessarius—karitas perfecta. Id est, ut diligatur Deus ex toto corde, toto animo,[3] tota uirtute, in sensu perfecto, in uoluntate bona, in cogitatu mundo, in uerbis diuinis, in operibus Deo placitis, et proximos nostros, id est omnes Cristianos, sicut nosmetipsos diligamus, quia caritas operit multitudinem peccatorum.[4] Karitas uera est amicum diligere in Deo et inimicum propter Deum.[5] Karitas enim omnium uirtutum obtinet principatum,[6] quia Deus karitas est. A Deo ergo et a regno Dei se separant qui semetipsos a karitate dissotiant.[7] Sine karitate namque quicquidem malum est, quamuis bonum forinsecus uideatur; ieiunium, elemosina, oratio, oblatio, humilitas, et cetera his similia bona nil proderunt, et nullum bonum est sine karitate.[8] Uę illi qui karitatem abicit, quia Deum abicit a semetipso.

Quartus gradus[a] est pacientia[b] uera. Id est, ut quandocumque a Deo qualiacumque flagella patimur, uel ab antiquo aduersario, id est (fo. 19ᵛ) a diabolo temptamenta, uel a proximo persecutiones, uel contumelias nullo modo uincamur; sed patienter in Dei laudibus sustineamus,[9] et semper Deo gratias referamus. Quia patientia uera est aliena mala unanimiter perpeti, et contra eum qui mala irrogat nullo dolore morderi.[10] Quia patientia uera est quę et ipsum amat quem portat,[11] et si quis tibi intulerit mala, ne irascaris; sed potius dole pro eo, quia Deus illi irascitur.[12]

Quintus gradus est humilitas sancta. Id est, in mente et in omnibus moribus atque in loquelis, et in stando et in sedendo, uel in ambulando uel in uestitu, semper humilitas ostendatur. Humilitas est, si, quando peccauerit in te frater tuus, antequam ille peccauerit, indulgeas ei.[13] Omnis utique labor sine humilitate uanitas est.[14] Qui etiam sibi uilis est per humilitatem, ante Deum[c] magnus est. Portate semper uerecundiam in uultu, de recordatione delicti.[15] Puluis estis et in puluerem sedetis. Cinis estis, in cinere uiuetis.[16] In summo honore summa uobis sit humilitas.[17]

Sextus gradus est mansuetudo. Id est, ut mites sitis, et humiles corde,[18] et in mansuetudine cuncta opera uestra perficiatis,[19] et ut sitis mansueti et quieti ad

---

[a] gradus] *scribal corr., orig.* modus   [b] pacientia] *scribal corr., orig.* penitentia
[c] Deum] *scribal insertion*

[1] Defensor, *Liber scintillarum*, xxxiii, 4.   [2] Cf. ibid. xxxiv, 10.
[3] Cf. ibid. i, 29.   [4] Ibid. i, 2.   [5] Ibid. i, 35.   [6] Ibid. i, 40.
[7] Ibid. i, 43.   [8] Cf. ibid. i, 9.   [9] Cf. ibid. ii, 22.   [10] Ibid. ii, 24.
[11] Ibid. ii, 28.   [12] Ibid. ii, 40.   [13] Ibid. iv, 51.   [14] Ibid. iv, 49.
[15] Ibid. iv, 44.   [16] C.f. ibid. iv, 45.   [17] Ibid. iv, 46.
[18] Cf. ibid. lxxi, 1.   [19] Ibid. lxxi, 9.

intelligenda uerba,[20] quę uilitas ex uerbis et ex lege Cristi nobis annuntiare curat. Quia sicut Lucifer in cęlo fulget, sic anima mitis coram Deo rutilat.[21]

Septimus gradus est indulgentia. Id est, si offers munus tuum ad altare, et ibi recordatus fueris quam[d] frater tuus habet aliquid aduersum te, relinque ibi munus tuum ante altare, et uade reconciliari prius fratri tuo, et tunc ueniens offeres munus tuum.[22] Si etiam dimiseritis hominibus peccata eorum, dimittet uobis et Pater uester qui est in cęlis. Si autem non dimiseritis hominibus, nec Pater uester dimittet uobis peccata uestra.[23] Itaque Cristi plebs, filii Dei, cum patientia supportate inuicem, donantes uobismetipsis si quis aduersus aliquem habet querelam. Sicut Deus donauit in Cristo uobis, ita et uos facite.[24] Non reddentes malum pro malo uel maledictum pro maledicto, sed e contrario benedicentes, quia in hoc uocati estis, ut benedicationem hereditate possideatis.[25] Unusquisque etiam talem indulgentiam accepturus est a Deo, qualem et ipse (fo. 20) dederit proximo suo.[26] Quisquis etiam illi qui in eum peccauerit dimittit ignoscendo peccatum, sine dubio elemosinam facit maximam.[27]

Octauus gradus est conpunctio cordis. Id est, memoria preteritorum[e] facinorum, consideratio peregrinationis in huius uite calamitate, recordatio pęnarum futurarum, desiderium supernę patrię quatenus ad Dei spem quantocius ualeat peruenire.[28] Beatus namque et ter beatus quisquis habet conpunctionem.[29] Conpunctio sanitas animę est. Conpunctio remissio peccatorum est. Conpunctio Spiritum sanctum ad se perducit, et Cristum in se habitare facit.[30]

Nonus gradus est oratio. Id est, ut orationi sitis instantes, orantes omni tempore in spiritu, uigilantes in omni instantia,[31] ut digni habeamini fugere omnia mala quę futura[f] sunt, et securi stare ante Cristi tribunal. Dum enim oramus, ad memoriam culpas reducamus. Cum Deo assistimus,[g] gemere et flere debemus, reminiscentes quam grauia sunt scelera quę commisimus.[32] Oratio debet esse pro uobismetipsis, pro omni populo catholico, pro amicis uel proximis, pro inimicis, et persequentibus uos. Pro nobis itaque qui pro uobis oramus, et uerbum Dei uobis nuntiamus, quia oratio munda diaboli tela exuperat;[33] inmundos spiritus euincit, demonia alligat.[34]

Decimus gradus est confessio pura, quia[h] qui abscondit scelera sua, non dirigitur. Qui autem confessus fuer[it], et relinquerit ea, misericordiam consequitur a Deo,[35] et mundat eum Deus ab omni iniquitate. Tempus confessionis est nunc; confiteri quę fecistis, quę in uerbo, quę in opere, quę in nocte, quę in die.[36] Confessio iustificat, confessio peccati ueniam dat.[37] Ideo confitemini nunc Domino et sanctis sacerdotibus, ut mundi et digni ante Cristi iudicium[i] peruenire mereamini.

Undecimus gradus est pęnitentia digna. Id est, ut ne tardetis conuerti ad Dominum, et ne differatis de die in diem,[38] sed conuertimini ad Dominum, et

---

[d] quam] *Defensor has* quia.   [e] preteritorum] *scribal corr., orig.* preteritarum
[f] futura] *scribal corr., orig.* facitis   [g] assistimus] *scribal corr., orig.* assistamus
[h] quia] *scribal corr., orig.* quam   [i] iudicium] *scribal corr., orig.* tribunal

[20] Cf. ibid. lxxi, 10.   [21] Ibid. lxxi, 21.   [22] Ibid. v, 1.   [23] Ibid. v, 2.
[24] Ibid. v, 3.   [25] Ibid. v, 5.   [26] Ibid. v, 8.   [27] Ibid. v, 21.
[28] Ibid. vi, 24.   [29] Ibid. vi, 28.   [30] Ibid. vi, 29.   [31] Ibid. vii, 5.
[32] Ibid. vii, 35.   [33] Ibid. vii, 48.   [34] Cf. ibid. vii, 49.
[35] Ibid. viii, 4.   [36] Ibid. viii, 12.   [37] Ibid. viii, 37.   [38] Ibid. ix, 7.

relinquite peccata;[39] quia Deus omnipotens est paratus accipere penitentiam peccatorum. Iam igitur cesset unusquisque peccare, quia satis alienus est a fide qui ad agendam penitentiam tempora senectutis expectat.[40] Festi- (fo. 20ᵛ) -nandum est unicuique ad Deum pęnitendo conuerti citius,[41] quia in hoc seculo tantum modo poenitentiam operantibus Dei misericordia subuenit. In futuro autem iam non operamur, sed rationem operum nostrorum ponimus[42] coram Deo et sanctis eius, et tunc unicuique recompensabitur secundum opera sua.

Duodecimus gradus est abstinentia. Id est, ut unusquisque festinet beatus esse esuriendo et sitiendo iustitiam;[43] quia qui se a cibis abstinet, et praue agit, dęmones imitatur. Ille autem bene a cibis abstinet, qui iustitiam Dei esurit, et a malis actibus uel a mundi delectionibus ieiunat.[44] Nichil enim prodest carnem abstinentia affligere, si mentem a uitiis non emendamus.[45]

Tercius decimus gradus est*ʲ* timor Dei; ut omnis Cristianus timorem Dei semper sibi ante oculos ponat, et semper sit memor omnium quę pręcepit Deus, semperque cogitet qualiter contemnentes Deum pro peccatis suis in Gehennam incidunt, animoque suo semper reuoluat ęternam uitam, quę Deum timentibus preparata est; et custodiat se omni hora a peccatis et uitiis, id est, cogitationum, linguę, oculorum, manuum, pedum. Ęstimet se a Deo semper respici de cęlis omni hora, et facta sua omni loco ab aspectu diuinitatis uideri, et ab angelis omni hora renuntiari. Quapropter cauendu[m] est nobis omni hora ne nos declinemus*ᵏ* in malum, ne aliquando Dominus omnipotens malis nostris contristetur, sed semper quod bonum est faciamus, ut ille lętus nobiscum, et nos lęti cum illo regnare mereamur in uita perhenni.

Quartus decimus gradus est uirginitas. Virgines ergo siue uiri siue feminę, si in uirginitate castitatis permanserint, angelis Dei efficiuntur ęquales.[46] Ubi ergo uirginitas mentis et corporis est, ibi et Deus manet.[47] Nichil prodest uirginitas, ubi operatur corruptio mentis.[48] Longa namque castitas post peccatum imitatrix est uirginitatis.[49] Quapropter qui uirgo est sit mente casta et corpore impolluto, agat gratias omnipotenti Domino, omnique deuotione (fo. 21) studeat usque in finem in eadem uiginitate permanere. Qui autem in se ipso cognoscit pollutam esse uirginitatem, doleat, gemat, redeatque per penitentiam ad integritatem mentis et corporis, ut cum uirginibus sanctis angelis beatis consotietur.

Quintus decimus gradus est iusticia. Id est, ut contra nullum aliquid iniuste, uel cogitando, uel loquendo, uel operando, disponas, sed unumquemque hominem cristianum scito proximum et fratrem tuum esse. Quapropter quod tibi non uis fieri, alio ne facias.

Sextus decimus gradus est misericordia, quam itaque mentibus cordium uestrorum fixa radice infigite, uerba Cristi animo reuoluentes. Dicit enim ipse: 'Beati misericordes, quoniam ipsi misericordiam consequentur.'[50] Et omni Cristiano iubendo dicit: 'Estote ergo misericordes, sicut et Pater uester misericors est'.[51] Estote inuicem benigni, misericordes;[52] induite uos uiscera misericordię.[53]

ʲ gradus est] *MS* est gradus   *ᵏ* declinemus] *scribal corr., orig.* declinamus

[39] Ibid. ix, 10.   [40] Ibid. ix, 29.   [41] Cf. ibid. ix, 51.   [42] Ibid. ix, 61.
[43] Cf. ibid. x, 1.   [44] Ibid. x, 39.   [45] Cf. ibid. x, 61.   [46] Ibid. xiii, 16.
[47] Cf. ibid. xiii, 21.   [48] Ibid. xiii, 4.   [49] Ibid. xiii, 25.
[50] Ibid. xliv, 1.   [51] Ibid. xliv, 2.   [52] Ibid. xliv, 4.   [53] Ibid. xliv, 5.

Quia beata est anima, et beatus uir in cuius pectore misericordia seruat facere misericordiam et iudicium. Quia misericordia et iudicium magis placent apud Deum quam uictimę oblationum.[54] Neque enim mereri apud Deum misericordiam poterit, qui misericors ipse non fuerit. Neque inpetrabit de diuina pietate aliquid in precibus, qui ad preces pauperis non fuerit humanus.[55] Quapropter, si aliquis inter uos deuiando corruat, uos qui in uia recta statis, ins[tr]uite in spiritu lenitatis et misericordię, uestram fragilitatem considerantes ne forte et uos cadatis.[56] Ita clementes estote in alienis delictis,[*l*] sicut in uestris, ut nec aliter uos, nec aliter alios preesetis, sed sic alios iudicate, ut iudicari cupitis.[57] Quia cum honera nostra inuicem portamus, conluctatorem nostrum diabolum confundimus et superamus, et Dominum nostrum, qui in cęlis est, honorificamus.[58]

Septimus decimus[*m*] gradus est elemosina, de cuius uirtute Cristus dicit: 'Date elemosinam, et ecce omnia munda sunt uobis.'[59] Qui faciunt elemosinam et iustitiam, saturabuntur in uita ęterna gaudio summo.[60] Quia sicut ignem ardentem extinguit aqua, sic elemosina extinguit peccata.[61] Duę sunt elemosinę, una (fo. 21ᵛ) corporalis: egenti dare quicquid potueris; altera spiritalis: dimittere a quo Iesus es,[62] et discordantes ad concordiam reuocare. Qui itaque inimicum diligit, et qui lugenti effectum conpassionis et consolationis impertitur, aut in quibuslibet necessitatibus consilium adhibet, elemosinam procul dubio facit.[63] Iccirco, nullus est qui excusationem habere ualeat inopię, qui non elemosinam porrigere possit.[64] Quapropter, dum tempus habemus, operemur bonum ad omnes homines.

Octauus decimus gradus est hospitalitas, quam in tantum Dominus ipse laudat, ut semetipsum dicat in hospite suscipi. Unde in diem magni concilii dicturus est hospitalitatem amantibus: 'Hospes fui, et suscepistis me.' Legimus namque in sanctis scripturis, et ipsum Dominum, nec non et sanctos angelos in similitudine hominum, ad hospicium hominum uenire.

Nonus decimus gradus est honor parentum. Dicit hoc uetus testamentum, dicit et nouum. Euangelium loquitur, os Domini loquitur: 'Honora patrem et matrem, ut bene tibi sit et sis longeuus super terram.'[65] Qui itaque Deum timet, honorat parentes.[66] Mala fama est qui relinquit patrem, et est maledictus a Deo qui exasperat matrem.[67] Honoret ergo omnis Cristianus patrem, et subditus sit illi, et gemitus matris sue non obliuiscatur.[68] Parentes nostros ut propria uiscera diligamus, si accedere nos ad seruitutem Cristi non prohi[bu]erint. Si autem prohibuerint,[*n*] nec sepulchra illis a nobis debentur.[69] Patres estote prudentes, et nolite ad iracundiam prouocare filios uestros, sed docete illos in disciplina et correctione Dei.[70] Quia honor patris, honor est filii. Et honor filii[*o*] est honor patris.

Uicesimus gradus est silentium moderatum, quia in multiloquio non effugietur peccatum.[71] Quapropter plebs Cristi, audi et intellige doctrinam Cristi. Antequam

---

l delictis] *scribal corr., orig.* debetis   *m* decimus] *scribal insertion*
n prohibuerint] *scribal corr., orig.* non prohibuerint   *o* filii] *scribal insertion*

[54] Cf. ibid. xliv, 12.   [55] Ibid. xliv, 23.   [56] Cf. xlv, 4.
[57] Ibid. xlv, 34.   [58] Ibid. xlv, 35.   [59] Ibid. xlix, 1.
[60] Cf. ibid. xlix, 4.   [61] Ibid. xlix, 13.   [62] Ibid. xlix, 41.
[63] Ibid. xlix, 39.   [64] Cf. ibid. xlix, 40.   [65] Ibid. lvi, 1.
[66] Ibid. lvi, 7.   [67] Ibid. lvi, 10.   [68] Ibid. lvi, 11.   [69] Ibid. lvi, 14.
[70] Ibid. lvi, 2.   [71] Ibid. xvi, 5.

loquaris, disce.[72] Scito quo tempore loquaris, considera quando dicas. Tempore congruo loquere, tempore congruo tace.[73] Linguosus homo imperitus est, sapiens paucis uerbis utitur. Sapientia breuem sermonem facit; stulticia autem multum loquitur.[74] Sit in uerbo mensura, sit in sermone statera, semper sint uerba omnis (fo. 22) Cristiani moderata.[75] Nichil loquatur Cristianus, nisi uerba utilia et moderata, et uerba aedificationis. Qui custodit os suum, custodit animam suam.[76]

Uicesimus primus gradus est consilium bonum. Id est, ut sine consilio nichil faciatis, ne post factum penitere incipiatis.[77] Cristianus homo cum bono Cristiano et cum uiro religioso tractet suam causam et suam necessitatem.[78] A mali uoluntate autem, consilium suum abscondat. Ante actum omnem uestrum consilium habete discretum et stabile.[79] In omni opere quod cogitatis facere, primum cogitate Deum; et si secundum Deum est quod cogitatis, diligenter examinate; et si[p] rectum est coram Deo, perficite illud. Si uero peruersum fuerit repertum, amputate illud ab anima uestra.[80]

Uicesimus secundus gradus est iudicium rectum, de quo Dominus ipse testatur dicens, 'Nolite iudicare, ut non iudicemini. In quo enim iudicio iudicaueritis, iudicabimini.'[81] Iustum iudicium iudicate.[82] Quapropter, filii Dei, tenete firmiter hunc gradum sancte scalę, et nullum ante iudicium condemnetis, sed ante probate et sic iudicate.[83] Nolite uosmetipsos in aliorum iudicio ligare ante Cristi tribunal, sed unusquisque uestrum semetipsum considerando iudicet. Quia omnis homo in semetipso habet sufficienter et plus quam indigeat iudicare et condempnare.

Uicesimus tertius gradus est exemplum bonum. Id est, ut exemplum prebeatis omnibus hominibus in uos considerantibus, in uerbis, in moribus, in conuersatione, in caritate, in fide,[84] et in omni bonitate. Debet ergo unusquisque qui hanc beatissimam scalam ascendere cupit, in omnibus semetipsum prebere exemplum bonorum operum.[85]

Uicesimus quartus gradus est uisitatio infirmorum. Quam namque Dominus omnipotens in die iudicii coram angelis suis in tantum commendat, ut semetipsum in infirmo uisitari testetur dicens: 'Infirmus fui, et uisitastis me.' Et item dicit: 'Quod uni ex minimis meis fecistis, mihi fecistis.' Quapropter karissimi omni studio uisitate infirmos, opem consolationis illis porrigendo, ut, in infirmo, Cristus a uobis uisitetur. Et Cristus uos uisitare uobisque aeternę felicitatis opem retribuere (fo. 22ᵛ) dignetur.

Uicesimus quintus gradus est frequentatio sanctorum Dei et sanctorum locorum in quibus sancti Dei requiescunt. Hoc sancto in euangelio ipsum Dominum qui peccatum non fecit, nec inuentus est dolus in ore eius, sępe et sępe fecisse legimus. Ibat Dominus Iesus in sanctam ciuitatem Ierusalem ad templum sanctum orare, non necessitate aliqua pregrauatus, sed itaque pro nobis et propter nos, ut nobis et illud exemplum suis actibus in semetipso proponeret, sicut et cetera proposuit. Iccirco frequentemus sanctos Dei in locis illis a Deo

---

[p] si] *scribal corr., orig.* sicut

[72] Ibid. xvi, 23. [73] Ibid. xvi, 41. [74] Ibid. xvi, 43.
[75] Cf. ibid. xvi, 43. [76] Ibid. xvi, 17. [77] Ibid. lxv, 18.
[78] Cf. ibid. lxv, 20. [79] Ibid. lxv, 22. [80] Ibid. lxv, 25.
[81] Ibid. lxxii, 1. [82] Ibid. lxxii, 2. [83] Ibid. lxxii, 22.
[84] Cf. ibid. lxxvi, 3. [85] Ibid. lxxvi, 5.

donatis. Quam si ipse Dominus qui nec alicuius cogitationum delicti fuit occupatus sanctum templum sępe et frequenter causa orationis uisitauit, quanto magis nos qui peccatis et criminibus diuersis obuoluti sumus, omni studio, omnique deuotione, frequentare debemus, ieiunando, uigilando, atque orando, sanctisque Dei suplicando, ut sanctis suis precibus omnipotentem Dominum profusis, nostra peccata nobis dimittantur, aeternaque felicitas nobis donetur.

Uicesimus sextus gradus est oblatio iusta et Deo dicata. Oblatio iusta odor suauitatis est in conspectu altissimi Dei, et sacrificium iusti acceptum est, et memoriam illius non obliuiscitur Deus.[86] Quapropter dignas oblationes Deo offerte, quia mors non tardat.[87] Nolite offerre munera praua, non enim illa suscipit Deus.[88] Itaque qui offert sacrificium ex substantia pauperis quasi qui uictimat filium in conspectu patris sui.[89] Magna est ergo purgatio peccatorum, assiduitas sacrificiorum. Iccirco purgate uos ab omni inquinamento corporum et mentium, ut digni efficiamini Deo omnipotenti munera offerre.

Uicesimus septimus gradus est decimam Deo esse soluendam. De quo ipse in sancto euangelio suo proclamat dicens: 'Omnem decimationem uestram distribuite.'[90] Et alibi ipse Dominus per prophetam suam iubendo loquitur: 'Inferte omnem decimationem in horreum nostrum, ut sit cibus in domo mea.'[91] Ecce fratres, decimę tributa sunt egentium animarum.[92] Quod si decimam dederitis, non solum habundantium fructuum recipietis, sed etiam sani- (fo. 23) -tatum corporum et animarum consequemini.[93] Non eget Dominus Deus, non premium postulat, sed honorem.[94] Deus autem omnipotens qui dignatus est totum dare quicquid boni habemus, decimam a nobis dignatus est repetere, non sibi, sed nobis sine dubio, profuturam.[95] Qui ergo sibi aut premium comparare aut peccatorum desiderat indulgentiam promereri, reddat decimam de omni substantia sua, et de nouem etiam partibus studeat elemosinam dare.[96]

Uicesimus octauus gradus est sapientia. Sapientia est timere Deum, abnegare seipsum a malis.[97] Prima sapientia est uitare malum; secunda sapientia est facere bonum.[98] Omnis qui secundum Deum sapiens est, beatus est.[99] Neminem diligit Dominus, nisi eum qui cum sapientia inhabitat.[100] Quapropter, potenti manu, tenete hunc sanctum gradum beatę sapientię. Et in omni re diligendo eam habere contendite, quia qui sapientiam diligit, Deum diligit, et per illam uitam hereditabit aeternam.[101]

Uicesimus nonus gradus est uoluntas bona. Uoluntas autem bona est, sic aduersa alterius, sicut nostra, pertimescere; nulli denegare quod tibi iuste inpendi desideras; necessitatem proximi non solum iuxta uires concurrere, sed prodesse, etiam ultra uires uelle.[102] Ecce fratres nullus se ante Cristi iudicium excusare ualet, quin possit hos sanctos gradus per passus iustitię scandere si uoluerit. Quia uere omnes hoc gradus, infantes et lactantes, iuuenes et senes, uiri et feminę, omnisque aetatis homines iam sępe ascensuros nouimus. Hunc itaque gradum, id

[86] Ibid. li, 7.   [87] Cf. ibid. li, 3.   [88] Ibid. li, 8.   [89] Ibid. li, 5.
[90] Ibid. xxix, 1.   [91] Ibid. xxix, 2.   [92] Ibid. xxix, 7.
[93] Ibid. xxix, 8.   [94] Ibid. xxix, 9.   [95] Ibid. xxix, 10.
[96] Ibid. xxix, 17.   [97] Ibid. xviii, 85.   [98] Ibid. xviii, 86.
[99] Ibid. xviii, 96.   [100] Ibid. xviii, 95.   [101] Cf. ibid. xviii, 48–9.
[102] Ibid. xlii, 13.

est bonam uoluntatem, pauper et pauperrimus habere potest, sicut et diues et potentissimus. Consolentur se pauperes, diuitias non habentes, et transcendant potentes diuitiis affluentes bona uoluntate sua. Quia nichil ditius nichilque dulcius Deo quam bona uoluntas. Nichil enim aliud a uobis querit Deus, nisi uoluntatem bonam[103] et opus perfectum.

Tricesimus gradus est huius sacratissimę scalę, perseuerantia in bono, de qua ipse Dominus in euangelio suo testatur: 'Qui perseuerauit usque in finem, hic saluus erit.'[104] Tunc enim placet Deo nostra conuersatio, quando bonum (fo. 23ᵛ) quod inchoamus, fine perseuerandi[q] complemus.[105] Quia in Cristianis non queruntur initia, sed finis.[106] Incassum quippe bonum agitur, si ante terminum uitę deseratur[r].[107] Semper in uita hominis finis quęrendus est, quia Deus omnipotens non respicit quales ante fuerimus, sed quales circa finem uitę assisterimus.[108] Unumquemque enim Dominus de suo fine, non de uita preterita iudicat.[109] Ex fine enim suo unusquisque aut iustificabitur, aut condemnabitur.[110]

Ecce fratres quales sint gradus huius gloriosissime scale audistis. Nunc queso audite et de firmissimis atque robustissimis lateribus eiusdem scalę cum quibus continentur et sustentantur prefati gradus. Unum ergo latus est sanctę scale corpus Cristi, id est, sanctum Eucharistium, quo corpus et animam nostram aptare et confirmare debemus, quatenus prefatos gradus sine aliquo inpedimento scandere ualeamus. Aliud latus est sanctę scalę, memoria sanctę abrenuntiationis, quam contra diabolum ante gratiam baptismatis gessimus, quam assidue in mente, in cogitatione, in locutione, in uisu, in auditu, in opere, diligere et habere debemus. Quisquis itaque hęc duo latera cęlestis scalę in semetipso non confirmat, id est, corpus et sanguinem Cristi digne et sedule non percipiendo, aut in mente memoriam sanctę abrenuntiationis[s] contra diabolum pugnando non habet, uacui sine dubio et inutiles illi sunt gradus predicti qui a quo[t] infigantur, uel in quo se contineant, omnino non habent, si latera desint. Quapropter, dilectissimi, incalescat mens uestra ad regna cęlestia, et nolite segnes esse ad erigenda latera uel inserendos gradus, sed in omnipotentis Dei opitulatione confidentes, erigite scalam beatissimam, per quam scandere ad Dominum gloriosissimum, et ad regnum felicissimum feliciter mereamini. Nolite Dominum omnipotentem spernere; nolite euangelium Cristi spernere; nolite sanctos angelos uel cęteros fideles Dei abicere; nolite uos ipsos perdere. Cognoscite Dominum eius pręcepta amando. Cognoscite uosmetipsos, cogitantes quid nunc sitis, quid futuri estis. Nunc ergo estis homines carnales, fragiles, mortales, et citius morituri, et post mortem (fo. 24) putredini, et uermibus subiciendi, omnique spurcitia redigendi. Hęc itaque corpora uestra post mortem patiuntur. Hęc cogitantes, et alta suspiria trahentes in cordibus uestris, scalam erectam ad omnipotentem Dominum[u] et ad suum regnum ascendite.

[q] perseuerandi] Lib. scint.: perseueranti
[r] deseratur] *scribal corr., orig.* desideratur
[s] abrenuntiationis] *scribal corr., orig.* abrenutionis
[t] quo] *scribal corr., orig.* qua   [u] Dominum] *MS* Dominum Dominum

[103] Ibid. xlii, 8.   [104] Ibid. xxii, 1.   [105] Ibid. xxii, 10.
[106] Ibid. xxii, 5.   [107] Ibid. xxii, 8.   [108] Ibid. xxii, 13.
[109] Ibid. xxii, 14.   [110] Ibid. xxii, 15.

Quo ad harum uirtutum perfectionem ualeatis scandere, per se in unaquaque perseuerate. Non enim qui ceperit,^{v} sed qui perseuerauit, saluus erit. Principium nostrę salutis est timor Domini. De timore, conpunctio. De conpunctione, abrenuntiatio. De abrenuntiatione rerum, nuditas. De nuditate, humilitas. De humilitate, mortificatio nascitur. De mortificatione pulsuntur^w uitia. De expulsione uitiorum, uirtutes pullulant. De pullulatione uirtutum, puritas cordis adquiritur. De puritate cordis, caritas possidetur,[111] que Deus est. Sicque ad summam perfectionis poteris peruenire. Hactenus de uirtutum institutionibus digessimus, a modo que sint octo principalia uitia disponimus. Primum uitium est castrimargię, quę gula est.[112] Numquam uitiorum stimulos prohibere poterit, qui desideria gulę refrenare nequiuerit. Numquam robustioribus eum conluctari posse confidas, quem in leuioribus uideris superari.[113] Qui moderamina uult participare uirtutum, necesse est gule submoueat appetitus. Inpossibile est saturum uentrem pugnam interioris^x hominis experiri, qui deicitur exteriori conflictu.[114] Nullus carne non deuicta legitime certabit.[115] Triplex enim natura est castrimargie, una quę horam preuenire compellit, alia quę nimia saturitate^y quarumlibet gaudet escarum, tertia quę acuratissimis aepulis delectatur.[116] Non solum crapula uini mentem inebriare consueuit, sed omnium escarum nimietas uacillare facit. Sodomitis causa subuersionis non uini crapula, sed saturitas extitit panis. Audi Dominum Iesum increpantem: 'Quid peccauit soror tua Sodoma, nisi quia panem suum in saturitate comedebat?'[117] Tantum frugalitatis unusquisque debet sibi indicere, quantum corporea pugna deposcit. Longa namque ieiunia, saturitate corporis subsequente, lassitudinem adquirunt. Districta ieiunia succedente superflua remissione uacuantur, et in castrimargię uitium conlabuntur. Melior est cotidiana refectio cum (fo. 24^v) moderatione, quam longum ieiunium subsequente ingluuie uacuatum. Nouit inmoderata inedia non modo mentis labefactare constantiam, sed etiam orationum efficatiam, reddere lassitudine corporis eneruatam.[118]

Secundum certamen est fornicationis, diuturnum pre cęteris, ac paucis ad purum deuictum, inmane bellum. Et cum a primo tempore pubertatis inpugnare incipiat humanum genus, non nisi cętera uitia superentur extinguitur. Nec sufficit solum corporale ieiunium ad^z consequendam castimonię puritatem, nisi precesserint contricio spiritus et oratio perseuerans, meditatio scripturarum, opus manuum, humilitas uera.[119] Quantum enim sublime est premium castitatis, tanto grauioribus inimici insidiis lacessitur. Et iccirco ut rex Babilonius cum clibano carnis extinguatur,[120] necessaria est cum subtractione ciborum uigilia nocturna, quia sicut custodia diei nocturnam preparat castitatem, ita uigilię nocturnę statum solidissimum premittunt.[121]

Tercius conflictus est aduersus filargiriam, quę amor pecunię dicitur, peregrinum bellum, extra naturam nec aliunde sumens principium quam de

---

^{v} ceperat] *scribal corr., orig.* perseuerat ^{w} pulsuntur] *MS* puluntur
^{x} interioris] *MS* mentioris ^{y} saturitate] *MS* satietate ^{z} ad] *MS* a

[111] Cf. Cassian, *De institutis coenobiorum*, iv. xliii.   [112] Cf. ibid. v. i.
[113] Cf. ibid. v. xi.   [114] Cf. ibid. v. xiii.   [115] Ibid. v. xvi.
[116] Ibid. v. xxiii.   [117] Ibid. v. vi.   [118] Ibid. v. ix.   [119] Cf. ibid. vi. i.
[120] Cf. ibid. vi. xvii.   [121] Cf. ibid. vi. xxiii.

tepidę mentis ignauia. Cetera uitiorum incitamenta uidentur in nobis habere principia, et quodammodo inuiscerantur.[122] Ad philargirię uero uitium propellendum, perfectio euangelica necessaria est qua dicitur: 'Si uis perfectus esse, uende que habes et da pauperibus, et thesaurizabis in cęlo',[123] et dimissa ulterius ne repetas. Nam qui retro aspicit, aptus regno Dei non erit. Nemo potest Deo et mamone seruire.[124] Non sola enim est cauenda possessio, nec effectus philargirię uitandus, quam ipsa uoluntas radicitus exstirpanda, quia nichil prodest pecunias non habere, si uoluntas manet possidendi.[125]

Quartum certamen[aa] est irę mortiferum uirus de recessibus animę nostre funditus eruendum.[126] Si quis enim ad perfectionem tendens hunc agonem cuperit decertare[bb] ab omni irę et furoris uicio alienus existat, quia audiat apostolum: 'Omnis ira et indignatio et clamor et blasphemia cum omni malitia tollatur a uobis.'[127] Ira enim uiri iusticiam Dei non operatur. Cuius (fo. 25) morbi hęc erit medicina perfecta: primum credendum est nobis nullo modo licere irasci, scientes nos nulla moderamina posse discernere sub ira, nec preces irati debere fundere. Nichil nobis continentia nec abrenuntiatio, nichil que ieiuniorum et uigiliarum nobis conferre poterunt, nisi ira mitigetur.[128] In quieto enim animo et tranquillo sedes Dei est, et beati pedes pacem portantes, et pacifici filii uocantur.

Quinto nobis certamine edacis tristicie stimuli retundendi sunt. Quę si passim per singulos incursus obtinendi animam nostram habuerit facultatem, ab omni nos separat diuine contemplationis intuitu ipsamque mentem suffocans labefactat. Tranquillum ac mitem quempiam perturbat, omnique salubri perdito consilio et cordis constantia perturbata uelut amentem facit hebrium sensum, et obruit desperatione pęnali.[129] Sed tristicia quę ex Deo est, penitentiam operatur et salutem. Seculi autem tristicia mortem ingeminat.[130] Illa quę mortem operatur, asperrima est, inpaciens, dura, plena rancore, merore, et uniuersos spiritales fructus euacuans.[131] Illa quę salutem operatur, oboediens est, affabilis, ut pote ex caritate descendens.[132] Perniciosam[cc] namque pellentes a nobis semper leti et immobiles perduremus, nec casibus deiecti nec prosperis elati, utraque caduca et mox transeuntia contemplantes.[133]

Sextum nobis certamen est contra accidiam, quod grecię[dd] achedian, nos uero tedium siue anxietatem possumus nuncupare. Hoc affinis est tristicie. Denique nonnulli hanc esse pronunciant meridianum demonem. Qui cum obsederit miserabilem mentem, horrorem loci, domus fastidium, fratrum cum eo commorantium tanquam neglegentium aspernationem gignit. Ad omne opus facit desidem atque inhertem.[134] Tunc huc illucque anxietate septus, sepiusque egreditur et ingreditur edem ac solem uelut tardius ad occasum properantem sepius intuetur. Et ita tetra nubilatus caligine, omni actu redditur ociosus,

---

[aa] certamen] *scribal corr., orig.* genus   [bb] decertare] *MS* decuntare
[cc] perniciosam] *the sense requires a noun to govern* perniciosam; De inst. coen. *supplies* passionem
[dd] grecie] *scribal corr., orig.* grece

---

[122] Cf. ibid. vii. i.   [123] Cf. ibid. vii. xvi.   [124] Ibid. vii. xv.
[125] Ibid. vii. xxi.   [126] Ibid. viii. i.   [127] Ibid. viii. v.
[128] Cf. ibid. viii. xxii.   [129] Ibid. ix. i.   [130] Cf. ibid. ix. x.
[131] Cf. ibid. ix. xi.   [132] Ibid. ix. xi.   [133] Ibid. ix. xiii.
[134] Ibid. x. i–ii.

ingemiscit se nichil proficere nec habere se fructum suspirat, ab omni questu inanem uacuumque conqueritur.[135] Sed uerus alleta[ee] Cristi, hunc quoque morbum de latebris anime festinet excludere, et contra hunc accidie spiritum utrubique contendat, et neque somni telo elisus concidat neque de loco in locum fugitiuus discedat,[136] sed resistendo superet.[137]

Septimum nobis certamen est contra spiritum cenodoxie, quam nos uanam siue inanem gloriam possumus appellare, multiformem, uariam atque subtilem, ita ut quibuslibet perspicatissimis oculis non dicam caueri sed preuideri deprehendiue uix possit,[138] tantoque perniciosior ad pugnam, quanto obscurior ad cauendum,[139] inpugnans omnes, ut qui non possunt carnaliter decipi, spiritalibus successibus acrius saucientur.[140] In habitu, (fo. 25^v) in forma, in incessu, in uoce, in opere, in uigiliis, in ieiuniis, in oratione, in remotione, in lectione, in scientia, in taciturnitate, in obedientia, in humilitate, et in multis his similibus militem Cristi uulnerare conatur, et uelut pernitiosus scopulus tumentibus undis obtectus inprouisum naufragium secundo nauigantibus uento, dum non cauetur, inportat. Itaque uiam regiam uolentem incedere per arma iusticię quę a dextris sunt et a sinistris oportet apostolica transire disciplina. Et ita nobis iter uirtutis dirigere conuenit, ut dextra leuaque si paululum quod deflectamus sciamus nos pernitiosissimis mox cautibus illidendos. Ideo per Salomonem monemur: 'Ne diuertaris ad dexteram neque ad sinistram', id est, ne tibi de uirtutibus blandiaris, nec in spiritalibus extollaris nec deflectens ad sinistram tramitem[ff] uitiorum gloriam tibi ex eis in tua confusione conferas. Nam cui sub specie honestę uestis cenodoxiam non potuit generare, pro squalida et inculta conatur inserere;[gg] quem non potuit per honorem deicere, humilitate subplantat.[141] Pulchre seniores naturam morbi huius in modum cepę pulborumque describunt, que uno coriata tegmine alio rursus inueniuntur induta totiensque repperiuntur obtecta, quotiens fuerint expoliata.[142] In solitudine[hh] quoque fugientem causa glorię persequi non desistit, et ita fit ut qui aduersarii conflictu non potuimus superari, nostri triumphi sublimitate uincamur.[143] Ideoque alleta Cristi, qui uerum ac spiritalem agonem legitime certare desiderat, hanc multiformem bestiam omnimodis superare festinet, cogitans illud Dauiticum: 'Dominus dissipabit[ii] ossa eorum qui hominibus placent.'[144]

Octauum nobis certamen est aduersus spiritum superbię. Qui morbus licet ultimus sit in conflictu uitiorum atque in ordine ponatur extremus, origine primus est, perfectos maxime temptans. Cuius duo sunt genera, unum spiritales pulsari,[jj] aliud quod etiam incipientes[kk] et carnales complectitur.[145] Nullum autem est

---

[ee] alleta] *the scribe consistently employs this spelling instead of the more common* athleta
[ff] tramitem] *MS* tramite [gg] inserere] *scribal corr., orig.* asserere
[hh] solitudine] *MS* solitudines
[ii] dissipabit] *scribal corr., orig.* dissipat; De inst. coen. *and* Ps. 52: 6 *read* dissipavit
[jj] pulsari] *the compiler has over-abbreviated here, providing nothing for the infinitive* pulsare *to depend on; in* De inst. coen. *it depends on* diximus ('unum hoc, quo diximus spiritales summosque pulsari')
[kk] incipientes] *MS* insipientes

[135] Cf. ibid. x. ii. [136] Ibid. x. v. [137] Ibid. x. xxv. [138] Ibid. xi. i.
[139] Ibid. xi. ii. [140] Ibid. xi. ii. [141] Ibid. xi. iii–iv. [142] Ibid. xi. v.
[143] Ibid. xi. vi. [144] Ibid. xi. xix. [145] Ibid. xii. i–ii.

uitium aliud, quod omnes uirtutes exhauriat, ut superbia.[146] Hoc uero cum possidet mentem, omnia fundamina uirtutum euertit.[147] Et ut grauissimam eius tyrannidis potentiam cognoscamus, angelum illum Luciferum nullo alio quam hoc (fo. 26) uitio deiectum inuenimus.[148] Quapropter alleta Cristi, qui spiritali agone legitime certans a Domino desiderat coronari, hanc ferocissimam bestiam ut deuoratricem cunctarum uirtutum omni modis festinet extinguere.[149]

Plus est id quod incessanter offertur quam quod per temporis interualla soluitur, et gratius uoluntarium munus quam regulares functiones, de hoc Dauid ait: 'Uoluntarie sacrificabo tibi.'[150] Merito hec tria tempora, id est tercia, sexta, nona, religionis sunt officiis deputata: in his promissionum perfectio est et summa nostrę salutis impleta. His tribus temporibus Danihel apertis fenestris preces Domino fudit. Hora namque tercia Spiritus sanctus super discipulos uenit.[151] Hora autem sexta, Dominus Iesus Cristus Saluator mundi oblatus est Patri. Eadem quoque hora Petro in excessu mentis ostensum est uas uelut linteum, quatuor initiis summissum, significans quadriformem euangeliorum fidem.[152] Hora uero nona inferna penetrans, nos liberauit. Eadem quoque hora Cornelius centurio orationum et elemosinarum Deo placitum expertus est. Petrum autem et Iohannem hac hora ascendisse in templum orationis obtentu nota.[153]

Uespertina autem sacrificia debere persolui euidenter probatur, que in ueteri testamento lege Mosayca offerri sanctiuntur. Unde Dauid: 'Eleuatio manuum mearum sacrificium uespertinum.' Quod de illo sacrificio uespertino intelligi potest, quod uespere a Domino Saluatore cenantibus apostolis traditur, cum initiaret ecclesie sacramenta, uel quod ipse die postero se ipsum sacrificium uespertinum eleuatione manuum suarum pro salute mundi obtulit Patri.[154] De matutina uero solennitate etiam illud nos instruit, quod in ipsa decantatur: 'Deus, Deus meus, ad te de luce uigilio.' In hac hora pater familias conduxit operarios in uineam suam.[155]

Gregorius in registro: Nos dicere consecrationem nullo modo possumus, quę ab excommunicatis est hominibus celebrata. Hec itaque tam patentia tamque manifesta sunt, ut dilucidari non egeant; patentissime namque simoniacorum sacerdotium[ll] et sacrificium irrita esse demonstrant: quamuis quidam scripserit, quod, sicut in baptismate simoniacorum, ita et eorundem sacrificio uirtus sancti Spiritus co-operetur, scilicet ut non eisdem sit uerum et salutare sacramentum sacrificium, sed his, quibus exhibent. Et idem ex premissis sententiis (fo. 26ᵛ) patrum apertissime refellitur,[mm] et maxime ex eo, quod dicitur: 'Sacrificia eorum tamquam panis luctus; omnes qui manducant eum, contaminabuntur.' Non enim exhibitio baptismatis et sacrificii Dominici corporis omnino simili sibi collatione referri ualent: nam necessitate urgente omni baptizato conceditur baptizare sub fidei interrogatione et nomine Trinitatis, et trina mersione,[nn] quod utique[oo] concessum est propter eum, qui periculo mortis urgetur, ne, si tunc ad

---

[ll] sacerdotium] *MS* sacerdotum   [mm] refellitur] *MS* refellit
[nn] mersione] *scribal corr., orig.* mercione   [oo] utique] *scribal insertion*

[146] Ibid. xii. iii.   [147] Cf. ibid. xii. iii.   [148] Ibid. xii. iv.
[149] Ibid. xii. xxxii.   [150] Ibid. iii. ii.   [151] Cf. ibid. iii. iii, 1–2.
[152] Cf. ibid. iii. iii, 3–4.   [153] Cf. ibid. iii. iii, 6–7.   [154] Cf. ibid. iii. iii, 9.
[155] Ibid. iii. iii, 10–11.

sacerdotem,*pp* cum non adfuerit, recurratur, subito non ualeat inuenire, qui baptismate redimatur. Solis autem sacerdotibus licitum est Dominicum corpus conficere: quod quidem non baptizato ilico morituro necessarium non est. Baptisma enim precedit Dominici corporis perceptionem ideoque necessarium est, per quemlibet baptizatum*qq* uirtute Sancti Spiritus sacramentum baptismatis efficiatur,*rr* quod et ordine et maiori necessitate quam Dominicum corpus a morituro expetitur. Magis namque dolendum est quempiam absque baptismo humanis rebus excedere, quam baptizatum absque Eucharisticę communione, quamuis nemo sine utroque saluetur, qui quidem utrumque possit sumere. Nam qui dixit: 'Nisi quis renatus fuerit ex aqua et Spiritu sancto, non intrabit in regnum Dei', idem dixit: 'Nisi manducaueritis carnem Filii hominis et biberitis eius sanguinem, non habebitis uitam in uobis.' Ideo autem dixi de potentia sumendi utrumque, quoniam paruulus modo renatus, non ualet carnem Dominicam manducare, licet sanguinem eiusdem uix ori infusum possit deglutire. Nam quod dicitur, 'nisi manducaueritis', de his, qui manducare possunt, accipiendum puto. Nemo enim dicit de eo, qui non potest manducare, 'nisi manducauerit', sed de eo, qui potest.[156]

Hereticus siquidem,*ss* qui catholicę ecclesię fidem relinquit et sui uel alterius erroris uiam seque diligit. Item iuxta beatum Isidorum: 'Qui sacram scripturam aliter interpretatur, quam flagitat sensus Spiritus sancti per quem scripta est, licet ab ęcclesia non recesserit, hereticus appellari potest. Scismaticus uero est, qui quidem rectam fidem confiteri se simulat, sed sanctorum patrum traditiones superbe contempnit et se aliqua maliuolentia ab unitate*tt* ęcclesię scindit. Hereticus est, qui non sequitur catholicam*uu* ueritatem; scismaticus est, qui non amplectitur catholicam pacem.'[157]

Innocentius Papa ait: 'Negligere quippe, cum possis deturbare peruersos, nichil est aliud quam fouere.'[158]

Ambrosius: 'Consentire est non solum mala scienter fieri permittere, sed et male facta non persequi.'[159]

Cauendum est et summopere precauendum est, ac per uirtutem Cristi sanguinis interdicendum est, ut nemo per simoniacam heresim regiminis locum in ęcclesia teneat quacumque datione, factione, calliditate, commoditate, aut per se aut per emissam personam. Cum Spiritus sanctus per os Gregorii dicat: 'Cur non uidetur? cur non perpenditur, quod benedictio talium in maledictionem*vv* conuertitur, quia ad hoc ut fiat hereticus, promouetur.'

Fraternę mortis crimen incurrit quisque cum potest fratrem (fo. 27) a morte minime defendit.

Quicumque furatur aliquid patri uel matri, et dicit hoc peccatum non est, homicidii particeps est. Pater noster sine dubio Deus est, qui nos creauit. Mater uero ęcclesia est, quę nos spiritaliter regenerauit in baptismate. Ergo qui furatur aliquid patri uel matri, homicida ante Dei uultum deputabitur.

pp sacerdotem] *MS* sacerdotum   *qq* baptizatum] *MS* baptismum
rr efficiatur] *MS* officiatur   *ss* siquidem] *the sense requires* siquidem est
tt ab unitate] *MS* a bonitate   *uu* catholicam] *MS* catholici
vv maledictionem] *MS* maledictione

[156] Deusdedit, *Libellus contra invasores et symoniacos et reliquos scismaticos,* ii ('A' text), 321–3.   [157] Ibid. 332.   [158] Cf. ibid. 335.   [159] Ibid. 336.

BIBLIOGRAPHY

MANUSCRIPTS

Aberdeen, University Library, MS 216
Berne, Burgerbibliothek, MS 334
Cambridge, Trinity College, MSS B.3.25, B.3.32, B.3.33, R.5.22, R.16.34, R.17.1
Cambridge, University Library, MS Kk.1.23
Dublin, Trinity College, MS 174
Durham Cathedral, MSS B.IV.6, B.IV.12
Exeter Cathedral, MSS 3500, 3507, 3525
Hereford Cathedral, MSS O.iii.1, O.iii.2, O.iv.8, P.i.3, P.i.5, P.i.6, P.i.10
London, BL, MSS Add. 34807, Cotton Julius B VII, Nero A I, Nero E I, Tiberius C I, Vespasian B X, Vitellius A VIII, Vitellius A XII, Vitellius D IX, Harley 3080, Royal App. 1, Royal 3 B xi, 5 A xiii, 5 B xiv, 5 B xvi, 5 E xvi, 5 E xix, 5 F xiii, 5 F xviii, 6 B xv, 6 C iv, 8 B xiv, 15 B xix, 15 C xi
Oxford, Bodleian Library, MSS Bodley 210, 319, 387, 392, 444, 516, 698, 731, 739, 752, 756, 765, 768, 781, 804, 815, 827, 835, Digby 96, Hatton 23, lat. bib. C. 8 (P), Laud lat. 49, Rawlinson C. 723, Rawlinson liturg. e 42, Tanner 165
Oxford, Keble College, MS 22
Oxford, Trinity College, MSS 4, 28
Paris, Musée des Archives Nationales, MS 138
Salisbury Cathedral, MSS 4-7, 9-12, 24-5, 33, 35, 37-8, 57-9, 61, 63-7, 78, 88-9, 96, 100-1, 106, 109-10, 112, 114-20, 124-5, 128-40, 150, 154, 157-60, 162, 165, 168-9, 172-3, 179-80, 197-8, 221-3
Vatican, Biblioteca Apostolica, MS lat. 143

PRINTED PRIMARY SOURCES

De abbatibus Abbendoniae, ed. J. Stevenson, *Chronicon monasterii de Abingdon*, RS (London, 1858), ii. 267-95.
Actus pontificum Cenomannis in urbe degentium, ed. G. Busson and A. Ledru, Archives Historiques du Maine, 2 (Le Mans, 1901).
AETHICUS ISTER (Pseudo-), *Aethici Istrici cosmographia Vergilio Salisburgensis rectius adscripta: Codex Leidensis Scaligeranus 69*, ed. T. A. M. Bishop, *Umbrae codicum occidentalium*, 10 (Amsterdam, 1966).
AMALARIUS, *Amalarii episcopi opera liturgica omnia*, ed. J. M. Hanssens, *Studi e testi*, 138-40 (1948-50).
AMBROSE, *De fide*, ed. O. Faller, CSEL 78 (Vienna, 1962).
—— *De sacramentis, De mysteriis*, ed. O. Faller, CSEL 73 (Vienna, 1955).
—— *De Spiritu Sancto*, ed. O. Faller, CSEL 79 (Vienna, 1964).

Anthologia latina, Pars prior: Carmina in codicibus scripta, ed. A. Riese, 2 vols. (Leipzig, 1894–1906).

AUGUSTINE, *De agone christiano, De mendacio,* ed. J. Zycha, CSEL 41 (Prague/Vienna/Leipzig, 1900).

—— *De natura et origine animae,* ed. C. F. Urba and J. Zycha, CSEL 60 (Vienna/Leipzig, 1913).

—— *La Règle de saint Augustin,* ed. L. Verheijen, 2 vols. (Paris, 1967).

AUGUSTINE (Pseudo-), *The Pseudo-Augustinian Hypomnesticon against the Pelagians and Celestians,* ed. J. E. Chisholm, 2 vols. (Fribourg, 1967–80).

—— *Pseudo-Augustini quaestiones veteris et novi testamenti cxxvii,* ed. A. Souter, CSEL 50 (Vienna/Leipzig, 1908).

BEDE, *Opera de temporibus,* ed. C. W. Jones (Cambridge, Mass., 1943).

—— *De temporum ratione liber,* ed. C. W. Jones, CCSL 123 B (Turnhout, 1977).

BEDE (Pseudo-), *De psalmorum librum exegesis: PL* 93. 477–1098.

—— *De sex dierum creatione: PL* 93. 207–34.

BONIFACE, *Aenigmata,* ed. F. Glorie, *Variae collectiones aenigmatum Merovingicae aetatis,* CCSL 133 (Turnhout, 1968).

BRUNO THE CARTHUSIAN (attrib.), *Expositio in psalmos: PL* 152. 637–1420.

CAESARIUS OF ARLES, *Sermones,* ed. G. Morin, 2 vols, CCSL 103–4 (Turnhout, 1953).

CASSIAN, *Conlationes xxiiii,* ed. M. Petschenig, CSEL 13 (Vienna, 1886).

—— *De institutis coenobiorum et de octo principalium vitiorum remediis,* ed. M. Petschenig, CSEL 17 (Prague/Vienna/Leipzig, 1888).

Cassiodori senatoris Institutiones, ed. R. A. B. Mynors (Oxford, 1937); tr. by L. W. Jones as *An Introduction to Divine and Human Readings* (New York, 1946).

Catalogi veteres librorum ecclesiae cathedralis Dunelm, Surtees Society, 7 (1838).

Charters and Documents Illustrating the History of the Cathedral, City, and Diocese of Salisbury in the Twelfth and Thirteenth Centuries, ed. W. R. Jones and W. D. Macray, RS (London, 1891).

CHATELAIN, E., *Paléographie des classiques latins,* 2 vols. (Paris, 1884–1900).

CICERO, *Tusculanarum disputationum libri quinque,* ed. T. W. Dougan, 2 vols. (Cambridge, 1905–34).

Commentarius anonymus in Micrologium Guidonis Aretini, ed. P. C. Vivell, Sitzungsberichte der Kaiserliche Akademie der Wissenschaften in Wien, phil.-hist. Klasse, 185/5 (Vienna, 1917), 3–92.

Councils and Ecclesiastical Documents relating to Great Britain and Ireland, ed. A. W. Haddan and W. Stubbs, 3 vols. (Oxford, 1869–73).

Councils and Synods with Other Documents Relating to the English Church, i, AD 871–1204, ed. D. Whitelock, M. Brett, and C. N. L. Brooke, 2 vols. (Oxford, 1981); ii, *AD 1205–1313,* ed. F. M. Powicke and C. R. Cheney, 2 vols. (Oxford, 1964).

Cummian's Letter, De controversia Paschali and the De ratione conputandi, ed. M. Walsh and D. Ó. Cróinín, Studies and Texts, Pontifical Institute of Medieval Studies, 86 (Toronto, 1988).

DEFENSOR OF LIGUGÉ, *Liber scintillarum,* ed. H.-M. Rochais, CCSL 117 (Turnhout, 1957).

DEUSDEDIT, *Libellus contra invasores et symoniacos et reliquos scismaticos*, ed. E. Sackur, *Libelli de lite imperatorum et pontificum* ..., ii, MGH (Hanover, 1892), 291–365.

De vita vera apostolica: *PL* 170. 609–64 (where it is attributed to Rupert of Deutz).

DÜMMLER, E., ed., *Poetae latini aevi Carolini*, i, MGH (Berlin, 1881).

EADMER, *Historia novorum in Anglia*, ed. M. Rule, RS (London, 1884).

EUSEBIUS, *Die Kirchengeschichte*, ed. E. Schwartz, 3 vols, GCS 9 (Leipzig, 1903–9).

EUSEBIUS 'GALLICANUS', *Collectio homiliarum*, ed. F. Glorie, 3 vols, CCSL 101–2 B (Turnhout, 1970–1).

Felix's Life of Saint Guthlac, ed. B. Colgrave (Cambridge, 1956).

FLORENCE OF WORCESTER, *Chronicon ex chronicis*, ed. B. Thorpe, 2 vols. (London, 1848–9).

GARLANDUS COMPOSITA, *Dialectica*, ed. L. M. de Rijk (Assen, 1959).

GELASIUS (Pseudo-), *Decretum Gelasianum de libris recipiendis et non recipiendis*, ed. E. von Dobschütz, *Texte und Untersuchungen zur Geschichte der altchristlichen Literatur*, 38/iv (Leipzig, 1912).

Gesta abbatum monasterii sancti Albani, ed. H. T. Riley, 3 vols, RS (London, 1867–9).

GOSCELIN OF ST BERTIN, 'The *Liber Confortatorius* of Goscelin of St. Bertin', ed. C. H. Talbot, *Studia Anselmiana*, fasc. xxxviii (*Analecta Monastica*, 3rd ser.) (Rome, 1955).

Gregorii I papae registrum epistolarum, ed. L. M. Hartmann, 2 vols, MGH, *Epistolae*, i–ii (Berlin, 1887–99).

HAIMERIC, *Ars lectoria*, ed. C. Thurot, 'Documents relatifs à l'histoire de la grammaire au moyen âge', *Academie des Inscriptions et Belles Lettres: Comptes rendus*, NS 6 (1870), 242–51.

HAIMO OF HALBERSTADT (Pseudo-), *Explanatio in psalmos*: *PL* 116. 191–696.

Hermanni monachi de miraculis s. Mariae Laudunensis: *PL* 156. 961–1018.

Hilaire de Poitiers sur Matthieu, ed. J. Doignon, 2 vols. (Paris, 1978–9).

HILARY (Pseudo-), *Tractatus Hilarii in septem epistolas canonicas*, ed. R. E. McNally, *Scriptores Hiberniae minores*, i, CCSL 108 B (Turnhout, 1973).

HILDEBERT OF LE MANS, *Epistolae*: *PL* 171. 141–312.

HONORIUS 'AUGUSTODUNENSIS', *Expositio psalmorum*: extracts in *PL* 172. 269–312.

JEROME, *Epistolae*: *PL* 22. 325–1224.

LANFRANC, *In omnes Pauli epistolas commentarii*: *PL* 150. 101–406.

LELAND, J., *J. Lelandi antiquarii de rebus Britannicis collectanea*, ed. T. Hearnius, 6 vols. (Oxford, 1715).

LETBERT OF LILLE, *In psalmos Davidis lxxv commentarius*: *PL* 21. 641–960.

Libellus de diversis ordinibus et professionibus qui sunt in aecclesia, ed. G. Constable and B. Smith (Oxford, 1972).

The Life of King Edward who Rests at Westminster, ed. F. Barlow (London, 1962).

METHODIUS (Pseudo-), *Revelationes*, ed. M. de la Bigne, *Maxima bibliotheca veterum patrum*, iii (Lyon, 1677), 727–34.

NEW PALAEOGRAPHICAL SOCIETY, *Facsimiles of Ancient Manuscripts, etc.*, ed.

E. M. Thompson, G. F. Warner, F. G. Kenyon, and J. P. Gilson, 2nd ser. (London, 1913–30).

ORDERIC VITALIS, *The Ecclesiastical History*, ed. M. Chibnall, 6 vols. (Oxford, 1968–80).

PASCHASIUS RADBERTUS, *De corpore et sanguine domini*, ed. B. Paul, CCCM 16 (Turnhout, 1969).

Pelagius's Expositions of Thirteen Epistles of St Paul, ed. A. Souter, Texts and Studies, 9 (1922–31).

RATRAMNUS, *De corpore et sanguine domini*, ed. J. N. Bakhuizen van den Brink, 2nd edn (Amsterdam/London, 1974).

Regesta Regum Anglo-Normannorum, 1066–1154, 4 vols: i, ed. H. W. C. Davis; ii, ed. C. Johnson and H. A. Cronne; iii–iv, ed. H. A. Cronne and R. H. C. Davis (Oxford, 1913, 1956, 1968–9).

La Règle du Maître, ed. A. de Vogüé, 3 vols. (Paris, 1964–5).

La Règle du Maître, ed. F. Masai (Brussels, 1953).

Les Règles des saints pères, ed. A. de Vogüé, 2 vols. (Paris, 1982).

REMIGIUS OF AUXERRE (Pseudo-), *Enarrationes in psalmos*: PL 131. 133–844.

Rouleau mortuaire du b. Vital, Abbé de Savigni, ed. L. Delisle (Paris, 1909).

The Salisbury Psalter: edited from Salisbury Cathedral, MS. 150, ed. C. Sisam and K. Sisam, EETS 242 (Oxford, 1959).

A Scottish Chronicle known as the Chronicle of Holyrood, ed. M. O. Anderson, Scottish Historical Society, 3: 30 (Edinburgh, 1938).

SIGEBERT OF GEMBLOUX, *Liber de scriptoribus ecclesiasticis*: PL 160. 547–88.

Statutes and Customs of the Cathedral Church of the Blessed Virgin Mary of Salisbury, ed. C. Wordsworth and D. Macleane (London, 1915).

VICTORINUS, Commentary on the Apocalypse, ed. J. Haussleiter, *Victorini episcopi Petavionensis opera*, CSEL 49 (Vienna/Leipzig, 1916).

WILLIAM OF MALMESBURY, *De gestis pontificum Anglorum*, ed. N. E. S. A. Hamilton, RS (London, 1870).

A Wulfstan Manuscript Containing Institutes, Laws and Homilies: British Museum Cotton Nero A.I, ed. H. R. Loyn, EEMF 17 (Copenhagen, 1971).

SECONDARY WORKS—PUBLISHED

ALEXANDER, J. J. G., *Norman Illumination at Mont St Michel 966–1100* (Oxford, 1970).

ALEXANDER, J. J. G. and GIBSON, M. T. (eds), *Medieval Learning and Literature: Essays presented to Richard William Hunt* (Oxford, 1976).

ALTANER, B., *Patrology*, tr. H. C. Graef (Freiburg/ Edinburgh/London, 1960).

BARRÉ, A., *Les Homélaires Carolingiens de l'école d'Auxerre*, Studi e testi, 225 (1962).

BECKER, W., 'The Latin Manuscript Sources of the Old English Translations of the Sermon *Remedia Peccatorum*', Medium Ævum, 45 (1976), 145–52.

BERGER, S., *Histoire de la Vulgate pendant les premières siècles du moyen âge* (Paris, 1893).

BESTUL, T. H., 'Ephraim the Syrian and Old English Poetry', *Anglia*, 99 (1981), 1–24.

BÉVENOT, M., *The Tradition of Manuscripts: A Study in the Transmission of St. Cyprian's Treatises* (Oxford, 1961).

Bibliotheca hagiographica latina, ed. Socii Bollandiani (Brussels, 1898–1901); *Supplementum* (Brussels, 1911); *Novum Supplementum*, ed. H. Fros (Brussels, 1986).

BISCHOFF, B., 'Wendepunkte in der Geschichte der lateinischen Exegese im Frühmittelalter', *Sacris Erudiri*, 6 (1954), 189–281; repr. in his collected papers, *Mittelalterliche Studien*, i (Stuttgart, 1966), 205–73; rev. and tr. in *Biblical Studies: The Medieval Irish Contribution*, ed. M. McNamara (Dublin, 1976), 74–160.

—— 'Living with the Satirists', in *Classical Influences on European Culture, AD 500–1500*, ed. R. R. Bolgar (Cambridge, 1971), 83–94; repr. in his collected papers, *Mittelalterliche Studien*, iii (Stuttgart, 1981), 260–70.

—— *Latin Palaeography: Antiquity and the Middle Ages*, tr. D. Ó. Cróinín and D. Ganz (Cambridge, 1990).

BISHOP, T. A. M., *Scriptores regis* (Oxford, 1961).

—— *English Caroline Minuscule* (Oxford, 1971).

—— 'The Prototype of the *Liber glossarum*', in *Medieval Scribes, Manuscripts and Libraries: Essays Presented to N. R. Ker*, ed. M. B. Parkes and A. G. Watson (London, 1978), 69–86.

BLOOMFIELD, M. W., GUYOT, B.-G., HOWARD, D. R., and KABEALO, T. B. (eds), *Incipits of Latin Works on the Virtues and Vices, 1100–1500 AD* (Cambridge, Mass., 1979).

BOUTEMY, A., 'Un grand abbé du xie siècle: Olbert de Gembloux', *Annales de la Société archéologique de Namur*, 41 (1934), 43–85.

BRETT, M., *The English Church under Henry I* (Oxford, 1975).

BRITISH MUSEUM, *Catalogue of Additions to the Manuscripts 1921–1925* (London, 1950).

BROOKE, C. N. L., 'Gregorian Reform in Action: Clerical Marriage in England, 1050–1200', *Cambridge Historical Journal*, 12 (1956), 1–21; repr. in his collected papers, *Medieval Church and Society* (London, 1971), 69–99.

—— 'Archbishop Lanfranc, the English Bishops, and the Council of London of 1075', *Studia Gratiana*, 12 (1967), 39–59.

—— 'The Archdeacon and the Norman Conquest', in *Tradition and Change: Essays in Honour of Marjorie Chibnall*, ed. D. Greenway, C. Holdsworth, and J. Sayers (Cambridge, 1985), 1–19.

—— 'Monk and Canon: Some Patterns in the Religious Life of the Twelfth Century', in *Monks, Hermits and the Ascetic Tradition*, ed. W. J. Sheils, Studies in Church History, 22 (Oxford, 1985), 109–29.

—— *The Medieval Idea of Marriage* (Oxford, 1989).

BROOKE, Z. N., *The English Church and the Papacy from the Conquest to the Reign of John*, 2nd edn (Cambridge, 1989).

BROWN, T. J., 'An Historical Introduction to the Use of Classical Latin Authors in the British Isles from the Fifth to the Eleventh Century', *Settimane di studio del Centro italiano di studi sull'alto medioevo XXII, 1974* (Spoleto, 1975), 237–93.

BYNUM, C. W., 'The Spirituality of Regular Canons in the Twelfth Century', in

Jesus as Mother: Studies in the Spirituality of the High Middle Ages (Berkeley, Calif., 1982), 22–58.

CHAPLAIS, P., 'William of Saint-Calais and the Domesday Survey', in *Domesday Studies: Papers read at the Novocentenary Conference of the Royal Historical Society and the Institute of British Geographers, Winchester 1986*, ed. J. C. Holt (Woodbridge, Suffolk, 1987), 65–77.

CHENEY, C. R., *From Becket to Langton: English Church Government 1170–1213* (Manchester, 1956).

—— 'The Earliest English Diocesan Statutes', *EHR* 75 (1960), 1–29; repr. with an additional note in his collected papers, *The English Church and its Laws 12th–14th Centuries* (London, 1982).

—— *English Synodalia of the Thirteenth Century*, 2nd edn (Oxford, 1968).

CHENU, M.-D., *Introduction à l'étude de s. Thomas d'Aquin* (Paris, 1954).

CONSTABLE, G., *Monastic Tithes from their Origins to the Twelfth Century* (Cambridge, 1964).

COWDREY, H. E. J., 'The Anglo-Norman *Laudes regiae*', *Viator*, 12 (1981), 37–78.

CROSS, J. E., 'More Sources for Two of Ælfric's *Catholic Homilies*', *Anglia*, 86 (1968), 59–78.

—— 'Towards the Identification of Old English Literary Ideas—Old Workings and New Seams', in *Sources of Anglo-Saxon Culture*, ed. P. E. Szarmach (Kalamazoo, 1986), 77–101.

—— *Cambridge Pembroke College MS. 25: A Carolingian Sermonary Used By Anglo-Saxon Preachers*, King's College London Medieval Studies, i (London, 1987).

—— 'Hiberno-Latin Commentaries in Salisbury Manuscripts before 1125', *Hiberno-Latin Newsletter*, 3 (1989), 8–9.

DE GHELLINCK, J., '"Originale" et "Originalia"', *Bulletin du Cange*, 14 (1939), 95–105.

—— *Le Mouvement théologique du xiie siècle*, 2nd edn (Bruges, 1948).

DE HAMEL, C. F. R., *Glossed Books of the Bible and the Origins of the Paris Booktrade* (Woodbridge, Suffolk, 1984).

DEKKERS, E., *Clavis patrum latinorum*, 2nd edn (Bruges, 1961).

DELEHAYE, H., 'Les Actes de s. Marcel le centurion', *Analecta Bollandiana*, 41 (1923), 257–87.

DELISLE, L., 'Canons du Concile tenu à Lisieux en 1064', *Journal des Savants*, 3: 66 (1901), 516–21; repr. in C. J. Hefele, *Histoire des Conciles*, tr. and ed. H. Leclercq (1911), iv. 1420–3.

DEROLEZ, R., *Runica manuscripta: The English Tradition* (Bruges, 1954).

Dictionnaire d'histoire et de géographie ecclésiastiques, vols. i– (Paris, 1912–).

Dictionnaire de spiritualité, fasc. i– (Paris, 1932–).

DOLBEAU, F., 'Un nouveau catalogue des manuscrits de Lobbes aux xie et xiie siècles', *Recherches augustiniennes*, 13 (1978), 3–36; 14 (1979), 191–248.

DUMVILLE, D., 'English Libraries before 1066: Use and Abuse of the Manuscript Evidence', in *Insular Latin Studies: Papers on Latin Texts and Manuscripts of the British Isles: 550–1066*, ed. M. W. Herren (Toronto, 1981), 153–78.

EDWARDS, K., 'The Cathedral of Salisbury', in *The Victoria History of the Counties of England, A History of Wiltshire*, ed. R. B. Pugh and E. Crittall (London, 1956), iii. 156–210.

EDWARDS, K., *The English Secular Cathedrals in the Middle Ages*, 2nd edn (Manchester, 1967).

ESPOSITO, M., 'On the Earliest Latin Life of St. Brigid of Kildare, *Proceedings of the Royal Irish Academy* (C), 30 (1912), 307–26.

ÉTAIT, R., 'L'Ancienne collection de sermons attribués à saint Augustin *De Quattuor Virtutibus Caritatis*', *Rev. bén.*, 95 (1985), 44–59.

FLINT, V. I. J., 'Some Notes on the Early-Twelfth-Century Commentaries on the Psalms', *RTAM* 38 (1971), 80–8.

—— 'The "School of Laon": A Reconsideration', *RTAM* 43 (1976), 89–110.

FOREVILLE, R., 'The Synod of the Province of Rouen in the Eleventh and Twelfth Centuries', in *Church and Government in the Middle Ages: Essays Presented to C. R. Cheney on his Seventieth Birthday*, ed. C. N. L. Brooke, D. E. Luscombe, G. H. Martin and D. Owen (Cambridge, 1976), 19–39.

—— and LECLERCQ, J., 'Un débat sur le sacerdoce des moines au xiie siècle', *Analecta monastica*, 4 (1957), 8–118.

GALBRAITH, V. H., 'The Date of the Geld Rolls in Exon Domesday', *EHR* 65 (1950), 1–17.

GEM, R., 'The First Romanesque Cathedral at Old Salisbury', in *Medieval Architecture and its Intellectual Context: Studies in Honour of Peter Kidson*, ed. E. Fearnie and P. Crossley (London, 1990), 9–18.

GIBSON, M. T., 'The Study of the "Timaeus" in the Eleventh and Twelfth Centuries', *Pensamiento*, 25 (1969), 183–94.

—— 'Lanfranc's "Commentary on the Pauline Epistles"', *Journal of Theological Studies*, 22 (1971), 86–112.

—— *Lanfranc of Bec* (Oxford, 1978).

—— 'The Twelfth-Century Glossed Bible', in *Studia Patristica*, xxiii, ed. E. A. Livingstone (Leuven, 1989), 232–44.

GNEUSS, H., 'A Preliminary List of Manuscripts Written or Owned in England up to 1100', *ASE*, 9 (1981), 1–60.

—— 'Anglo-Saxon Libraries from the Conversion to the Benedictine Reform', *Settimane di studio del Centro italiano di studi sull'alto medioevo XXXII, 1984* (Spoleto, 1986), 643–88.

GREEN, W. M., 'Mediaeval Recensions of Augustine', *Speculum*, 29 (1954), 531–4.

GREENFIELD, K., 'Changing Emphases in English Vernacular Homiletic Literature, 960–1225', *Journal of Medieval History*, 7 (1981), 283–97.

GREENWAY, D. (ed.), J. Le Neve, *Fasti Ecclesiae Anglicanae, 1066–1300*, ii: *Monastic Cathedrals* (London, 1971); iv: *Salisbury Cathedral* (London, 1991).

—— 'The False *Institutio* of St Osmund', in *Tradition and Change: Essays in Honour of Marjorie Chibnall*, ed. D. Greenway, C. Holdsworth, and J. Sayers (Cambridge, 1985), 77–101.

GULLICK, M., 'The Scribe of the Carilef Bible: A New Look at Some Late-Eleventh-Century Durham Cathedral Manuscripts', in *Medieval Book Production: Assessing the Evidence, Proceedings of the Second Conference of The Seminar in the History of the Book to 1500*, ed. L. L. Brownrigg (Los Altos Hills, 1990), 61–83.

HARTMANN, W., 'Psalmenkommentare aus der Zeit der Reform und der Frühscholastik', *Studi Gregoriani*, 9 (Rome, 1972), 313–66.

HOLT, J. C., '1086', in *Domesday Studies: Novocentenary Conference, Royal Historical Society and Institute of British Geographers, Winchester 1986*, ed. J. C. Holt (Woodbridge, Suffolk, 1987), 41–64.

HOLTZ, L., *Donat et la tradition de l'enseignement grammatical* (Paris, 1981).

HOPE, W. H. ST JOHN, 'Report on the Excavation of the Cathedral Church of Old Sarum in 1913', *Proceedings of the Society of Antiquaries of London*, 2nd ser., 26 (1913–14), 100–17.

HUMPHREYS, K., 'The Early Medieval Library', in *Paläographie 1981: Colloquium des Comité International de Paléographie München, 15.-18. September 1981*, ed. G. Silagi (Munich, 1982), 59–70.

HUNT, R. W., Review of C. W. Jones (ed.), *Bedae opera de temporibus* in *Medium Ævum*, 16 (1947), 62–4.

—— 'The Introductions to the "Artes" in the Twelfth Century', *Studia mediaevalia in honorem admodum reverendi patris Raymundi Josephi Martin* (Bruges [1948]), 85–112; repr. in his collected papers, *The History of Grammar in the Middle Ages*, ed. G. L. Bursill-Hall (Amsterdam, 1980), 117–44.

—— 'Studies on Priscian in the Twelfth Century: II', *Medieval and Renaissance Studies*, 2 (1950), 1–56; repr. in his collected papers, *The History of Grammar in the Middle Ages*, ed. G. L. Bursill-Hall (Amsterdam, 1980), 39–94.

HUYGENS, R. B. C., *Accessus ad auctores; Bernard d'Utrecht; Conrad d'Hirsau* (Leiden, 1970).

JAMES, M. R., *A Descriptive Catalogue of the Manuscripts in the Library of Corpus Christi College, Cambridge*, 2 vols. (Cambridge, 1912).

—— *A Catalogue of the Medieval Manuscripts in the University Library Aberdeen* (Cambridge, 1932).

KEALEY, E. J., *Roger of Salisbury* (Berkeley, Calif., 1972).

KER, N. R., 'Manuscripts from Salisbury Cathedral', *Bodleian Library Record*, 3, no. 31 (1951), 121.

—— 'Salisbury Cathedral Manuscripts and Patrick Young's Catalogue', *The Wiltshire Archaeological and Natural History Magazine*, 53 (1949–50), 153–83.

—— 'Sir John Prise', *The Library*, 5: 10 (1955), 1–24.

—— *Catalogue of Manuscripts Containing Anglo-Saxon* (Oxford, 1957).

—— 'Three Old English Texts in a Salisbury Pontifical, Cotton Tiberius C I', in *The Anglo-Saxons: Studies in some Aspects of their History and Culture Presented to Bruce Dickins*, ed. P. Clemoes (London, 1959), 262–79.

—— *English Manuscripts in the Century after the Norman Conquest* (Oxford, 1960).

—— *Medieval Manuscripts in British Libraries*, vols. i– (Oxford, 1969–).

—— 'The English Manuscripts of the Moralia of Gregory the Great', in *Kunsthistorische Forschungen Otto Pächt zu seinem 70. Geburtstag*, ed. A. Rosenauer and G. Weber (Salzburg, 1972), 77–89.

—— 'The Beginnings of Salisbury Cathedral Library', in *Medieval Learning and Literature: Essays presented to Richard William Hunt*, ed. J. J. G. Alexander and M. T. Gibson (Oxford, 1976), 23–49.

—— 'Copying an Exemplar: Two Manuscripts of Jerome on Habakkuk', in *Miscellanea codicologica F. Masai dicata*, ed. P. Cockshaw, M. Garand, and P. Jodogne (Ghent, 1979), 203–10.

KNOWLES, D., BROOKE, C. N. L., and LONDON, V. C. M. (eds.), *The Heads of Religious Houses: England and Wales 940–1216* (Cambridge, 1972).

KOTTJE, R., 'Klosterbibliotheken und monastische Kultur in der zweiten Hälfte des 11. Jahrhunderts', *Zeitschrift für Kirchengeschichte*, 4: 18 (1969), 145–62.

LAMBOT, C., 'La Tradition manuscrite des sermons de saint Augustin pour la Noël et l'Épiphanie', *Rev. bén.*, 77 (1967), 217–45.

LAPIDGE, M., 'The Present State of Anglo-Latin Studies', in *Insular Latin Studies: Papers on Latin Texts and Manuscripts of the British Isles 550–1066*, ed. M. Herren (Toronto, 1981), 45–82.

—— 'The Study of Latin Texts in Late Anglo-Saxon England: The Evidence of Latin Glosses', in *Latin and the Vernacular Languages in Early Medieval Britain*, ed. N. Brooks (Leicester, 1982), 99–140.

—— 'Surviving Booklists from Anglo-Saxon England', in *Learning and Literature in Anglo-Saxon England: Studies presented to Peter Clemoes on the Occasion of his Sixty-fifth Birthday*, ed. M. Lapidge and H. Gneuss (Cambridge, 1985), 33–89.

LECLERCQ, J., 'The Renewal of Theology', in *Renaissance and Renewal in the Twelfth Century*, ed. R. L. Benson and G. Constable (Oxford, 1982), 68–87.

LEYSER, K., 'Liudprand of Cremona, Preacher and Homilist', in *The Bible in the Medieval World: Essays in Memory of Beryl Smalley*, ed. K. Walsh and D. Wood (Oxford, 1985), 43–60.

LOWE, E. A., 'A Manuscript of Alcuin in the Script of Tours', in *Classical and Medieval Studies in Honour of Edward Kennard Rand*, ed. L. W. Jones (New York, 1938), 191–3; repr. in Lowe's collected papers, *Palaeographical Papers 1907–1965*, ed. L. Bieler (Oxford, 1972), i. 342–4.

McKITTERICK, R., *The Carolingians and the Written Word* (Cambridge, 1989).

MANITIUS, M., *Geschichte des lateinische Literatur des Mittelalters*, 3 vols. (Munich, 1911–31).

MARSHALL, P. K., MARTIN, J., and ROUSE, R. H., 'Clare College MS. 26 and the Circulation of Aulus Gellius 1–7 in Medieval England and France', *Mediaeval Studies*, 42 (1980), 353–94.

MARTIN, H., *Catalogue des manuscrits de la Bibliothèque de l'Arsenal*, 9 vols. (Paris, 1885–94).

MASKELL, W., *Monumenta ritualia ecclesiae Anglicanae: The Occasional Offices of the Church of England According to the Old Use of Salisbury*, 2nd edn, 3 vols. (Oxford, 1882).

MASON, J. F. A., 'The Date of the Geld Rolls', *EHR* 69 (1954), 283–9.

MICHAUD-QUANTIN, P., *Sommes de casuistique et manuels de confession au moyen âge (xii–xvi siècles)*, *Analecta mediaevalia Namurcensia*, xiii (Louvain, 1962).

MILDE, W., 'Der Bibliothekskatalog des Klosters Murbach aus dem 9. Jahrhundert', *Beihefte zum Euphorion*, 4 (1968).

MINNIS, A. J., *Medieval Theory of Authorship: Scholastic Literary Attitudes in the Later Middle Ages*, 2nd edn (Aldershot, 1988).

MORIN, G., 'Le Pseudo-Bède sur les Psaumes, et l'*opus super psalterium* de Maître Manegold de Lautenbach', *Rev. bén.*, 28 (1911), 331–40.

Musset, L., 'Recherches sur les communautés de clercs séculiers en Normandie au xie siècle', *Bulletin de la Société des Antiquaires de Normandie*, 55 (1961, for 1959–60), 5–38.

Mynors, R. A. B., *Durham Cathedral Manuscripts* (Oxford, 1939).

Nortier, G., *Les Bibliothèques médiévales des abbayes bénédictines de Normandie: Fécamp, Le Bec, Le Mont Saint-Michel, Saint-Évroul, Lyre, Jumièges, Saint-Wandrille, Saint-Ouen* (Paris, 1971).

Ogilvy, J. D. A., *Books known to the English, 597–1066* (Cambridge, Mass., 1967).

—— 'Books known to the English, 597–1066: *Addenda et Corrigenda*', *Mediaevalia*, 7 (1984), 281–325.

Omont, H., *Catalogue générale des manuscrits des bibliothèques publiques de France*, i–ii, *Rouen* (Paris, 1886–8).

Parkes, M. B., 'The Handwriting of St Boniface: A Reassessment of the Problems', *Beiträge zur Geschichte der Deutschen Sprache und Literatur*, 98 (1976), 161–79.

—— 'The Influence of the Concepts of *Ordinatio* and *Compilatio* on the Development of the Book', in *Medieval Learning and Literature, Essays Presented to Richard William Hunt*, ed. J. J. G. Alexander and M. T. Gibson (Oxford, 1976), 115–41.

—— 'Punctuation, or Pause and Effect', in *Medieval Eloquence: Studies in the Theory and Practice of Medieval Rhetoric*, ed. J. J. Murphy (Berkeley, Calif., 1978), 127–42.

—— 'A Note on MS Vatican, Bibl. Apost., lat. 3363', in *Boethius, His Life, Thought and Influence*, ed. M. T. Gibson (Oxford, 1981), 425–7.

—— 'A Fragment of an Early-Tenth-Century Anglo-Saxon Manuscript and its Significance', *ASE*, 12 (1983), 129–40.

—— 'The Date of the Oxford Manuscript of *La Chanson de Roland* (Oxford, Bodleian Library, MS. Digby 23)', *Medioevo Romanzo*, 10 (1985), 161–75.

Pollard, H. G., 'The Construction of English Twelfth-Century Bindings', *The Library*, 5: 17 (1962), 1–22.

Rella, F. A., 'Continental Manuscripts acquired for English Centers in the Tenth and Early Eleventh Centuries: A Preliminary Checklist', *Anglia*, 98 (1980), 107–16.

Reynolds, L. D. (ed.), *Texts and Transmission: A Survey of the Latin Classics* (Oxford, 1983).

Robinson, I. S., 'The Bible in the Investiture Contest: The South German Gregorian Circle', in *The Bible in the Medieval World: Essays in Memory of Beryl Smalley*, eds. K. Walsh and D. Wood (Oxford, 1985), 61–84.

Robinson, P. R., 'Self-Contained Units in Composite Manuscripts of the Anglo-Saxon Period', *ASE*, 7 (1978), 231–8.

—— 'The "Booklet": A Self-Contained Unit in Composite Manuscripts', *Codicologica*, 3 (1980), 46–69.

Rochais, H.-M., 'Les Manuscrits du "Liber scintillarum"', *Scriptorium*, 4 (1950), 294–309.

—— 'Contribution à l'histoire des florilèges ascétiques du haut moyen âge latin: Le "Liber scintillarum"', *Rev. bén.*, 63 (1953), 246–91.

RÖMER, F., *Die handschriftliche Überlieferung der Werke des heiligen Augustinus*, 2/i, *Grossbritannien und Irland, Werkverzeichnis*, Österreichische Akademie der Wissenschaften phil.-hist. Klasse, Sitzungsberichte, 281 (Vienna, 1972).

ROUSE, R. H. and ROUSE, M. A., 'The *Florilegium Angelicum*: Its Origin, Content and Influence', in *Medieval Learning and Literature: Essays Presented to Richard William Hunt*, ed. J. J. G. Alexander and M. T. Gibson (Oxford, 1976), 66–114.

—— 'The *Registrum Anglie*: The Franciscan "Union Catalogue" of British Libraries', in *Manuscripts at Oxford: An Exhibition in Memory of Richard William Hunt (1908–1979)*, eds. A. C. de la Mare and B. C. Barker-Benfield (Oxford, 1980), 55–6.

SCHULLIAN, D. M., 'The Anthology of Valerius Maximus and A. Gellius', *Classical Philology*, 32 (1937), 70–2.

SIEGMUND, A., *Die Überlieferung der griechischen christlichen Literatur in der lateinischen Kirche bis zum zwölften Jahrhundert* (Munich, 1949).

SIMS-WILLIAMS, P., 'Thoughts on Ephrem the Syrian in Anglo-Saxon England', in *Learning and Literature in Anglo-Saxon England: Studies presented to Peter Clemoes on the Occasion of his Sixty-fifth Birthday*, ed. M. Lapidge and H. Gneuss (Cambridge, 1985), 205–26.

SMALLEY, B., 'Master Ivo of Chartres', *EHR* 50 (1935), 680–6.

—— 'Gilbertus Universalis, Bishop of London (1128–34), and the Problem of the "Glossa Ordinaria"', *RTAM* 8 (1936), 24–60.

—— 'La Glossa Ordinaria: Quelques prédécesseurs d'Anselme de Laon', *RTAM* 9 (1937), 365–400.

—— *The Study of the Bible in the Middle Ages*, 3rd edn (Oxford, 1983).

SOUTHERN, R. W., 'The Place of England in the Twelfth-Century Renaissance', *History*, 45 (1960), 201–16; repr. with some alterations in his collected papers, *Medieval Humanism* (Oxford, 1970), 158–80.

—— *St Anselm and His Biographer* (Oxford, 1963).

STEGMÜLLER, F., *Repertorium biblicum medii aevi*, 11 vols. (Madrid, 1940–80).

THOMSON, R. M., 'The Library of Bury St Edmunds Abbey in the Eleventh and Twelfth Centuries', *Speculum*, 47 (1972), 617–45.

—— 'A Thirteenth-Century Plautus Florilegium from Bury St. Edmunds Abbey', *Antichthon*, 8 (1974), 29–43.

—— *Manuscripts from St Albans Abbey 1066–1235*, 2 vols. (Woodbridge, Suffolk, 1982).

—— 'British Library Royal 15 C. xi; A Manuscript of Plautus' Plays from Salisbury Cathedral (c.1100)', *Scriptorium*, 40 (1986), 82–7.

—— 'The Norman Conquest and English Libraries', in *The Role of the Book in Medieval Culture*, ed. P. Ganz (Turnhout, 1986), ii. 27–40.

—— *William of Malmesbury* (Woodbridge, Suffolk, 1987).

—— *Catalogue of the Manuscripts of Lincoln Cathedral Chapter Library* (Cambridge, 1989).

THORNDIKE, L. and KIBRE, P., *A Catalogue of Incipits of Mediaeval Scientific Writings in Latin*, 2nd edn (London, 1963).

VAN DEN EYNDE, D., 'Literary Note on the Earliest Scholastic *Commentarii in Psalmos*', *Franciscan Studies*, 14 (1954), 121–54.

VAN DER HORST, K., *Illuminated and Decorated Medieval Manuscripts in the University Library, Utrecht: An Illustrated Catalogue* (The Hague, 1989).

VAN DER VYVER, A., 'Les Œvres inédites d'Abbon de Fleury', *Rev. bén.*, 47 (1935), 125–69.

VEZIN, J., 'Observations sur l'emploi des réclames dans les manuscrits latins', *Bibliothèque de l'École des Chartes*, 125 (1967), 5–33.

—— 'Manuscrits des dixième et onzième siècles copiés en Angleterre en minuscule caroline et conservés à la Bibliothèque Nationale de Paris', *Humanisme actif: Mélanges d'art et de littérature offerts à Julien Cain*, ii (Paris, 1968), 283–96.

WALLER, K., 'Rochester Cathedral Library: An English Book Collection based on Norman Models', *Les Mutations socio-culturelles au tournant des xie-xiie siècles. Colloque international du CNRS: Le Bec-Hellouin, 11–16 juillet 1982* (Paris, 1984), 237–50.

WALTHER, H., *Initia carminum ac versuum medii aevi posterioris Latinorum*, Carmina Medii Aevi Posterioris Latina, i (Göttingen, 1959).

WARNER, G. F. and GILSON, J. P., *British Museum, Catalogue of Western Manuscripts in the Old Royal and King's Collections*, 5 vols. (London, 1921).

WEBBER, T., 'Salisbury and the Exon Domesday: Some Observations Concerning the Origin of Exeter Cathedral MS 3500', *English Manuscript Studies 1100–1700*, 1 (1989), 1–18.

—— 'Patrick Young, Salisbury Cathedral Manuscripts and the Royal Collection', *English Manuscript Studies 1100–1700*, 2 (1990), 283–90.

WIELAND, G. R., 'The Glossed Manuscript: Classbook or Library Book?', *ASE*, 14 (1985), 153–73.

WILMART, A., 'Le Commentaire sur les Psaumes imprimé sous le nom de Rufin', *Rev. bén.*, 31 (1914–19), 258–76.

—— 'Les Sermons d'Hildebert', *Rev. bén.*, 47 (1935), 12–51.

WORMALD, F., *English Kalendars before AD 1100*, Henry Bradshaw Society, 72 (London, 1934).

—— 'An Eleventh-Century Copy of the Norman *Laudes regiae*', *BIHR*, 37 (1964), 73–6.

ZETTEL, P. H., 'Saints' Lives in Old English: Latin Manuscripts and Vernacular Accounts: Ælfric', *Peritia*, 1 (1982), 17–37.

SECONDARY WORKS—UNPUBLISHED

CARTER, P., 'An Edition of William of Malmesbury's Treatise on the Miracles of the Virgin Mary', 2 vols., D.Phil. thesis (Oxford University, 1959).

DRAGE, E. M., 'Bishop Leofric and the Exeter Cathedral Chapter (1050–1072): A Reassessment of the Manuscript Evidence', D.Phil. thesis (Oxford University, 1978).

GILLESPIE, V. A., 'The Literary Form of the Middle English Pastoral Manual with Particular Reference to the *Speculum christiani* and Some Related Texts', D.Phil. thesis (Oxford University, 1981).

MᴄIɴᴛʏʀᴇ, E. A., 'Early Twelfth-Century Worcester Cathedral Priory, with Special Reference to Some of the Manuscripts written There', D.Phil. thesis (Oxford University, 1978).

Mᴏʀʀɪsʜ, J. J., 'An Examination of Literacy and Learning in England in the Ninth Century', D.Phil. thesis (Oxford University, 1982).

Rᴀᴛʜʙᴏɴᴇ, E., 'The Influence of Bishops and of Members of Cathedral Bodies in the Intellectual Life of England, 1066–1216', Ph.D. thesis (London University, 1935).

Rᴇʟʟᴀ, F. A., 'Some Aspects of the Indirect Transmission of Christian Latin Sources for Anglo-Saxon Prose from the Reign of Alfred to the Norman Conquest', B.Litt. thesis (Oxford University, 1977).

Zᴇᴛᴛᴇʟ, P. H., 'Ælfric's Hagiographic Sources and the Latin Legendary Preserved in B.L. MS Cotton Nero E i+CCCC MS 9 and Other Manuscripts', D.Phil. thesis (Oxford University, 1979).

INCIPIT EXPOSITIO BEDE PRESBYTERI· ET VASIS eius ac vestibus
SACERDOTII· CAPITVLA LIBRI PRIMI· I· Moyses in monte dñi
cum iosue ascendens· aaron & ur ad regim̄ pop̄li reliquit· ij· Idem
·vij· die ad altiora montis uocatus· xl· diebz, ac noctibz ibi cū dño montē·
·iij· fili isrł pinguas dño offerre· et sc̄m arcū facere iubentur· iiij· Descr̄
pō arc̄· v· Propitiatorii & cherubin· VI· mense· Vij· vasorū et
& panum propitiationis & thuris· Viij· Candelabri· Viiij· Lucer
narū eius & emūctoriū· INCIPIT LIBER PRIMVS·
Locuturi iuuante dño de figura tabernaculi· & uasorū· atq; uten_
siliū eius· primo situ loci & circumstantias rerum· quomodo se se
habuerunt· quando aut̄ fieri precepta sunt· inspicere atq;
intentius considerare debemus· Omnia aut̄ sicut apłs ait· in figura
contingebant eis; scripta sunt aut̄ propter nos omnia· udelicz ñ solū
facta uel uerba que sacris litteris continentur· uerū & iā locorum·

1a. Scribe i (lines 1–6 'arce'); scribe xii (lines 6–14)

Inter has scilicet creaturarū mirabilem & speciosā uarieta ·X·
tē· ex qua pulcherrima unuisica formatarū estat rerū· de
q̄ dict̄; Erant oīa ualde bona; Bona ū· q̄ ab uno c̄dita
sunt creatore· s̄ ñ sic bona sicut creator· q̄ solus summū & inco
mutabile bonū; Homo solus ad imagin̄ & similitudin̄ e
diuinis creat· ee· legit· & felicissimi hoſt· qui paradisus dicit
habitator constituitus· uniq; tantū in epulis· phibit· qua ten
tam facilis mandati obseruatione· celeste meretretur bea _
titudin̄·7 Sed inuidia ruentis angti· de beatitudine sua
łui mandati transgressor effect· e· atq; in huius exilii sic co
mmat· e· ei creatur erū noſa derelict· e· miseria & penali moſti
c̄ditione· multat·7 Sed miatissim creator· nolens facturā ima _
ginis suę aeternaliō pire; Misit filiū suū unigenitū dm̄ pq

1b. Scribe ii

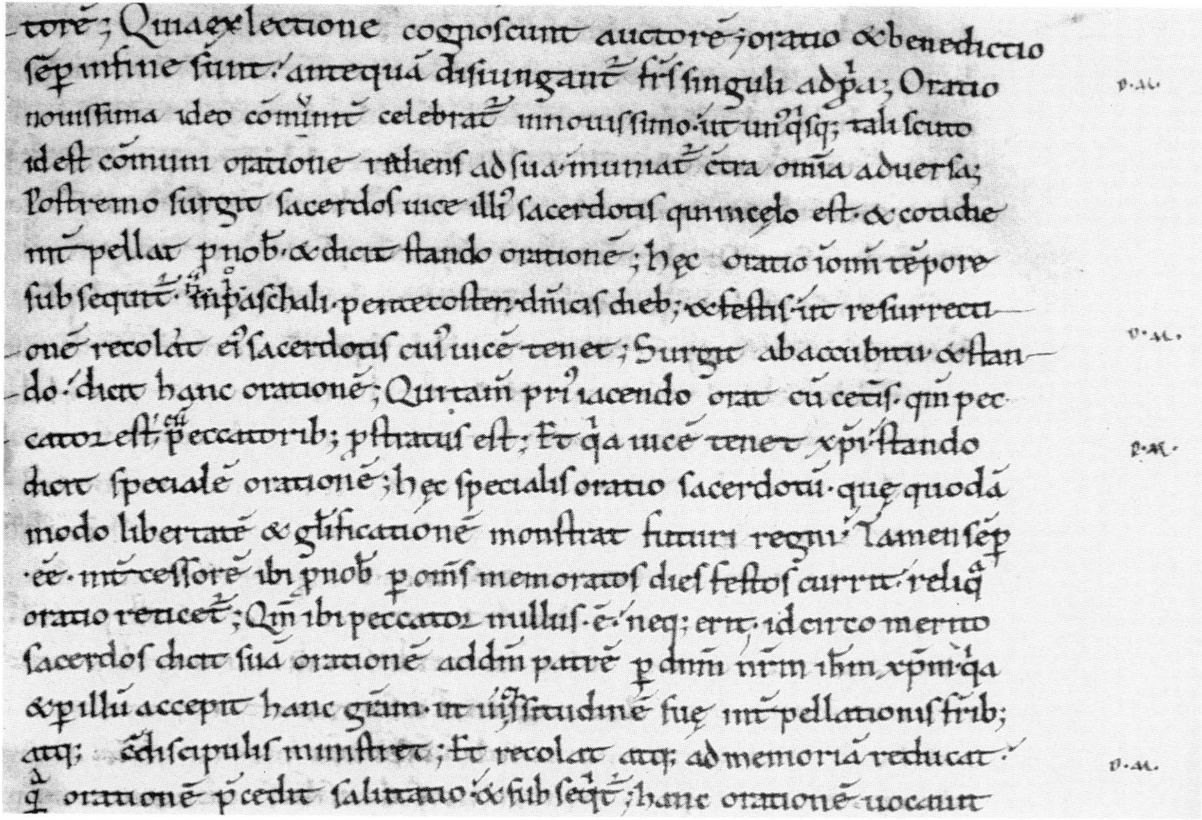

2. Scribe iii

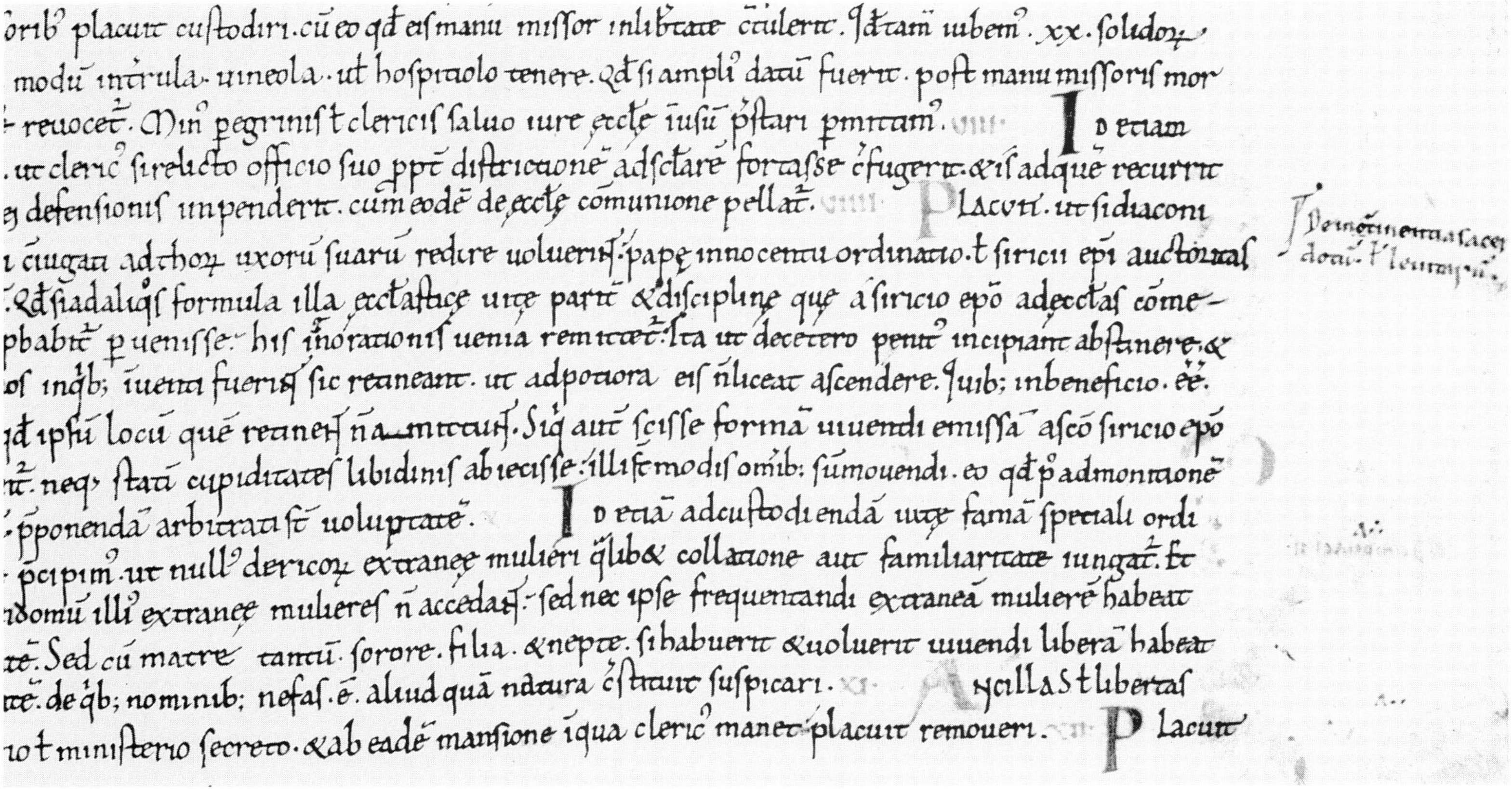

3. Scribe v

aliud n̄ nosse n̄ amare cū habeat id ē nouerit. Sed cū

uideā nonnullos non ob aliqd uerbi grā discere

numeros: n̄ ut eadē disciplina pecuniosi fiant aut

hoīb; placeant. quā cū didicerint ad eundē fine refer

que sibi cū discerent pposuerant Neq; ullā disciplinā

aliud sit habere quam nosse. & fieri potest ut habeat

aliqd qd habere hoc sit qd nosse nequea & tam qnqm

bonum q̄ nsfruit n̄ aute frui sin amat. nec habet igit quod

amandū ē. qn q̄uit etiam si amare possit quin habet. Nemo

igit beatā uitam nouit & miser ē. Qm si amanda ē sic ē hoc ē

eam nosse quod habere. Que cum ita sino quid ē aliud beate

uiuere nisi aeternū aliquid cognoscendo habere. gtnuū ē

enim deq solo recte fidit quodam ante auferri nnpotest. Idq3

ipsum ē quod nihil sit aliud habere quam nosse. Omnium

enī rerū pstantissimū est qd aeternū ē. Et ppterea id habere

non possum n̄ ea re qua pstantiores sum id ē mente.

Quicqd aute mente habetur noscendo habet. nullū q;

bonū pfec te noscit qd n̄ pfec te amatur. neq; ut sola

mens potest cognoscere. ita & amare sola potest. Nāq;

amor appetitor qdā ē & uidem etia ceteris animi partib;

inesse appetit. Qui si menti ratione q; consentiat in tali

pace & tranqllitate uacabit. licebit mente ōteplari.

qd aeternū est. Ergo etia ceteris suis partib; amare anim

debet. hoc tā magnū qd mente noscendū est. Et qm id

qd amat efficiat ex se amante. necesse sit ut sic amatū

qd aeternū ē aeternitate animū afficiat. Quocirca

4. Scribe ix (lines 1–7, 14 'nosse' –26); scribe xi (lines 8–14 'quam')

sublimissimu eode ordine quo petruf ceteriq; apti afctm fr uoluntarie fufce-
piffe: q uocationif fue pclara pncipia cupiditatif ac phylargirie peftifero fine
cfumanf. ufq; ad traditione dni crudeliffim parricida prupit? Aut quid
obfuit paulo qd repente cecat ad uia falutif uelut inuit uidet attract? qui
poftea dnm toto animi feruore fecut. initiu neceffitatif uoluntaria deuotione con-
fumanf. glofam tantif uirtutib; uita incoparabili fine cclufit? Totu q infine
confiftit. inquo potell quif &optime cuerfionif initiu dedicat? inferior pnegli-
gentia repiri. &neceffitate atqae adnom monachi pftendu effici pamore
di diligentiamq; pfectuf; VI. Nunc deabrenuntiationib; differendu eft.
quaf trefee. & patrum traditio. &fcripturaru fcarum demonftrat auctorita
quafq; uniquenq; nrm omi ftudio oportet implere; Prima e. qua corporali
uniuerfaf diuitiaf mundi facultatifq; cfempnim; Seda qua moraf acutia
affectufq; priftinof animi carnifq; refpuim; Tertia. qua mte nram depfen
uniuerfif acuifibilib; euocantef. futura tantu in cfeplam. & ea que funt
inuifibia concupifcim? Que tria ut fimul pficiant? etia abrahe legi-
m dnm pcepiffe cu dicit ad eu. Exi de tra tua & de cognitione tu
& de domo patrif tui. Primu dix de tra ide de facultatib; mundi
hui opib; q tremf. Sedo decognatione tua ide de cufatione & mo-
rib; uirtufq; porib; que nobif a nra natiuitate coherentia: uelut
affinitate quada & confanguinitate cognata funt. Tercio de domo
patrif tui. ide omi memoria mundi hui que oculof occurrit ob-
tutib; . De duob; eni patrib; fiue de illo q deferend. fiue de eo qui
expetend e. ita p d auid ex pfona dicant Audi filia & uide
& inclina aure tua . & obliuifcere poplm tuu & domu patrif tui.
a qui dic audi filia. pat utiq e. Et illu qui cui domu ut poptm

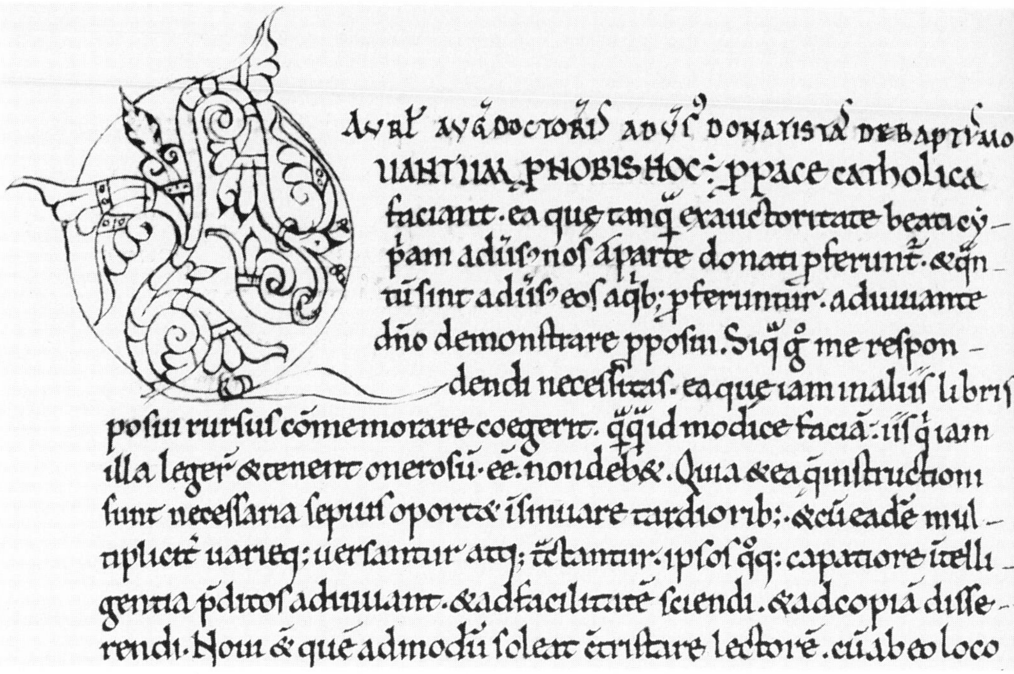

6*a*. Scribe 3

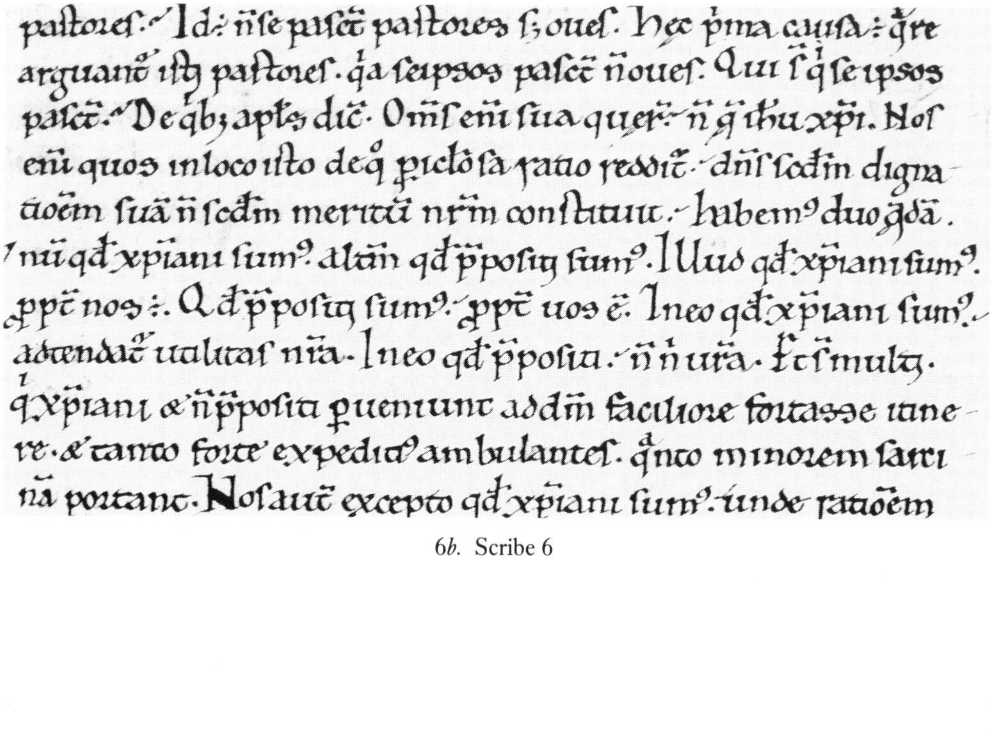

6*b*. Scribe 6

Xpc̄	Eucharistiam	Aecclesia
Incipabilis.	Sumendam.	Sumens.
Invescibilis.	Urscendam.	Vescens.
Dat	Datam	Accipit
Ab ipso.	Ex ipso.	Corpus eius.

7. Scribe 3 (lines 1–32 'sermone') scribe 7 (lines 32 'dominum' –35)

damnatione penaru̅ ſalueris inqua o̅ib; fidelib; declinet iudicas ſca̅m
uero eccleſiam rene que qg dn̅i patre omnipotente & unigenitu̅ filiu̅
eſt ſubin xp̅m dm̅ nr̅m & ſc̅m ſp̅m concordi   conſona ſubſtan
tie racione profitetur filiumqʒ . dm̅ natu̅ ex uirgine & paſſu̅ proſa
lite humana acreſurrexiſſe amoracuſ   carne quinatur; ē . cre
dit . Eiuſdeqʒ uenturu̅ iudice omniu̅ ſperat inqua & remiſſio pecca
torii & carniſ reſurrectio predicatur ſuerii deremiſſione peccatoru̅
ſufficere debere& ſola credulitaſ quiſ eni̅ cauſaſ aut racionem requirat
                  principaliſ; ē & tamen cu̅ torren̅ ſuiſ regeſ liberaltaſ
nonſit obnoxia abhumana temeritate diſcutitur   largitio .
Solent eni cuminuiſione dicere aduerſu̅   qd̅ ipſi noſ decipi
amuſ quiputemuſ crimina   miſta ſiunt uerbiſ poſ_
te purgari & aiunt   qui homicidii committ homicida non ad eſſe aut ad uter non undem quia adulterii perpetrauit .
Quomodo ergo huiſ cemodi criminiſ reuſ   nobiſ effici ſubito uidē
& ſuruſ fiad adhec ut dixi meliuſ fide qua racione reſpondeo · rex
enim . ē . omniu̅ qui promiſit terre celi queuēthiſ.ē . qui hec pollicetur

8. Scribe 8

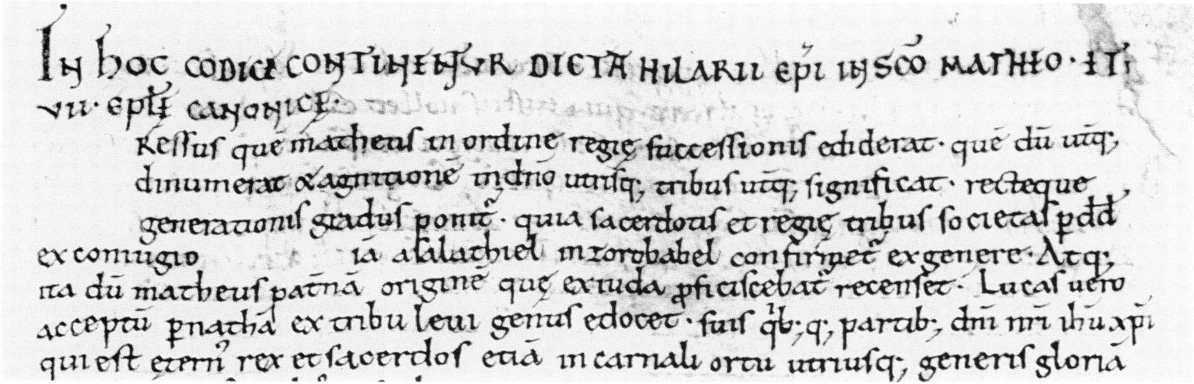

9a. Scribe 9

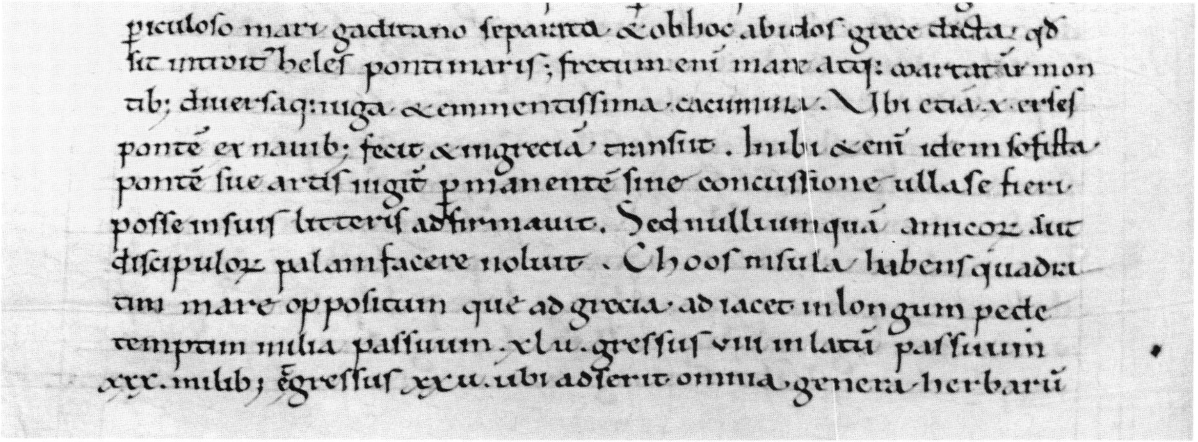

9b. Scribe 12

IN NOMINE SANCTE TRINITATIS.

Scripturarum divinarum mole q[uis]q[ue] affimm nequit potiri quodam privilegio brevis elucubratissimis flosculis
medullatus tenella condiri. Ne nos tenebre sis comprehendant dum lucem habemus currere s[anc]tis gradibus satagamus. ne hereditate[m] promissam culpa n[ost]ri quod absit amitt-
tamus.

Primus gradus est sacratissime scale. fides recta cum op[eri]b[us]
iustitie. idest ut in patrem et filium et in sp[iritu]m s[anctu]m p[er]fecte
credat. in s[an]c[t]a trinitate unum d[omi]n[u]m cognoscat. in uno deo s[anctam]
trinitate[m] noverit coeternum et coequalem d[e]i filium deo p[at]r[i].
et deo sp[irit]u s[an]c[t]o. Quia qui incredulus est filio d[e]i. non videbit
vitam. sed ira d[e]i manet sup[er] eum.

Sec[un]d[u]s gradus est spes firma in d[omi]n[u]m. idest ut unusquisque spe[m]
sua[m] in deo ponat. de omni re de p[re]sentibus atq[ue] de futuris bonis
spem habeat q[ui]cq[ui]d boni l[oquitur] cogitet l[oquitur] faciat a deo sibi remunerari
di et spem habeat indulgentie peccatorum. si se veraciter
ad d[omi]n[u]m convertat p[er] penitentiam. Desp[er]atio aut[em] peior est omni
peccato. quia auget peccatum.

Tertius gradus est in[mi]rune necessarius. karitas p[er]fecta. id[est]
ut diligat d[eu]s ex toto corde. toto animo. tota virtute. in sensu p[er]fecto. in voluntate bona. in cogitatu mundo. in verbis
divinis. in op[eri]bus deo placatos. et primos n[ost]ros .i. om[ne]s [christ]i-
anos sicut nosmetipsos diligam[us]. quia c[a]ritas op[eri]t multitudinem peccatorum. Karitas vera est amicum diligere in deo. et
inimicum p[ro]pt[er] d[omi]n[u]m. karitas enim om[n]iu[m] virtutum obinet p[ri]n-
cipatum. quia d[eu]s karitas est. A deo q[uoque] a regno d[e]i se separant. qui
semetipsos a karitate dissociant. Sine karitate namq[ue] quicq[ui]d e[st]

10. Scribe 11

amcnda mangustaq; lapide mansim uino consilio notuos si dr uro regali
puero regnum patris sui conqsusse. que mandauit apostolica auctoritas de
uuilfridbo epo sead implere do spoponidin. Shain postuoa mutacis annus
munuax. onicio curta os cu gerantzo manucia niam conuert fiut. Apos ramus
de angusta libata. fugias immaf nisregnu accepim? Porm hec uerba finite
sunt. epi sibi mituo separat abalus intre eper aliqndo cuies archi eps aliqndo
si sapienassima uirgo adsteda. Shui sci consilu tas sinus exatte ut orsepi
Shex cu optimaas; suis pure pars coodia cu wilfridbo epo iniere qin iniere
se utaq; adfinem utre sseruauer reddeirxet edtuo optima coenobia
que sunt inbrripis Shin aguthalder ig etu omib. redirab; suis er
illa die oms epise minuce oscalauar Shamplexrauxer panes;
frangenxer comunicauer gras agenxer deo oms sci hui beatitudis
suis inpace xpi adsua loca reneaxiunt
IRABILIS DS insen funt qui pamore
coraus gede saluuofaiu pace animas pretula coronauit Sh
hi maxuna beatuudo grxtaq; pares tam illox q plonga spatia

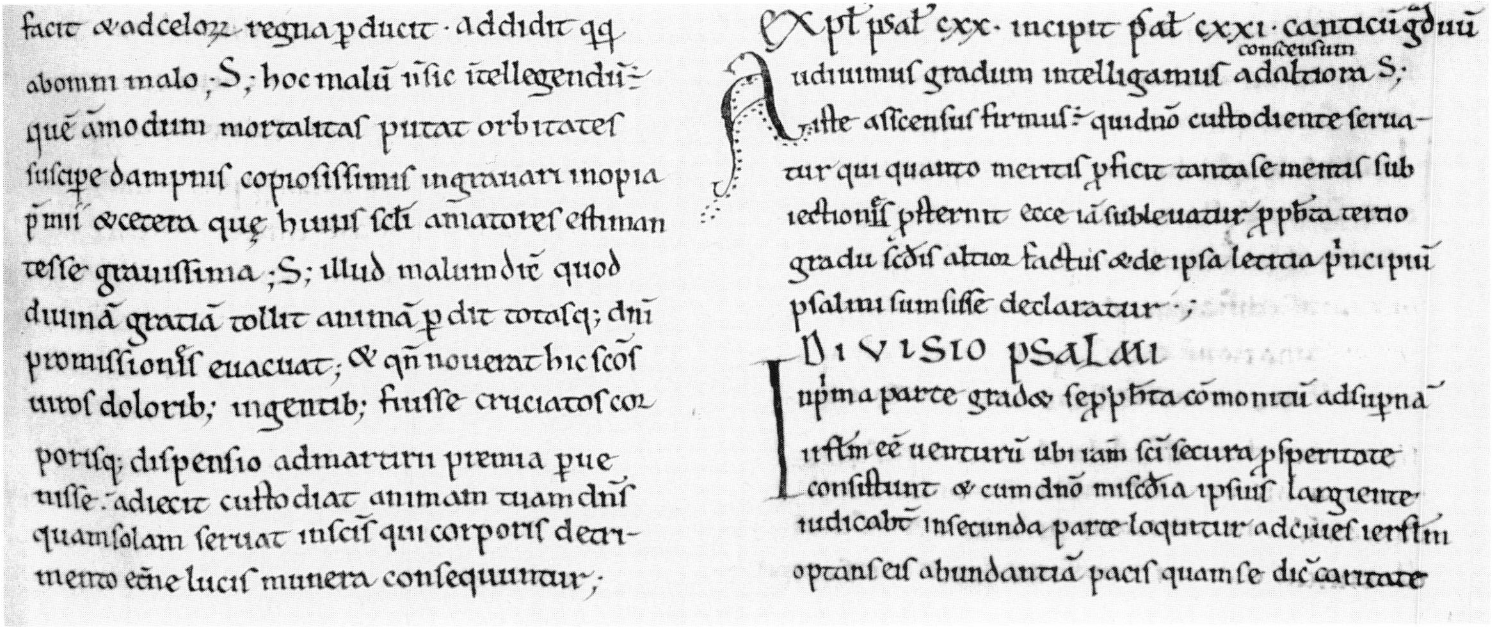

12. Scribe 14

dñi felici sorte prūpit. Ī uideuſ bona futū
ſcti. que ei ſe credebat largitatib; adipiſci.
Ē ceuī paſſer inuenit ſibi domū & ꞇaur nidū
ſibi reponat pulloſ ſuoſ.
Cū ſupi anima corpᵒq; dixerit in dñi exulta
cione gaude. hic autū iſta dᵒſo genera ad
q̄ndā ſimilitudinē cōūidandāpoſinſte diuoſ
cū. paſſer eſt nimia uelocitate celerrim̄.
q̄ uiſiluit habitare ū pariū, ſ, domū ſibi in
parietū foraminib; deſiderant exq̄rit.
Qᵈ dū inuenit nimio gaudio leᵒ exultat.
q̄a ſe diūſariū adūſitatū ultᵒ patere
ū credū inſiduſ. Sic anima iocunda
tur dū incelox regno manſionē ſuā
ſenſerit. ee. p̄paratā. Cūꞇ ū abſti
uentie moderatione caſtiſſim̄ eſt.
q̄ una cantū copulatione contetᵘ
filuſ ſuuſ nidū edificare cognoſci
tur. q̄ ū ut paſſer p̄paratā domū
repit. ſ; nouā ſibi de db; dā parti
culiſ fabricare contendit. huic
caro nr̄a ū irrite cōparat̄. que

13. Scribe 15

Aut qn petit filius eius ouum . nuqd porrig illi scorpione si q̄ uos cu sitis mali nostra
bona data dare filiis urīs . quanto mag̅ pr̄ ur̄ celestis dabit bona petentib; se
Quādiu g̅ uiuim in isto s̄c̄lo die tribulationis patim . qa ad dn̄o pugnam siue bene sit nob
scdm s̄c̄m dies t̄bulationis ꝫ qdiu tēp puguationis . Tc̄ en̄i tn̄sit t̄bulatio qn finitas
puguatio . Tc̄ aut finiet puguatio qn i patria nr̄a celestia adimeti angl̄is scit cu rege
nr̄o dn̄o ih̄u xp̄o sine fine uiuim . ꝯ̄ sine fine gaudebim . ꝫ regnabim . Ibi eni
amabim ꝫ laudabim . ꝫ gaudebim . ꝫ uidebim . Eua sc̄ aut dn̄u q̅ edificat in nob s̄c̄a apl̄s
Ipsa eni q̅ necessaria sc̄ i isto s̄c̄lo fides . spes . karitas . fides ut credam . Spes ut ex
spectem . Karitas ut amem . Fides aut pisces ꝫ qa qm pisces i aq̅ natat . ꝫ ide
uiuit . Sic ꝫ p baptismu fides accipit ꝫ uiuit i s̄c̄lo . Ouu aut qr spes ꝫ qa pullus
ndu uidet . s; adhuc spat . Sic eni ait apl̄s . Spe eni salui facti sum . Spes aut q̅ uidet
n̄ spes qd eni uidet q̅s qd spat . Si aut qd n̄ uidem spam p patientia expectam .
Patientia nr̄a calefac ouu . Vide q̅nta patientia hꝫ gallina qn calefac ouum .
uix inde surgit . ut ut modicu manducet ꝫ redeat . Hꝫ pus patientia ut i uemat
spea de filiis leticia . Karitas aut qa totu uincit . pani coparat . sine q̅ nulla
mꝭ ca pot uiuere . i . sine d̄o ut q̅ n̄ hꝫ karitate pat ut n̄ht . qn ad m̄sā panis p
pone . Pome illuc ꝫ pmi m̄ṃ . s; leuat inde . ꝫ panis ibi ꝫ . Alii alii ponuntur
ꝫ leuant . panis tn̄ usq; i fine pseuerat . Ergo petam . grani . pulsem . ut dn̄s n̄
q̅ scit nob pdesse i isto s̄c̄lo . ꝫ det nob . ꝫ i tuto uita gtnā qua pmisit . ꝫ iste nob
ꝫ ipse faciet q̅ uiuit ꝫ regnat in trinitate i s̄c̄la s̄c̄lo amen . CAꝗ̄ XVII
INCIPIT PAVCA PROBLESMATA DE ENIGMATA EX TO MIS.
Vet̄ testamtu idō dr̄ . qa ueniente nouo cessauit . De q̅ apl̄s meminit . Vetā
transient . ꝫ ecce om̄a noua iā facta sc̄ . Testamtu aut idō dr̄ noui . quia om̄a inouat .
Non eni illud discunt n̄ h̄oes renouati ex uetustate p gram . ꝫ punientes iā ad testamtu
nouu q̅ꝫ regnu celoy . Hebrei aut uet̄ testamtu i . xxii . numant . eod i pncipio sc̄
xxii . opa fecit . Hā pmo die . VII . opa . i . matiā i forme . angl̄os . luce . celos supiores .
tru . aquā . atq; aere . Scda aut die firmamtu tot . Tercia die maria . semina . sationes .
plantaria . Quarta die sole . luna ꝫ stellas . Quinta die . pisces . ꝫ reptilia aq̅ru ꝫ uolatilia .
Sexta die bestias . pecudes . ꝫ reptilia tr̄e ꝫ h̄oem . Facta sc̄ omia . xxii . opa in uii . dieb; .
Itc̄ xxii . gnationes sunt . ab adā usq; ad iacob ex cui gente nat̄ q̅ni iudeoy cu dn̄i
dedit xxii . elemta quib; costat diuine legis doctrina i xxii . libros a genesi usq;
istorios diuidunt . hebrei in iiii . ordines legis ꝫ ꝓphetaru ꝫ agyographoy .
DE ORDINE . CAꝗ̄ NIS . APVD . HEBREOS . ET GRECOS . ET LATIHOS . SCD̄m HIEROHYOV .
Primi ordo legis i qinq; libris accipit . quoy pmi ꝫ bresit . q̅ꝫ genesis . Scd̄ elesmoth .
q̅ꝫ exodus . Terti uaiecra . q̅ꝫ leuitic . Quart uagetabor . q̅ꝫ numer . Quintus

14. Scribe 16

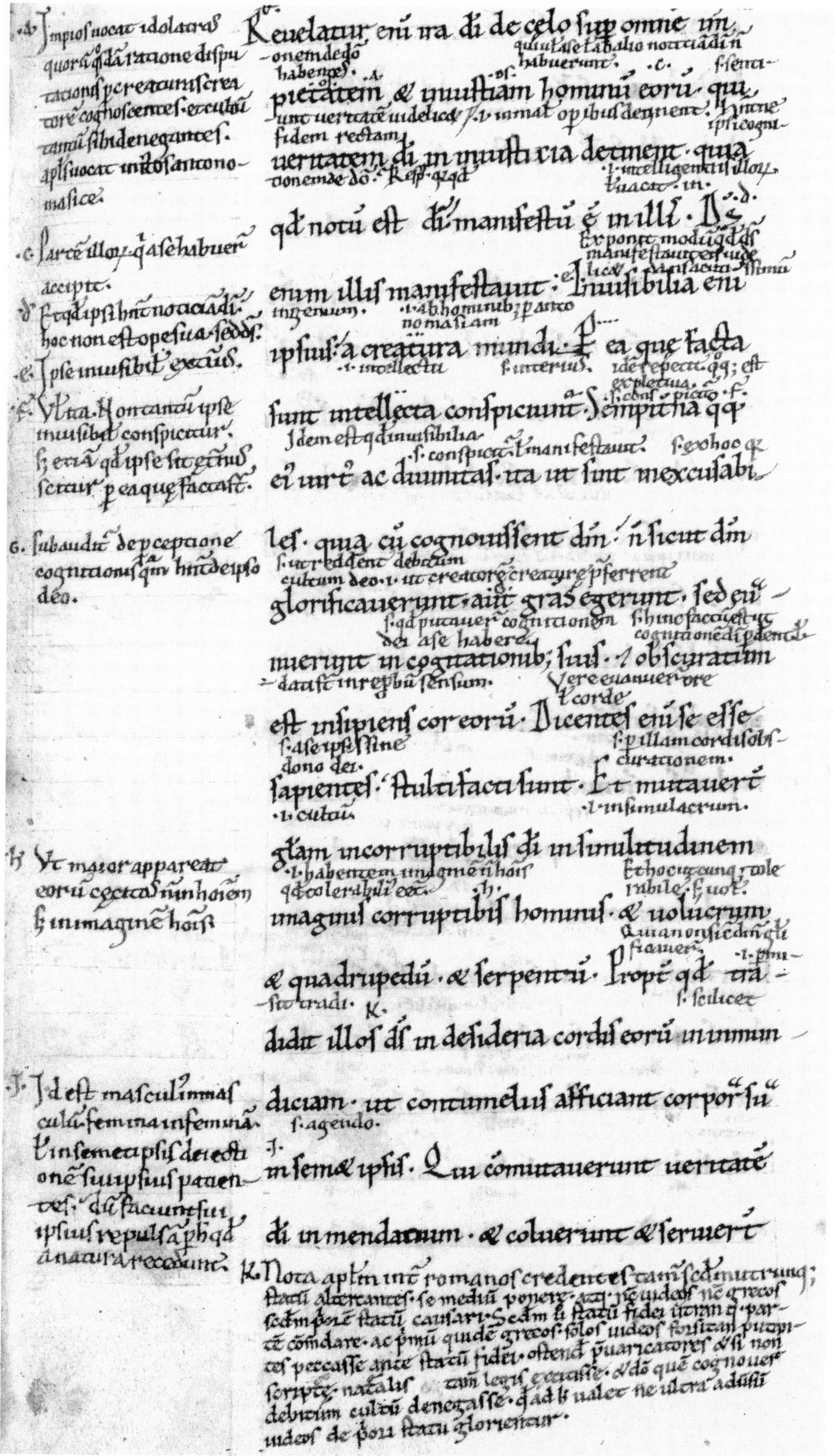
Revelatur enī ira dī de celo sup omnē im-
pietatem & iniustitiam hominū eorū qui
ueritatem dī in iniustitia detinent. quia
qd notū est dī manifestū ē in illi. Ds
enim illis manifestauit. Inuisibilia enī
ipsius a creatura mundi. p ea que facta
sunt intellecta conspiciunt. Sempitna qq
eī uirt ac diuinitas. ita ut sint inexcusabi-
les. quia cū cognouissent dm̄. n sicut dm̄
glorificauerunt. aut gras egerunt. sed eu-
nuerunt in cogitationib; suis. & obscuratum
est insipiens cor eorū. Dicentes enī se esse
sapientes. stulti facti sunt. Et mutauert
glām incorruptibilis dī in similitudinem
imaginis corruptibilis hominis. & uolucrum
& quadrupedū. & serpentiū. Propt qd tra-
didit illos ds in desideria cordis eorū in inmun-
diciam. ut contumeliis afficiant corpora sua
in semet ipsis. Qui commutauerunt ueritatē
dī in mendacium. & coluerunt & seruiert

15. Pauline Epistles with glosses (s. xi ex)

ponendo festinationem resurrectionis sue sic dicens.

Ds in adiutorium meum intende .i. te intentum adhoc ut me adiuues prebe. Ii-
Adiuua ut resurgam . & ñ cum mora . s; odñe ad adiuuandum me festina .i. festi-
natam da resurrectionem p terciam diem · qr ñ differas resurrectionis mee fructu
usq; ad cõmunem resurrectionem · s; indilate fac ut resurgam uth utilitas qua iam
dicam in sequatur. qr confundantur bona confusione. & de peccatis erubescant. &
pri rtuereant .i. timeant incurrere penas gehenne quia initium sapientie dñi
amor. Ons illi scl timeant qui querunt animam meam in morte detinere. Tria
inimicor genera uult hic notare. facientes. & anime sue inquisitores & uolentes. & applau-
dentes de quibus statim subiungit. qui dicebant magistr bone. & hoc e qr sequitur:
Auertantur retrorsum .i. qui prius uolebant preesse. fiant sequaces & erubescant
de peccatis suis qui uolunt michi mala. scl consentientes. atqz qui dicebant michi sub
adulatoria uoce. euge. euge. Erubescentes auttant ñ cum mora s; statim. he bre-
uit. & factores & consentientes. & adulatores erubescant. & conuertantur. s; & alij
qui iam confisi sunt: quorum fidem corroborandam dixi. exultent exterius ap
primos. & letentur intus ipsis. Ctius intiqz exultent. & letentur. ñ tn de se gloriam
s; inte a quo hut letari. & exultare qui querunt te. quia alij ñ hut inte letari & exultare: & dicant apud primos. magnificetur dñs .i. dñm faciant p dicatione sua
magnum reputari. qui diligunt salutare tuum .i. saluationem tuã. & qr p te
st saluati. & qui me diligunt salutare tuum p que genu saluas humanum. de
redicant. Magnificus e dñs. qr nos tam potent saluauit. De se ñ dicant. Ego egenus
.i. indicans meam salutem. & & alior. & paup sum. id e insufficiens p me ad eã
inquirendam .i. recognoscant se impotentes p se. & sic orent adte. Ds adiuua
me. ut possim quã desido salutem habe. / Adiutor ms. facta inpositione ad
primam orationem de se reiteratur. Intende in adiutorium dixi. ut resurgam
& intm adiutor ms sis. & coopator inbonis. & liberator ms es tu .i. prectort a
malis. Et pt li dñe. ne moreris inданda resurrectione s; ad adiuuandum me
uite odie Speraui. ipsi dst ps. filior ionadab. &   Sfestina mihe tcia
prior captuior. Vt filior ionadab. & qui pri captiui ducti sunt. hic titulus
tangit historiam. quomodo filij ionadab in prima captiuitate in babilo-
niam ducti sunt quibus pat ionadab pcepit. ut non biberent uinum. & in
tabnaculis morarentur. Ionadab qui inptatur spontaneus dñi xpm figura-
uit. qui filijs & imitatorib; suis pcepit. ut non bibant uinum .i. trene uolup-
tan ñ inhereant. & intabnacul .i. in milicia dñi habitare consuescant. Spontaneus dñi fuit xpc. qr dño patri usq; ad mortem factus e obediens. Exponit aut sic titulus. Psiste attribuit ipsi dst .i. xpo qui xpo loquitr inhoc ps
Ps dico filior ionadab .i. imitator xpi qr aduutilitatem eor agit. filior ionadab .i. prior captuior qr qui nc sunt filij xpi. pri filij adam iniquitate
a diabolo sunt ducti. Nam ñ fuit prl ut ait aptls. qr spuale. s; qr animale.
Animales qppe in adam fuimr. & in carne uiuentes. in xpo ñ spuales. Ad:

NOTES TO THE PLATES

Each plate is reproduced at the same size as the original.

PLATE 1

(*a*) Salisbury Cathedral, MS 165, fo. 23 (detail). The beginning of a copy of Bede, *De tabernaculo* (note the absence of elaborate decoration). Scribe i copied lines 1–6 'arce', acting as a director, by setting the line-spacing at the beginning of a new text; scribe xii copied lines 6 'V. Propitiatorii'—14. Both scribes have employed small, informal, 'academic' hands. Note the difference in appearance of the duct of the two hands, which indicates the absence of a house style of script: scribe i's hand is firm, angular, and laterally compressed, whilst scribe xii's hand exhibits lighter pen strokes, and the letter forms are generally rounded. Distinctive features of scribe xii's hand are the splayed **ct** and **st** ligatures (for example, line 14 'facta', line 10 'circumstantias').

(*b*) Salisbury Cathedral, MS 165, fo. 135 (detail). From a copy of Alcuin, *De fide sanctae et individuae Trinitatis.*
Copied by scribe ii, who wrote a well-developed, vigorous 'academic' hand. When writing swiftly (as here), he was liable to employ variant forms of the same letter, especially complicated forms such as **g** (compare, for example, line 9 'angeli' with line 10 'transgressor'). His hand exhibits a number of distinctive characteristics: a liking for suprascript **s** as a space-saver, the archaic **rt** ligature (e.g. line 11 'mortis'), and the *punctus versus* sometimes formed with the '**7**' placed to the right of the point instead of below it (e.g. line 9, after '-titudinem').

PLATE 2

Salisbury Cathedral, MS 154, p. 153 (detail). From a copy of Amalarius, *Liber officialis.* Copied by scribe iii who wrote the most regular and accomplished hand of all the Group I scribes. His hand exhibits features of both English Caroline minuscule (e.g. the formation of the letter **g** (line 2 'singuli') and the ampersand (line 5)) and small 'academic' hands (e.g. **a** without a headstroke (line 2 'antequam') and **d** with a curved shaft (line 4 'aduersa')).

PLATE 3

Salisbury Cathedral, MS 78, fo. 128 (detail). Copied by scribe v, who employed a small 'academic' hand, generally upright, with tall ascenders. He made a frequent use of the **NT** ligature (e.g. line 6 'uoluerint'). Salisbury 78 contains a copy of Lanfranc's abbreviation of Pseudo-Isidore, Decretals and Canons of Councils, which has been extensively annotated by scribe i in order to facilitate its use for reference purposes. This plate illustrates two sets of marginal annotations: a series of *nota* marks in the form of the letter **a** accompanied by different patterns of dots, and a subject heading 'De incontinentia sac[er]dotum. uel leuitarum'.

PLATE 4

Salisbury Cathedral 168, fo. 14. Augustine, *De diversis quaestionibus lxxxviii.* One of the smallest of the Group I books, with a written space of only 146 x 105mm. Scribe ix copied lines 1–7 and 14 (last two words)–26. Scribe xi copied lines 8–14. Scribe ix wrote a distinctive, highly expert, small 'academic' hand which is characterized by a firm duct, the careful treatment of the tops of ascenders, and a contrast between thick and thin strokes. Ascenders are at least, if not more than, twice the height of minims; the height of the **ct** and **st** ligatures is particularly exaggerated (e.g. line 18 'perfecte' and line 6 'potest'). Scribe xi also wrote a small, well-formed hand. Its principal distinctive feature is the ampersand (e.g. line 9 'habet'), in which the final upward stroke is finished with a pronounced horizontal serif to the right.

PLATE 5

Salisbury Cathedral, MS 10, fo. 22 (detail). Cassian, *Collationes.* The hands of three scribes appear here, the changes of hand occurring mid-sentence: scribe vi copied lines 1–4; scribe iii (see notes to Pl. 2) copied lines 5–14 'tantum', and scribe viii copied lines 14 'modo'–25. The hand of each scribe is readily identifiable. Scribe vi's hand lacks the firm, upright pen-strokes characteristic of scribe iii's hand; vertical strokes have a tendency to curve, and serifs are formed with less care. Scribe viii wrote a distinctive small hand. The somewhat clumsy, backward-leaning two-tier **s** and **f** are particularly characteristic features of his hand (e.g. line 17 'facultatibus' and line 20 'sunt'). Note also his *punctus elevatus,* with the 'tick' facing to the right (e.g. line 25, after 'filia'). Note that the initial in line 9 was added later, and is incorrect: it should be an **N**.

PLATES 6–10. SALISBURY SCRIBES IN THE EARLY TWELFTH CENTURY: THE GROUP IIA SCRIBES

PLATE 6

(*a*) Salisbury Cathedral, MS 64, fo. 9. The beginning of book ii of Augustine, *De baptismo.* Copied by scribe 3. His hand is more formal and calligraphic than that of any other Group II scribe: letters are upright and regular, and vertical strokes are finished with carefully formed serifs. The line-drawn initial **Q** is typical of the initials which occur in manuscripts copied by Group II*a* scribes 3 and 6.

(*b*) Salisbury Cathedral, MS 64, fo. 81 (detail). Augustine, *De pastoribus.* Copied by scribe 6 who wrote a distinctive hand which exhibits a conscious element of style. Ascenders are reduced in height, and round **s** is frequently employed in preference to long **s**, not only in final positions but sometimes also in the middle of a word (e.g. line 2 'seipsos'). Final **i** (e.g. line 8 'multi'), is sometimes elongated, and curves to the left.

PLATE 7

Salisbury Cathedral, MS 61, fo. 34 (detail). Heriger, *De corpore et sanguine domini.* Scribe 3 (see notes to Pl. 6) copied lines 1–32 'sermone', neatly incorporating a diagram within the text block; scribe 7 copied lines 32 'dominum'—35. Scribe 7's hand may be distinguished from that of scribe 3 on the basis of certain details, the most obvious of which are the common mark of abbreviation (e.g. line 32 'dominum'), formed with a down-up-down stroke, and the letter **g**, which resembles an arabic 8 (line 32 'ignarum'; compare with the form of **g** employed by scribe 3, line 30 'cathegorico').

PLATE 8

Salisbury Cathedral, MS 162, fo. 15ᵛ (detail). Rufinus, Commentary on the Apostles' Creed. Copied by scribe 8. Distinctive features of his hand are the ampersand formed with a descender extending well below the ruled line, and the angle of the serifs on the tops and bottoms of vertical strokes. Note the pattern of gaps left by the scribe, which probably indicates that his exemplar was damaged. Annotations (s.xiii) in the left-hand margin indicate that the book, even in its imperfect state, remained in use at Salisbury in the later Middle Ages.

PLATE 9

(*a*) Salisbury Cathedral, MS 124, fo. 3 (detail). The beginning of a copy of Hilary of Poitiers, Commentary on St Matthew's Gospel. This manuscript also contains the Irish Pseudo-Hilary's commentary on the seven Catholic Epistles. The heading here indicates that the scribe was under the impression that both commentaries were by Hilary of Poitiers. Copied by scribe 9, who wrote an uncalligraphic hand. The letter **g** (e.g. line 4 'agnitionem'), formed with a sharp angle at the top right-hand corner of the lower lobe, is his most distinctive letter form.

(*b*) Salisbury Cathedral, MS 110, fo. 22ᵛ (detail). Aethicus, *Cosmographia.* Copied by scribe 12. The splayed *litterae notabiliores* (e.g. line 3 'Ubi'), employed to introduce each *sententia*, are a distinctive feature of his hand. The ruling pattern typical of the Group II books is visible in the bottom left- and right-hand corners of the plate.

PLATE 10

Salisbury Cathedral, MS 162, fo. 19 (detail). The beginning of the *Scala virtutum.* Copied by scribe 11. His hand exhibits some traces of the influence of English Caroline minuscule: note, for example, the generally upright character of the hand, the horizontal serifs added to the feet of minims, and **a** (e.g. line 5 'gradibus') formed with a pronounced headstroke. Note the simple but effective manner in which the text is arranged on the page: each 'gradus' (step) begins on a new line, and is introduced by a *littera notabilior.*

PLATES 11–14. SALISBURY SCRIBES IN THE EARLY TWELFTH CENTURY:
THE GROUP IIB SCRIBES

PLATE 11

Salisbury Cathedral, MS 223, fo. 54 (detail). *Vitae sanctorum.* Scribe 17 copied lines 1–8; scribe 14 copied lines 9–16. Note the proportions of the two hands: in both, ascenders are, for the most part, less than twice the height of minims. Scribe 14's hand exhibits some of the clumsiness apparent in the hand of the scribe of the Salisbury *titulus* in the Mortuary Roll of Abbot Vitalis of Savigny (*c.* 1122–3). Note that the space left for a two-line initial **M** has not been filled.

PLATE 12

Salisbury Cathedral, MS 59, fo. 175 (detail). Cassiodorus, *Expositio psalmorum.* Copied by scribe 14, apparently from an exemplar copied by an insular scribe. Note the initial **A** (column b, line 2) which imitates insular initials both in the form of the letter and in the decorative dotting which surrounds it. Note also the 'diminuendo' effect employed at the beginning of the rubric for the explicit to the commentary on Psalm 120 (column b, line 1), a device developed by Irish scribes to indicate important divisions within a text. The scribe has evidently experienced some difficulty in ruling for two columns: the left-hand vertical ruling of column b is not perpendicular to the horizontal.

PLATE 13

Salisbury Cathedral, MS 59, fo. 85 (detail of column b). Cassiodorus, *Expositio psalmorum.* Copied by scribe 15, a scribe who has attempted to write a larger version of an 'academic' hand: note the somewhat heavy and ponderous minim strokes. This manuscript, in common with many of the Salisbury books, contains several leaves of parchment which are of poor quality and lack straight edges. In this example, it is clear that the parchment was already imperfect before the scribe began to write, since, for the last fourteen or so lines of the column, he was forced to reduce the length of each line of writing.

PLATE 14

Salisbury Cathedral, MS 115, fo. 20 (detail). This plate illustrates the beginning of a copy of the so-called Irish Reference Bible. Copied by scribe 16, who wrote an idiosyncratic 'academic' hand which is smaller than the hands of the other Group II*b* scribes. Its distinctive appearance is achieved by the employment of thin pen-strokes, a preference for the tironian *nota* for 'et', and splitting the tops of ascenders. The small size of script and the heavy employment of abbreviations have enabled the scribe to fit a considerable amount of text onto a single page.

PLATES 15 AND 16. THE STUDY OF THE BIBLE ON THE EVE OF SCHOLASTICISM

PLATE 15

Oxford, Keble College, MS 22, fo. 6. Pauline Epistles with glosses. Group I scribe viii copied the Pauline text which occupies the central column. Scribe xiv wrote all but the first line of the gloss in the lower margin. Scribe i wrote the remainder of the marginal glosses and all of the interlinear glosses. He also corrected punctuation and added syntax marks to the Pauline text: in line 6, for example, he indicated that what was originally written as two *sententiae* ('Inuisibilia enim ipsius a creatura mundi' and 'Per ea quę facta sunt intellecta conspiciuntur') should form a single *sententia*. He then added syntax marks to help the reader construe the *sententia*; these marks consist of a sequence of dots which indicate the order in which the words should be read: one dot is placed above 'Inuisibilia' (line 5), two above 'intellecta' (line 7), three above 'creatura' (line 6), and four above 'per' (line 6). Note that the page was designed from the outset to receive glosses: the lines of biblical text are widely spaced to enable the addition of interlinear glosses, whilst the margins have also been ruled with more closely spaced lines for the addition of more lengthy glosses. Scribe i has employed letters of the alphabet in sequence as *signes de renvoi* to link text and marginal glosses.

PLATE *16*

Salisbury Cathedral, MS 160, fo. 98 (detail). Anonymous commentary on the Psalms (attributed elsewhere to Master Ivo of Chartres). Copied by a scribe in a small 'academic' hand similar to the kinds of hands employed by many Salisbury scribes. However, since I have not identified this hand in any other book associated with Salisbury, it is possible that this book was not produced at Salisbury. A combination of such features as the consistent use of the ampersand rather than the tironian *nota* for 'et', the generally rounded character of the script, the comparatively small number of abbreviations, and dry-point ruling, suggest an early twelfth-century date.

INDEX OF MANUSCRIPTS CITED

ABERDEEN, University Library
  216: 12, 15, 38, 68, 132 n., 143
ANGERS, Bibliothèque Municipale
  306: 60 n.
AVRANCHES, Bibliothèque Municipale
  84: 148 n.
  159: 52 n.

BAMBERG, Staatsbibliothek
  Patr. 23 (B.III.13): 54 n.
  Patr. 134 (B.V.25): 117 n.
BERNE, Burgerbibliothek
  334, ii: 91 n., 96 n., 97, 99
BORDEAUX, Bibliothèque Municipale
  35: 117 n., 123 n.
BOULOGNE-SUR-MER, Bibliothèque Municipale
  48: 57
  82: 71
BRUSSELS, Bibliothèque Royale
  444–52: 49, 50
  1246–9: 14 n.
  5351: 64

CAMBRIDGE, University Library
  Gg.5.35: 72
  Ii.2.4: 69
  Kk.1.23: 9 n.
CAMBRIDGE, Corpus Christi College
  9: 40 n., 70, 154 n.
  130: 48
  184: 55
  187: 54, 55
  192: 71
  194: 117 n.
CAMBRIDGE, Fitzwilliam Museum
  McClean 101: 152 n.
CAMBRIDGE, Peterhouse
  74: 48
  114: 117 n.
CAMBRIDGE, St John's College
  5: 53–4
CAMBRIDGE, Trinity College
  B.3.25: 72–3
  B.3.32: 54
  B.3.33: 51 n., 52 n., 59
  B.4.27: 76
  B.11.2: 71
  B.16.3: 71 n.
  B.16.44: 47–8
  O.7.9: 148 n.

CAMBRIDGE, Trinity College (*cont.*)
　　R.5.22: 75
　　R.16.34: 23, 41, 64–5, 86, 131 n., 158
　　R.17.1: 109 n.
COLOGNE, Dombibliothek
　　79: 57

DUBLIN, Trinity College
　　174 (B.4.3): 12, 13, 23, 24, 40, 70, 143, 158
　　371 (D.1.26): 71 n.
DURHAM, Dean and Chapter Library
　　B.IV.6: 72–3
　　B.IV.12: 56–7
　　B.IV.24: 103 n.

EDINBURGH, National Library of Scotland
　　Adv. 18.4.3: 148 n.
EINSIEDELN, Stiftsbibliothek
　　302: 72
ETON COLLEGE
　　48: 51 n.
EXETER, Dean and Chapter Library
　　3500 (Exon Domesday): 13, 14, 16
　　3507: 69, 74, 144 n.
　　3525: 152 n.

FULDA, Landesbibliothek
　　Bonifatianus 1 (Codex Fuldensis): 62 n.

HEREFORD, Cathedral Library
　　O.iii.1: 57
　　O.iii.2: 35–6, 46, 57
　　O.iv.8: 73
　　P.i.3: 54
　　P.i.5: 51 n.
　　P.i.6: 56
　　P.i.10: 56
　　P.vi.2: 47

KARLSRUHE, Badische Landesbibliothek
　　Aug. CCXXII: 62 n.

LEIDEN, Bibliotheek der Rijksuniversiteit
　　Scaliger 69: 71
LE MANS, Bibliothèque Municipale
　　15: 51 n.
　　143: 60 n.
LINCOLN, Cathedral Library
　　134: 49
LONDON, British Library
　　Additional 18332: 57
　　Additional 21084: 55
　　Additional 23944A: 46, 57
　　Additional 34807: 117 n., 123 n.
　　Additional 40165A: 45–6, 57
　　Arundel 180: 148 n.
　　Cotton Julius B VII: 117 n., 122

Cotton Nero A I: 78 n., 152 n.
Cotton Nero E I: 40 n., 70, 154 n.
Cotton Tiberius C I: 10, 12, 13, 16, 23, 24 n., 75, 143–4, 145 n., 159
Cotton Vespasian B VI: 74
Cotton Vespasian B X: 71
Cotton Vitellius A XII: 12, 14, 23, 41, 63, 69, 74, 144–5, 159
Harley 865: 49–50
Harley 3080: 72, 73
Royal 3 B xi: 104
Royal 5 A xiii: 51 n.
Royal 5 B xiv: 73
Royal 5 B xvi: 72–3
Royal 5 E xvi: 13, 19 n., 20, 21, 68, 145
Royal 5 E xix: 12, 13, 14, 15, 38, 145
Royal 5 F xiii: 15, 23
Royal 5 F xviii: 13, 20, 22, 24 n., 145–6, 153 n, 159
Royal 6 B xv: 22, 23, 46, 59, 159
Royal 6 C iv: 53–4
Royal 8 B xi: 75
Royal 8 B xiv: 13, 146
Royal 11 E vi: 55 n.
Royal 13 B v: 55
Royal 15 B xix: 24, 72, 159, 165–6
Royal 15 C xi: 13, 20, 21, 22, 23, 24 n., 41, 63–4, 86, 146, 159
Royal App. 1: 23, 38, 43, 50, 168–9
LONDON, Lambeth Palace
  149: 52, 53, 68
  185: 66
  372: 152 n.
  1229, nos. 14 and 15: 152 n.

MONTE CASSINO, Archivio della Badia
  384: 62 n.
MUNICH, Bayerische Staatsbibliothek
  Clm 8113: 53
  Clm 11730: 117 n.
  Clm 14492: 54 n.

NAPLES, Biblioteca Nazionale
  Vindob. lat. 4: 62, 166 n.

OXFORD, Bodleian Library
  Additional C. 181: 47
  Bodley 134: 47
  Bodley 145: 47
  Bodley 149: 50
  Bodley 201: 54
  Bodley 218: 79 n.
  Bodley 319: 68
  Bodley 387: 51 n.
  Bodley 391: 46
  Bodley 392: 12, 13, 20, 114 n., 132 n., 136–7, 146
  Bodley 444: 12, 13, 36, 132 n., 146
  Bodley 516: 77, 78, 79
  Bodley 698: 24, 27, 28, 36 n., 37 n., 43, 58, 60 n., 159–60
  Bodley 718: 69
  Bodley 731: 117 n., 122, 123 n.

OXFORD, Bodleian Library (*cont.*)
Bodley 739: 53–4
Bodley 752: 53–4
Bodley 756: 12, 13, 14, 15, 20, 90 n., 132 n., 134, 147
Bodley 765: 12, 13, 14, 15, 37 n., 39, 52 n., 59, 132 n., 147
Bodley 768: 12, 15, 21, 51, 58, 132 n., 147
Bodley 781: 109 n.
Bodley 804: 52 n.
Bodley 815: 73
Bodley 827: 53–4
Bodley 835: 12, 13, 15, 36 n., 58, 132 n, 147
Digby 23: 27
Digby 96: 124–8
Douce 140: 78 n.
Fell 1, *see* Salisbury Cathedral, MS 222
Fell 3, *see* Salisbury Cathedral, MS 223
Fell 4, *see* Salisbury Cathedral, MS 221
Hatton 23: 75
Lat. bib. c. 8 (P): 77, 79
Laud Lat. 49: 85 n., 95
Rawlinson C.723: 12, 14, 36 n., 38, 132 n., 147
Rawlinson G.139: 65
Rawlinson Liturg. e. 42: 117 n., 122
Tanner 3: 79 n., 84 n.
Tanner 165: 60 n., 61 n.
OXFORD, Keble College
22: 12, 13, 14, 15, 28 n., 40, 87–101, 102, 111, 130 n., 140, 147–8, 200–1, Pl. 15
OXFORD, Magdalen College
Lat. 207: 102 n.
OXFORD, Trinity College
4: 54
28: 74
OXFORD, University College
191: 134 n.

PARIS, Bibliothèque de l'Arsenal
236: 51 n.
PARIS, Bibliothèque Nationale
lat. 440: 103
lat. 614A: 38 n., 61, 165 n.
lat. 943: 69
lat. 1751: 51 n.
lat. 3645: 117 n.
lat. 4952: 64
lat. 8207: 117 n.
lat. 12005: 61, 66
lat. 12006: 103
lat. 12207: 52 n.
lat. 12208: 52 n.
lat. 13365: 54 n.
lat. 17398: 50
PARIS, Musée des Archives Nationales
138 (Mortuary Roll): 22, 25, 26, 27

RHEIMS, Bibliothèque Municipale
376: 57

ROUEN, Bibliothèque Municipale
  478: 50
  488: 60 n.

ST GALL, Stiftsbibliothek
  29: 57
  89: 59
  150: 59
SALISBURY, Cathedral Library
  4: 23, 36 n., 39 n., 58, 160
  5: 23, 38, 62, 90 n., 160
  6: 12, 13, 36 n., 37 n., 73, 148
  7: 24, 160
  9: 13, 20, 23, 24, 36 n., 59, 148–9, 160–2
  10: 12, 13, 14, 17, 20, 41, 75, 78, 80, 84–5, 114 n., 133 n., 149, 198, Pl. 5
  11: 22, 23, 162
  12: 13, 20, 22, 24 n., 40, 61, 66, 68, 80, 114 n., 115 n., 149, 162
  24: 13, 14, 36 n., 38, 58, 133 n., 149
  25: 12, 14, 15, 17, 20, 23, 36 n., 38, 58, 133 n., 149
  33: 13, 14, 15, 17, 19, 20, 38, 59, 149–50
  35: 24, 27, 36 n., 37 n., 43, 50, 54, 60 n., 162
  37: 12, 15, 20, 38, 60, 76, 133 n., 150
  38: 77, 78
  57: 23, 24, 25, 27, 36 n., 162–3
  58: 23, 24, 26, 27, 36 n., 163
  59: 24, 27, 28, 36 n., 163, 200, Pls. 12 and 13
  61: 22, 23, 28, 37 n., 40, 101, 148 n., 163–4, 199, Pl. 7
  63: 12, 13, 14, 36 n., 37 n., 54, 150
  64: 23, 25, 28, 37 n., 164, 198–9, Pls. 6a and 6b
  65: 23, 24 n., 28, 37 n., 47, 164
  66: 142 n.
  67: 12, 13, 15, 17, 19, 20, 36 n., 38, 58, 133 n., 150
  78: 12, 13, 16 n., 21, 48, 101, 131 n., 133 n., 134–5, 135 n., 150, 197–8, Pl. 3
  88: 12, 13, 20, 21, 35, 36, 46, 133 n., 150–1
  89: 77, 79–80
  96: 77, 79
  100: 77, 142 n.
  101: 23, 76, 164
  106: 12, 13, 20, 36 n., 37 n., 39, 41, 55–6, 133 n., 151, 154 n.
  109: 15, 23, 28, 37 n., 56–7, 151, 164
  110: 23, 24, 41, 70–1, 85, 164, 199, Pl. 9b
  112: 23, 68, 165
  114: 13, 15, 36 n., 37 n., 38, 151
  115: 24, 38, 61, 159, 165–6, 168 n., 200, Pl. 14
  116: 23, 28, 36 n., 37 n., 39 n., 58, 166
  117: 77, 79
  118: 22, 23, 37 n., 166
  119: 12, 13, 16 n., 151
  120: 13, 14, 151
  124: 23, 38, 58, 61–2, 66, 166, 199, Pl. 9a
  125: 23, 167
  128: 12, 13, 14, 15, 20, 21 n., 36 n., 37 n., 39, 51 n., 52, 53, 58, 68, 133 n., 135 n., 151
  129: 12, 13, 43, 60, 76, 133 n., 152
  130: 23, 40, 75, 101, 167
  131: 22, 23, 25–6, 28, 161 n., 167
  132: 15
  133: 77, 79

SALISBURY, Cathedral Library (*cont.*)
  134: 77, 79, 84
  135: 12, 13, 133 n., 152
  136: 23, 167
  137: 24, 27, 36 n., 167
  138: 12, 13, 14, 15, 20, 24 n., 37 n., 47, 152
  139: 23, 25, 26, 36 n., 55, 167–8
  140: 12, 13, 14, 15, 36 n., 39 n., 53–4, 133 n., 152, 153 n.
  150: 78 n.
  154: 12, 13, 70–1, 133 n., 152–3, 197, Pl. 2
  157: 77 n.
  158: 41, 74–5, 76–7, 133
  159: 12, 21, 36 n., 38, 133 n.
  160: 77, 80, 87, 102–11, 140, 201, Pl. 16
  162: 15 n., 23, 24, 38, 40, 116–22, 153, 168, 171–83, 199, Pls. 8 and 10
  165: 8 n., 12, 13, 14, 15, 23, 24 n., 26, 36 n., 37 n., 73, 74 n., 133 n., 153–4, 168, 197, Pls 1*a* and 1*b*
  168: 12, 13, 14, 15, 21, 36 n., 37 n., 154, 198, Pl. 4
  169: 13, 14, 20, 22, 24 n., 37 n., 40, 41, 56, 59–60, 115 n., 154, 168
  172: 77, 78
  173: 77, 79
  179: 12, 13, 14, 15, 154, 161 n.
  180: 77, 79
  197: 23, 25, 37 n., 38, 40, 43, 50, 60 n., 168–9
  198: 23, 28, 36 n., 37 n., 133, 169
  221 (formerly Oxford, Bodleian Library, MS Fell 4): 12, 13, 14, 15, 20, 21, 24, 40, 70, 154–6, 169
  222 (formerly Oxford, Bodleian Library, MS Fell 1): 12, 13, 14, 15, 18, 19, 20, 40, 70, 154 n., 156–7, 169, 170
  223 (formerly Oxford, Bodleian Library, MS Fell 3): 24, 27, 40, 169–70, 200, Pl. 11

TOKYO, Professor T. Takamiya
  21: 77, 79
TRIER, Stadtbibliothek
  14: 99
TURIN, Biblioteca Nazionale
  G.V.7: 60, 67

UTRECHT, Universiteits-bibliotheek
  86: 14

VALENCIENNES, Bibliothèque Municipale
  197: 103
VATICAN CITY, Biblioteca Apostolica Vaticana
  Vat. lat. 143: 91, 96–7, 98–9
  Vat. lat. 3307: 64
  Vat. lat. 5762: 66
  Vat. lat. 10807: 117 n.
  Pal. lat. 167: 66
  Reg. lat. 1260: 71 n.

WORCESTER, Cathedral Library
  F 92: 57

GENERAL INDEX

Texts which lack authorship (genuine or attributed) are indexed by title; those texts which lack an established title are indexed under the heading 'anonymous texts'. Aspects of book production and palaeographical terms (for example, parchment, punctuation, English Caroline minuscule) are grouped under the general heading 'palaeography'. Books of the Bible are listed in the order in which they appear in the Bible.

Abbo of Fleury 74
  'De differentia circuli et sperae' 144
Abelard, Peter 83
Abingdon, Abbey:
  manuscript from 124 n.
  specialist scribes at 29
Adalbert of Metz: *Speculum Gregorii*
  attrib. to 76
Ælfric 62, 70
Aethicus Ister (Pseudo-): *Cosmographia*
  70–1, 164, 199
Ailwinus, *magister* 83
Alcuin:
  De animae ratione 153
  De fide sanctae et individuae Trinitatis
    153, 197
  De Trinitate ad Fredegisum quaestiones
    xxviii 153
  on Ecclesiastes 79
  on Song of Songs 38, 145
Aldhelm (St): *De virginitate* 78
Alexander, bishop of Lincoln 30, 66
Amalarius of Metz: *Liber officialis* 70, 71,
  133 n., 152, 197
Ambrose (St), bishop of Milan 31, 34, 39,
  58, 89, 149, 165
  attribution of *Scala virtutum* to 123
  Works:
  De apologia prophetae David 57, 164
  De benedictionibus patriarcharum, see
    De patriarchis
  De excessu fratris 132 n., 147
  De fide 36 n., 39 n., 53–4, 133 n., 152
  De fuga saeculi 159
  De Gedeon 57, 164
  De Iacob et vita beata 159
  De incarnatione dominicae sacramento
    152
  De Ioseph patriarcha (*De prophetis*)
    36 n., 147
  De Isaac vel anima 36 n., 159
  De mysteriis 50–1, 57, 132 n., 147, 164
  De paenitentia 132 n., 147

De patriarchis (*De benedictionibus*
  patriarcharum) 132 n., 147
De prophetis, see *De Ioseph patriarcha*
De sacramentis 50–1, 132 n., 147;
  extracts 148 n.
De spiritu sancto 133 n., 152
De viduis 51 n., 132 n., 147
De virginibus 51 n., 147
De virginitate 51 n., 132 n., 147
Epistola lxiii 132 n., 147
Exhortatio virginitatis 51 n., 132 n., 147
see also Saints, lives of
Ambrose (Pseudo-):
  De lapsu virginis consecratae 51 n.,
    132 n., 147
  on the Pauline Epistles, *see*
    Ambrosiaster
  sermon 'Mirum satis' 57, 164
Ambrosiaster:
  on Pauline Epistles 89, 90, 132 n., 135,
    147
  Quaestiones cxxvii veteris et novi
    testamenti 43, 60, 76, 133 n., 152
Ambrosius Autpertus: *De conflictu*
  vitiorum et virtutum 163
Angers:
  Abbey of Saint-Aubin, manuscript from
    60 n.
  manuscript from region of 54
anonymous texts which lack established
  titles:
  'De baptismo' 149
  'De carne superbię sermo' 161
  'De circumcisione' 160
  'De columba' 148–9
  'De consecratione ecclesiarum' 159
  'De diuersis locis' 148
  'De genealogia Iob' 149
  'De his qui hebrietatem diligunt' 161
  'De illo latrone' 149
  'De inspiratione hominis' 149
  'De Lazaro et Diuite' 149
  'De monachis' 161

anonymous texts which lack established
    titles: (*cont.*)
  'De qualitate anime' 160
  'De quattuor temporibus anni' 161
  'De sepulchro' 148
  'De stella' 149
  'De tempore natiuitatis Cristi' 148
  'De Trinitate interrogatio' 165
  'Expositio de oratione dominica' 161
  'Expositio simboli' 161
  Note on works of six days of Creation
    168
  'Oportet enim nos timere uerbum
    domini' 161
  poem, 'Nec Veneris nec tu uini tenearis
    amore' 158
  'Sententia apostoli' 161
  'Sermo de caritate' 161
  'Sermo de misericordia' 161
  'Sermo [ ] Moysi. Timor domini effugiat
    omnem maliciam . . .' 161
  see also commentaries; homilies;
    prayers; scientific texts; *summa de
    divinis officiis*
Anselm of Laon 82, 104
Arator 107
  De actibus apostolis 84
Arnobius Iunior: *Conflictus de Deo trino
    et uno* 163
artes (liberal arts) 41, 83–6
  influence on biblical exegesis 92, 94–5,
    98–9
  see also grammar; logic; rhetoric
auctoritates 125, 134, 140
Augustine (St), bishop of Hippo 31, 32,
    34, 39, 42–3, 89, 105, 123 n., 129,
    149, 165
  'Catalogus librorum Augustini' 162 n.
  life of, by Possidius, extracts 168, 169;
    epitome 166
  verses on, 'Mentitur qui te totum legisse
    fatetur' 166
  Works:
  Ad inquisitiones Ianuarii (*epp.*
    54–5) 37 n., 133 n., 168, 169
  Confessiones 36 n., 37 n., 73, 148;
    extracts 166, 169
  Contra adversarium legis et prophetarum
    36 n., 37 n., 51, 52, 151
  Contra Faustum Manichaeum 36 n.,
    37 n., 39 n., 58, 166
  Contra Iulianum 37 n., 46–7, 152,
    164
  Contra mendacium 37 n., 39, 51, 52 n.,
    59, 132 n., 147
  Contra sermonem Arianorum 37 n., 51,
    52, 151

De adulterinis coniugiis 20, 37 n., 39,
    51, 52, 53, 133 n., 135, 151
De agone christiano 36 n., 37 n., 54,
    133 n., 150, 162, 169
De baptismo 37 n., 164
De beata vita 36 n., 43, 60, 159–60
De civitate Dei 43; extract 163
De cura pro mortuis gerenda 37 n., 51,
    52 n., 59, 132 n., 133 n., 147, 169
De decem chordis (*sermo 9*) 166
De disciplina christiana 150, 151, 154
De diversis quaestionibus lxxxiii 36 n.,
    37 n., 154
De doctrina christiana 36 n., 37 n., 84,
    133 n., 151
De duabus animabus 37 n., 43, 60, 160
De fide et operibus, extract 163
De fide et symbolo 36 n., 37 n., 133 n.,
    169
De genesi ad litteram 36 n., 37 n., 38,
    58, 151
De genesi ad litteram imperfectus 37 n.,
    38, 43, 60, 169
De gratia novi testamenti (*Quaestiones v
    de novo testamento*) (*ep.* 140) 36 n.,
    37 n., 150
De haeresibus 36 n., 72–3
De immortalitate animae 168
De libero arbitrio 36–7 n., 39, 67, 151
De magistro 37 n., 166
De mendacio 37 n., 39, 51, 52 n., 59,
    132 n., 147
De natura boni 37 n., 39, 150, 151, 163
De natura et origine animae (*De anima
    et eius origine*) 37 n., 51, 52, 133 n.,
    151
De nuptiis et concupiscentia 37 n.,
    46–7, 152, 164
De octo quaestionibus Dulcitii 37 n., 41,
    55–7, 133 n., 151, 154, 164
De opere monachorum 37 n., 40, 169
De ovibus (*sermo 47*) 164
De pastoribus (*sermo 46*) 164
De peccatorum meritis 37 n., 164
De presentia Dei (*ep.* 187) 168
De quantitate animae 36 n., 151
De spiritu et littera 37 n., 164
De symbolo 162
De unico baptismo 37 n., 164
De urbis excidio 133 n., 169
De utilitate credendi 37 n., 150
De vera religione 36 n., 37 n., 151
De videndo Deo (*ep.* 147) 37 n., 130
De vita et moribus clericorum (*sermones
    355–6*) 169
Enarrationes in Psalmos 25, 26, 36 n.,
    43, 110, 162, 163

Enchiridion 78
Homilies on St John's Gospel 17, 36 n.,
  38, 43, 58, 133 n., 150
Letters 43, 133 n., 152, 154, 163, 164,
  168, 169; extract 162; see also *Ad
  inquisitiones Ianuarii, De gratia novi
  testamenti, De presentia Dei, De
  videndo Deo*
Quaestiones v de novo testamento, see
  De gratia novi testamenti
Retractationes 35, 36, 54, 133 n., 150;
  extracts 148, 150, 162, 163, 169
Sermons 41, 56, 133 n., 143, 147, 151,
  154, 163, 169; see also *De decem
  chordis, De ovibus, De pastoribus, De
  vita et moribus clericorum*
Soliloquia 79
Speculum 36 n., 43, 60, 162
*Tractatus in epistolam Iohannis ad
  Parthos* 76
Augustine (Pseudo-) 43
  Adversus quinque haereses, see
    Quodvultdeus
  Contra Felicianum, see Vigilius
    Thapsensis
  De cantico novo, see Quodvultdeus
  De cataclismo, see Quodvultdeus
  De conflictu vitiorum et virtutum, see
    Ambrosius Autpertus
  De duodecim abusivis saeculi 154
  De ecclesiasticis dogmatibus, see
    Gennadius
  De essentia divinitatis 74
  De quarta feria tractatus, see
    Quodvultdeus
  De quattuor virtutibus caritatis, see
    Quodvultdeus
  De symbolo ii–iv, *see* Quodvultdeus
  De tempore barbarico, see
    Quodvultdeus
  De unitate sanctae Trinitatis 145
  De vita christiana, see Pelagius
  Dialogus quaestionum lxv 154;
    extract 165
  'Epistola ad diuersos' 169
  Hypomnesticon 49–50, 56–7, 58, 162,
    164, 168
  *Quaestiones cxxvii veteris et novi
    testamenti, see* Ambrosiaster
  'Rule of St Augustine' (*Regula
    Augustini*) 40, 59–60, 115, 168
  Sermons 143, 148, 150, 151, 154, 161,
    162, 163, 169
  Tractatus de carne superba 161 n.
  'Tractatus de fide' 169
Aulus Gellius: *Noctes Atticae* (*florilegium*
  of extracts from) 41, 64–5, 86, 158

Bath: manuscript from 73
Bec, Abbey:
  manuscripts from 47, 52 n.
  school at 6
Bede (St) 32, 34 n., 62
  De aetatibus saeculi (letter to
    Plecguin) 41, 63, 159
  De die iudicii 154
  De tabernaculo 74, 133 n., 153, 197
  De temporum ratione 74, 77, 133 n.
  on Samuel 167
  on Tobit 168
  on Luke 38, 133 n., 150
  on the Apocalypse 38, 68, 132 n., 143
Bede (Pseudo-):
  De sex dierum creatione 149 n.
  on the Psalms 94, 104–9
Benedictine rule 115, 122–3
Berengar of Tours 91, 96, 99, 101
Berengaudus: on the Apocalypse 38, 152,
  153
Bible:
  glossed books of 30; the *Gloss* (*Glossa
    ordinaria*) 88; Pauline Epistles
    39–40, 87–102, 111, 147–8, 200–1
  individual books: Genesis 39, 111;
    Deuteronomy and Numbers 79;
    Psalms 39, 79, 111; Matthew's Gospel
    39, 111, 119, 124; Pauline Epistles
    39, 111, 124
  note on the historical interpretation of
    35, 151
  study of 31, 34–6, 39, 86–111, 140
  see also commentaries; Irish Reference
    Bible
bibliographical guides 35, 36
Bobbio, Abbey: manuscripts from 60,
  66–7, 115
Boethius:
  De consolatione philosophiae 84
  De differentiis topicis 92, 94
  on *Isogoge* of Porphyry 108
Boniface (St) 62 n., 78 n.
  Aenigmata (riddles) 72, 166
  see also Saints, lives of
book collections, content of:
  Anglo-Saxon 32–4, 81, 114
  continental 37
  English (post-Conquest) 42–3, 81,
    114
  monastic 114
  Norman 37
  see also Bury St Edmunds; Durham;
    Leofric; Mont Saint-Michel; Salisbury;
    Worcester
Bruno the Carthusian: commentary on the
  Psalms attrib. to 105–9

Burton-on-Trent, Abbey: manuscript from 46

Bury St Edmunds, Abbey:
book collection 43
library catalogue 83
manuscript from 47

Caesarius (St), archbishop of Arles:
Epistola 2 148
sermons 114, 132 n., 136, 143, 146, 160, 161
calendar 145
canon law texts 121–2, 131
canons promulgated after Battle of Hastings 143
'De regula Gangrensis concilii' 162
'Responsiones Nicholai papę ad consulta Bulgarorum' 162
see also councils and synods; Isidore (Pseudo-)
canons:
regular 113, 115, 128
secular 113, 128, 129
Canterbury:
manuscripts from 47, 72, 78, 79 n.
and transmission of texts 6, 46, 47, 48, 57–8
Canterbury, Abbey of St Augustine:
manuscripts from 46, 49, 51 n., 54 n., 66, 78
Canterbury, Christ Church Cathedral Priory 18, 30, 78
manuscripts from 9 n., 48, 50, 51 n., 53–4, 55, 71, 72–3, 76
Carolingian book collections and learning 34, 37, 41, 66, 84, 105
Cassian, John 165
Collationes 17, 75, 114, 133 n., 137, 149; extract 161 n.
De institutis coenobiorum, as source for *Scala virtutum* 117, 120–1, 168 n., 171, 179–82
Cassiodorus 31, 86, 105, 165
Institutiones 34, 35, 46, 84, 87, 151
on Psalms 36 n., 105, 163, 200
Chalcidius: on the *Timaeus* 85, 164
Chrodegang, rule of St 115
Cicero:
De inventione 85 n., 92, 95 n.
De officiis 41, 64, 86, 158
Topica 85 n., 92
Tusculan Disputations 41, 64, 67, 86, 159
Clement (Pseudo-): *Recognitiones* (tr. Rufinus) 162
commentaries on the Bible 38–9
on Genesis 39; *see also* Augustine

on Exodus, *see* Origen
on Leviticus, *see* Origen
on Samuel, *see* Bede
on Tobit, *see* Bede
on Job, *see* Gregory I
on Psalms, *see* Augustine, Bede (Pseudo-), Bruno the Carthusian, Cassiodorus, Honorius 'Augustodunensis', Ivo of Chartres, Lanfranc, Letbert of Lille, Manegold of Lautenbach, Remigius (Pseudo-)
on Ecclesiastes, *see* Alcuin
on Song of Songs 39, 145, 146; *see also* Alcuin
on Isaiah, *see* Jerome
on Jeremiah, *see* Jerome
on Ezekiel, *see* Jerome
on Matthew's Gospel 39; *see also* Hilary (bishop of Poitiers), Jerome
on Luke, *see* Bede
on John's Gospel, *see* Augustine
on Pauline Epistles 39; *see also* Ambrosiaster, Bible: glossed books of, Lanfranc, Pelagius
on Catholic Epistles, *see* Hilary (Pseudo-)
on Apocalypse 39; *see also* Bede, Berengaudus, Jerome, Victorinus
see also Irish Reference Bible
computistical texts 69, 77
Corbie, Abbey 37, 80
manuscripts from 52 n., 54 n., 61, 66, 115
councils and synods:
Lateran IV (1215) 131, 132
Lisieux (1064) 64, 131, 158
London (1075) 2
of Province of Rouen 130–1
see also canon law
Cummian: *Epistola* (*Epistola Cummiani*) 41, 63, 159
Cyprian (St), bishop of Carthage 34, 45–6, 59
Ad Demetrianum 159
Ad Donatum 159
Ad Fortunatum 159
Ad Quirinum 159
De bono patientiae (*De patientia*) 59 n., 148, 159
De catholicae ecclesiae unitate 59 n., 148, 159
De habitu virginum 159
De lapsis 159
De mortalitate 59 n., 148, 159
De opere et eleemosinis 59 n., 148, 159
De oratione dominica 36 n., 59 n., 132 n., 147, 148, 159
De zelo et livore 159

Letters 159
Quod idola dii non sint 159
Sententiae episcoporum de haereticis baptizandis 159
see also Saints, lives of
Cyprian (attrib.):
De aleatoribus 159
De laude martyrii 159
'Dicta' 160

Decretum Gelesianum 35, 150, 153, 165
Defensor of Ligugé: *Liber scintillarum*, as source for *Scala virtutum* 116, 117–20, 168 n., 171, 172–8
Deusdedit, canonist: *Libellus contra invasores et symoniacos*, as source for *Scala virtutum* 117, 121–2, 168 n., 171, 183
De vita vera apostolica 127–8
dialectic, *see* logic
Dialogus Egberti 144
Disticha Catonis 84
Domesday Survey 3, 16, 56 n.
see also Exon Domesday
Drogo of Paris 96, 99
Durham Cathedral Priory 18
book collection 42–3
manuscripts from 18 n., 48, 56, 72–3

Einsiedeln, Abbey 72 n.
Ephraim Syrus 32, 33 n.
De beatitudine animae 167
De compunctione chordis 167
De die iudicii 167; extracts 161
De die iudicii et de resurrectione 167
De luctaminibus 167
De paenitentia 167
Epistola Cummiani, see Cummian
Eucharist, texts on doctrine of 39–40, 95, 100–1, 148 *see also* Heriger of Lobbes; Paschasian *catena*; Paschasius; sacraments
eucharistic miracle stories 153
Eucherius 165
Eusebius, bishop of Caesarea 32
Historia ecclesiastica (tr. Rufinus) 26, 36 n., 54–5, 167
Eusebius 'Gallicanus': Sermons 114, 132 n., 136–7, 146
Eutropius: *Sermo de districtione monachorum* 40, 162
Everard of Calne, archdeacon 138
Exeter Cathedral: manuscripts from 18 n., 50, 52 n., 53, 54, 68, 69, 71, 73, 78
see also Leofric
Exon Domesday 7, 13, 16, 17

see also Domesday Survey; Wiltshire Geld Accounts

Fathers of the Church, works of, *see* patristic texts
Faustus of Riez: *De ratione fidei* 165
Fécamp, Abbey: manuscript from 80
Fleury, Abbey 37, 74
manuscript from 71 n.
florilegia 34, 64, 116, 160
see also Aulus Gellius; *Florilegium Angelicum*; *Scala virtutum*; Valerius Maximus
Florilegium Angelicum 41
Florus of Lyons: *Collectaneum* 89, 90
Freculphus of Lisieux: *Chronicon* 151
Fulgentius (Pseudo-), bishop of Ruspe: *Sermo ix* 161

Garlandus Composita: *Dialectica* 94
Gaudentius, bishop of Brescia (Brixiensis): *Tractatus xv* (*De Machabeis*) 158
Gembloux, Abbey: manuscripts from 64, 67
Gennadius of Marseilles:
De ecclesiasticis dogmatibus 153
De viris inlustribus 35, 36 n., 150
Gilbert de la Porrée 103, 104
Gloucester, Abbey: manuscript from 51 n.
Godwin, cantor (precentor) 123
Meditationes Godwini 7, 116, 123–8, 131, 137, 141
Goscelin of St-Bertin 3 n., 40 n.
grammar 83, 140
see also *artes*
Gregory I, pope 31, 34 n., 42, 58, 165
Cura pastoralis (Alfred's translation) 69, 75
Dialogues 79
Letters 160
Moralia in Iob 14 n., 17, 38, 59, 149; epitome (*Speculum Gregorii*) 76; extracts 165
see also Saints, lives of
Gregory Nazianzenus 165
Orationes 59, 79; *Ad cives nazianzenos gravi timore perculsos* (*De Hieremiae prophetae*) 59, 148
Guido of Arezzo: *Micrologus* 94
Gunter of Le Mans, archdeacon 138
Guy of Étampes 82–3

Haimericus: *Ars lectoria* 86 n.
Haimo (Pseudo-): on the Psalms 104–10
Helperic: *De computo* 77
Herbert Losinga, bishop of Norwich 45
Hereford Cathedral: manuscript from 47

Hereman, bishop of Salisbury 2, 3 n., 40 n., 76
Heriger of Lobbes: on the Eucharist 40, 101, 163, 199
Hilary of Poitiers (St) 39, 43, 61–2
  De synodis 160
  De Trinitate 36 n., 39 n., 58, 160; extracts 148
  on Matthew 38, 58, 61, 66, 166, 199
  see also Saints, lives of
Hilary (Pseudo-): on Catholic Epistles 38, 43, 61–2, 166, 199
Hildebert, bishop of Le Mans 66, 82
homiliaries 34, 57
  of St-Père de Chartres 145
  see also Paul the Deacon
homilies, anonymous 145, 146
Honorius 'Augustodunensis': on the Psalms 104–7, 109
Hubald, archdeacon 85, 138–9
Hugutio of Pisa: definition of *auctoritas* 134

Institutio Osmundi, see Osmund
Irish Reference Bible 38, 61, 63 n., 165–6, 200
Isidore of Seville 165
  Allegoriae 35, 36, 146, 151
  De differentiis, extracts 145, 167
  De ecclesiasticis officiis, extract 35, 151
  De miraculis Christi 68, 145
  De natura rerum 144
  De ortu et obitu patrum 35, 36, 132 n., 146, 151
  De viris inlustribus 35, 150
  Liber synonymorum 145
  Libri etymologiarum 68, 165; extracts 145, 146, 159
  Libri sententiarum 160; extract 161
  Prooemia 35, 36, 146, 151
  Quaestiones in vetus testamentum 76, 133 n., 152; extracts 160, 164
Isidore (Pseudo-):
  Decretals (*Collectio Lanfranci*) 16 n., 47–8, 101, 131, 133 n., 134, 150, 198
  Lamentum paenitentiae, see Sisbertus Toletanus
  Liber de variis quaestionibus adversus Iudaeos 167
  'Versus beati Isidori' 148
Isidorian world diagram 144
Ivo of Chartres, pupil of Gilbert de la Porrée 103
  commentary on the Psalms attrib. to 102–11, 201

Jerome (St) 8, 31, 34, 42, 89, 165
  Altercatio Luciferiani et Orthodoxi 168
  De viris inlustribus 35, 36 n., 150
  on Isaiah 17, 36 n., 38, 58, 133 n., 149
  on Jeremiah 36 n., 38, 58, 133 n., 149
  on Ezekiel 36 n., 38, 133 n., 136, 147
  on Matthew 36 n., 167
  recension of Victorinus on the Apocalypse 143
  see also Saints, lives of
Jerome (Pseudo-):
  'Admonitio Ieronimi de esu corporali' 161
  De duodecim scriptoribus 153
  Epistola 42, Ad Oceanum 160
Jocelin, bishop of Salisbury 20
John of Salisbury, bishop of Chartres 65
Jumièges, Abbey: manuscript from 60 n.
Junilius Africanus 165

ladder of virtues, see *Scala virtutum*
Lanfranc, archbishop of Canterbury 44–5, 47, 51, 98, 99, 101
  Collectio Lanfranci 16 n., 47–8, 101, 131, 133 n., 134, 150, 198
  on the Psalms 104
  on Pauline Epistles 89, 91, 96, 98
Laon:
  canons of 30
  schools at 6, 66
Laudes regiae 79–80
Leland, John 8 n., 124 n.
Le Mans: manuscripts from 60 n., 66
  see also Hildebert, bishop
Leofric, bishop of Exeter: books donated by 68, 73, 76
Letbert of Lille: on the Psalms 104–9
Libellus de diversis ordinibus 128–9
Liber glossarum 80, 84–5
Liber graduum, see Scala virtutum
liberal arts, see *artes*
Liège:
  Abbey of St Laurent: manuscripts from 14 n.
  schools at 67, 85 n., 94 n.
Lincoln Cathedral: books of 43 n.
Lobbes, Abbey 67 n.
logic (dialectic) 83, 91, 98, 140
  see also *artes*
Lorsch, Abbey: manuscript from 66
Low Countries 14 n., 67

Mainz: manuscript from 53
Manegold of Lautenbach 99, 104
  commentary on the Psalms attrib. to 94 n., 104 n.

marriage 125, 126–7
Martianus Capella:
   De nuptiis philologiae et mercurii 84
   see also Remigius of Auxerre
Meditationes Godwini, see Godwin
Methodius (Pseudo-): *Revelationes* 133 n.,
   146, 153, 159
Mont Saint-Michel, Abbey: book
   collection of 37
Mortuary Roll of Abbot Vitalis of Savigny:
   Salisbury *titulus* 22, 25, 26, 27,
   200
Murbach, Abbey 35 n.

Naples: manuscript from region of 62
Nigel, bishop of Ely 30, 66

Odo, bishop of Bayeux 67
Odo of Tournai 67
Olbert, abbot of Gembloux 67 n.
Order of consecration of a virgin 143
Orderic Vitalis 67, 85 n.
Orders of benediction of abbess, abbot,
   bishop, monk 143, 144
Origen:
   on Exodus 36 n., 38, 133 n.
   on Leviticus 36 n., 38, 133 n.
originalia 134, 141, 142
Osmund, bishop of Salisbury 2, 3, 4, 16,
   17, 24, 30, 40 n., 45, 67, 80 n., 113,
   142
   foundation charter of 4, 113
   Institutio Osmundi 4, 83
   as scribe 10, 137

palaeography:
   abbreviations 18, 63, 102, 200, 201
   annotations (*notae*) 16 n., 41 n., 76,
      78 n., 131, 132–7, 141, 198, 199; see
      also *signes-de-renvoi*, syntax marks
   binding 9, 10, 16
   booklets 8, 10, 12, 141, 143 n., 158
   book lists 33; *see also* Bury St
      Edmunds, Peterborough, Saewold,
      Worcester
   catchwords 20, 27, 30
   corrections 11, 12, 15, 19, 20–1, 23, 26,
      29, 88, 100, 133–4, 201
   decoration and initials 9, 14 n., 17, 19,
      21, 28, 37 n., 87, 102, 197, 198, 200
   dimensions 8, 87, 102, 198
   exemplars 17, 25, 41, 44, 75, 76, 77,
      199; acquisition of 43, 44–5, 58,
      65–6, 67, 77, 81; collation with a
      second exemplar 20, 25–6, 27, 29,
      53, 54–5, 68; from Anglo-Saxon
      centres 68–70, 73–4, 76; imported

45–8, 51–2, 53–4, 56–7, 60, 63, 66,
   German 64, Norman 49–51, 64, 65;
   in insular script 62–3, 200; reference
   to in colophon 146 n.
insular features: abbreviations 49, 62–3;
   decoration 28, 200
layout: long lines 9, 19; two columns 9,
   19, 27; three columns 85; *see also*
   ruling
notae, see annotations
origin and provenance of particular
   manuscripts: Africa 45; Brittany 71,
   79; Continent 74, 76, 79, *see also*
   Gembloux, Lorsch, Mainz, St Gall,
   Werden; England 51 n., 78 n., 79, *see*
   also Abingdon, Bath,
   Burton-on-Trent, Bury St Edmunds,
   Canterbury (Christ Church),
   Canterbury (St Augustine's), Durham,
   Exeter, Hereford, Rochester,
   St Albans, Sherborne, Winchester,
   Worcester; France 46, 74, 80, *see*
   also Angers, Bec, Corbie, Fécamp,
   Fleury, Jumièges, Tours; Italy 61,
   78 n., 79, 96, 115, *see also* Bobbio,
   Naples; Wales 79
parchment 9, 10, 16, 29, 200
punctuation 29; correction of 100, 201;
   forms of 14 n., 24 n., 197, 198
quire formation 8, 17, 19, 25
quire signatures 19, 20, 27; *see also*
   catchwords
ruling 9, 10, 19–20, 27, 87, 102, 199,
   200, 201
scribal collaboration, patterns of 10, 12,
   16, 17, 22, 25, 29, 30, 31, 88
scribal practices 19–20, 27, 30
scribes, *see* Abingdon, St Albans,
   Salisbury
script: duct 11; hierarchy of script
   37 n.; house-style of script 9, 30, 197;
   letter forms 14 n., 15 n., 18, 19, 22 n.,
   23 n., 24 n., 26, 27, 197–201; ligatures
   18, 197, 198; serifs 14 n., 18, 23 n.,
   27, 198, 199
script, varieties of: Anglo-Saxon square
   minuscule 71; book hands 18, 28;
   Carolingian minuscule 9, 77;
   continental minuscule 14 n., 77, 80,
   85; English Caroline minuscule 14 n.,
   15, 19, 26, 60 n., 72, 76, 197, 199;
   German hands 75 n.; of Salisbury
   scribes 9, 11, 17–19, 26–7; small
   'academic' hands 10, 11, 15 n., 17–18,
   19, 23 n., 26–7, 102, 197, 198, 200,
   201
scriptoria, monastic 18, 28, 30

Palaeography (*cont.*)
  signes-de-renvoi 55, 87, 201
  syntax marks 201
Paris, schools 30, 83
Paschasian *catena* on the Eucharist (the
    Exaggeratio) 39, 40, 100–1, 148 n.,
    163
Paschasius:
  De corpore et sanguine domini 40, 75,
    101, 167; extracts 39, 100, 148,
    153 n.
passional, *see* Saints, lives of
patristic texts 31, 141, 142
  in Anglo-Saxon England 32–4
  in England after the Conquest 37, 58,
    60
  in medieval book collections 32, 34 n.,
    37
  used as sources for glosses on Pauline
    Epistles 88–90, 96, 97
  see also auctoritates; *originalia*;
    Salisbury book collection
Paul, abbot of St Albans 44–5
Paul the Deacon: homiliary of 154
Paulinus of Aquileia: *Liber
    exhortationis* 167
Pelagian *Libellus fidei ad Innocentium
    papam* 149
Pelagius:
  De vita christiana 168
  on Pauline Epistles 38, 62, 89, 90 n.,
    160
  see also Pelagian *Libellus fidei*
penitentials 34
  penitential miscellany 79
Peterborough, Abbey: book list 33 n.
Philip of St Edward, canon 20–1
Plautus: *Comoediae* 41, 42, 63–4, 86,
    146, 159
Pontifical: additions to 10, 16, 75, 143–4
prayers 144, 159
Priscian: gloss on 83
Prise, Sir John 56 n.
Prosper of Aquitane:
  De gratia et libero arbitrio 57, 164
  Epigrammata 84
  *Responsiones Prosperi contra
    Pelagianos* 57, 164

Quodvultdeus, bishop of Carthage:
  Adversus quinque haereses 150
  De cantico novo 162
  De cataclismo 162
  De quarta feria tractatus 160
  De quattuor virtutibus caritatis 160
  De symbolo ii–iv 162
  De tempore barbarico 160

Ramsbury 2, 3 n., 29
Registrum Anglie 60, 61 n., 62 n.
Regula magistri 61, 115 n.
Remigius of Auxerre:
  on Martianus Capella 41, 80, 84
  on Sedulius 79, 84, 85
Remigius (Pseudo-): on the Psalms 104–9
Rhabanus Maurus: *De computo* 144
rhetoric 91–4, 97, 125, 140
  see also artes
Richard Poore, bishop of Salisbury 131,
    141, 142
  statutes of 132, 141
Robert, archdeacon 138
Rochester, Cathedral Priory 18, 30
  manuscripts from 18 n., 47, 51 n., 53,
    55
Roger, bishop of Salisbury 30, 45, 66, 82,
    83
Rufinus of Aquileia: on the Apostles'
    Creed (*De symbolo*) 141, 168, 199
Rule of Augustine, *see* Augustine
    (Pseudo-)
Rule of the Four Fathers 40, 61, 66, 80,
    115, 162
runic alphabets 145

sacraments 120, 121–2, 129, 130
  see also Eucharist
Saewold, abbot of Bath: list of
    books 33 n.
St Albans, Abbey:
  manuscripts from 49–50, 53, 54, 55
  specialist scribes at 29
  see also Paul, abbot of
Saint-Évroul, Abbey 34 n., 50
St Gall, Abbey: manuscripts from 59
Saints, lives of 40, 70
  Abdon and Sennen 156
  Achatius 158
  Adrianus, *see* Hadrianus
  Aegydius 158
  Afra 143
  Agapitus 156
  Agatha 155
  Agnes 155
  Albinus, bishop of Angers 155
  Alexander I, pope, Eventius and
    Theodulus 155
  Alexis 170
  Amalberga 158
  Amandus (Amand) 155
  Ambrose, bishop of Milan 155
  Ammon 169
  Anastasia 157 n.
  Andrew, Apostle 143, 157 n.
  Anianus 157 n.

Apollinaris of Ravenna 156
Arcadius 170
Asclas 155
Audoenus (Ouen) 156
Audomar (Omer) 156
Augustine, bishop of Hippo 156;
   extracts 166, 168, 169
Babylas 155
Barnabas, Apostle 143
Bartholomew, Apostle 156
Basil the Great, bishop of Caesarea 154
Basilides and his companions 156 n.
Bathildis 158
Benedict and Scholastica 157 n.
Bertin 156
Blasius (Blaise) 169
Boniface (Bonifatius) 156, 169
Briccius (Brictius) 157 n.
Brigid of Kildare 155
Caesarius 157 n.
Callistus (Calixtus) pope 157 n.
Cassianus, bishop of Autun 156
Cecilia 157 n.
Christina 157 n.
Chrysanthus and Daria 157 n.
Chrysogonus 157 n.
Clement 157 n.
Columba 157 n.
Concordius 170
Conon 155, 170
Cornelius, pope 156
Cosmas and Damian 157
Crispina 143
Crispinus and Crispinianus 157 n.
Cuthbert 40 n., 170
Cyprian, bishop of Carthage 156, 157,
   158
Cyprian and Justina 157
Denis, *see* Dionysius
Didymus and Theodora 143
Dionysius (Denis), bishop of Paris,
   Rusticus, and Eleutherius 157
Dioscurus 170
Domitilla and her companions 155
Donatus 156
Eleutherius and Anthia 155
Eligius 157 n.
Epipodius 170
Erasmus, bishop 156
Eugenia 157 n.
Eulalia 157 n.
Euphemia 143, 156
Euplus 156
Eupraxia (Euphrasia) 143
Eusebius 156
Eustace 157 n.
Eutyches, Victorinus and Maro 155

Faith, *see* Fides
Faustinus and Victor 157 n.
Felicitas and Perpetua 155
Felicity and her seven sons 156
Felix, bishop (Pope Felix II) 156
Felix, bishop of Thibiuca 154
Felix, priest 154–5
Fides (Faith) 170
Firminus I, bishop of Amiens 157
Forty martyrs (Quodraginta
   martyres) 155
Four crowned martyrs (Quattuor
   coronati) 157 n.
Fructuosus, Augurius, and Eulogius 155
Fursey 155
Gallicanus 156
Gaugeric 156
Genesius 156
Geneviève (Genovefa) 154
George 155
Germanus, bishop of Paris 155
Gertrude 169
Gervasius and Protasius 155
Getulius, Cerealis, and their companions
   156 n.
Gordianus and Epimachus 155
Gregory I, pope 155
Guthlac 70, 158
Hadrianus and his companions 156
Hieronymus, *see* Jerome
Hilary, bishop of Poitiers 154
Hippolytus 156
Honoratus, bishop of Arles 170
Hucbert (Hubert) 157 n.
Hyacinth 156
James the Greater, Apostle (Iacobus
   maior) 156
James the Less, Apostle (Iacobus
   minor) 155
Jerome (Hieronymus) 157
John, abbot of Parrano (Iohannes
   Penariensis) 169–70
John, Apostle and Evangelist 157 n.
John the Baptist 170
John and Paul 156
Jude, Apostle 157 n.
Judoc 157 n.
Julian and Basilissa 154, 158
Juliana of Nicomedia 155
Julianus of Brioude 158, 170
Julius 170
Lambert, bishop of Maastricht 156
Laurence 156
Leodegar (Léger), bishop of Autun 157
Leonard 158
Longinus 157 n.
Lucianus 154

Saints, lives of (*cont.*)
  Lucy 157 n.
  Lucy (Luceja) 143, 157 n.
  Lucy and Geminianus 156
  Luke, Apostle 143
  Maccabees 158
  Marcellinus and Peter 156
  Marcellus 155
  Marcellus I, pope 155
  Marinus 157 n.
  Mark, the Evangelist 155
  Martin of Tours 156, 157 n.
  Martina 154
  Mary, the Blessed Virgin, and Mother of
    God 157 n., 170
  Mary of Egypt 155
  Matthew, Apostle 157
  Maurice and his companions 157
  Maurus 157 n.
  Maximilian 170
  Maximus 157 n., 170
  Medard, bishop of Tournai 156
  Menna 157 n.
  Michael, Archangel: apparition on Mt.
    Gargano 157; apparition on Mons
    Tumba 170
  Modestus and Crescentia 156
  Nereus and Achilleus 155
  Nicholas of Myra 143
  Nicomedes 155
  Omer, *see* Audomar
  Ouen, *see* Audoenus
  Pancratius 155
  Pantaleon 156
  Parmenius 156
  Paternus 158
  Patrick 155, 169
  Patroclus 155
  Paul, Apostle 156
  Peter, Apostle 156
  Petronilla and Felicula 155
  Philip, Apostle 155
  Piatus 157
  Polycarp, bishop of Smyrna 155
  Polychronius 156, 170
  Potitus 155
  Praxedis 156
  Primus and Felicianus 156
  Processus and Martinianus 156
  Pudentiana 155
  Quadraginta martyres, *see* Forty martyrs
  Quattuor coronati, *see* Forty crowned
    martyrs
  Quentin (Quintinus) 157 n.
  Quiriacus 155
  Remigius, bishop of Rheims 157
  Richarius (Riquier) 157

Rufina and Secunda 156
Rufinus and Valerius 158
Sabina 156
Sabina (Savine) 156
Sabinianus (Savinien) 170
Sabinus 157 n.
Salvius (Sauve) 170
Saturninus 157 n.
Sebastian and his companions 155
Seven sleepers (Septem dormientes)
  156
Seraphia 156
Sergius and Bacchus 157
Servatius, bishop of Tongern 158
Silvester 157 n.
Simon, Apostle 157 n.
Simplicius, Faustinus, and Beatrix 156
Sixtus II, pope 156
Sosthenes and Victor 143
Spes, Fides, Caritas, and Sapientia 143
Speusippus, Eleusippus, and Melasippus
  (Meleusippus) 155
Stephen, 1st martyr 143
Stephen I, pope 156
Sulpitius 155
Symphorianus 156
Symphorosa and her seven sons 156
Thecla 143
Theodore 157 n., 170
Theodoretus (Theodorus) 155, 170
Theodosia 155
Theodota 143
Theogenes 154
Theophilus 'the penitent' 155
Thomas, Apostle 157 n.
Thyrsus, Leucius, Callinicus, and their
  companions 155
Torpes 155, 170
Trudo (Trond) 157 n.
Tryphon 155
Ursinus, bishop of Bourges 170
Valentine 155
Vedast (Vaast) 157
Victor and Corona 143
Vincent, of Saragossa 143, 155
Vitus 156
Wandregesil (Wandrille) 157 n.
Wilfrid 40 n., 170
Winnoc 156, 157 n.
Zoe 170
Salisbury (Old Sarum) 1–2, 3, 16–17
  archdeacons 16 n., 138; *see also*
    Everard of Calne, Gunter of Le Mans,
    Hubald, Robert, Thomas Chobham
  archischola 83
  bishops, *see* Hereman, Jocelin, Osmund,
    Richard Poore, Roger

book collection, content of 6, 31; canon law texts 130–1; classical and secular texts 41–2, 43, 84–6, 140; compared with Anglo-Norman collections 37, 42–3, 81; compared with Anglo-Saxon collections 6, 32–4; computistical texts 41; influence of Cassiodorus, *Institutiones* 34–6, 87; patristic texts 6, 31–2, 34, 36–9, 42–3, 58, 112, 140, 142; Saints' lives 40; texts of moral and spiritual guidance 40, 114–16
book production at 5, 8–30, 81
books imported to 75–81

Canons:
late 11th and early 12th c. 2–3, 16, 30, 66, 80; *see also* Alexander, bishop of Lincoln; Nigel, bishop of Ely
biblical and theological studies 6, 39–40, 99–102, 111–12, 129–30, 140–1; *see also* Bible, commentaries
choice of texts for book collection 31, 34, 36, 37–42
conduct of religious life and spiritual interests 4, 6–7, 113–16, 129–32; *see also* Godwin, *Meditationes, Scala virtutum*
contacts with Continent and continental schools 6, 30, 43, 60, 65–7, 80, 85, 111–12
interest in pastoral activity and reform 129–32, 134–7
scribal activities 5, 28–9, 131
secular studies 41–2, 84–6
13th c. 141–2

cantor (precentor) 3; *see also* Godwin
cathedral: at Old Sarum 1–2, 29; at new Salisbury 8
chancellor 3, 21, 83
chapter, structure, and organization 1, 2–4; *see also* cantor, chancellor, dean
dean 3, 66
diocese and see 2, 8, 29, 76, 131–2
and the Domesday Survey 7, 16–17
magister scholarum 82–3; *see also* Ailwinus, Guy of Étampes
precentor, *see* cantor
scribes 5, 7, 10–30, 31 n., 40, 47, 50, 53, 55, 59, 61, 62–3, 64, 68, 76, 81, 87, 88, 100, 101, 102, 122, 197–201; annotations of 41 n., 131, 132–9; dates of scribal activity 16–17, 24–5; manuscripts copied by 12–15, 16, 22–4, 143–70; nature of activity 5, 11, 17–21, 25–9, 30; numbers of 11–12, 22; *see also* palaeography

and transmission of texts: Anglo-Saxon textual traditions 68–74; classical texts 63–5, 67; Salisbury manuscripts which contain unique English witness to particular texts 6, 61–3, 144 n.; Salisbury manuscripts which contain unique English witness to particular textual traditions 6, 58–60, 65; textual traditions shared with other post-Conquest English manuscripts 45–58, 72–3; *see also* palaeography: exemplars
Samson, bishop of Worcester 67
Sarum, Use of 122, 123
Sarum *Martyrologium* 40, 122–3
Scala virtutum (*Liber graduum*) 7, 40, 116–23, 124, 125, 127, 131, 168, 171–83, 199
schools, continental 6, 10, 30, 80, 84, 85, 111–12, 141
see also Bec; Laon; Liège; Paris
scientific texts, anonymous 144–5
Sedulius: *Carmen Paschale* 84
see also Remigius of Auxerre
Seneca: *De beneficiis*, extracts 41, 64, 86, 158
Sermo arianorum 51, 52, 151
Sherborne, Abbey 3 n., 69
manuscripts from 69, 75
Sherborne, see and diocese 2, 16, 29, 76
Sisbertus Toletanus: *Lamentum paenitentiae* 148
Smaragdus: *Diadema monachorum* 40, 68, 114, 149
summa de divinis officiis (treatise on rites and observances of the Church) 152
Symphosius (Scholasticus): *Aenigmata* 166

Terrentius (Irish grammarian) 36 n.
Tertullian: *Apologeticum* 145, 159
Theodulf of Orleans: *De processione Spiritus sancti* 150
Thomas I, archbishop of York 67
Thomas Chobham 131, 132, 141
Thurstan, abbot of Glastonbury 67
Tournai 67
Tours: manuscripts from 54, 79
Twelfth-Century Renaissance 140–1

Utrecht, Abbey of St Paul 14 n.

Valerius Maximus: *Factorum et dictorum memorabilium libri* (*florilegium* of extracts from) 41, 64–5, 86, 158
Victorinus: on the Apocalypse 132 n., 143

Vigilius Thapsensis: *Contra Felicianum* 153, 154, 162
Vitalis, abbot of Savigny, *see* Mortuary Roll

Werden: manuscript from 99
William I, king of England 16
William of Malmesbury 28 n., 65
  on acquisition of books at Salisbury 10, 16, 45
  on Hubald, archdeadon 85, 138–9
  on Osmund, bishop of Salisbury 3 n., 10, 16, 45
  on Salisbury canons 30
William of Rots, abbot of Fécamp 67

William of St Calais, bishop of Durham 42–3
Wiltshire Geld Accounts 7 n., 13, 14, 16
  see also Domesday Survey; Exon Domesday
Winchester: manuscript from 74
Worcester, Cathedral Priory 30, 78
  book collection 42
  book list 79 n., 84 n.
  manuscripts from 40 n., 51 n., 69–70, 71, 74, 75, 78 n., 79 n., 154 n.
Wulfstan II, bishop of Worcester 69 n.

Young, Patrick: catalogue of Salisbury manuscripts 8 n., 77, 103